50 BEST PLACES
Fly Fishing the Southeast

KEVIN HOWELL & WALKER PARROTT

Stonefly Press

Copyright © 2019 by Stonefly Press

All rights reserved, including the right of reproduction of this book in whole or in part in any form.

640 Clematis St. #588
West Palm Beach, FL 33402
FAX: 877-609-3814

For information about discounts on bulk purchases, or to book the author for an engagement or demonstration, please contact Stonefly Press at inquiries@stoneflypress.com, or visit us at Stoneflypress.com.

stoneflypress.com

Library of Congress Control Number:
_____

Stonefly Press
Managing Partner: Patrick Kelley
Managing Partner: Terry Gunn
Managing Partner: Khellar Crawford
Acquiring Editor: Robert D. Clouse
Cartographer: Mike Boruta
Copy Editors: Rick Kughen, Nicole Kraft, and Rachel Rosolina
Proofreader: Charlotte Kughen
Front Cover Photo: Tom Branch Falls, J.E.B. Hall

*This book is dedicated to our fathers
Don R. Howell and Peter Parrott.
Thank you for the countless hours and effort
you invested in taking us fishing.*

Contents

Acknowledgments vi
About the Authors vii
Foreword by Bob Clouser ix
Introduction x
The Southeast xiii

I FARM PONDS

1. Farm Ponds 5

II FLORIDA

2. Lower Keys 13
3. Upper Keys 17
4. Ten Thousand Islands 23
5. South Florida 27
6. Mosquito Lagoon/Indian River 33
7. Tampa Bay 41
8. Florida Panhandle 47
9. St. Johns River 57

III GEORGIA

10. Chattahoochee River 65
11. Flint River 73
12. J. Strom Thurmond Reservoir (Clarks Hill) 79
13. Savannah River 85
14. Lake Sidney Lanier 93
15. Dukes Creek 99
16. Toccoa River 105

IV SOUTH CAROLINA

17. Chattooga River 113
18. Lake Jocassee 119
19. Saluda River and Broad River 125
20. Hilton Head Island 133
21. Charleston Low Country 139

V NORTH CAROLINA
22. Harkers Island *149*
23. Neuse River *155*
24. Roanoke River *161*
25. Deep Creek *167*
26. Lake Norman *171*
27. South Mills River *177*
28. Big East Fork of the Pigeon River *183*
29. Davidson River *191*
30. French Broad River *197*
31. Tuckasegee River *205*
32. Hazel Creek *213*
33. Cataloochee Creek *219*
34. Nantahala River *227*

VI TENNESSEE
35. South Holston River *235*
36. Wautaga River *241*
37. Holston River *247*
38. Little River *253*
39. Abrams Creek *259*
40. Tellico River *265*
41. Clinch River *271*
42. Collins River *277*
43. Caney Fork *283*
44. Hiwassee River *289*

VII KENTUCKY
45. Cumberland River *297*

VIII VIRGINIA
46. New River *305*
47. James River *311*
48. Shenandoah River *315*
49. Mossy Creek *232*

IX WEST VIRGINIA
50. North Fork of the South Branch of the Potomac River *331*

Acknowledgments

Any book is a challenge but a guide book that covers one fourth of the United States and three distinctly different fisheries is a major undertaking. Walker and I certainly could not have accomplished this composition without a lot of help behind the scenes.

We owe a special debt of gratitude to all the chapter contributors. These contributors gave up days on the water or time out of fly shops to help us make this book a success. Not to mention giving up some of their favorite fishing locations and fly patterns. They also add a lot of notoriety to this book as most of them have been published in articles and books more times than either of us have.

Thanks to Patrick Williams, Louis Cahill, Gene Slusher, Honson Lau, Jeb Hall, Rob Fightmaster, Kelly Bandlow, David Knapp, David Cannon, Daniel Munger, and others for the contribution of some wonderful photography that helps bring this book to life.

Stonefly Press for their faith and belief in us, along with countless hours of emails and phone calls they have tolerated from us.

Vanessa Rollins for all the proofreading and editing she did to prevent us from sounding like the crusty old fishing guides we truly are.

John Rich, Jeff Furman, Nick Roberts, Landon Lipke, J.E.B. Hall, and the rest of the staff at Davidson River Outfitters for covering our trips and shop hours while we roamed the Southeast in search of photos, contributors and fish.

Finally and most importantly to our wives, families and dogs who have allowed us to literally roam the Western Hemisphere in pursuit of our passion. For it was their support years ago when we walked away from the 9-5 jobs, that allowed us to build the knowledge to compile this book.

About the Author

KEVIN HOWELL—Kevin Howell is the owner of Davidson River Outfitters; he also is an author, lecturer, fly-fishing instructor, and guide. Kevin is a Signature fly Designer for Montana Fly Company. A 2018 inductee to the Fly Fishing Museum of the Southern Appalachians Hall of Fame and a 2018 inductee to the Legends of the Fly Hall of Fame as well. Kevin has been guiding the waters of North Carolina, South Carolina, and East Tennessee for 25 years. When not guiding he can be found fishing with his wife Mellissa, and sons David and Andrew.

Kevin Howell with a Canadian Smallmouth bass. Andrew Howell.

WALKER PARROTT—Growing up on the South Carolina coast, Walker Parrott was introduced to fishing as a child, catching redfish, trout, jacks, and other inshore species. While completing high school in Sandpoint, Idaho, Walker was introduced to mountain trout fishing. He wanted to stay in the mountains, but live in the Southeast. After completing Brevard College with a bachelor's degree in experimental education, Walker settled in Brevard, North Carolina where he could fish the streams and rivers for trout and bass. After college, Walker took a job with an environmental engineering firm, which he soon left to pursue his passion of fishing, landing at Davidson River Outfitters. Now, too many years later, Walker is managing Davidson River Outfitters guide service and guiding and hosting anglers to Andros Bahamas, Argentina, and Montana. Between working with a great staff in the shop and guiding trout, smallmouth, and musky trips, he has the perfect balance. While trout are the staple, Walker likes to float for smallmouth bass and musky in Tennessee, North Carolina, and Virginia. When Walker is not guiding or pacing the fly shop, Walker can be found mountain biking, kayaking, taking long walks on the beach, fishing, and hanging out with his wife Nicole, and dogs, Mojo, Mia, Cassidy, and Catch 'em.

Walker Parrott with an Argentinian Golden Dorado. Kevin Howell

What dreams are made of, releasing a spectacular colored fall brown trout

Foreword

I have known Kevin Howell and Walker Parrott for years as friends and fishing partners. Their knowledge and time spent on the waters described in this book are outstanding. They have assembled an all-star group of guides, writers, and shop owners to give an in-depth look into the fly fishing opportunities in the Southeast. This book is a must-read for anyone attempting to fish throughout the Southeastern United States.

Kevin and Walker take you through the main coldwater resources of their beloved region. Many species of trout native and stocked abound in these selected waters. If you are interested in warmwater species, such as panfish, bass, and musky, this book will help you with these destinations, tool. Kevin and Walker also cover some of the best saltwater locations in the Southeastern United States, and they show you the flies and lures to use, tell you when and where to fish, provide information about hatches that are critical to the fly angler.

If you are looking for one book that will make your travel and fishing a success and lead you to creating many exciting memories, this book is for you.

Bob Clouser

Introduction

As the manager and the owner of a fly-fishing shop, the one question that we are repeatedly asked is where to fish and what to use. And if anglers are traveling, they want to know if there are any good guides in the area they will be fishing. We have had several clients comment over the years that we should put our knowledge into a book. When David Gray approached me to write *50 Best Places Fly Fishing the Southeast*, I saw just that opportunity to get the knowledge into a book. However, the fisheries in the Southeast are more diverse than any other region in the United States. I asked David if I could get Walker Parrott, my good friend and shop manager for the past 15 years, to assist, because I felt he had knowledge of certain fisheries and areas that I felt needed to be in the book, and I thought that maybe he could help me find the balance of saltwater, warmwater, and coldwater locations.

Over the years, we have seen many guidebooks and where-to books end up on coffee tables or recycled at the local thrift shop. Our goal was to create a book that would get thrown in your car or duffel bag every time you headed to a new destination, be it with friends or on the family vacation. A book that gave you the simple information that is so often requested by our clients: Where do I go? How do I get there? What do I use once there, or what guide service should I talk to? We wanted a book with good maps, excellent photography, and the knowledge and wisdom of the local experts. We called a lot of our fellow guides and industry experts to help us with the book.

The challenge of this book was that we were limited to 50 locations and only 250 pages. This book could have easily been *50 Best Trout Fisheries in the Southeast*, or *50 Best Warmwater Fisheries*, or *50 Best Saltwater Places to Fly Fish in the Southeast*. Most chapters had to be condensed down to be the bare necessities to meet the space criteria. For example, rivers like the New River and French Broad River cover hundreds of miles and countless target species, so for this book, we limited a lot of locations to certain sections that, for whatever reason, we felt were better than others. This guidebook is not the Holy Grail of guidebooks or the guidebook gospel by any means. We wrote and had contributors write chapters that we thought the angling public should know about. Some locations are well-known, and no one will question why they made the book—other places you have never heard of and will wonder why we included it (until you go there and fish).

We struggled with the states of Alabama and Mississippi—not because of a lack of great fishing but rather a lack of a fly-fishing presence. Lakes like Guntersville Lake, Pickwick Lake, and countless other waters offer great warmwater fishing opportunities, but there were so few fly-fishing guides or shops. We knew that anglers would have difficulty finding supplies and information, so for that reason, we felt we should concentrate on places that have a little more defined presence in the fly-fishing world.

The contributors to this book are a virtual who's who of Southeast anglers; you are going to read words by champion tournament anglers, guides, and captains who are often booked more than a year in advance. These captains and guides know and understand their fisheries from working their waters year after year, day after day.

When they suggest you should not take a hard boat down that section of river, listen to what they have to say. Chances are they have tried it in a hard boat at low water and left a nice gel-coat path for others to follow. Paying attention to small, subtle fishing tips can make the difference between catching fish and being eaten alive by no-see-ums while you are stuck on a mudflat waiting for the tide to come in.

Always keep in mind that Mother Nature, the Tennessee Valley Authority (TVA), and Duke Energy can make or break your experience. The most important piece of gear you should pack for any trip is your common sense. Before you get going, take two to four minutes and look at the radar, hourly weather prediction, stream flows, and projected water releases. Driving all the way to the South Holston or into the Cataloochee Valley to discover there is too much water or not enough water, or that it is muddy and blown out, will put a kink in your plans. Sometimes your plans just don't pan out, but paying attention to water levels can help.

If you get blown out, or the water levels or temperatures won't let you fish the location you are headed to, look at the suggested places to eat, get a cold adult beverage, or go check out the recommended places to see when you are in town.

The Bobby N. Setzer State Fish Hatchery in Pisgah National Forest in North Carolina is a pretty cool place to check out, and kids love to feed and watch the fish.

We hope the suggested places to fish will help you find your next greatest place to visit and fish. Use the guides and outfitters recommended for a reference and point of contact. Get in touch with them for day-to-day reports. If they cannot help, they will know who can. Keep in mind that guiding is not a nine-to-five job. If the suggested guide does not respond the day of your inquiry, give them a few days. Long days in peak seasons can make it hard to catch up on mail and return phone calls.

Remember that fisheries are cyclical, as are most things in life, and some years are better than others. As for the lodging and restaurants in the guide, they are suggestions—as managers and employees change, so do the businesses. As for the guides and outfitters, remember to shop with them and use their services, because if they were not around, chances are you would not be reading about that particular fishery or have anyone to provide you with up-to-date information.

Have a great time exploring new ponds, lakes, rivers, or coastal waters. Always take the time to meet the local anglers—we guarantee that you will discover, as we have, that there are a lot of colorful and entertaining fly fishermen out there.

Good Fishing,
Kevin Howell and Walker Parrott

Authors Walker Parrott left and Kevin Howell right with a low country double. Capt Kai Williams

The Southeast

The first challenge of this book was to define what the Southeast is; it seems everyone has a different opinion. For the purpose of this book, we have decided that the Southeast is defined by the Mississippi River on the west, the states of West Virginia and Virginia to the north, and the Gulf of Mexico and the Atlantic Ocean to the south and east. These ten states represent approximately 25 percent of the nation's population.

The geography of the Southeast is more varied than any other part of the contiguous United States. It is home not only to Mount Mitchell (the highest point east of the Rocky Mountains) but also includes thousands of miles of shoreline of the Atlantic Ocean and the Gulf of Mexico. It is the only place in the world where fly anglers can catch a mountain trout in the morning, make a four-hour car ride and land redfish in the afternoon, and stop off for some bass and carp action in between. At the same time, anglers have to plan carefully, because the angler that wants to fish Harkers Island and the Davidson River in North Carolina on the same trip need to realize that they are separated by an eight-hour drive. Yet, the Davidson River and Charleston, South Carolina, are separated by only 3 ½ hours.

The History

Over the years, fly fishing has undergone many transitions. Most anglers associate fly fishing in the United States as having its beginnings in New England, slowly finding its way west and then south. However, the first flies known to be fished in the Southeast were by the Cherokees in the 1500s (more than 200 years earlier than the New England anglers). The Cherokees would take a bone from a deer and wrap a flicker feather or piece of deer hair around the hook in a reverse fashion and lash it to the hook with rawhide and rudimentary cement. The fly was then tied on a string that was attached to a long Calcutta cane (an early form of the modern tenkara fishing. The fly would then be allowed to float downstream and twitched back up-stream, eliciting strikes from the native brook trout of the Southern Appalachians.

Most early fly fishing in the Southeast took place in streams and creeks of what is today the Great Smoky Mountain National Park, Cherokee National Forest, Nantahala National Forest, and Pisgah National Forest. For most anglers, this was a substance practice instead of sportfishing. For the most part, the Southern fisheries were secluded and kept quiet until the end of World War II, mainly because of the remoteness of the Southern mountains.

Not only do you have Many pioneers in trout fishing hailed from the South, including Don and Dwight Howell, Walter Babb, Eddie George, George "Cap" Weise, G. Neil Daniels, Cato Holler, and Fred Hall. All these people fought for conservation and were leading innovators in the Southeast trout-fishing scene. While these guys were standing in cool mountain streams, another group of anglers was pioneering a totally new side to the sport of fly fishing in the Southeast. Anglers like Flip Pallot, Jose Wejebe, Lefty Kreh, Joe Brooks, Billy Pate, and Stu Apte were changing the whole aspect of fly fishing by focusing on saltwater fly fishing. Today the Southeast has become a melting pot for fly anglers where anglers carry not only Parachute Adams but also Tarpon Toads and Clouser Minnows in their packs. Today, the fly fishing scene in the Southeast is being driven by names like , Gary Merriman, Kevin Howell, Walker Parrott, Wanda Taylor, Louis Cahill, Don Kirk, Jon and Paul Cave, Bill Oyster, and countless other highly talented fishing guides and writers—many of whom contributed to this book.

The Water

Defining the 50 best places to fish in the Southeast was the largest challenge we faced when we started this book. Not only does the Southeast offer great trout fishing, especially in North Carolina, Tennessee, and Northeast Georgia, but it offers some of the best saltwater fishing in the world. (Not to mention the thousands of miles of exceptional bass rivers and shoreline; after all, the B.A.S.S. tour spends more time in the Southeast than any other area.) So how do you pick? You could easily pick 50 spots that were just trout or 100 that were salt water. We wanted a list that everyone who read the book could go to, fish at, and walk away from with the same feeling that we had the first time we set foot in that location.

Trying to pick the best meant leaving out some streams that, while we felt they should be included, we knew from a professional standpoint the stream did not have the ability or infrastructure to handle added pressure. It also meant leaving out saltwater fisheries that probably should have been included; however, if we included one of those, then we would have had to drop a warmwater or coldwater selection. In the end, we ended up compromising on a mix of saltwater, coldwater, and warmwater locations (some of which you will have never heard of, and yet all will recognize the other locations). Our intent was not to give away all the secret locations, although I am sure there will be some of those e-mails. In reality, though, all the information in this book is already out in the world somewhere—we were just the guys who collected it, collaborated on it, and consolidated it all in one place.

Some of the locations (like the Watauga River, for example) cross state lines, with one state or the other having the better fishing. With that said, the constraints of this book meant we may not be able to cover the entire river like we would have preferred. So we choose to focus on the better part of the fishery.

While we knew the fisheries and had fished them, we were by no means the experts on some of the fisheries. So, when David Gray and Robert Clouse approached us about this book, we agreed to it only if we could follow the format that Terry and Wendy Gun had used: getting the local expert to write about their own fishery.

You will notice that there is one special chapter in this book dedicated to ponds, be they saltwater, blackwater, or cold mountain spring-fed ponds. For so many of us in the Southeast, this is where we got our introduction to the fly rod. Casting a Sneaky Pete or similar popper to bluegill and bass with a leader made of 8-weight test Berkley Trilene on an old Eagle Claw rod with a Pflueger reel. To us, the pond is the quintessential fishing location in the Southeast. To this day, we still find ourselves spending as much time on a pond as possible and wondering, "When was the last time someone fished here?"

Access

There is a huge debate facing the country now as to who owns the water and the access to it. The Southeast is no different. Some streams are totally private, and access is not allowed under any circumstance, while other streams can be accessed by paying a rod fee. The concern should not be over what is private and what is not private. After all, there have been countless court battles over access and the fact is what is private is private and filing another lawsuit or complaining about it is not going to change that. The battle should be on how we as anglers ensure what is left as public remains that way. In North Carolina alone, the vast majority of mountain trout water is located on privately owned land. Over the past several years, plenty of places I fished as kid have been closed to access because of anglers' misuse and abuse of places that the landowner had been gracious enough to allow anglers to fish. So don't leave your trash, don't crawl into someone's garden when you need to use the restroom, and don't threaten to sue landowners because you got injured on their property. As an angler, you are accepting a certain level of risk when you step into the water.

Seasons

This is a tough part to write about and explain the hows and why nots. There is not a perfect time to fish—just go. Fishing is an outside sport so far. Who knows? Maybe trout ponds and tidal creeks will be in the mall sometime soon. Maybe Bass Pro Shops will offer tarpon fishing next to the camo coveralls. While I mention that in jest, sometimes, I think that we anglers just want it right now. Recommended seasons can help anglers plan for a day trip or multi-day jungle journey. Understanding seasons, weather patterns, and temperature changes will definitely help an angler avoid a fishing disaster.

Trout fishing in the Southeast is a year-round event. The months of July, August, and early September are the slowest trout fishing of the year (especially in Northeast Georgia). In the Carolinas, summer trout fishing is great if it is a rainy summer and can be a little tough in the dryer years. The flip side to that is that while Buffalo, New York, and Cincinnati, Ohio, are shoveling snow, the trout fishing in the Southeast is offering 50-degree days and phenomenal fishing activity. Of course, the fall and spring fishing is some of the finest fishing of the year, with the months of April, May, October, and November being the best trout fishing.

The warmwater opportunities in the Southeast are also a year-round event; however, some target species are better caught at different times of the year. For the guys chasing stripers on a fly, the fall, winter, and early spring are the best. For smallmouth bass in the rivers, the hotter the weather, the better the fishing. For carp, it is all about the spring and summer.

Salt water is also a year-round opportunity. The best redfish bite often occurs in the dead of winter, yet the tarpon run in Tampa is May through July on average. The biggest problem anglers encounter on the big salt pond is weather and tides. Spring months tend to have huge tides, sometimes as high as 10 feet. Tide charts can easily be found online, and anglers should pay attention to weather and wind predictions. You do not want to run through Bouge Inlet on an outgoing tide with a 30-mph east wind pushing you—that will not end well.

We highly suggest that for your first few trips to a new area, regardless of how seasoned an angler or boat operator you are, that you hire a professional, licensed guide for that area. Every area has its differences. For example, you need to know how to time a float with TVA releases; otherwise, it is a five-mile walk down the Watauga River, pulling your drift boat over the rock ledges because the TVA turned the water release off. How about navigating around the Knuckle in rough seas while your fishing partner is fighting a false albacore off Cape Lookout? Mess that one up and you are a statistic.

With the different weather patterns and fishing opportunities in the Southeast, fishing can be accomplished all year long and in almost any weather scenario. If you're on the coast dealing with 30-mph winds, try the many ponds that the coast has to offer. If the tailwater you have been waiting to fish for months has the incorrect water levels, try walking up a Rhododendron-lined mountain stream and catching brookies.

Etiquette

As our streams, lakes, and bays get more crowded, it seems as if etiquette and common sense have been left on the bank. We have all been there. You arrive at your favorite fishing spot only to discover that someone else beat you there—be sure to leave them as much room as you would want them to leave you. It seems a lot of people just pile on top of other anglers these days. But stop and ask yourself, "If I were fishing there, would I like it if he walked in and started casting over my drift?" We suggest leaving a minimum of 100 yards (one football field) between you and the other wade angler. If you are floating, ask the anchored boat or the wade angler which side he would prefer you pass on. If water levels do not permit, then wait until they do or the angler finishes fishing the area you have to pass through. If you are on the lake, bay, or ocean, leave at least 100 yards between you and the other boat. We have seen countless flies cut off because people came charging into a pod of fish and ran over the line of someone fighting a fish. Again, if you were hooked up, you would be really irritated if someone ran over your line and cut your fish off. Also, that buffer is for safety as much as anything else—you do not want to knock someone off course or be knocked off course when navigating around safety hazards. Remember the golden rule: do unto others as you would have them do unto you!

FARM PONDS

1 · Farm Ponds

▶ **Location:** There is one within 30 minutes of your house.

Man-made ponds have been around since the Middle Ages, when they were constructed near the castles and stocked with fish to provide food for the house during the winter months when other food supplies were hard to come by. During colonial American times, salt ponds were constructed in the low country of South Carolina and Georgia to propagate rice production.

In response to the Dust Bowl of the early 1930s, the U.S. Congress passed Public Law 74-46 on April 27, 1935, in which it recognized that "the wastage of soil and moisture resources on farm, grazing, and forest lands . . . is a menace to the national welfare." It established the Soil Conservation Service (SCS) as a permanent agency under the U.S. Department of Agriculture. In 1994, the SCS name was changed to the Natural Resources Conservation Service (NRCS) to be more in line with their broader scope of operations.

During the late 1940s and continuing through the 1950s, the SCS offered financial and design assistance to farmers and landowners with large tracts of land for the sole purpose of building ponds on their property. The purpose of the ponds was to create a stable and reliable source of water and a form of recreation on the farms across the United States. Today, it is estimated that there are more than two million ponds in the United States, which account for nearly 20 percent of the nation's standing water supply. North Carolina alone has more than 16,000 man-made ponds.

Today, many ponds are constructed in large subdivisions for recreational activities such as swimming, fishing, canoeing, and other outdoor activities, while others are built in subdivisions as a method to reclaim wetlands for building houses or for drainage and irrigation purposes. Regardless of why or when the pond was built, chances are your neighborhood pond has fish in it.

For many Southern anglers, the farm pond represents their introduction to fishing and fly fishing. Most of us started fishing for bluebill in the local pond with a Calcutta cane, a length of line, and live crickets. Once we were old enough, usually around age ten, we were introduced to a fly rod and

Farm pond outside of Anderson, South Carolina. Kevin Howell

Jeb Hall with a black water pond largemouth. J.E.B. Hall

popping bug. When presented correctly, it would catch more bluegills than the live cricket and would also fool the weary old mossy-backed largemouth bass so common in Southern ponds.

For this book, we are going to cover three types of ponds:

Mountain ponds (coldwater)
Coastal and Piedmont regions (blackwater ponds)
Salt ponds (those that are present and have an occasional influx of salt water, based on tides)

For our purposes, we are going to consider mountain ponds to be constructed at or above 1,500 feet above sea level. The mountain ponds are found in Western North Carolina, Upstate South Carolina, Northeast Georgia, East Tennessee, Southwest Virginia, and West Virginia. Mountain ponds are typically clear and deep, have cooler water temps, and are usually fed by a small stream or spring. They are typically stocked with bluegills and largemouth bass. Typically, the fish in these ponds do not grow as large as their kin in the ponds at lower elevations, mainly due to a shorter growing season and consistently cooler temperatures. Ponds at or above 2,000 feet are often stocked with mountain trout.

Ponds in the Piedmont and coastal regions of the Southeast, including the borrow pits of Florida, are usually stocked with largemouth bass, bluegill, catfish, and occasionally, shell crackers (known as redear sunfish in other parts of the country). These ponds tend to be shallower and warmer, which results in large fish as well as murkier water. These ponds typically have vegetation in them ranging from duckweed, to lily pads, to hydrilla. The other common thing found around these ponds in the Southeast are American alligators and cottonmouth snakes (also known as water moccasins), both of which, when threatened, will be more than willing to stand their ground and defend what they believe to be their territory. While very few people are bitten by the cottonmouth annually, anglers should always be observant when around ponds in the Southeast. As for the alligators, they are a lot easier to spot. Keep in mind that a large alligator can run 30 mph across land, which is faster than most people (unless you are related to Usain Bolt). However, alligators rarely

Top. Andrew and David Howell fishing a pond. Kevin Howell

Inset. Farm ponds are a great place to get kids started fly fishing. Andrew Howell with a small pond bass that ate a popping bug. Kevin Howell

Above. Always be cognizant of your surroundings while fishing ponds in the deep South. Fish aren't the only things that bite. Kelly Bandlow

Below left. Walker Parrott with a lowcountry black drum. Gonzalo Flego

attack humans. When humans approach the water, alligators usually simply slide off into the water and disappear. Alligators that stand their ground are typically guarding a nest, and when they hiss or do not slide off into the water, anglers should not approach them or disturb the area.

Salt ponds are typically found from the South Carolina coast around to the Mississippi River. Salt ponds usually have some type of water exchange through a tidal flood gate. Salt ponds typically hold redfish, flounder, sheepshead, black drum, and some might even have tarpon and snook. Salt ponds are more commonly found along golf courses, housing developments, or old Southern plantations. Anglers can expect to encounter alligators in the salt ponds, too. Most developments keep the gators trapped out so that Fluffy (the neighbors' little white poodle) doesn't get eaten when he is out for his morning walk.

➤ **Hatches:** There are a lot of differences in the what flies will work best when fishing ponds throughout the Southeast. Anglers who are fishing in mountain ponds will want to carry some olive and black Woolly Buggers in sizes 6-10 and sparkle minnows in size 6. If bluegill and bass are present, small poppers such as a Mini Pop in size 6 or Boogle Bug in size 6 will always produce fish in the warmer months. In mountain ponds, anglers will want to use a 9-foot leader tapered to 3X because of the clearer water and spooky fish.

In blackwater ponds, anglers will want to carry streamers such as Clouser Minnows in size 2, Lefty's Deceivers in size 2-3/0, or crayfish patterns such as a size 6 Near Nuff Crayfish for bass in the cooler months. During the warmer months, Dahlberg Divers or Boogle Bugs in size 2 will always produce some bass. Bluegill and other panfish can always be picked up on small poppers and almost any small beadhead nymph dropped below the popper. In blackwater ponds, anglers can get by using a 7-foot leader and will probably only need to be tapered to 12-pound test. In many cases, anglers will be able to fish as heavy as 15-pound tippet.

Anglers who are targeting fish in salt ponds will want to fish Clouser Minnows size 6 to 1/0, Kwans in size 6 to size 2. Remember, fish in salt ponds are still saltwater fish and primarily feed on shrimp, small fish, and crabs. Any fly that mimics these forage items will probably work. Tidal influences might affect what the fish are feeding on based on how much water is being pumped in or out the flood gates. Anglers will want to fish a saltwater tapered leader that is tapered down to a light 20-pound tippet.

➤ **Tackle:** For gear, it will greatly depend on what part of the Southeast you are in. For bluegill, a 2-weight with a good selection of popping bugs will provide hours of entertainment. For the largemouth, a Sage Bass rod or a good 7- to 8-weight fly rod will be sufficient. Anglers should match that to a 9-foot leader tapered to a delicate 10- to 12-weight test. Poppers will often work year-round in these ponds; however, a good selection of Clouser Minnows or large trout streamers will often catch the larger fish that do not want to come to the top. For salt ponds, a good 8-weight rod will be all you need. Match it to a 9-foot leader tapered to about a 16-weight test. Shrimp and crab patterns that you would typically use for the species in the pond will easily suffice.

Kevin Howeel with a nice Davidson River brown trout. Walker Parrott

KEVIN HOWELL—Kevin Howell is the owner of Davidson River Outfitters; he also is an author, lecturer, fly-fishing instructor, and guide. Kevin is a Signature fly Designer for Montana Fly Company. A 2018 inductee to the Fly Fishing Museum of the Southern Appalachians Hall of Fame and a 2018 inductee to the Legends of the Fly Hall of Fame as well. Kevin has been guiding the waters of North Carolina, South Carolina, and East Tennessee for 25 years. When not guiding he can be found fishing with his wife Mellissa, and sons David and Andrew.

Kevin Howell with a large black drum from a lowcountry salt pond. Gonzalo Flego

FLORIDA

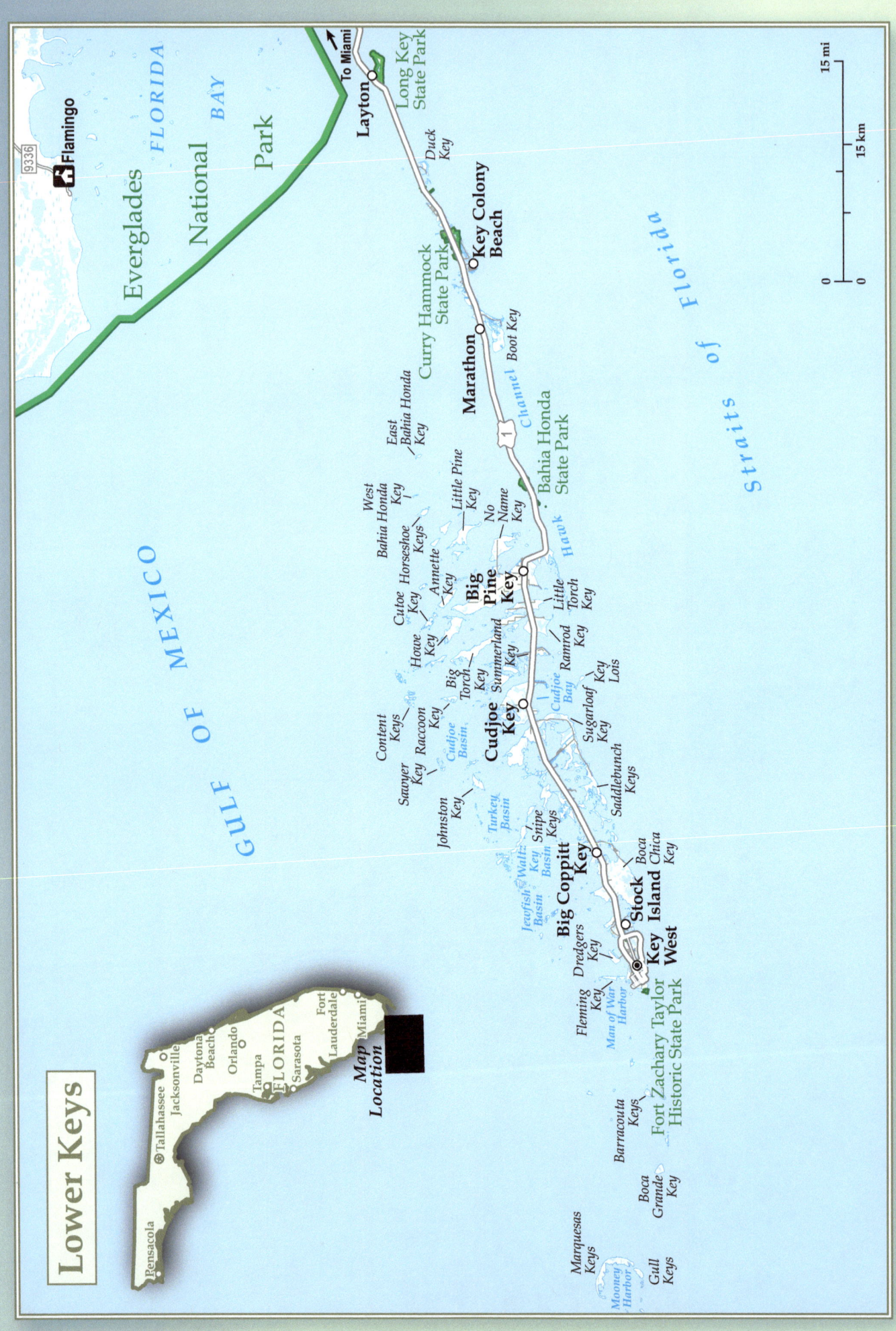

2 · Lower Keys

➤ **Location:** Key West is 129 miles southwest of Miami, and 106 miles from Havana, Cuba. Arriving in Miami International Airport, anglers can rent a car and access all the Keys and Key West.

With the busy cruise ship and tourist industry, Key West can be full of tourists and anglers alike. If you need to warm up in the winter months, Key West gets more than 3,000 hours of sunshine annually. It is also home to crowds of tarpon, bonefish, permit, and many not-so-glamorous species. Key West is the end of the road (literally), and it has been known to be the end to a lot of marriages, relationships, and bank accounts. Yes, the fly fishing can be good enough to just pack it up and go.

It is only fitting that the crown jewel of Southeastern fly fishing is at the farthest point you can travel in the Southeast; Key West and the Lower Keys are the birthplace of saltwater fly fishing. Key West is where the pioneers of saltwater fly fishing began poling their skiffs and clients to the large schools of migrating tarpon, permit, and bonefish that inhabit the gin-clear waters of the Lower Keys. These pioneers, fishermen, and guides included men, such as Stu Apt, Flip Pallot, and Steve Huff, just to name a few.

Key West and the Lower Keys have miles of turtle grass and sand-covered flats, and the nourishing warm waters that surround them provide perfect habitat for what is considered "the big three" of saltwater fly fishing: tarpon, bonefish, and permit. In fact, Key West and the Lower Keys include one of the few places in the world that anglers can catch all the species of the big three (or grand slam).

Key West and the Lower Keys can provide great fly fishing year-round for tarpon, bonefish, and permit. However, there are better times than others, depending on what you want to target and how you want to target them. The big three are the staple for anglers, but the varieties of saltwater fish can be endless. We can always catch something on any given charter. Depending on weather, winds, and tides, anglers can have their hands full with potential catches. Starting around mid-February and running through mid- to late-April, the larger migrating tarpon start trickling into the backcountry of the Lower Keys. Tarpon move in from the deeper water and "lay up" in shallower areas. This is the start of "laid up" tarpon fishing. This is the period when, on the right days, anglers can find massive schools of fish, sometimes in the hundreds, moving from channel to channel. In late June, as the larger tarpon make their way farther north, anglers can stay busy with shrimp hatches that occur in the backcountry. At times, anglers can find early mornings with juvenile tarpon crushing shrimp and floating crabs on top. These conditions can provide an excellent opportunity to target tarpon with topwater flies. When the sun gets high in the sky, set your sights on bonefish and permit to finish out the slam. Having

Mangroves growing in Florida Bay. Walker Parrott

a slick, calm day with no wind will help anglers sight-fish. This time of year ultimately provides you your best chance to grab the slam as the season extends to late fall. Rods, reels, leaders, tippets, and flies can be provided by your guide, but if you're one who likes bringing your own equipment, here are some suggestions.

➤ **Tackle:** I would suggest bringing a few fast-action rods ranging from 8-weight to 12-weight. Having a wide weight range of proper rods and tackle can help anglers conquer the grand slam. Reels can be the most important part battling such great gamefish. Make sure you have a reel with a sealed drag with lots of stopping power and a fine-tuned drag, such as Hatch Reels. As far as fly lines, anglers need to be rigged

On the Run. Lower Keys tarpon screams across the flat. Capt. Joel Dickey

with weight-forward tropical taper floating lines. Remember, this is the tropics, and the improper fly lines can actually transform into a smear of plastic due to the warm temperatures of the Keys and Key West. I recommend to my clients to bring an extra spool with a clear floating line for each reel. This is an absolute must for calm, clear days, as fish can become extremely wary and picky in these conditions. Tarpon and bonefish become a little spooky with seasonal angling pressure, and clear lines really do help.

Leaders and tippets should be species specific. I recommend checking with your guide for the correct leader and tippet formula for perfect presentation and the correct bite tippets. Guides usually have a leader formula that is tried and true. Ask before you get on the boat for a great day of fishing. Believe me, you do not want to travel all this way south with the incorrect leaders and lines.

Proper clothing and correct boat gear can make or break the day fishing in the tropics. Clothing will need to be breathable with the highest SPF rating possible. I also suggest wearing too much sunscreen. Long pants and long shirts need to cover any bare skin, helping anglers hide from the sun. Oh yeah, don't forget to bring a Buff or similar sun mask for your face! Avoiding sun burn the first day will help on days two and three. Seriously, here in sunny Florida, the sun will bake you like a Christmas turkey if you are not prepared. A small boat bag with sunscreen, raingear, and snacks will help anglers enjoy the full day. Having some gear is better than having nothing. Summer thunderstorms can kick up here in a minute, and being prepared with the proper raingear can save a foul-weather day.

When anglers visit the Lower Keys, there are some ideal places to stay that cater to the avid and expert angler alike. On Little Torch Key, you can stay at Dolphin Marina or Parmer's Resort, which is also located on Little Torch Key. When traveling this far south, you are basically staying on a rock that splits the Gulf of Mexico and the Atlantic Ocean. This does not mean there is a shortage of great places to eat, however. While you are visiting the Keys and Key West, stop in and curb your appetite at the Square Grouper on Cudjoe Key, Blue Heaven in Key West, and the Hogfish Bar and Grill on Stock Island.

Crushed popper. Barracuda can liven up any slow day in the lower Keys. Walker Parrott

Flight or fight. Massive poon takes the battle to the air. Capt. Joel Dickey

Capt. Joel Dickey with a trophy lower Keys permit. Joel Dickey

CAPT. JOEL DICKEY is a full-time guide in the Florida Keys and Key West. He lives with his family on Big Pine Key. Capt. Joel is fortunate to be on pro staff programs with Thomas & Thomas, Hatch Reels, Airflo, and Towee Boats. Capt. Joel has been featured on several covers of nationally distributed fly-fishing magazines, along with being featured in one of the industry's top-selling DVDs, Rise. He is also a contributor to popular blogs and magazines in the industry. Capt. Joel specializes in sight fishing for tarpon, bonefish, and permit. His website is www.captainjoeldickey.com, and he can be reached at captsilverking@aol.com for bookings.

CLOSEST GUIDES AND OUTFITTERS

Capt. Joel Dickey
305-619-7769
captsilverking@aol.com

Capt. Bruce Chard
captpermit@aol.com

The Angling Company
333 Simonton St.
Key West, FL 33040
305-292-6306
www.anglingcompany.com

CLOSEST LODGING

Dolphin Marina and Cottages
28530 Overseas Hwy.
Little Torch Key, FL 33042
800-553-0308
www.dolphinmarina.net

Parmer's Resort
565 Barry Ave.
Little Torch Key, FL 33042
305-872-2157
www.parmersresort.com

CLOSEST RESTAURANTS

The Square Grouper Bar and Grill
22658 Overseas Hwy.
Summerland Key, FL 33042
305-745-8880

Blue Heaven Restaurant
729 Thomas St.
Key West, FL 33040
305-296-8666

Hogfish Bar and Grill
6810 Front St.
Stock Island, FL 33040
305-293-4041

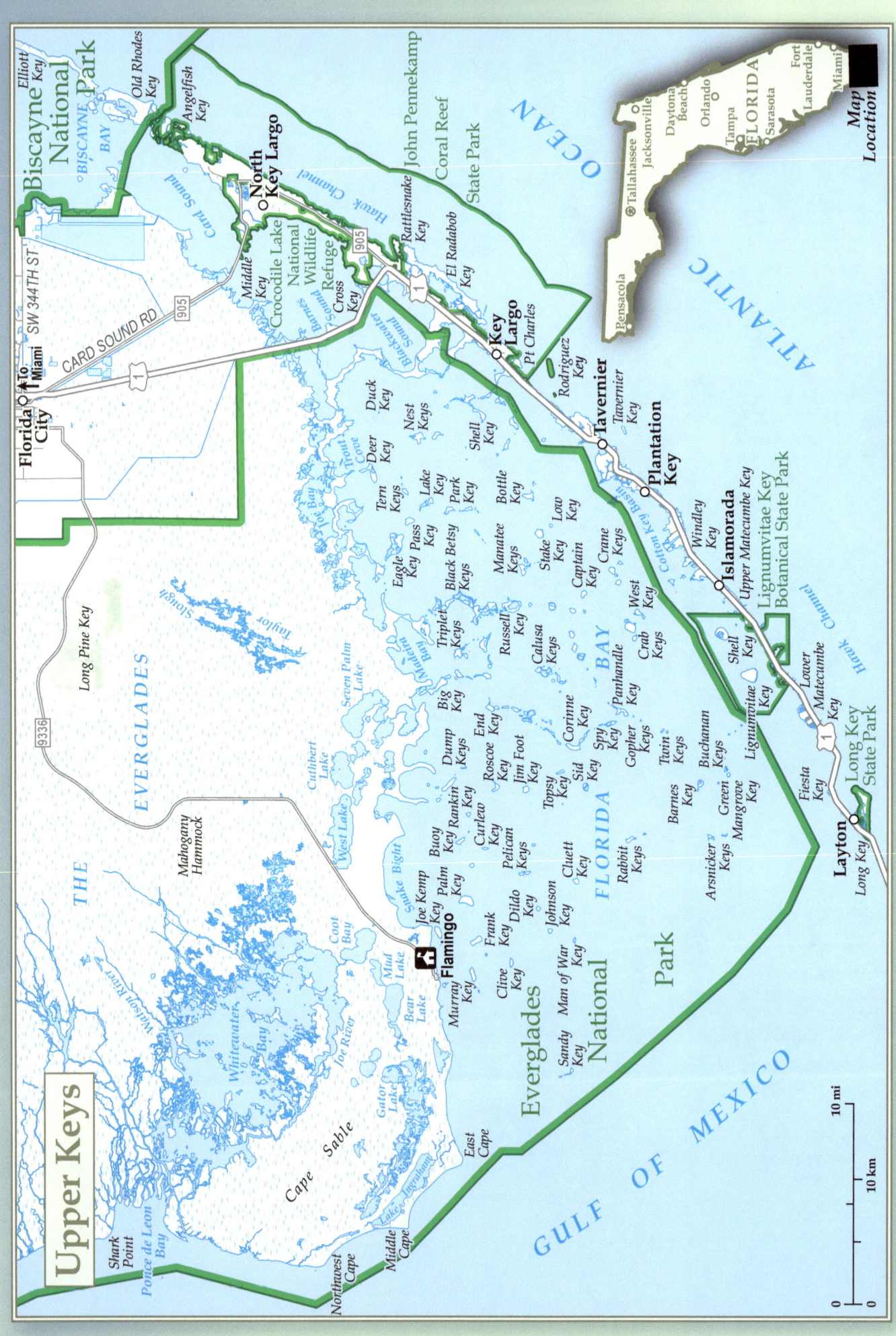

3 · Upper Keys

➤ **Location:** Islamorada, Village of Islands, made up of several Keys (including Upper and Lower Matecumbe and Plantation Keys), sits only 74 miles south along U.S. Route 1, and 82 miles north of Key West. Fly into Miami, rent a car at the new and safe car rental center, and drive south—it's about two hours to paradise.

When I tell people I live in the Florida Keys, most equate that with Key West. But Key West is like another country for us, another 90-mile drive south and, quite frankly, a totally different vibe. Islamorada is situated in the Upper Keys, which are more connected to the Everglades and the mainland than the rest of the Keys. It is easy and accessible.

Islamorada has long promoted itself as the Sport Fishing Capital of the World—and rightly so. The variety of inshore and offshore opportunities are endless, coupled with a variety of accommodations and dining opportunities that rival the best big cities have to offer.

There is really no "roughing it" when visiting Islamorada—the fishing, the food, the spas, and the sunsets never get old—and if it does, well, then this lifestyle is just not for you.

We chose to move here permanently several years ago, relocating the family from the hustle and craziness of downtown Miami to the laid-back home of fishing guides, soccer moms, and world record tailing bonefish. It was the best decision of our lives, and we've never looked back. Life in Islamorada is as it should be—calm, family oriented, and without the road rage and stress of an overcrowded concrete time bomb.

The variety of species available and types of flats within a boat ride make Islamorada extremely versatile in most weather conditions. It's a place that's comfortable for novices and the biggest of challenges in the world for fly-fishing experts. The food and accommodations are world-class, and it's easy to get here.

For those who haven't been here, it's on their lists. For those who come, it's the place to which they always return.

➤ **Hatches:** People visit Islamorada to relax, honeymoon, and dive, but mostly they come to fish. And for fly fishermen, it has always been a bucket-list destination and the retirement-home dream.

Primarily, fly fishermen come to Islamorada to target the "glamour" species: bonefish, permit, tarpon, redfish, and snook. There is really no other place in the world that will regularly give you shots at all five glamour species in the

Angler and guide in search of tailing fish. Honson Lau

same day. The series of islands running to the southwest from Miami make up the Florida Keys, providing a variety of flats encompassing Florida Bay and Everglades National Park to the north and extensive oceanside flats protected by a reef system only four miles offshore. The Gulf Stream sits a few miles farther away and can be accessed in a skiff on calm days.

Bonefish—There is nowhere else in the world that 10-plus-pound bonefish are regularly caught than Islamorada. In fact, more world records have come from the nutrient-rich waters of famous "downtown Islamorada" than from any other locale. These fish are not easy and it is definitely the PhD of all flats fishing. Fish here grow to more than 15 pounds, and have been known to bring experienced flats fisherman to their knees. Bonefish require specialized techniques and are ultra-spooky. The Bahamian phrase "long strip, mon" doesn't get it done and is regularly met with disdain.

Jumping 'poons in the upper Keys. Honson Lau

Boatside hookup in the upper keys. Honson Lau

We catch bonefish year-round, but the biggest fish are typically caught in the fall. For sheer numbers of fish, the summers can be fantastic for tailing fish. Typical fishing is 10–15 shots per day with days with more than 20 shots considered great.

Tarpon—Tarpon fishing creates the most excitement of the year, and it's easy to see why—with 6 feet of muscle in shallow water that eat 2-inch flies better than bait, what's not to love? Tarpon bring out the egos and testosterone. It is the singular fish that causes fights between guides on the water and back at the dock. Prime time tarpon season is April through July, when the big schools are migrating up and down the ocean and throughout the backcountry. But we catch big tarpon 12 months a year, and the best fishing of the year typically happens when we have summer-like conditions in the winter. Rising water temperatures and light winds bring the big giants out of the Gulf and up onto the warmer banks of Florida Bay to feed.

Permit—For my taste, permit are psychological head cases. Do everything right, over and over, and you can still get refusals. But then again, some days they are very aggressive and multiple strikes happen. There is very little rhyme or reason. When I first started fishing for permit back in the mid-1990s, we used to say it took ten perfect casts to get one to eat. That number has dropped significantly with the development of new flies and techniques, and many anglers—some of which are as crazy as the quarry they pursue—only target permit. It's like a cult to many, a passion that drives them to all ends of the world's flats to find. However, unlike tarpon and bonefish, the gratification of doing it right is not always enough. For that reason, despite catching several dozen over the years myself, I will always consider them a glorified jack!

Permit love warm weather, so the toughest months to pursue them are the winter months. Big tides, clear skies, and strong winds to mask your presence are the typical preferred permit conditions.

Redfish—Many times, when the weather is poor or fishing has been tough, we comment, "Thank God for redfish!" Arguably the most consistent fishing we have, redfishing in Everglades National Park is simply outstanding. And over the last several years, the population has crept east. Now, several great days are had within five to ten minutes of Islamorada.

Redfish are fun for novice and expert alike. Novices get to take many shots in a day at tailing and mudding fish, and it gives them lots of work on seeing and casting to feeding fish. Experts use redfish to refine and hone skills and to practice putting the fly on the plate—I've always said doing a lot of redfishing will seriously improve your tarpon fishing and bonefishing. Redfishing is strong 12 months a year.

Snook—An estimated 250,000 snook were killed in 2010 when a cold front dropped air temperatures into the low 30s and water temps into the 50s. Along with a quarter million snook, the cold killed countless tarpon, bonefish, ladyfish, jacks, sharks, and other species. Backcountry snook are most susceptible to cold, and they had nowhere to go. Fast-forward to 2016, and many snook regulars believe the fishing is rebounding.

Snook are targeted all over Florida Bay, including the No Motor Zone, but the fishery close to Islamorada in and around the main Keys also can be outstanding. Snook that are sight-fished with a fly and can be extremely aggressive, like their freshwater cousin, the largemouth bass. They pounce on topwater gurgler patterns, so surface bites can be quite common.

We fish for snook year-round, but the fishery can change day-to-day without a lot of pattern. The best time of year for exploring the extreme backcountry is winter.

We fish for all of the glamours year-round, and while there are historically preferred seasons for each species, everything is weather dependent.

Spring (April, May, June)
  Prime time big tarpon season
  Great bonefishing for big mudders
  Excellent permit fishing

Summer (July, August, September)
  Excellent baby tarpon fishing
  Tailing bonefish and redfish in big tailing schools
  Snook up on the flats

Fall (October, November, December)
  Most record bonefish caught
  Biggest redfish of the year
  Good permit on big tides

Winter (January, February, March)
  Big laid-up tarpon fishing (weather pending)
  Great snook fishing in the very backcountry and No Motor Zone
  Great trout, jacks, sharks, and barracuda

Upper Keys tarpon putting gear and man to the test. Honson Lau

Shallow water redfish in the upper Keys. Honson Lau

▶ **Tackle:** If you're visiting Islamorada and fishing with a guide, the basics will be provided. Rods, reels, flies—my grandfather always said if we had those three things, we could forget everything else. Most fly fishermen become equipment junkies at some point along the way, so here is a list of things to bring on your trip if you fit that description:

- **Rods**—I recommend 9-weights for bonefish, redfish, and snook. For permit and baby tarpon, use 10-weights. Employ 12-weights for big tarpon.
- **Reels**—I've always advised anglers to buy the best reel you can afford. Abel, Tibor, and Nautilus reels will last a lifetime.
- **Lines**—Almost exclusively floating, I prefer Monic Floating Tropical Clear lines for everything except tarpon. I use Scientific Anglers Mastery Series Tarpon Taper lines for big tarpon unless it gets slick-calm on the ocean, and then I switch to Monic Floating Tropical Clear.
- **Flies**—Until you develop intimate knowledge, rely on your guide to provide the right food for the right fish at the right time.
- **Raingear**—The number one forgotten item. Get rained on in August, and then run 40 mph through the Everglades, and you will think it is winter.
- **Lunch**—Most guides appreciate lunch, but it's always good to ask ahead of time. Go heavy on water—I recommend eight bottles per person, per day during a trip. You will stay hydrated and feel fresh after a day on the water.
- **Clothing**—Long-sleeve shirts and pants, gloves, a hat, and a face mask with liberal sunscreen is the only way to go. Covering your skin actually keeps you cool in the hot sun.
- **License**—Not necessary if you are with a guide.

A typical fishing day out of Islamorada will be eight hours on the water, leaving you plenty of time to relax by the pool or have a tropical cocktail on the beach. There are a variety of mostly water-based activities you can do, but most fly fishermen tend to focus on refueling the body, talk about broken leaders and guide mistakes, and prepare for the next day's tailers.

▶ **Fun Activities:** It's hard not to want to just fish night and day when you're in Islamorada. Many clients come to town, fish all day, and then want to go wading on their own in the evening. But if you bring your family and want a few other fun things to do, here are a couple of suggestions:

Drive to Key West for the day—It's only 90 miles, and a completely different Keys experience. Eclectic and crazy, Key West is primarily a party town but it does have quality things to experience for the whole family, such as the aquarium and Ernest Hemingway Home & Museum.

Go to Robbie's Dock—Hang out at Robbie's for hours, eat lunch, shop for local trinkets, but mostly, go to hand-feed the big tarpon. For a couple of dollars, you can get eyeball-to-eyeball with hundreds of these ancient creatures, study how they inhale a bait, and maybe even get some tarpon mouth scrapes on your arms.

Check out Theater of the Sea—This is one of the oldest dolphin shows in the world. You can also see sea lion and parrot shows which rival those found anywhere. They also have a fascinating shallow water lagoon system filled with our favorite glamour species to study!

Tim with a great upper Keys bonefish. Honson Lau

TIM MAHAFFEY is the only angler in history to win all of the major fly-fishing invitational tournaments in the Florida Keys—the Gold Cup Tarpon Tournament, the Don Hawley Tarpon Tournament, the Spring Fly Bonefish Invitational (four times), and the Fall Fly Bonefish Invitational (two times). After 21 tournament wins, he switched to the back of the boat and recently guided Heidi Nute to the largest tarpon ever caught on fly by a lady angler—a 152.8-pound giant.

CLOSEST FLY SHOPS

Florida Keys Outfitters
81219 Overseas Hwy.
Islamorada, FL 33036
305-664-5423
tackle@floridakeysoutfitters.com
http://www.floridakeysoutfitters.com/

Fly Shop of Miami/Fort Lauderdale
8243 S. Dixie Hwy.
Miami, FL 33143
305-669-5851
theflyshop02@bellsouth.net
www.flyshopofmiami.com

CLOSEST GUIDES AND OUTFITTERS

Capt. Tim Mahaffey
Flatshead Fishing Charters
305-219-8201
tim@flatshead.com

Capt. Duane Baker
Florida Keys Flats Fishing Guide
305-852-0102
duanebaker40@bellsouth.net

Capt. Eric Herstedt
Florida Light Tackle Charter
954-592-1228
capterichersted@bellsouth.net

Florida Keys Outfitters
81219 Overseas Hwy.
Islamorada, FL 33036
305-664-5423
tackle@floridakeysoutfitters.com
www.floridakeysoutfitters.com

CLOSEST LODGING

The Breezy Palms
80015 Overseas Hwy.
Islamorada, FL 33036
305-664-2361
www.breezypalms.com

Cheeca Lodge & Spa
81801 Overseas Hwy.
Islamorada, FL 33036
305-664-4651
www.cheeca.com

CLOSEST RESTAURANTS

Kaiyo
81701 Old Highway
Islamorada, FL 33036
305-664-5556
www.kaiyogrill.com

Marker 88
88000 Overseas Hwy.
Islamorada, FL 33070
305-852-9315
www.marker88.info

Lorelei
96 Madeira Rd.
Islamorada, FL 33036
305-664-2692
loreleicabanabar.com

S.A.L.T.
82779 Overseas Hwy.
Islamorada, FL 33036
305-664-9094

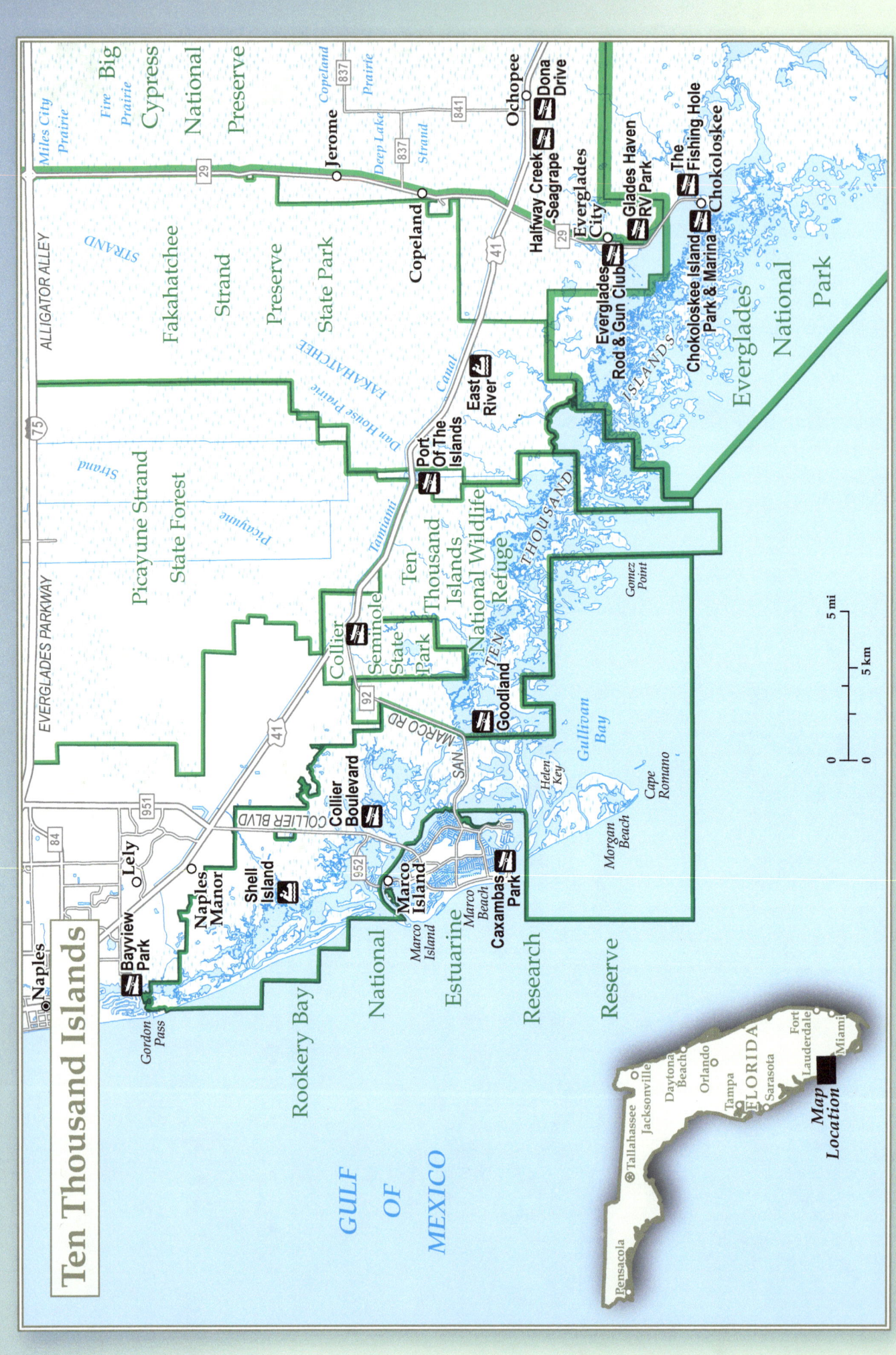

4 · Ten Thousand Islands

➤ **Location:** Ten Thousand Islands, located in Southwest Florida, span from Naples to Everglades City. Naples is located an hour south down Interstate 75 from Southwest International Airport in Fort Myers. The beautiful setting of Naples and Marco Island provides anglers and the family with endless options for fishing, dining, and relaxing. The ease of access to a variety of different types of water is what sets Ten Thousand Islands apart from the rest of South Florida. From baby tarpon in the backcountry lakes to snook on the beach, and everything in between, the year-round opportunities will keep an angler occupied no matter the season.

Ten Thousand Islands is composed of myriad rivers, creeks, bays, bars, and islands. All of this shallow water provides prime habitat for many great saltwater gamefish. Tarpon roll along the beaches and basins, redfish meander along oyster bars, and snook prowl the labyrinth of mangrove roots in search of their next meal. Many offshore species migrate past the islands as well, giving an angler shots at jack crevalle, mackerel, cobia, and bonito (false albacore).

The seasons and water temperature dictate where to find the fish. The cooler temperatures of winter and early spring keep fish in search of warmer water up the rivers, creeks, and oyster bars. A series of warm days may even bring resident tarpon out of hiding as they search for a secluded bay to enjoy the warmth of the sun. This early season is also great for kayak fishing the many backcountry lakes and creeks as the bug count is down and the fish enjoy the warmer tannin-stained water. As spring turns to summer, anglers chase fish out of the backcountry and out along the beautiful beaches, passes, and outside points of the islands. Summer is also the start of the rainy season, which can dirty up the water, so a little searching may be in order to find sight-fishable water. The plus side is that the afternoon rainstorms really fire the fish up and the fishing can be phenomenal afterward—just don't forget the bug spray! Late summer and fall are prime time. Bait is around in mass quantities and every gamefish around starts to fatten up for the upcoming winter. This is a great time to try for a backcountry slam (snook, redfish, seatrout, and tarpon).

Fly selection is fairly simple in Ten Thousand Islands. Baitfish flies, such as Deceivers, EP Minnows, and Tom's Tantrum, will catch anything that swims in Southwest Florida and beyond. Generally, small baitfish flies and shrimp patterns will be used in the cool, clear water of winter then increase in size as the seasons progress. Summer is a great time to throw topwater flies, because you never know what might blow-up on it! For sight-fishing here, the key is to have

Kelly Bandlow with a backcountry redfish. Kelly Bandlow

a fly that lands softly and a hook that is always sharp. More than likely, the fly will be tied to a 9-foot leader with a "bite" tippet of 40-pound fluorocarbon that's about 12 to 18 inches in length. Clear water in winter may call for a bite tippet of 20-pound, and tarpon can increase it up to 80-pound fluorocarbon.

For anglers short on time to fish the gulf, beaches on the coast of Naples and Marco Island are a great option. Gordon Pass and the Naples Pier provide anglers walking the beaches with lots of structure to fish. Doctors Pass, Clam

Above. Kelly Bandlow with a micro poon. Kelly Bandlow

Inset. Wade fishing for micro poons. Josh Almond

Pass, and Wiggins Pass all have easy access and have some beautiful water to fish. Fly selection on the beach is a little different; here, smaller is better. Flies in the 1 1/2- to 3-inch range that imitate shrimp or small baitfish are key. The white, sparsely tied patterns seem to do the trick for color and style. Be sure to stay on the sand as snook, jacks, and redfish will cruise right in the wash where the water meets the sand. Anglers wading in the water will miss fish as they swim behind them. Leaders are also slightly different for beach fishing as well. Longer leaders in the 10- to 12-foot range with a 25- to 30-pound fluorocarbon bite tippet will get more eats than a standard backcountry leader. Fishing the dock lights at night is another great option for a quick trip. The same flies used on the beach work well for snook in the lights. Fly fishing the lights is great fun and offers amazing sight-fishing opportunities, although it is limited to anglers with access to a boat or paddle craft.

▶ **Tackle:**

Snook/Redfish/Baby Tarpon
- 9-foot, 7-weight
- 9-foot, 8-weight
- 9-foot, 9-weight

Full-size Tarpon
- 9-foot, 11-weight
- 9-foot, 12-weight

Winter time redfishing can be great in 10,000 Islands. Josh Almond

Above right. Josh Almond surf fishing for snook. Josh Almond

JOSH ALMOND grew up fishing the lakes and streams of northern Michigan and has been fly fishing since he was eight years old. After spending several years in the mountains of Western North Carolina, he has found his way south to Naples, Florida. He has traded wading for trout, musky, and smallmouth for poling a skiff for tarpon, snook, and redfish. The snook photo is courtesy of Capt. Wright Taylor of www.flyfishmarco.com.

CLOSEST FLY SHOPS
Mangrove Outfitters
4111 E. Tamiami Trl.
Naples, FL 34112
239-793-3370
www.mangroveoutfitters.com

Fly Shop of Miami
8243 S. Dixie Hwy.
Miami, FL 33143
305-669-5851
theflyshop02@bellsouth.net
www.flyshopofmiami.com

CLOSEST GUIDES AND OUTFITTERS
Capt. Paul Nocifora
239-206-0177
www.gladesflyfishing.com

Capt. Wright Taylor
239-821-9203
www.flyfishmarco.com

Capt. Tom Shadley
239-793-3370
www.mangroveoutfitters.com

Mangrove Outfitters
4111 E. Tamiami Trl.
Naples, FL 34112
239-793-3370
www.mangroveoutfitters.com

Captain Pete's Bait and Tackle
550 Port O Call Way
Naples, FL 34102
239-643-4466

CLOSEST BOAT RAMPS
Goodland Boating Park
740 Palm Point Dr.
Goodland, FL 34140
239-389-4247

Port of the Islands Marina
525 Newport Dr.
Naples, FL 34114
239-389-0367

CLOSEST LODGING
Naples La Quinta Inn and Suites
1555 Fifth Ave. S.
Naples, FL 34102
239-793-4646
www.laquintanaplesdowntown.com

The Boathouse Motel
1180 Edington Pl.
Marco Island, FL 34145
239-642-2400
www.theboathousemotel.com

CLOSEST RESTAURANTS
Randy's Fish Market
10395 Tamiami Trl. N.
Naples, FL 34108
239-593-5555
www.randysfishmarketrestaurant.com

Tacos and Tequila Cantina
4834 Davis Blvd.
Naples, FL 34104
239-732-8226
www.tacosandtequilanaples.com

The Snook Inn
1215 Bald Eagle Dr.
Marco Island, FL 34145
239-394-3313
www.snookinn.com

The Parrot Bar and Grill
1100 Sixth Ave. S., #6
Naples, FL 34102
239-435-7900
www.theparrotbarandgrill.com

CLOSEST HOSPITALS OR URGENT CARE
NCH Baker Hospital Downtown
350 Seventh St. N.
Naples FL 34102
239-624-5000
www.nchmd.org

North Naples Hospital
1190 Health Park Blvd.
Naples FL 34110
239-552-7000
www.nchmd.org

Naples Urgent Care
713 SW Health Pkwy., Ste. 1
Naples, FL 34109
239-597-8000
www.naplesurgentcareonline.com

5 · South Florida

▶ **Location:** Boca Raton is on the east coast of Florida, 35 minutes north of Fort Lauderdale, 30 minutes south of West Palm Beach, and one hour north of Miami. There are major airports in each of the aforementioned cities, making travel convenient.

"Where do you fly fish around here?" is the most common question asked by non–fly fishers who come into my fly shop in Boca Raton. It has a simple answer: "Anywhere there is water." Boca may be that place your family heads to visit grandma and grandpa, or where you take a quick flight to for that weekend business meeting, but to us locals who live and breathe fly fishing, there are plenty of opportunities within an hour's drive.

Walking the beaches in Palm Beach County make for a perfect easy-access saltwater adventure. The beach fishing is a year-round thing, but the "glory fishing" occurs from late April to mid-October with big snook and tarpon being the main events. People are surprised when I tell them you can see 30-pound snook swimming at your feet right up on the shore or tarpon corralling bait in only 3–4 feet of water.

Access to the beaches of Palm Beach are up and down A1A Scenic & Historic Coastal Byway, which runs parallel to the ocean. You can't fish the public beaches between the lifeguard stations while lifeguards are on duty. In Palm Beach County, they generally work from 9:00 a.m. and 5:20 p.m. You can use the public access to walk past the guard towers. These beaches are open to the public up to the high-water mark (typically where the sand ends) and are fishable 24/7.

Tarpon show up in May, and we get a big push through the beginning of July. Schools of 40- to 150-pound fish will travel in 20 feet of water passing the coast. Individuals and pods of fish will break off from the bigger schools to capture bait in the shallows. These fish can be 20–80 feet from shore and will eat a properly presented Pilchard or Glass Minnow fly. These well-oxygenated tarpon are very difficult to land, even if you are specifically targeting them with 11- or 12-weight rods. But the sight of a leaping tarpon right next to shore is a thrill, whether it's landed or not.

Fly fishing for snook kicks in as the tarpon thin out in July and August. Snook will cruise the beaches, looking for food to carry them through this spawning season. Pilchard and Glass Minnow patterns, such as Scott Hamilton's Eat Me fly

Fishing the canals around Boca Raton. Kelly Bandlow

and the EP Perfect Minnow, work well. Clear intermediate lines on 8- and 9-weights work best. Bite tippets of 25- to 40-pound fluorocarbon are required to protect against rough mouths and sharp gill plates. It's a sight-fishing experience, so a stripping basket helps with your line management.

Nighttime fishing in the Intracoastal Waterway for snook and tarpon is a year-round fishery on dock lights and bridge pilings. We like to do this in flats boats rigged with trolling

A healthy, colorful peacock bass.

motors. Throw small white baitfish or shrimp patterns under dock lights, and cast large black and purple mullet patterns near the bridges. I use 6- to 9-weight with clear intermediate lines and a 30-pound bite tippet for the lights. I use a 10-weight with a fast-sinking line on the bridges to handle larger flies and fish.

Fly fishing offshore in Palm Beach County is world-class. Blackfin tuna up to 35 pounds and false Albacore up to 20 pounds dominate the summer months. They feed along a natural reef in 100 feet of water. We typically employ live chum Pilchards and Glass Minnows to get the fish fired up. We hunt for dolphinfish in the spring and fall a little farther out in the Gulf Stream, searching for weed lines and floating debris. Fish will hang around structures and will also get lit up on live chum. Nine to twelve weights work well with intermediate lines, and Eat Me flies on leaders with fluorocarbon bite tippets. The wintertime brings the Gulf Stream extremely close to Palm Beach. This warmer water brings different species to our coast, such as Spanish mackerel, kingfish, cobia, big jack crevalle, permit, ladyfish, and bluefish. Fishing takes place much closer to shore, as the offshore swells keep all but the biggest boats in close. All these species present a lot of food to a huge spinner shark migration that shows up from February to the beginning of April. We fish for spinners with 12- to 14-weight, with big size 7/0 orange deer-hair flies on floating lines. Our leaders are usually straight 50-pound into size 7 wire (certainly not IGFA regulation, but this helps avoid line breakage on their sandpaper-like skin).

Freshwater fishing in South Florida is a blast. The local area is checker boarded with canals and lakes where access is more determined by finding a parking space than finding a fishing spot.

The largemouth fishing is best from October through May. We use 6- to 8-weight rods, with an 8 being best to handle the wind with larger flies and dealing with fighting bass though weeds. Tropical floating lines with 10- to 16-pound leaders will cover most of your needs, but sinking lines work well dragging bottom-bumping flies.

South Florida cichlid. Kelly Bandlow

Colorful south Florida cichlid. Kelly Bandlow

A good selection of poppers can range from a size 10 to big size 4/0 Frogs. Colors in both light and dark with bright chartreuses, yellows, and olive all will produce fish. Subsurface flies must cover different parts of the water column. High-riding baitfish patterns tied with bulky heads are effective. These include Mike Connor's Glades Minnow and Enrico Puglisi's Everglades Special. I enjoy fishing Barr's Meat Whistles as my deeper fly. It gets down weighted by a conehead and has a rabbit tail that wiggles enough to drive bass crazy.

There are many introduced species that thrive in the heat of the summer, including cichlids and peacock bass. The hotter, the better for these South American exotics. (Spots that have bass typically sustain populations of exotics.) The peacocks eat flies that include a lot of chartreuse and orange. I fish weighted flies like Clousers and Ehlers's Grim Reaper deep near structure. Cichlids will crush a small chartreuse foam popper and fight like a bluegill on steroids.

South Florida canals are full of exotic species. Kelly Bandlow

CLOSEST FLY SHOPS

Ole Florida Fly Shop
6353 N. Federal Hwy.
Boca Raton, FL 33487
561-995-1929
www.oleflorida.com

Bass Pro Shops
200 Gulf Stream Way
Dania Beach, FL 33004
954-929-7710

Gander Mountain
100 Gander Way
Palm Beach Gardens, FL 33403
561-627-5642
www.gandermountain.com

CLOSEST GUIDES AND OUTFITTERS

Capt. Scott Hamilton
Palm Beach and Jupiter (offshore and inshore)
561-745-2402
blueh2ofly@aol.com
www.flyfishingextremes.com

Capt. Dave Saddler
Intracoastal Palm Beach-Miami (nighttime)
Biscayne Bay (daytime)
954-254-2971
turtlegrasscharters@yahoo.com
www.turtlegrasscharters.com

Capt. Ron Doerr
Palm Beach and Jupiter (offshore and inshore)
561-512-5560
fish@captainronbiteme.com
www.captainronbiteme.com

Capt. Mark Giacobba
Intracoastal, Everglades (nighttime fishing in fresh water and saltwater)
561-789-2983
pesceflies@aol.com
www.gladesoutfitters.com

CLOSEST LODGING

The Colony Hotel and Cabaña Club
525 E. Atlantic Ave.
Delray Beach, FL 33483
561-276-4123
www.colonyflorida.com

The Seagate Hotel and Spa
1000 E. Atlantic Ave.
Delray Beach, FL 33483
877-577-3242
www.theseagatehotel.com

➤ **Tackle:** For the beach, I recommend 8- to 9-weight for snook, and 11- and 12-weight for tarpon. Use clear intermediate line and tapered leaders with a 12- to 20-pound class tippet with a 25- to 40-pound bite tippet. A wire bite tippet is necessary for barracuda or mackerel and bluefish in winter. Stripping baskets help immensely with line control. I recommend sandals or wading shoes to help in the rocky areas.

For offshore, I recommend 9- to 14-weight, clear intermediate and faster sinking density compensated lines. If I chose two outfits for all around offshore, it would be a 10-weight with an intermediate and a 12-weight with a fast sinker. Use boat shoes or sandals with nonmarking soles.

For fresh water, use 6- to 8-weight, tropical floating line with leaders of 8- to 16-pound tippets. Weedguards on flies help in most situations. Always wear shoes, not sandals, when walking the banks to protect yourself from fire ants.

➤ **Regulations:** Please refer to Florida Fish and Wildlife Conversation Commission's website for updated regulations: www.myfwc.com.

Darren Selznick.

DARREN SELZNICK is the owner of Ole Florida Fly Shop in Boca Raton, Florida. He grew up fly fishing throughout New England and graduated from Louisiana State University with a degree in fisheries management. After college, he guided in southern Colorado. He's passionate about fly tying, tying commercially, and teaching students since 2003, when he took over the reins of Ole Florida.

Sailfish Marina Resort
98 Lake Dr.
Palm Beach Shores, FL 33404
561-844-1724
www.sailfishmarina.com
(marina/inlet access)

The Breakers
1 South County Rd.
Palm Beach, FL 33480
888-273-2537
www.thebreakers.com
(private beach access)

Peanut Island Campground
6500 Peanut Island Rd.
Riviera Beach, FL 33404
561-845-4445
(access by boat only, water taxi available out of Sailfish Marina)

CLOSEST RESTAURANTS

Little Moir's Food Shack
103 S. U.S. Route 1, #D3
Jupiter, FL 33477
561-741-3626
www.littlemoirs.com/food-shack

Rhythm Cafe
3800 A. South Dixie Hwy.
West Palm Beach, FL 33405
561-833-3406

V&S Italian Deli
2621 N. Federal Hwy.
Boca Raton, FL 33431
561-395-5206

Guanabanas
960 N. Hwy. A1A
Jupiter, FL 33477
561-747-8878

The Funky Buddha Lounge and Brewery
2621 N. Federal Hwy.
Boca Raton, FL 33431
561-368-4643

CLOSEST HOSPITALS OR URGENT CARE

JFK Medical Center North Campus
2201 45th St.
West Palm Beach, FL 33407
561-842-6141
http://jfknorth.com/

Delray Beach Medical Center
5352 Linton Blvd.
Delray Beach, FL 33484
561-498-4440
www.delraymedicalctr.com

Boca Raton Regional Hospital
800 Meadows Rd.
Boca Raton, FL 33486
561-955-7100
www.brrh.com/

6 · Mosquito Lagoon / Indian River

> **Location:** Mosquito Lagoon is situated on Florida's east-central coast and extends from Ponce de Leon Inlet near the town of New Smyrna Beach to its southern terminus at Kennedy Space Center, an area that encompasses about 36,000 submerged acres.

A major portion of the lagoon is federally managed by Merritt Island National Wildlife Refuge and Canaveral National Seashore and thus retains an overwhelming percentage of natural habitat. For more than a century, its prolific fishery has maintained a legendary status with anglers and the sport of saltwater fly fishing can trace some of its roots to the area beginning in the 1870s, when James Henshall (of Book of the Black Bass fame) wrote about using fly tackle to catch various marine gamefish in nearby interconnected backwaters of the Indian River. W. H. Gregg also documented Mosquito Lagoon's outstanding fishing in his book Where, When, and How to Catch Fish on the East Coast of Florida (1902). To this day, the lagoon offers truly world-class saltwater fly-fishing opportunities—often in pristine settings that have changed little since Henshall and Gregg visited.

Tarpon, snook, jack crevalle, bluefish, ladyfish, pompano, and black drum are among the great gamefish that are seasonally abundant in Mosquito Lagoon, but it's the unique opportunities to catch redfish and spotted seatrout that have gained the area its well-deserved notoriety as an outstanding saltwater fly-fishing destination. Not only are both species found in prolific numbers throughout Mosquito Lagoon, but they also attain world record proportions. Redfish grow to more than 40 pounds and 10-pounders are common. The largest "gator" trout will top 10 pounds and 6-pound specimens are taken with regularity. Further contributing to Mosquito Lagoon's reputation is the fact that it offers a unique opportunity to stalk these two fish by sight fishing in clear water in the same manner used on bonefish flats. It's big-league flats fishing at its best and can be very challenging, yet highly rewarding when everything comes together.

Redfish and spotted seatrout are closely related members of the Sciaenedae, or drum, family and have many similar characteristics and habits, including a preference for the same kinds of prey and habitat. Consequently, techniques that work for redfish are usually just as effective for seatrout. As a matter of fact, it's common to catch one species while looking for the other.

Seven-, eight-, and nine-weight gear is ideal for seatrout and redfish in Mosquito Lagoon. Use the lighter gear for small flies or when there is little wind. If it's windy or a situation calls for a larger or weighted fly, a 9-weight outfit provides a distinct advantage. Under most circumstances, though, an 8-weight outfit makes a good all-around choice. A floating line will handle most situations, but a sink-tip line is more productive for fishing deeper holes and drop-offs. Leaders

Winter months offer clear water and great redfishing in the lagoon. Capt. Jon Cave

should be around 9 to 10 feet long, with a tippet ranging from 12- to 16-pound test. Just make sure to add a 20- to 30-pound test monofilament shock tippet to withstand the redfish's abrasive mouth and, to a lesser degree, that of the seatrout as well.

Summertime Indian River Redfish. Capt. Jon Cave

Facing. With Mosquito Lagoon being so shallow anglers can exit the boat and wade a lot of the no motor zones for tailing redfish. Capt. Jon Cave

Studies have shown that crabs are a favorite prey of redfish while seatrout demonstrate a preference for penaeid shrimp and small finfish. Regardless, a match-the-hatch approach to fly selection isn't necessary since both fish are opportunistic predators and will feed rather indiscriminately on a variety of prey. Any selection of flies should include Cave's Wobbler (the original spoon fly that does not spin when stripped quickly), Clouser Minnows, Dorsey's Kwan, a bendback, Popovic's Siliclone, and any popper variation. Since redfish have the down-turned (inferior) mouth of a bottom-feeder, flies fished along the bottom work best as reds often have trouble ingesting topwater presentations. When redfish are tailing, unweighted inverted patterns (with the hook point riding up) reduce the chances of hang-ups in the grass and are also less likely to spook fish. In contrast, seatrout have an up-turned mouth that is indicative of fish that prefer to feed on prey above them or at the same level, and they will often go out of their way to strike a noisy popper. Nevertheless, both fish will strike at all levels of the water column—top to bottom.

Grass flats, approximately 2–3 feet deep and marked with sandy potholes, are the ideal habitat for reds and trout. Other prime locations include drop-offs, the downcurrent side of small tidal flows and rivulets, sand and mud holes, oyster and sandbars, submerged structure, creek mouths, and the edges of spartina grass and mangroves. Regardless of habitat, a nearby plentiful food source is usually a prerequisite to finding fish.

There are several ways to access the lagoons. Small skiffs, canoes, kayaks, and other light watercraft provide easy access to all areas, and launch sites are conveniently located on the lagoon's perimeter. Furthermore, miles of dirt roads parallel a large portion of shoreline where a fly fisher is only a few steps away from great wade fishing. Guides are available as well, but to my knowledge, Paul Cave (www.backwatersguideservice.com) and John Turcot (www.backcountryonfly.com) are the only ones who cater specifically to fly fishers.

The southern end of Mosquito Lagoon consists mostly of open flats marked with an occasional island. The bottom is a mixture of grass, sand, and mud. In contrast, the upper

Capt. Paul Cave releasing a Mosquito Lagoon redfish. Capt. Jon Cave

one third is a maze of islands where oyster bars are plentiful and the water is sometimes darker than it is to the south. Regular tidal movement is strongest in the northern part of the lagoon closest to Ponce Inlet, but decreases proportionately farther south and is mostly imperceptible in the southernmost reaches. Water movement outside of tidal zones is largely the result of wind-driven currents, and sustained winds from the same direction can raise the water level on the windward side of the lagoon to form a sort of "wind tide" or seiche. Exposed areas can become highly productive as wind-driven currents raise the water level sufficiently enough for fish to swim and vice versa. Oppositely, the water level drops on the leeward shoreline, and fish tend to move to deeper flats, drop-offs, holes, and depressions when that happens. Furthermore, rainfall, runoff from adjoining watersheds, and the influx of water from freshwater streams and marshes can also affect depth. Keep in mind that redfish and seatrout normally face into a current (wind-driven or tidal) when they are cruising—adjust your fly-fishing tactics accordingly so that any presentation appears to be naturally moving away from them.

The most consistent fishing for reds and trout is between October and July, when temperatures are relatively cool. However, the quality of fishing drops significantly during the hottest months when shallow-water sight fishing is limited to either very early in the morning or late in the evening when the water is coolest. Winter cold snaps will send fish scrambling for the protective warmth of deep water, such the holes at Eddy Creek and Eldora.

Mosquito Lagoon offers many unusual contrasts—natural beauty next to space-age technology, peaceful manatees sharing the water with noisy watercraft, and pristine wetlands bumping up against New Smyrna Beach condos. Despite these curious dynamics, or perhaps even partly because

Above. Mosquito Lagoon offers some exceptional winter fishing for redfish and trout. Capt. Jon Cave

Below. No motor zones make for some great kayak fishing for trout and redfish in the Lagoon. Capt. Jon Cave

Below. The large Sea Trout of Mosquito Lagoon are as popular of a target species as redfish. Capt. Jon Cave

Above. Battling a shallow water Mosquito Lagoon redfish. Capt. Jon Cave

Inset. Mosquito Lagoon is known for its large gator sea trout. Capt. Jon Cave

of them, Mosquito Lagoon remains one of North America's premier saltwater fisheries and an epicenter for those who like to sight fish for big reds and seatrout with fly gear.

▶ **Regulations:** In general, a saltwater fishing license is required for anyone over 16 unless fishing with a licensed guide. For more info on licenses and additional regulations on other species, visit www.myfwc.com.

  Specific Regulations:
  - Redfish Regulations—Size limit is not less than 18 inches or more than 27 inches.
  - Daily recreational bag limit is one per day in the Red Drum South Management Zone (includes all of Mosquito Lagoon).
  - Seatrout Regulations—Size limit is not less than 15 inches or more than 20 inches (exception: may possess one over 20 inches).
  - Daily recreational bag limit is four per day in the Spotted Seatrout Southeast Management Zone (includes all of Mosquito Lagoon).

Base of Operations:
- Titusville, Florida (near southeast end of Mosquito Lagoon)
- New Smyrna Beach, Florida (at north end of Mosquito Lagoon)

JON CAVE is an author, lecturer, fly-fishing instructor, and guide. His credentials also include a master of science in natural resources with special concentration in the fields of fisheries and water resources. He has been a professional fly-casting and fly-tying instructor for over 30 years and is the founder of the longest established fly-fishing school in the South. Jon has taught thousands of students and trained guides at many international locations. He is a member of the Sage Ambassador Advisory Staff, Rio Fly Line Advisory Staff, and Umpqua's Contract Tyer Program. Jon created the widely popular Rattler Fly patterns and his groundbreaking Wobbler Spoon-fly is prominently exhibited in the American Museum of Fly Fishing as the forerunner of all such patterns. His articles, casting tips, columns, and photographs have been featured in most fly-fishing publications. Furthermore, Jon is the author of *Performance Fly Casting* and *Fly-Fishing Odyssey, The Pursuit of Great Gamefish*. His work is also included in several anthologies, including *Gray Ghosts* and *Lefty's Deceivers: Fly-Fishing Wisdom from The Masters* and *Feather Brain*. The results of his research on the hooking mortalities of fish have been published in several prestigious scientific journals, including *Progressive Fish Culturist* and *Journal of Freshwater Ecology*. Also, he presented those findings at the University of Notre Dame before the Indiana

Capt. Jon Cave with a summertime Mosquito Lagoon redfish.

Academy of Science. Jon is only one of a handful of individuals to be honored with the prestigious Federation of Fly Fishers Silver King Award for his contributions to saltwater fly fishing. He currently holds a seat on the advisory council for the Atlantic States Marine Fisheries Commission and has served on the board of governors for the Federation of Fly Fishers Casting Certification Program.

CLOSEST FLY SHOPS

Come prepared. No full-service fly shops are available in Titusville or New Smyrna Beach although New Smyrna Outfitters, a general tackle store in New Smyrna Beach, does carry some fly gear.

New Smyrna Outfitters
402 Canal St.
New Smyrna Beach, FL 32168
386-402-8853
www.newsmyrnaoutfitters.com

CLOSEST LODGING

Titusville/Kennedy Space Center KOA Campground
4513 W. Main St.
Mims, FL 32754
800-562-3365
www.koa.com/campgrounds/titusville

Loughman Lake Lodge
1955 Hatbill Rd
Mims, FL 32754
321-268-2277
http://www.airboatridesatloughman.com/
(limited cabin rentals)

CLOSEST RESTAURANTS

Dustin's BBQ
1208 S. Ridgewood Ave.
Edgewater, FL 32132
386-423-5299
www.dustinsbarbq.com

Louis's BBQ
2191 N. U.S. Route 1
Mims, FL 32796
321-264-1446

JB's Fish Camp
859 Pompano Ave.
New Smyrna Beach, FL 32169
386-427-5747
www.jbsfishcamp.com

Goodrich Seafood Restaurant and Oyster House
253 River Rd.
Oak Hill, FL 32759
386-345-3397
www.goodrichseafoodandoysterhouse.com

Dixie Crossroads
1475 Garden St.
Titusville, FL 32796
321-268-5000

CLOSEST MAJOR AIRPORTS

Daytona International

Sanford/Orlando International

Orlando International

7 · Tampa Bay

➤ **Location:** Tampa Bay, Florida, is known as a great place to live and visit as it boasts the country's best beaches, superb weather, and a thriving bay area of more than 4 million people. But how many of you think of Tampa for world-class fly fishing and sight casting? If you find yourself visiting or passing through Tampa, consider hitting the water and experiencing some of Florida's finest fishing!

One of the reasons Tampa's fishery is so good is its geographical location and makeup. Take the largest bay in Florida and place it on the transition from tropical to subtropical climates, and you end up with a fishery that gets just enough seasonal changes to support awesome year-round fishing for a multitude of species. Add to this clean water, shallow flats, and an endless mix of light sand and lush grass and you have a fly fisherman's dream destination!

Tampa has been a best-kept secret for fly fishing for tarpon, redfish, snook, and trout with many other species to add to the mix. The seasonal balance allows visitors to experience great fishing throughout the year with great things to do for the family as well. Let's take a look at a few reasons that earn Tampa a spot on the Southeast's top 50.

Winds can make or break your trip. Anyone who has been blown out in the Keys knows this. Tampa enjoys some of the best fly-fishing winds found in the saltwater world. Much of the year, Tampa's winds match the fishery to make for happy fly anglers and guides. In the winter, Tampa will have many north- and east-wind days, which play in perfectly with the bay's shallow-water flats found on the north and east sides. As the season switches over from spring to summer, On Most days, Tampa wakes up to a southeast trade wind that switches on the water/coast to an onshore west wind by early afternoon. Imagine starting your tarpon day with an 8 mph offshore wind and the sun at your back! This makes for flat calm water and dream conditions! Then, as the morning progresses, the morning breeze dies a mile or two per hour until about 11 a.m. when the wind dies completely, signaling the soon-to-come daily sea breeze. This daily switching of the winds can make for some of the best fly-fishing conditions possible.

Tampa is a year-round fishery. When January is blowing its cold winds to the north, Tampa has crisp air, blue skies, and gin-clear waters for sight casting! This makes for some stellar redfishing, which resembles bonefishing more than redfishing. Many yearly fly anglers come this time of the year to practice this humbling part of our sport. Think redfishing is easy or boring? Come down to Tampa in the winter

Spring morning on Mailbox Pool. Pond in the River Guide Service

and see why some anglers find Tampa redfish to be a true sight-casting challenge equal to bonefish!

During the winter, fishing around Tampa is at its high point for convenience. Great redfishing can be found within minutes of the airport and eliminates any excuses for not grabbing a guide and hitting the water. In fact, there are hotels on the water within minutes of the airport where you can catch and even wade for redfish, big lunker gator trout, and snook. Flying in for a couple days with meetings? Hit the water for a half day and see how beautiful this fishery truly is!

As spring marches in, the Tampa fishery is in full swing. All species are in motion and on the hunt for food. The winter redfish and backcountry snook are joined with resident bay tarpon looking to warm up and start eating. These resident poon (a local name for tarpon) have been eagerly awaiting the warming sun rays that come with March. Nothing feels as good to a poon than the warm surface-temp water. It gets so intoxicating that they will keep elevating until their whole back is sticking out of the water! That's exciting stuff! Like the winter redfish season, the waters of Tampa Bay itself are your best pick for these early-season poons. This is a happy time for both fish and fishermen. For many, it is a good time to catch a few last flats fish before switching focus to the world-class gulf fishing that is about to start.

By May, the hunt for tarpon is in full swing. This is the time to be a local or visit Tampa, as this is the highpoint of the fishing season with some spectacular world-class tarpon fishing! The white sand, gin-clear waters, and perfect weather conditions make for epic sight casting for big fish. This part of the Gulf features a complex system of flats, bars, and channels, which the tarpon move through. Being at the right place at the right time can make all the difference. It is highly recommended to find a fly-fishing guide with years of experience when targeting these giants. Tampa is known for larger-than-average size fish with most fish averaging more than 100 pounds and many in the 125- to 150-pound range! Bringing your significant other? How about setting her (or him!) up on a white sand beach within yelling distance of you while you sightcast to schools of tarpon? That's Tampa!

Tampa, being the largest bay in Florida, always has an option for you. Don't have a boat, or not looking to hire a guide? No problem—walk the beach! The beaches to the west of Tampa offer great snook fishing from May through September. Tampa Bay features a great mix of mangroves and backwaters, as well as the spawning habitat of the barrier islands and beaches and thus is a great destination for snook. The start of summer marks the time when snook move out to the beaches for their yearly spawn. Big females will be seen cruising the beaches with no shortage of small to midsize males looking for fun. This makes for exciting, and many times frustrating, fishing as huge snook send the message that they have something else in mind. It's worth the challenge and effort as there is something really special about walking the beach and catching a nice shallow-water beach snook on a fly!

With the coming of fall comes great nighttime fishing for dock snook. The bay area has many dock lights that are left on all night for anglers to enjoy some great sight casting

Facing. Upper Tampa Bay redfish caught while wade fishing. Capt. Dave Chouinard

Redfish are the most common fly rod target in the Tampa Bay area. Capt. Dave Chouinard

during the quiet hours. If you haven't tried night fishing, try it—you will have a blast! If daytime is more your thing, then the fall brings big gator trout and schools of redfish. Tampa is known for great trout fishing and over the past five years, it has even gotten better. Trout 25 to 30 inches are caught on a fairly regular basis during the winter. Often, you can sightcast to them on edges and potholes across the area.

Fall also brings some surprising false albacore fishing! Yes, albies! These little tunny (a common name for false albacore) are known on the East Coast, but many Tampa visitors are surprised to see schools of little tunny busting bait in the Tampa area!

The waters around Tampa Bay are also some of the cleanest on the west coast of Florida. They offer spectacular sight fishing for tarpon, redfish, snook, trout, and much more. If you're into the team sport of poling a skiff and sight casting to fish, then Tampa is your place. It is one of the few places you can bring your entire family and mix world-class

Capt. Dave Chouinard prepares to release a Tampa Bay tarpon. Capt Dave. Chouinard

accommodations, amusements, and fishing to create a trip of a lifetime that everyone can enjoy equally. This is what puts Tampa high on the list of the Southeast's top 50 places to fly fish!

▶ **Tackle:** The gear needed for fishing the Tampa Bay area is very dependent on the targeted species and the time of year. For the Tarpon anglers will want an 11or 12 weight rod with both floating and intermediate lines. For redfish Anglers will want a 7- to 9-weight with an 8-weight being the preferred rod. Anglers should carry both a floating and an intermediate fly line. For Snook and Albacore, anglers should bring an 8-10 weight rod with floating, intermediate, and sinking lines. Leaders should be tapered 12- to 20-pound test depending on the targeted species. Anglers also should pack some shock leader, especially for the Snook and Tarpon. Kwans, Crimps (or similar crab or shrimp patterns) and small baitfish imitations, such as Clouser Minnows and Rattle Minnows, will work for redfish and trout. For Snook and Albacore, the best choices of flies will be small baitfish patters ranging from sizes 4 to 1/0. Tarpon will focus on baitfish patterns, tarpon toads, and similar patterns. Remember that these fish see a lot of flies, so anything you can do to make your fly a little different or a little more realistic will usually result in more strikes.

For more than 23 years, **Dave Chouinard** has been a passionate fly shop owner, guide, instructor, and fly-fishing industry sales rep. At the age of 21, he opened his first fly shop in the Northeast. Then, in 2008, he migrated south and became a fly shop owner and guide on the west coast of Florida. Today, Dave is the owner of Chouinard Outdoor Associates, a leading fly-fishing industry rep group in the Southeast.

Capt. Dave Chouinard with a Key West Bonefish. Capt. Dave Chouinard

CLOSEST GUIDES AND OUTFITTERS
Tampa Fly Guides
charters@tampaflyguides.com
www.tampaflyguides.com
(Finding specialized fly fishing guides is key to your success with a complex fishery such as Tampa Bay. Tampa Fly Guides is a collaborative effort of Tampa's top five fly guides, all in one place. You can't go wrong with any of these top Tampa guides.)

CLOSEST RESTAURANTS
Dunedin Brewery
937 Douglas Ave.
Dunedin, FL 34698
727-736-0606
www.dunedinbrewery.com

Tampa Bay Brewing Company
1600 E. Eighth Ave.
Ybor City (historic neighborhood)
Tampa, FL 33605
813-247-1422
tampabaybrewingcompany.com

Al's Finger Licking Good Bar-B-Que
1609 Angel Oliva St.
Tampa, FL 33605
813-956-0675
www.alsybor.com

CLOSEST LODGING
The Westin Tampa Bay
7627 W. Courtney Campbell Cswy.
Tampa, FL 33607
813-281-0000
www.westintampabay.com
(Winter fishing—minutes from Tampa international airport and endless flats fishing. Offers a sandy beach and spectacular views of Tampa bay. Boat and jet ski rentals are available, too.)

DoubleTree Suites Tampa Bay
3050 N. Rocky Point Dr. W.
Tampa, FL 33607
813-888-8800
(Guides can pick you up at the hotel dock and you can be fishing within minutes! Cast from their dock and catch some fish, too.)

Grand Hyatt Tampa Bay
2900 Bayport Dr.
Tampa, FL 33607
813-874-1234
www.grandtampabay.hyatt.com
(This hotel is set on a nature preserve on one of the best winter wading redfish flats on Tampa Bay! Summer fishing features some of the best tarpon action you'll find.)

Loews Don CeSar Hotel
3400 Gulf Blvd.
St. Pete Beach, FL 33706
727-360-1881
www.loewshotels.com/don-cesar
(This hotel is known for its dining and 11,000-square-foot spa, Oceana.)

The Tradewinds—St. Pete Beach—playground!

TradeWinds Island Grand
5500 Gulf Boulevard
St. Pete Beach, FL 33706
727-367-6461
(This hotel is very kid friendly with a 20-acre beachfront.)

The Vinoy Renaissance
501 Fifth Ave. NE
St. Petersburg, FL 33701
727-894-1000
(This hotel includes an 18-hole golf course, 12-court tennis complex, and a private marina.)

8 · Florida Panhandle

➤ **Location:** The Emerald Coast is the unofficial name for a coastal area in the state of Florida on the Gulf of Mexico. It is 4 1/2 hours from Birmingham, Alabama, six hours from Atlanta, Georgia, and four hours from New Orleans, Louisiana. You can fly commercially into Northwest Florida Beaches International Airport in Panama City, Northwest Florida Regional Airport in Valparaiso, or Pensacola International Airport in Pensacola.

Located in northwest Florida, the panhandle stretches about 100 miles through five counties (Escambia, Santa Rosa, Okaloosa, Walton, and Bay), from Pensacola to Panama City. The Emerald Coast encompasses three major bays: Pensacola Bay System, Choctawhatchee Bay, and the St. Andrews Bay System. Pensacola marks the Western boundary of the Emerald Coast. Here you will find Pensacola Bay, which includes Escambia Bay and East Bay. Located in the middle, Choctawhatchee Bay opens to the Gulf at the Destin Harbor. The St. Andrew Bay System (North, East, and West Bay) in Panama City marks the Eastern most portion of the Emerald Coast.

This area derives its name from the emerald-green appearance of the water. The sugar-white color of the quartz sand creates this emerald hue. Crystal clear sand flats provide an incredible backdrop from which to sight a large variety of Gulf Coast gamefish. These waters are teeming with large groups of baitfish, crabs, and shrimp. The inshore waters can be divided into three parts: shallow-water grass flats, deepwater bay flats and shoals, and surf. Close to the inlets and along the surf offer the best wade-fishing opportunities. Inside the bays, large areas of lush turtle grass flats are perfect for sight fishing tailing redfish and speckled trout (also known as spotted sea trout). Poling skiffs or kayakers have the easiest access to these areas. Wade anglers will find grassy areas difficult to navigate.

There are many public boat ramps available along the Emerald Coast. Big Lagoon State Park in Pensacola has accesses for both boaters and kayakers, as well as good areas for wade anglers. Inside the lagoon and along the surf are productive for a variety of inshore species. Access to Choctawhatchee Bay at the Charles E. Cessna Landing Boat Ramp on Hogtown Bayou is a good central location. This is located on the south shore of Choctawhatchee Bay. The area is best for boaters and kayakers looking to fish the grass flats found only a short distance from the ramp. St. Andrews State Park in Panama City Beach provides boaters, kayakers, and wade anglers access to the Gulf beaches and St. Andrews Bay. From this park, you can fish the rock jetties lining the pass to the Gulf. You can approach the rocks either by foot or boat. Due to the heavy current and large boat traffic, kayaks are not recommended in the pass.

When fishing shallow-water flats, most anglers prefer a 9-foot, 8-weight outfit, rigged with a floating line, and a 10-foot, 16-pound tapered leader. A mix of natural-colored crab, shrimp, and finger mullet imitations will produce redfish and speckled trout throughout the year. A size 2 EC Grass

Amberjack will test the physical capabilities of the best anglers. Capt. Jason Stacey

Shrimp is a good choice for targeting tailing redfish. These fish can be easily spooked due to the clear, shallow water. A quiet, accurate presentation is essential for success.

On deeper bay flats in 3–10 feet of water, anglers will benefit from clear intermediate lines rigged with 7 ½-foot tapered leaders, tipped with a 30- to 60-pound fluorocarbon shock tippet. Depending on the season and water temperature, bull redfish, Spanish mackerel, speckled trout, jack crevalle, tripletail, and tarpon can all be caught here with regularity. Look for tripletail suspended or lying flat on the surface next to crab pot floats or any sizable obstruction. Use a size 2 EC Crazy Critter to entice these picky eaters.

Night fishing in the bay around underwater dock lights is very productive during warmer months. For night fishing, a 9-foot, 7-weight rigged with a clear intermediate tip line and a 9-foot, 16-pound leader works well. An assortment of small Glass Minnow and baitfish imitations can produce a good number of fish.

Near the inlet and along the beach, anglers can expect to encounter a large variety of inshore and nearshore species, many very large. These include bull redfish, tarpon, pompano, Spanish mackerel, cobia, false albacore, and jack crevalle. Medium to large, brightly colored surface poppers and translucent baitfish imitations produce well in these areas. I recommend 9-foot, 10- to 11-weight rods for larger species and 9-foot, 7- to 8-weight rods for all others. A 7 ½-foot tapered leader, tipped with a 30- to 60-pound fluorocarbon shock tippet, is the norm. Surf anglers are becoming fond of 12-foot, 7- to 8-weight switch rods. Switch rods allow for added distance and less fatigue when doing a lot of repetitive casting in the surf.

The following tables will help you choose the right fly and target the right species at the right time of year.

Capt. Jason stacey with Jack Cravelle caught while wading the beach in the panhandle. Capt. Jason Stacey

Naturals	Months Available	Fly Imitation	Size
Pilchard (White Bait)	April–October	· ZEP Pilchard · Polar Fiber Minnow · Crease Fly	2, 1, 1/0
Pogey (Menhaden)	August–October	· EP Peanut Butter · Bob's Banger	2, 1/0, 2/0
Blood Minnow	July–October	· Gummy Minnow · Surf Candy · Super Hair Clouser	2, 1
Pinfish	January–December	· EP Pinfish · Polar Fiber Minnow	2, 1, 1/0
Mullet	January–December	· EP Finger Mullet · Rattlin' Mullet · Clouser Minnow	1, 1/0
Glass Minnow	January–December	· Surf Candy · Super Hair Clouser	6, 4, 2
Crab	January–December	· Merkin · EP Crab · Grand Slam Crab · Kwan	4, 2, 1
Shrimp	January–December	· Supreme Hair Shrimp · EC Grass Shrimp · EC Crazy Critter	4, 2

Battling a silver king. Capt. Jason Stacey

Season	Target Species	
Winter (December–February)	Fair:	
		· Speckled sea trout
	Good:	
		· False albacore
		· Redfish
Spring (March–May)	Fair:	
		· Blue fish
		· Tarpon
	Good:	
		· Redfish
	Best:	
		· Speckled sea trout
		· Pompano
		· Cobia
		· Jack crevalle
		· Spanish mackerel
Summer (June–August)	Fair:	
		· Cobia
	Good:	
		· Redfish
		· Speckled sea trout
		· False albacore
		· Jack crevalle
		· Spanish mackerel
		· Blue fish
	Best:	
		· Tarpon
Fall (September–November)	Fair:	
		· Spanish mackerel
		· Tarpon
	Good:	
		· Speckled sea trout
		· Tripletail
		· Jack crevalle
	Best:	
		· Redfish
		· False albacore
		· Blue fish

▶ **Regulations:**
- Redfish—Two fish per person, per day; eight-fish vessel limit; no fish may be less than 18 inches or more than 27 inches
- Spotted seatrout—Five per angler, per day; Fish must exceed 15 inches and be less than 20 inches total length (may possess one fish longer than 20 inches included in bag limit)
- Florida pompano—Six fish per angler, per day; 11 inches fork length
- Tripletail—Two fish per person, per day; 15 inches (total length, not fork length)
- Cobia—One per person, per day (or six per vessel, whichever is less); 33 inches fork length

▶ **Tackle:** I recommend 9-foot, 7- to 12-weight rods with floating and intermediate lines. Leaders should be 7 ½–10 feet tapered to 12- to 20-pound. I suggest 30- to 60-pound fluorocarbon shock tippet for tarpon and toothy species. Stainless pliers are recommended.

Florida Panhandle false albacore. Capt Jason Stacey

Facing. Fly anglers on the Emerald coast never know when they are going to have the opportunity to catch a fish like this beautiful American Red Snapper. Capt. Jason Stacey

Above. Hooked up to a bull redfish on the Emerald Coast. Capt. Jason Stacey

51

One fish, two fish, redfish, bluefish. Multiple species are common in the Florida Panhandle. Capt. Jason Stacey

Redfish release. Capt. Jason Stacey

Releasing a Jack Cravelle on the beach. Capt. Jason Stacey

CAPTAIN JASON STACY lives happily with his wife and children in Northwest Florida where he is a full-time fly-fishing guide. He is a certified instructor by the Federation of Fly Fishers and owner of the Emerald Coast Fly Fishing School. He has gained an intimate knowledge of this area and its species by spending more than 200 days a year on the water.

Capt Jason Stacey.

CLOSEST FLY SHOPS

Old Florida Outfitters
30 Watercolor Blvd. E., #101
Santa Rosa Beach, FL 32459
850-534-4343
www.oldfloridaoutfitters.com

Apalach Outfitters
32 Avenue D
Apalachicola, FL 32320
850-653-3474
fish@apalachoutfitters.com
www.apalachoutfitters.com

Orvis
625 Grand Blvd., Ste. 101
Sandestin, FL 32550
850-650-2174

CLOSEST GUIDES AND OUTFITTERS

Capt. Jason Stacy
Shallow Water Expeditions
30 Watercolor Blvd. N., Ste. 101
Santa Rosa Beach, FL 32459
850-534-4349
www.shallowwaterexpeditions.com

CLOSEST LODGING

WaterColor Inn & Resort
34 Goldenrod Cir.
Santa Rosa Beach, FL 32459
888-991-8878
www.watercolorresort.com

Courtyard Sandestin at Grand Boulevard
100 Grand Blvd.
Miramar Beach, FL 32550
850-650-7411

Hampton Inn & Suites
13505 Panama City Beach Pkwy.
Panama City Beach, FL 32407
850-230-9080

CLOSEST RESTAURANTS

Hunt's Oyster Bar
1150 Beck Ave.
Panama City, FL 32401
850-763-9645
www.huntsoysterbar.com

Old Florida Fish House
5235 E. County Rd. 30A
Santa Rosa Beach, FL 32459
850-534-3045
www.oldfloridafishhouse.com

Nick's
7585 Florida 20 West
Freeport, FL 32439
850-835-2222
www.nicksseafoodrestaurant.com

The Red Bar
70 Hotz Ave.
Santa Rosa Beach, FL 32459
850-231-1008
www.theredbar.com

Bud and Alley's Waterfront Restaurant
2236 E. County Rd. 30A
Seaside, FL 32459
850-231-5900
info@budandalleys.com
www.budandalleys.com

AJ's Seafood & Oyster Bar
116 Harbor Blvd.
Destin, FL 32541
850-837-1913
info@ajs-destin.com
www.ajsdestin.com

CLOSEST HOSPITALS OR URGENT CARE

Sacred Heart Hospital
5151 N. Ninth Ave.
Pensacola, FL 32504
850-416-7000
www.sacred-heart.org

Sacred Heart Hospital on the Emerald Coast
7800 U.S. Route 98 W.
Miramar Beach, FL 32550
866-591-3600
www.sacred-heart.org

Sacred Heart Urgent Care Center
6665 Pensacola Blvd.
Pensacola, FL 32504
850-416-2000
www.sacred-heart.org

Bay Medical Center
615 N. Bonita Ave.
Panama City, FL 32401
850-769-1511
www.sacred-heart.org

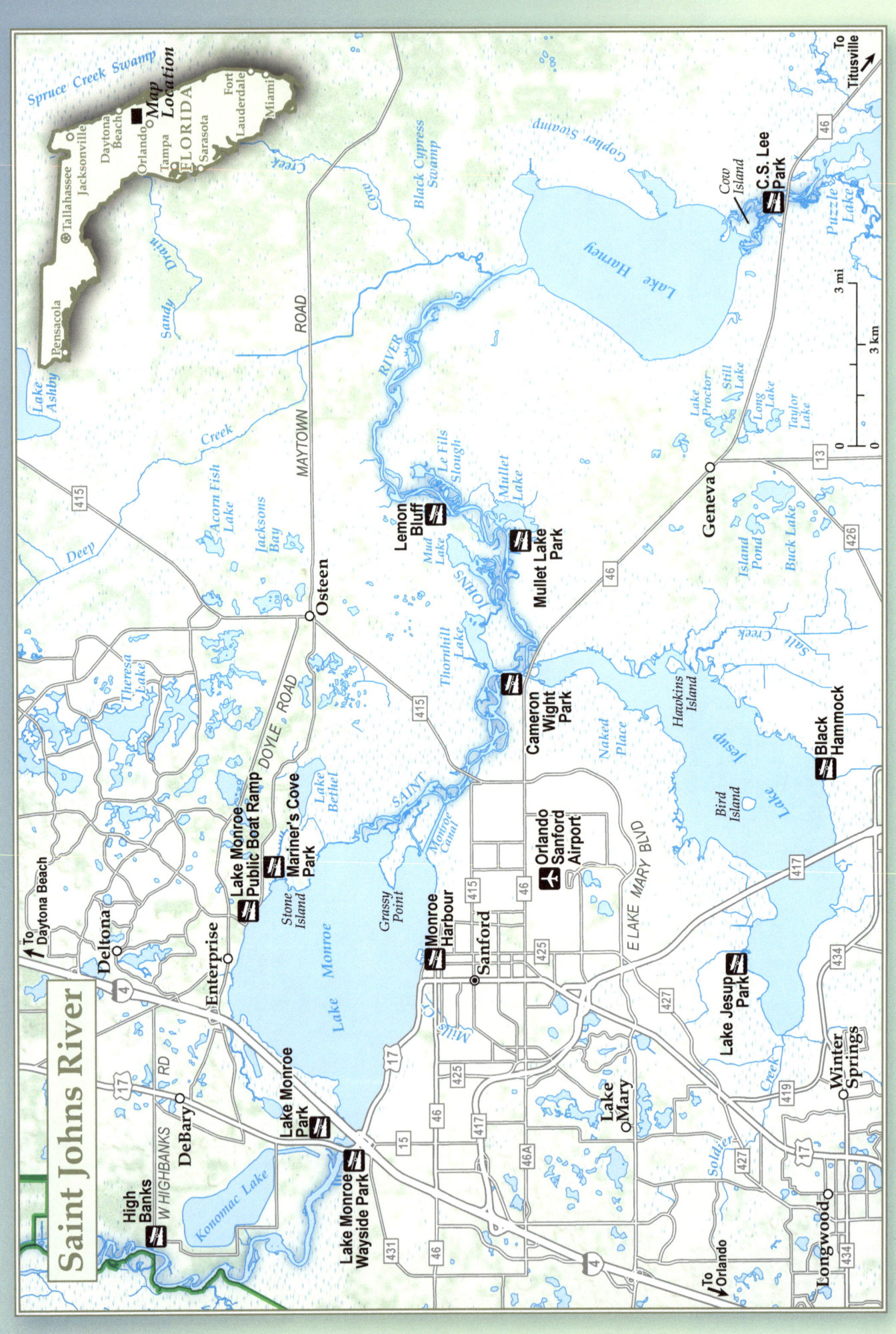

9 · St. Johns River

▶ **Location:** Seminole Indians called it "Welaka," or "river of lakes," a perfect description for the many lakes that are connected to one another along the more than 250-mile course of Florida's St. Johns River. The entire river has long been recognized as a premier freshwater fishery, but it's the wild and undeveloped uppermost section between Lake Monroe and the headwaters near Lake Hell n' Blazes that offers the best fly-fishing opportunities. That stretch of water is unmatched as fertile habitat for a variety of warmwater gamefish, a dynamic mixture of lush aquatic vegetation, braided waterways, deep cutbanks, remote wilderness, and a prolific forage base of small finfish. In addition, the comparatively shallow depth allows fly fishers to wade and cast from the banks—provided they keep an eye out for curious alligators and the occasional cottonmouth.

▶ **Largemouth Bass:** In his journal from the 1760s, pioneer naturalist William Bartram described using a fly-like Florida Bob to catch plentiful "green trout" (his term for largemouth bass) on the St. Johns. Although Bartram was inclined to exaggerate, the upper St. Johns has remained a legendary largemouth fishery and arguably offers the finest fly fishing for black bass in the world.

The largemouth bass population in the upper river is exclusively the Florida subspecies *Micropterus floridanus* (Florida largemouth bass). One of their predominant characteristics is the ability to attain a greater size than their closely related northern cousin, *Micropterus salmoides* (largemouth bass). Ten-pounders are not uncommon and specimens weighing more than 15 pounds are reported from time to time. Since bass in the St. Johns have to contend with currents, they become very strong and are more formidable fighters than their comparatively lethargic counterparts who reside in enclosed bodies of stillwater. During peak periods, it's not unusual for a skilled fly fisher to land as many as 50 bass in a day, and specimens exceeding 6 pounds can be taken with regularity.

The best bass fishing generally occurs during the driest months when the river is at its lowest—usually sometime between the end of October and the first of June. As the water level drops, bass increasingly concentrate in the deepest pools where they can easily be located with a few casts. At times, the fish will assemble in large schools and thrash the surface in a feeding frenzy as they prey on pods of small baitfish swept along in the current. These melees generally last only a few seconds, after which another attack may take place in a different location, usually within close proximity of the previous one. Unless a fly is delivered during the fracas, the chances of a hook-up drop significantly. There is little time for false casting—one backcast is the rule. Consequently, employing a saltwater-style speed-cast is critical to consistent success in those situations.

Other highly productive areas for bass include the edges of deep cutbanks, sharp bends, any location with a converging or diverging channel, shorelines with thick vegetation (littoral zone) that are directly adjacent to the main current, submerged structure, and the mouths of tributaries. After a rain shower, bass will also often gather where small rivulets of runoff empty into the river.

Angler battles a fiesty upper St. Johns River largemouth. Capt. Jon Cave

Capt. Jon Cave with a nice St. Johns largemouth. Capt. Jon Cave

Wading the upper St. Johns River. Capt. Jon Cave

Popping bugs and Clouser Minnows are far-and-away the most productive flies for St. Johns bass. I carry both patterns in a variety of colors, but when bass are focusing on bait pods and feeding selectively, flies that are predominately white or pearl overwhelmingly draw the most strikes as they closely match the light-colored prey. Extremely large flies that are top producers for largemouth in many lakes aren't nearly as effective in the St. Johns riverine environment in which bass of all sizes show a marked preference for small- to medium-sized patterns tied on hook sizes 1–6.

▶ **American Shad:** Each year, one of the most prolific, yet little known, runs of anadromous fish occurs during the winter months as American shad migrate from the sea to spawn near the St. Johns headwaters. After a 4–5-year absence, the fish are instinctively returning to their birthplace to produce a new generation. Florida has the southernmost migration, but there are other runs of American shad in many rivers along the Atlantic Seaboard. Tags indicate the fish travel from as far away as Canada's Bay of Fundy.

The American shad is the largest of the herrings. In Florida, they average 2–3 pounds, and 5-pounders are caught with regularity. In rivers to the north, the average size is somewhat larger, mostly because some of the northern fish are repeat spawners. Contrastingly, those in the St. Johns die after reproducing—probably the result of making such an exhaustingly long trip, but also because the warmer water saps the fish of the energy necessary to return to the Atlantic.

Shad begin to enter the river mouth at Jacksonville sometime in December when seasonal temperatures begin to cool the water. Male shad, or "bucks," are the first to arrive, followed shortly thereafter by the larger female "roe"

Releasing a St. Johns largemouth. Capt. Jon Cave

Raz Reid displays an American shad. Capt. Jon Cave

shad. Once the fish enter the river, they wind their way to the uppermost reaches south, or upstream, of Lake Monroe where 80 percent of the river's fall occurs and currents are the strongest. There, females release their eggs freely in the moving water while males swim alongside and disperse milt. The strong flow of water facilitates the fertilization process by mixing eggs and milt together. The height of spawning activity occurs in January, February, and March when water temperatures hover in the mid-60s.

The shad's preference for a location with a strong current should be the foremost consideration in selecting a productive fishing spot. Places with the swiftest flow include the main channel, the edges of steep banks, deep holes, the outside bank of sharp turns, and drop-offs. Among the locations with the best opportunities to fly fish for shad are those in the vicinity of Mullet Lake, Lemon Bluff, Highway 50, Lake Harney, Hatbill Park, and Puzzle Lake.

Shad are filter-feeders that nourish themselves by opening their mouths with gills flared to strain food, mostly plankton, from the water as they swim. However, studies by biologists indicate that shad, like many other anadromous fish, stop feeding once they enter freshwater environs. Some skeptical anglers question that scientific research because they have witnessed shad pursuing minnows (a rather common occurrence) in spawning locations and mistake that behavior for feeding when, instead, the shad (like spawning salmon and steelhead) probably regard the smaller fish as egg-eating predators and are chasing them from the breeding area. Despite the fact that they don't feed in fresh water, shad can be enticed to strike small flies if they are presented effectively. Flashy patterns tied on size 6 hooks and weighted with a set of bead-chain or extra-small dumbbell eyes are standard for the St. Johns River.

The presentation needs to be made at either a 90-degree angle to the current or, preferably, just slightly downstream. To allow the fly sufficient time to sink, dead-drift it with an occasional mend until it is quartering downcurrent. Then simply strip the fly slow enough to feel it occasionally bump the bottom. On the other hand, there are occasions when shad inexplicably prefer a faster retrieve with the fly closer to the surface—so it pays to experiment a little to find the most productive method.

There are many other species to pursue on the St. Johns with fly gear, including sunshine bass, black crappie, various bream, gar, and bowfin. Since walk-in fishing opportunities are limited, a kayak, canoe, or motorized skiff is needed to access the river's best fishing. Once you arrive at a likely spot, you have the options of casting from the boat, walking the bank, or wading. Be aware that the upper river is a maze of channels and dead-end sloughs and it's extremely easy to get lost in this remote area. Those unfamiliar with the watershed should take along a map and move about cautiously.

▶ **Regulations:** In general, a freshwater license is required for anyone over 16 unless fishing with a licensed guide. For more info on licenses and species regulations, visit www.myfwc.com.

▶ **Tackle:** To handle the vast majority of situations with largemouth bass, I recommend using 6- to 8-weight outfits matched to a floating line, but a sink-tip line can come in handy during cold snaps when fish seek refuge in deep water. Leaders should be 8–10 feet long with tippet sizes of 0X or larger to ensure adequate turnover of large and/or weighted flies. Any assortment of flies should include Clouser Minnows, popping bugs, and eel/worm streamers.

For American shad, I suggest employing 5- to 7-weight outfits with either a sinking, sink-tip, or floating line, depending on where the fish are located in the water column. Leaders can range up to 10 feet long with a 0X tippet size being a good all-around choice. Local patterns prevail (my favorite for over 30 years is Cave's Red-headed Killer $\frac{1}{32}$- to $\frac{1}{64}$-ounce jig-fly that resembles a minnow with an egg in its mouth), but weighted bonefish flies can be used in a pinch.

The following locations are great places to use as a base of operations when fishing Saint Johns River.

- Greater Orlando, Florida
- Titusville, Florida
- Sanford, Florida
- Cocoa, Florida
- Melbourne, Florida

Top. Capt. Paul Cave releases a largemouth back to the river. Capt. Jon Cave

Bottom. Capt. Paul Cave with a nice gar from the St. Johns. Capt. Jon Cave

CLOSEST FLY SHOPS

Harry Goode's Outdoor Shop
1231 E. New Haven Ave.
Melbourne, FL 32901
321-723-4751
hgos1946@gmail.com
www.harrygoodes.com

Travel Country Outfitters
1101 E. Altamonte Dr.
Altamonte Springs, FL 32701
407-831-0777
www.travelcountry.com

Bass Pro Shops
5156 International Dr.
Orlando, FL 32819
407-563-5200

Orlando Outfitters
2814 Corrine Dr.
Orlando, FL 32803
407-896-8220
www.orlandooutfitters.com

CLOSEST GUIDES AND OUTFITTERS

Capt. Paul Cave
Backwaters Guide Service
407-718-7920
(Captain Paul Cave is the only full-time fly-fishing guide operating regularly on the Saint Johns River. He also guides on Mosquito Lagoon, Indian River, and the Sebastian Inlet.)

CLOSEST LODGING

Titusville/Kennedy Space Center KOA Campground
4513 W. Main St.
Mims, FL 32754
800-562-3365
www.koa.com/campgrounds/titusville

Lake Loughman Lake Lodge
1955 Hatbill Rd
Mims, FL 32754
321-268-2277
http://www.airboatridesatloughman.com/

Manatee Hammock Campground
(near Indian River Lagoon, south of Titusville and east of Orlando)
321-264-5083
https://registration.brevardcounty.us/webtrac/wbwsc/webtrac.wsc/wbsplash.html?ccode=BRV02

Wickham Park Campground
(near Brevard Community College in Melbourne, Florida)
321-255-4307
https://registration.brevardcounty.us/webtrac/wbwsc/webtrac.wsc/wbsplash.html?ccode=BRV03

JON CAVE is an author, lecturer, fly-fishing instructor, and guide. His credentials also include a master of science in natural resources with special concentration in the fields of fisheries and water resources. He has been a professional fly-casting and fly-tying instructor for over 30 years and is the founder of the longest established fly-fishing school in the South. Jon has taught thousands of students and trained guides at many international locations. He is a member of the Sage Ambassador Advisory Staff, Rio Fly Line Advisory Staff, and Umpqua's Contract Tyer Program. Jon created the widely popular Rattler Fly patterns and his groundbreaking Wobbler Spoon-fly is prominently exhibited in the American Museum of Fly Fishing as the forerunner of all such patterns. His articles, casting tips, columns, and photographs have been featured in most fly-fishing publications. Furthermore, Jon is the author of *Performance Fly Casting* and *Fly-Fishing Odyssey, The Pursuit of Great Gamefish*. His work is also included in several anthologies, including *Gray Ghosts* and *Lefty's Deceivers: Fly-Fishing Wisdom from The Masters* and *Feather Brain*. The results of his research on the hooking mortalities of fish have been published in several prestigious scientific journals, including *Progressive Fish Culturist* and *Journal of Freshwater Ecology*. Also, he presented those findings at the University of Notre Dame before the Indiana Academy of Science. Jon is only one of a handful of individuals to be honored with the prestigious Federation of Fly Fishers Silver King Award for his contributions to saltwater fly fishing. He currently holds a seat on the advisory council for the Atlantic States Marine Fisheries Commission and has served on the board of governors for the Federation of Fly Fishers Casting Certification Program.

Capt. Jon Cave

Long Point Park Campground
(near Sebastian Inlet in southern Brevard County)
321-952-4532
https://registration.brevardcounty.us/webtrac/wbwsc/webtrac.wsc/wbsplash.html?ccode=BRV04

CLOSEST RESTAURANTS
Jolly Gator Fish Camp
4650 E. Florida 46
Geneva, FL 32732
407-349-5554

Loughman Lake Lodge
1955 Hatbill Rd
Mims, FL 32754
321-268-2277
http://www.airboatridesatloughman.com/

Lone Cabbage Fish Camp
8199 W. King St.
Cocoa, FL 32926
321-632-4199

Gators Riverside Grill
4255 Peninsula Point
Sanford, FL 32771
407-688-9700
www.gatorsriversidegrille.com

CLOSEST BOAT RAMPS
Boat ramps are readily available throughout the river's length. The easiest to access are generally adjacent to highway bridges and in county parks. Visit http://www.stjohnsriverkeeper.org/the-river/boat-ramps/ for a map showing many boat ramps along the river.

CLOSEST MAJOR AIRPORTS
Orlando International Airport
1 Jeff Fuqua Blvd.
Orlando, FL 32827
407-825-2001

Sanford/Orlando International Airport
1200 Red Cleveland Blvd.
Sanford, FL 32773
407-585-4000

Orlando Melbourne International Airport
1 Air Terminal Pkwy.
Melbourne, FL 32901
321-723-6227

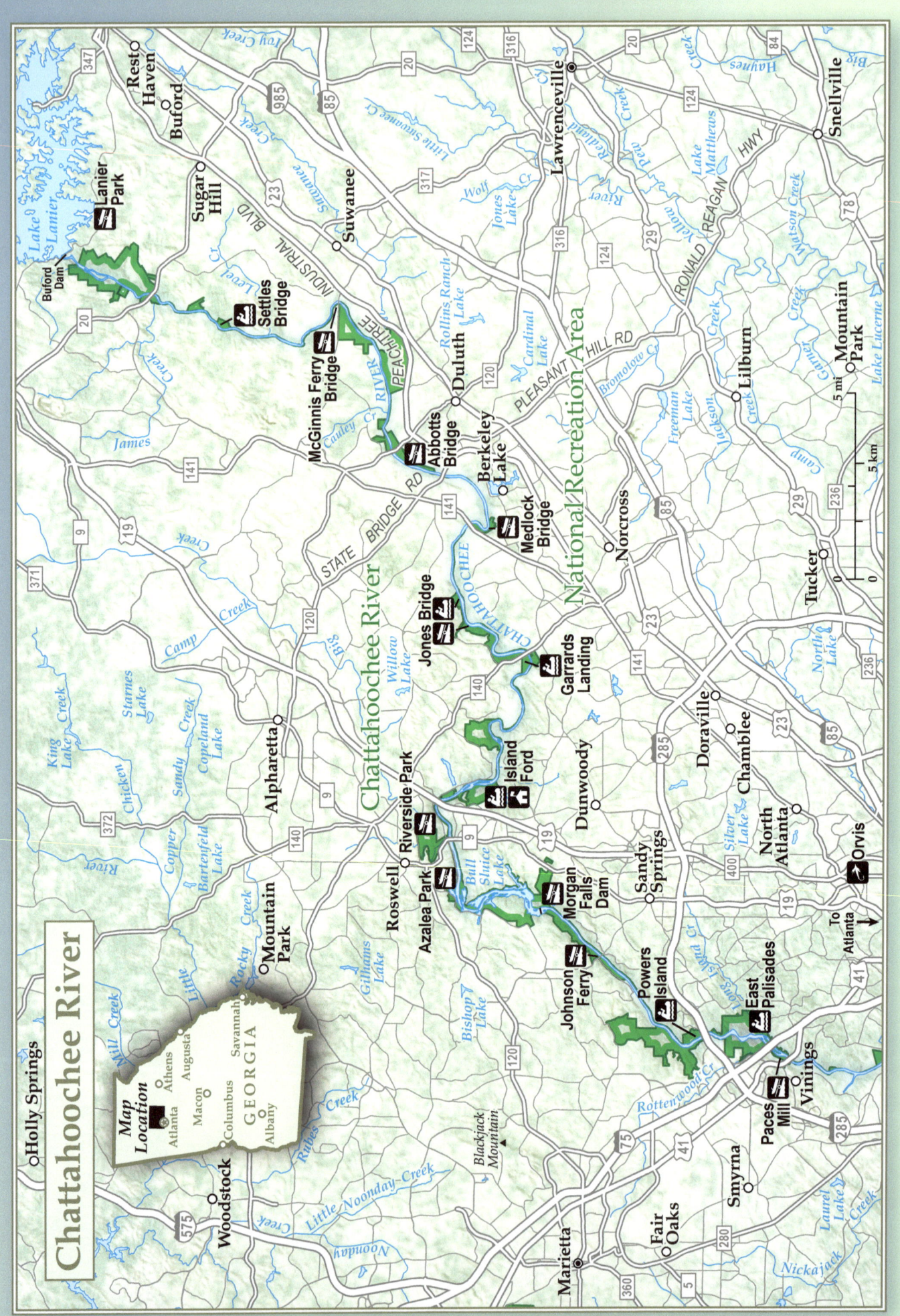

10 · Chattahoochee River

➤ **Location:** The Chattahoochee River has long been held as the Peach State's premier trout fishery. For roughly 40 miles, the cool waters of the river hold trout, making it one of the longest stretches of viable trout water in the Southeast. The river also boasts the state's largest brown trout record (20 pounds, 14 ounces) with brown trout naturally reproducing in the upper regions between Buford Dam and Morgan Falls Dam. Thanks to cold discharges from the depths of Lanier Lake, the waters below Buford Dam provide a year-round fishery to anglers who travel from great distances to sample Georgia's top tailrace.

➤ **Upper River:** Floating the Chattahoochee affords the angler the ability to hopscotch shoals, fish deeper pools with authority, and gain access to the mostly private stretches on the upper river below Buford Dam. Productive floats include the stretch between Morgan Falls Dam and Abbots Bridge and Abbots Bridge to Jones Bridge Park. The first is the longer of the two, 13 miles in total length and is best fished either in a jet-powered river boat or drift boat with an oarsman of solid fortitude.

Wading anglers are very limited on the upper stretch to a few hundred yards of shoals directly below Buford Dam, the shallow braided runs that parallel Jones Bridge Park, and another access point at Island Ford near the Chattahoochee Park Center. These areas offer the wading angler ample opportunity to roam at will with plenty of pocketwater and deeper runs. Weekends can be crowded, so be courteous to your fellow anglers and give them space.

points for floating or wading since much of the lower river corridor is bordered by the Chattahoochee National Park. Floating anglers can access the river at Morgan Falls, Johnson Ferry Park, Powers Island Park, and Paces Mill Park. All of these access points, save Powers Island, have ramp access for larger boats with ample parking. Drift boats, rafts, and personal watercraft are best used below Morgan Falls as the river becomes rocky and the angler must navigate a pair of Class II rapids just below Georgia 285.

For floating anglers, look for any change in current, seams, and shallow riffles to hold fish. Also, ledges near deep runs can often yield a surprising catch if you wish to ease a streamer down using a Type III sinking line. Many float anglers fish from the boat through the deeper pools and runs, then wade in the shallow riffles and shoals that dot the river. Wading anglers can find hundreds of yards of wadable shoals at

Canadian geese and blue heron are commonly encountered on the Hooch. Louis Cahill

➤ **Lower River:** The Chattahoochee below Morgan Falls Dam changes drastically in temperature and access compared to the upper river. Warmer temperatures make this an ideal stretch for the state's Delayed Harvest program, which runs from Sope Creek downstream to U.S. Route 41. During the Delayed Harvest season, anglers have a number of access Powers Island Park, Whitewater Park, and Paces Mill Park. These also happen to be the areas where the heaviest concentrations of fish and hatches seem to be located, making it the perfect quick getaway from work or that out of town business meeting.

The uniqueness of the Hooch is that you can trout fish right through the middle of a metropolitian area. Louis Cahill

Left. Stripers are abundant in the Hooch in the summertime, their favorite meal is fresh rainbow trout. Louis Cahill

One important bit of information would be there is no set generation schedule for Morgan Falls Dam. You must rely on the average discharge graph provided by the USGS and, unless you are monitoring the dam's outflow (which is typically on a one-hour lag time), watch the water levels on a nearby rock or other permanent structure in the river. If you notice the water line creeping up, exit the water immediately.

Following the Delayed Harvest season, the river warms, becoming inhospitable to trout who are replaced in short order by a modest run of striped bass which run upriver from West Point Lake. These striped bass average between 4 and 8 pounds; however, a few larger ones are caught every year. While their numbers are not overly plentiful, dedicated anglers who know where the fish live are consistently successful. One such angler is Rob Smith from the Fish Hawk Fly Shop in Atlanta. Rob guides on the lower river for stripers during the season and possesses the skills (and secret flies) to entice even the finickiest striper.

The Chattahoochee has many faces and many opportunities. From trout to stripers and a few shoal bass mixed in for good measure, there is something to get the blood pumping in any angler, no matter their disposition. For up-to-date

Broken fast water is a great place to look for rainbows. Louis Cahill

hatch information, fishing conditions, and general fly-shoppery, contact The Fish Hawk in Atlanta or Cohutta Fishing Company in Cartersville. Guided angling is available through River Through Atlanta Guide Service or either of the fly shops mentioned above.

▶ **Hatches::** Hatches on the upper river consist of caddisflies, Blue-winged Olives, and Light Cahills. While other bugs are present in good numbers, these are the most consistent hatches. Caddisflies typically begin in February with the small black caddisflies. For these little guys, a black Elk-hair Caddis (size 18) is about all you need. Look for the stronger hatches from Medlock Bridge downstream to Island Ford Park.

Following the black caddisflies, brown and tan caddisflies begin to emerge in March and continue through much of June. Elk-hair Caddis, X-Caddis, Harrop's Fertile Caddis, and Hemingway Caddis (sizes 14–16) will all do the trick. Rigging a dropper of an emerging caddis pupae or soft-hackle Pheasant Tail in one size smaller than the dry will typically yield more fish to the net. Cahills are present April–June with Compara-duns and parachutes (sizes 12–16) being all you need. Fish these light-colored mayflies just below riffles, especially around Jones Bridge and Island Ford. Blue-winged Olives are present year-round and the trout will key in on these diminutive mayflies at any emergence. Spotlight Blue-winged Olives, Sprout Blue-winged Olives, Harrop's Flat-wing Blue-winged Olive Emerger, and Mayhem Emergers (sizes 20–22) tied on 6X tippet with long leaders are the way to tempt trout into your offering. Many of the fish will be small, but the brightly colored hues of a wild brown trout in hand far outweigh the lack of inches on the tape.

Hatches on the lower river are slim, with caddisflies in the spring months yielding the most consistent dry-fly action. March–May can provide decent hatches of brown and tan caddisflies. The fish are not overly picky, so standard Elk-hair Caddis (sizes 14–16) and Harrop's Fertile Caddis (sizes 14–16) cover most bases for braided or slower water. Most anglers prefer to ply the lower river's waters with a double-nymph rig suspended by an indicator or by straight-line "euro" nymphing. For this, San Juan Worms in various colors (size 10), Y2K Bugs, Hot Head Sow bugs (sizes 10–12), Lightning Bugs (sizes 14–18), Prince Nymphs (sizes 12–16), and the ubiquitous Pheasant Tail (sizes 14–18) are fly box staples.

The Hooch offers a lot of great nymphing runs like this one. Louis Cahill

➤ **Tackle:** For larger trout, many anglers prefer casting streamers in the long pools that form a good portion of the river. The entire upper river between the dam and Island Ford is home to some very large brown trout. For these fish, go big or go home. Large streamers such as Galloup's Fat Head, Articulated Sculpins, and Game Changers fished on sinking lines will often tempt the larger trout into heart-stopping follows and short strikes if not a crushing take. Put the 5- and 6-weights back in the rod tubes and break out the 7- and 8-weight rods loaded with 250–300 grain sinking heads. Get deep and work the fly like a wounded baitfish. You have to entice a big trout to eat. You may not always see the take, but fish every cast like a 10-pound brown is following your fly, because it just might be!

If the trout are not rising and chucking big junk isn't your thing, feel free to drop a couple of nymphs below an indicator rig and get to work. Look for trout to hold in the braids, tailouts of pools, and seams. Fish a searching pattern such as a Psycho Prince Nymph, San Juan Worm, Hot Head Sow bug, Tungsten Redemption, or another brightly colored pattern (sizes 10–16) for the top fly, and drop a more natural pattern such as a Poxyback Baetis, Pheasant Tail, Split Case Blue-winged Olive, or Blue-winged Olive soft-hackle (sizes 16–20) off the back. These combos are proven on Chattahoochee trout so long as you're getting the fly down into the zone.

Should you wish to try it on your own, floating is the best method and searching the deeper pools with 8-weight rods and sinking lines tends to be the ticket. Flies such as Cowen's Magnum Baitfish, Seeker Baitfish, and Psychedelic Herring (all 2/0) are productive searching patterns for these migrating linesides. If you happen to tie into one of these, make sure your drag is tight and hope you remembered to tie solid knots on your 20-pound leader, because they will all be tested.

With no generation, much of the shoals on the Hooch can be easily waded. Louis Cahill

A canoe is a great way to navigate between shoal where there is no generation. Louis Cahill

James Buice releasing a striper on the lower Hooch. Louis Cahill

After graduating college with a degree in political science, JAMES BUICE quickly realized that the life of the law was not for him. He began guiding the mountains of Northern Georgia, Tennessee, and North Carolina for trout and striped bass. Also, he has had the pleasure of fishing North America, Central and South America, the Caribbean, the South Pacific, and Canada for saltwater species, Atlantic salmon, steelhead, and anything else that he could find. James has had the offer to write for several national publications, he has authored a book, and he now works as a manufacturer representative for Scott Fly Rods, Nautilus Reels, Airflo, and Echo Rods, among others.

CLOSEST FLY SHOPS

The Fish Hawk
3095 Peachtree Rd. NE
Atlanta, GA 30305
404-237-3473
www.thefishhawk.com

Cohutta Fishing Company
39 S. Public Sq.
Cartersville, GA 30120
770-606-1100
store@cohuttafishingco.com
www.cohuttafishingco.com

Orvis
3275 Peachtree Rd.
Buckhead Sq., Suite 210
Atlanta, GA 30305
404-841-0093

CLOSEST GUIDES AND OUTFITTERS

River Through Atlanta
710 Riverside Rd.
Roswell, GA 30075
770-650-8630
www.riverthroughatlanta.com

Cohutta Fishing Company
39 S. Public Sq.
Cartersville, GA 30120
770-606-1100
store@cohuttafishingco.com
www.cohuttafishingco.com

CLOSEST LODGING

Hampton Inn
915 Ronald Reagan Blvd.
Cumming, GA 30041
770-889-0877

Sheraton Suites Galleria
2844 Cobb Pkwy. SE
Atlanta, GA 30339
770-955-3900
www.sheratonsuitesgalleriaatlanta.com

CLOSEST RESTAURANTS

Swheat Market Deli
5 E. Main St.
Cartersville, GA 30120
770-607-0067

Ate Track Bar and Grill
28 N. Wall St.
Cartersville, GA 30120
470-315-4367

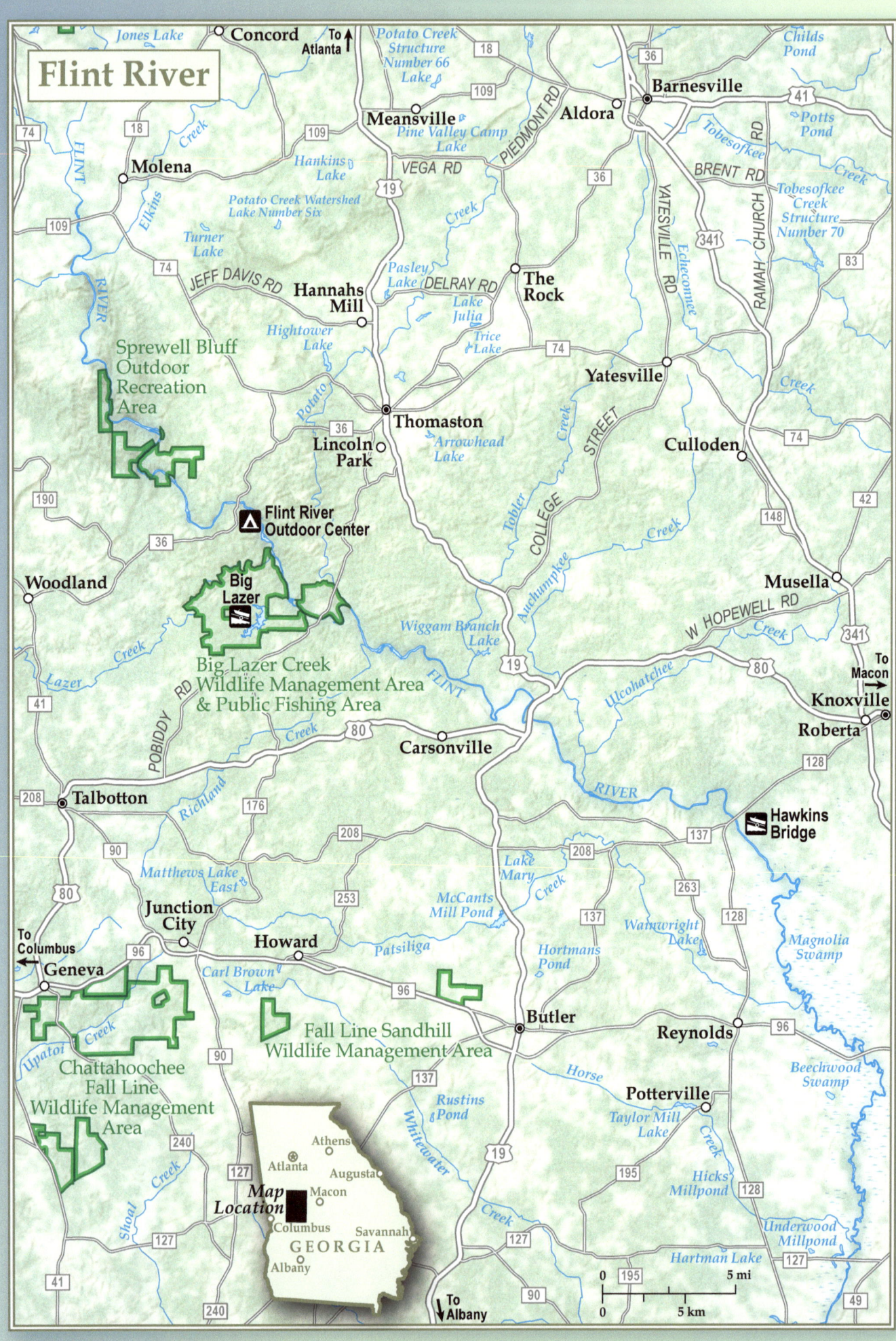

11 · Flint River

➤ **Location:** The fall line section of the Flint River is located in West Central Georgia about 50 miles south of Atlanta (less than an hour's drive), three hours from Birmingham, Alabama, one hour from Macon, Georgia, and less than an hour from Columbus, Georgia. You can fly into Atlanta.

The Flint is one of only 40 rivers in the U.S. that flow more than 200 miles without a dam. Beginning from underground springs just south of Atlanta, the Flint flows almost 350 miles, ultimately merging with the Chattahoochee River to become the Apalachicola River and reaching the Gulf of Mexico. Just below Atlanta, the river flows through a broad floodplain, which helps moderate its flow and cleanse the water. Then the Flint encounters the fall line, and its character changes completely.

The fall line here is a series of mountain ridges where crystalline rock was forced to the surface by a geologic fault some 30–50 million years ago. As the river cuts through these ridges and drops from the Piedmont to the Atlantic Coastal Plain, the elevation change is rapid, more than 400 feet in an 80-mile section. The flora and fauna from both regions flourish. Spanish moss and needle palms grow adjacent to wild azaleas and rhododendron. Among the numerous rare plant and animal species, you also find the shoal bass.

The shoal bass (Micropterus cataractae or "waterfall bass") was not officially recognized as a separate species of black bass until 1999. It is unusual to have a species relegated to a single river system, but that is the case with the shoal bass. This system includes only the Flint, Chattahoochee, and Apalachicola rivers and their tributaries. Because of numerous dams and habitat degradation, only the Flint now offers ideal shoal bass habitat, and the population elsewhere is limited mainly to isolated pockets. The fall line section of the Flint holds the largest concentration of shoal bass and offers a rarity in American angling—a native fish in its native environment that has never been stocked.

Long sections of shoals, some up to a mile or more long, are common on the Flint and are ideal for wade fishing. Some are available to the walk-in angler—these include Sprewell Bluff Outdoor Recreation Area near Thomaston and Big Lazer Wildlife Management Area near Manchester. Both offer walking access to more water than several anglers could fish in a day. Between the shoals are deeper narrow runs, which can be difficult to wade; thus, anglers often use canoes or kayaks to move between shallow shoal areas.

Notice the numerous rock out croppings associated with the fall line. David Cannon

A canoe outfitter located right on the river offers camping, shuttles, and canoe and kayak rentals. The water is mostly Class I and Class II whitewater and suitable even for novice paddlers.

March through October is the prime time for fishing the Flint, but the shoal bass is uniquely adapted to this river, so even the high water temperatures in midsummer don't put the fish off. Though air temperatures can often reach the mid-to-upper 90s this time of year, wet wading the shallow rushing water of the Flint is a cool and refreshing activity. Winter

Above. Typical Flint River shoals. David Cannon

Inset. Dragonflies are one of the favorite foods for shoal bass. David Cannon

Facing top. Numerous shoals on the Flint provide great habitat for the shoal bass. David Cannon

usually moves the fish into the deeper holes downriver, and their metabolism slows considerably.

Heavy rains can raise water levels and mud the river quickly, so check the water levels on the USGS website when planning a trip. The gauges at Molena and Carsonville are closest to the upper and lower borders of prime fishing. Ideal levels are under 7 feet and 4 feet, respectively, but the rate of rise or drop can be the best indication of clarity.

Shoal bass, like its cousins in the black bass family (largemouth, smallmouth, spotted bass, and so on), are generally very opportunistic feeders and will eat a wide variety of flies. Major forage includes crayfish, hellgrammites, dragonfly and damselfly nymphs, and many baitfish like small sunfish, darters, and minnows. Topwater bass bugs such as the Stealth Bomber and deer-hair poppers are often quite effective, along with Woolly Buggers, dragonfly nymphs, and all manner of streamers. Popper-dropper rigs with a large nymph tied to the hook bend of a large popper with 18 to 36 inches of tippet are also popular.

Though the shoal bass is closely related to the largemouth, fishing for them is more like trout fishing in many respects. Different even from river smallmouth, the shoal bass will move right into whitewater to feed. The river is very wide in the shoal areas but is usually divided into numerous different flows and fishes, more like ten trout streams laid side-by-side (but without the streamside vegetation to hamper backcasts).

An assortment of techniques is necessary for maximum success. Shoal bass like not just the big runs and deep pools, but they also lie in the deep, narrow slots in seemingly shallow, slower water. Many of these slots will be less than 12 inches wide, and the rocks severely undercut at the bottom—if the fish are not feeding aggressively on topwater baits, it is necessary to dead-drift a nymph so that it gets all the way down to the fish's level. Eddies behind rocks are good targets, but shoal bass also love the "push" water in front of the current obstructions. Especially in the summer with its typical low water, the fishing can become quite technical. During low-light conditions, shoal bass will often feed aggressively and

Inset. Hellgrammite's are another staple food source for the bass in the Flint. David Cannon

Left. Zach displaying a chucky Flint River shoalie. David Cannon

Below. Wanda fishing among the blooming spider lillies on the Flint. David Cannon

Kent Edmonds with a monster Flint River shoalie. David Cannon

Lone angler enjoying a late summer evening on the Flint. David Cannon

obviously in the shallows, but usually anglers are throwing to likely spots rather than to visible fish.

The river also offers numerous other species, including largemouth and spotted bass, bluegill and redbreast sunfish, gar and catfish.

➤ **Regulations:**
- For any combination of black bass species, the daily limit is ten.
- The minimum length is 12 inches for largemouth and 15 inches for shoal bass.
- There are no limits for other species.

➤ **Tackle:**
- 9-foot, 4- or 7-weight rods with floating weight-forward line
- Leaders 7–10 feet with 0–4X tippet
- Waders are seldom needed

Kent Edmonds with a Flint River shoal bass. David Cannon

KENT EDMONDS operates Fly Fish GA (www.flyfishga.com) and has been fishing the Flint with a fly for over 25 years. He was the Southeast Fly Fishing Forum's Instructor of the Year in 2013 and also operates The Habersham Mill Fly Fishing School in partnership with Jimmy Harris. His fly designs are sold commercially worldwide, and his articles are seen in numerous outdoor and fishing publications.

CLOSEST FLY SHOPS

Brannen Outfitters
106 Fairview Dr.
Perry, GA 31069
478-224-1616
www.brannenoutfitters.com

Ivey's Outdoor and Farm Supply, Inc.
108 N. Westover Blvd.
Albany, GA 31707
229-432-0622
info@iveysalbanyga.com
www.iveysalbanyga.com

The Fish Hawk
3095 Peachtree Rd. NE
Atlanta, GA 30305
404-237-3473
www.thefishhawk.com

Alpharetta Outfitters
79 S. Main St.
Alpharetta, GA 30009
(678) 762-0027
hello@alpharettaoutfitters.com
www.alpharettaoutfitters.com

Fly Box Outfitters
840 Ernest W. Barrett Pkwy. NW, Ste. 568
Kennesaw, GA 30144
866-460-2507
info@flyboxoutfitters.com
www.flyboxoutfitters.com

Cohutta Fishing Company
39 S. Public Sq.
Cartersville, GA 30120
770-606-1100
store@cohuttafishingco.com
www.cohuttafishingco.com

CLOSEST GUIDES AND OUTFITTERS

Fly Fish GA
Kent Edmonds
Thomaston, GA 30286
706-647-2633
www.flintriveroutdoorcenter.com

CLOSEST RESTAURANTS

The Bulloch House
47 Bulloch St.
Warm Springs, GA 31830
706-655-9068
www.bullochhouse.com

Moore's Whistling Pig Cafe
572 S. Main Ave.
Pine Mountain, GA 31822
706-663-4647

Idle Hour Pub
124 Bull St.
LaGrange, GA 30240
706-845-1167

CLOSEST HOSPITALS OR URGENT CARE

West Georgia Medical Center
1514 Vernon Rd.
LaGrange, GA 30240
706-882-1411
http://www.wghealth.org/contact/

Upson Regional Medical Center
801 W. Gordon St.
Thomaston, GA 30286
706-647-8111

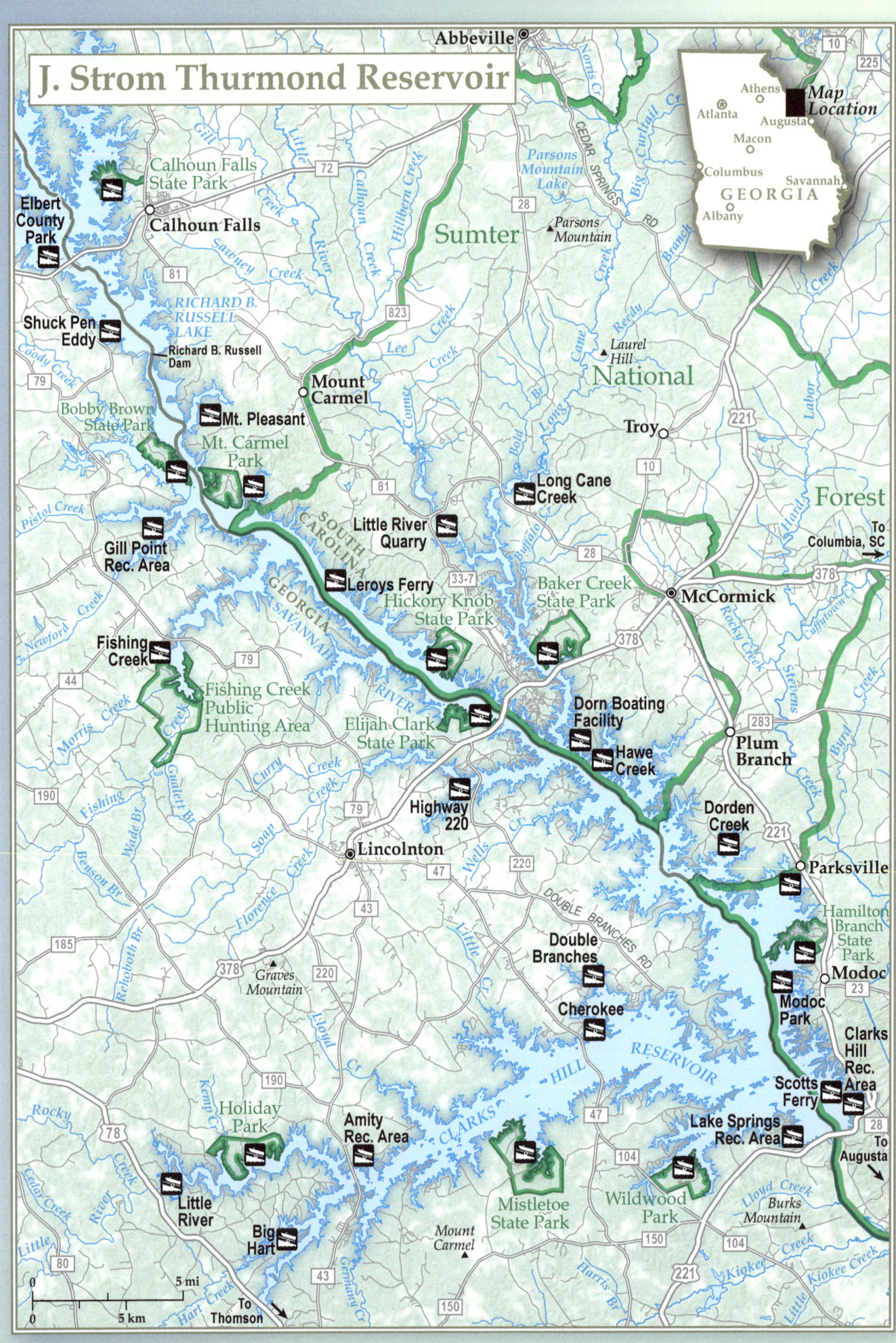

12 · J. Strom Thurmond Dam & Lake at Clarks Hill

▶ **Location:** More commonly known as Clarks Hill Reservoir, this reservoir is located about 30 minutes north of Augusta, Georgia, on the Savannah River. It is about two hours southwest of Atlanta, Georgia, and one hour west of Columbia, South Carolina. Anglers can base out of McCormick, South Carolina, Lincolnton, Georgia, or Thomson, Georgia. While you will need a boat to fish, anglers can fly into Augusta, Georgia, or Columbia, South Carolina.

Clarks Hill Reservoir was the first of three U.S. Army Corp of Engineers (USACE) dams to be constructed on the Savannah River. Commissioned by Congress in 1944, construction of the project began in 1946, and the lake began to fill in 1951. Clarks Hill is the third largest reservoir east of the Mississippi River; it covers 71,000 acres, with just more than 1,200 miles of shoreline. In 1988, the project was congressionally renamed J. Strom Thurmond Dam and Lake at Clarks Hill to honor Senator Thurmond from South Carolina. However, Georgia and most residents of the area around the lake were not in favor of the name change. In 1999, Georgia passed a resolution renaming the lake in the state of Georgia as Clarks Hill; to this day there is still quite a bit of controversy over the name, and the local residents still refer to the lake as Clarks Hill. Regardless of the name, the lake has found itself the center of several B.A.S.S. (Bass Anglers Sportsmen Society) tournaments, along with other well-known tours. In fact, it was here in 1976 that my father, Don R. Howell, won the United Bass Fisherman's Silver Cup Trail, defeating all of the legendary names, such as Roland Martin, Jimmy Houston, and Bill Dance (only to give up professional bass tournaments a year later to spend more time fishing with me). Clarks Hill Reservoir is currently listed as one of the 100 Bass Fisheries by B.A.S.S.

Clarks Hill is home to largemouth bass, striped bass, hybrid (bodie) bass, catfish, longnose gar, crappie, shell crackers, bluegills, chain pickerel (jack fish), and carp, just to name a few. The lake has a strong forage base of gizzard and threadfin shad. However, it's the blueback herring that drive the striper and hybrid fishing, as well as the largemouth bass fishing in the late spring. The lake is a striper and hybrid destination to many. Clarks Hill receives an annual stocking of 500,000 striper fingerlings and an additional 550,000 hybrid fingerlings.

Anglers will find everything from long, shallow sloping points, submerged islands, and blow-throughs to 40-foot deep creek channels and rock bluffs. While there has never been a shortage of cover for largemouth bass in the lake, the intense drought that Georgia suffered (which ended in late 2013) saw the lake reach record lows of nearly 22 feet. This prolonged drought allowed trees and grasses to grow to

Early morning sunrise across Clarks Hill. Kevin Howell

more than eight feet tall in places around the lake. The lake returned to full pool in 2013 and 2014, allowing fish to spawn in the shelter of all the new growth, not to mention all of the nutrients and food that was found in the new growth. This has provided a lot of one- and two-year-old class bass that will hopefully grow and prosper in the years to come. To fully understand the lake and all the structure, anglers need to visit the lake during the winter drawdown.

Due to its location, Clarks Hill offers excellent fishing from late September to late June. From late June through mid-September, surface water temperatures can range between 80 and 92 degrees Fahrenheit, bringing fishing to a halt. During the months of July, August, and September, the region around the lake can experience daily high temperatures that average 95–105 degrees daily for 60-plus days straight. Not only do the fish not want to feed on these days, but you may resemble a lobster after as little as three hours in the intense heat and sun. Any stripers and hybrids caught in this time are dead by the time they reach the surface, and most do not venture above the thermocline. The USACE has taken measures to provide more oxygen to the reservoir in the area around the dam to help the hybrids and stripers better survive the summer heat.

The best fishing of the year begins on the lake in mid-February, when the daily temperatures range into the high 50s and low 60s. As soon as you string three of these days in a row, the bass will begin to move shallow—first to the points close to the creek channel that are covered in the dark chunky sedimentary rock of the area. While they are opportunistic feeders, they are primarily focused on crayfish. As the water temperature warms into the upper 50s, the bass will spread out into the shallows and start to associate with any type of cover they can find in preparation for spawning. Anglers can target the bass with almost any subsurface pattern they favor, and

Top. Rocky points offer great crayfish habitat for early season bass. Kevin Howell

Inset. David Howell with a fall largemouth bass. Kevin Howell

once the water reaches 62 degrees and stays there overnight, anglers can find good action on top, fishing Dahlberg Divers and popping bugs around the abundant shoreline structure.

Full moons in April and May will bring the blueback herring spawn. Bass, along with stripers, hybrids, and countless other species will move to the long shallow points that drop into the deep channels, the countless submerged islands, and blow-throughs to feed on the congregated spawning blueback herring. When this occurs, anglers can find fish on Pole Dancers, Pencil Poppers, and Dahlberg-style flies. However, anglers that ply the water with an intermediate line and a fly like a Cowen's Baitfish or Howell's Herring find more and larger stripers and largemouth, as well as species such as catfish and pickerel that are shallow feeding on the herring.

By the end of May, the stripers, hybrids, and largemouth are beginning to move out to deep offshore ledges, creek channels, and other deepwater structures.

Once the water begins to cool in the early fall, the fish will move back shallow. October can provide some of the best topwater action of the year to anglers who fish frog patterns over the hydrilla mats. As fall progresses, the baitfish will migrate up the many creeks, bringing all of the gamefish with them. Anglers will find plenty of action as far up the creeks as they can go. Stripers, hybrids, and largemouth will be plentiful and gorging themselves on the shad for the coming cold weather.

Top. David Howell working a fly over a submerged tree in Clark Hill. Kevin Howell

Bottom. Abundant shoreline structure visible during winter draw down. Kevin Howell

By the time December and January roll around, the fishing becomes more dependent on the weather pattern that week. If you can string three days of nice mild weather together, you will find fish shallow—especially on the rocky points and deeper creek channel banks. However, a passing cold front

Kevin Howell with a Clarks Hill longnose gar caught during the herring spawn. Kevin Howell

will more than likely lay the fish down for a few days (especially for fly anglers).

Anglers can find countless ramps and parks to launch a boat. Some of the more popular areas are Elijah Clark State Park, Wildwood Park, Hickory Knob State Park, Amity Recreation Area, and Dorn Fishing and Boating Facility, just to name a few.

▶ **Tackle:** To successfully fish Clarks Hill Reservoir, anglers will need to gear up differently than when chasing bass on a river. Anglers will need to have a set of fly lines spooled on extra spools for a quick exchange. Over the years, I have learned to travel with a floating line (specifically a Rio Outbound Short) so that I can deliver a heavy fly a long distance with a single backcast. However, the most common line a lake angler will use is an intermediate sinking line, such as a Rio Tropical Intermediate Line. Finally, anglers are going to want a line that will put them on the bottom, such as a Rio Leviathan Sink Tip. Outside of casting poppers at structure, I encourage a 60–80 foot cast from clients—this allows your fly to remain in the strike zone longer. Anglers will also want a mix of monofilament and fluorocarbon leaders and tippet, depending on whether they want a fly to sink or ride up off the bottom.

For rods, I would recommend a 9-foot, 7- to 10-weight for the largemouth bass, depending on the size of the fly, the bass you are targeting, and how heavily they are embedded in structure or hydrilla mats. For stripers and hybrids, an 8- to 9-weight rod is ideal (except in April and May, when I prefer to use a 10-weight, as you can hook some monster fish during the herring spawn, and I prefer the added advantage of the 10-weight during that time frame).

Chuck Walker with a Clarks Hill largemouth. Kevin Howell

Kevin Howell with a fine Argentinian Brown. Gonzalo Flego

KEVIN HOWELL—Kevin Howell is the owner of Davidson River Outfitters; he also is an author, lecturer, fly-fishing instructor, and guide. Kevin is a Signature fly Designer for Montana Fly Company. A 2018 inductee to the Fly Fishing Museum of the Southern Appalachians Hall of Fame and a 2018 inductee to the Legends of the Fly Hall of Fame as well. Kevin has been guiding the waters of North Carolina, South Carolina, and East Tennessee for 25 years. When not guiding he can be found fishing with his wife Mellissa, and sons David and Andrew.

CLOSEST GUIDES AND OUTFITTERS

At the time of writing there are no fly guides working the lake, consult Rivers and Glen for possible guide services that cater to fly anglers.

CLOSEST FLY SHOPS

Rivers & Glen Trading Company
Surrey Shopping Center
387 Highland Ave.
Augusta, GA 30909
www.riversandglen.com
706-738-4536

CLOSEST LODGING

Hickory Knob State Resort Park
1591 Resort Dr.
McCormick, SC 29835
864-391-2450
www.southcarolinaparks.com/hickoryknob

Elijah Clark State Park
2959 McCormick Hwy.
Lincolnton, GA 30817
706-359-3458
www.gastateparks.org/ElijahClark

CLOSEST RESTAURANTS

Soap Creek Lodge and Restaurant
2498 Soap Creek Lodge Rd.
Lincolnton, GA 30817
706-359-3125

Michelle's Restaurant
131 Augusta Street
McCormick, SC 29835
1-864-852-9500

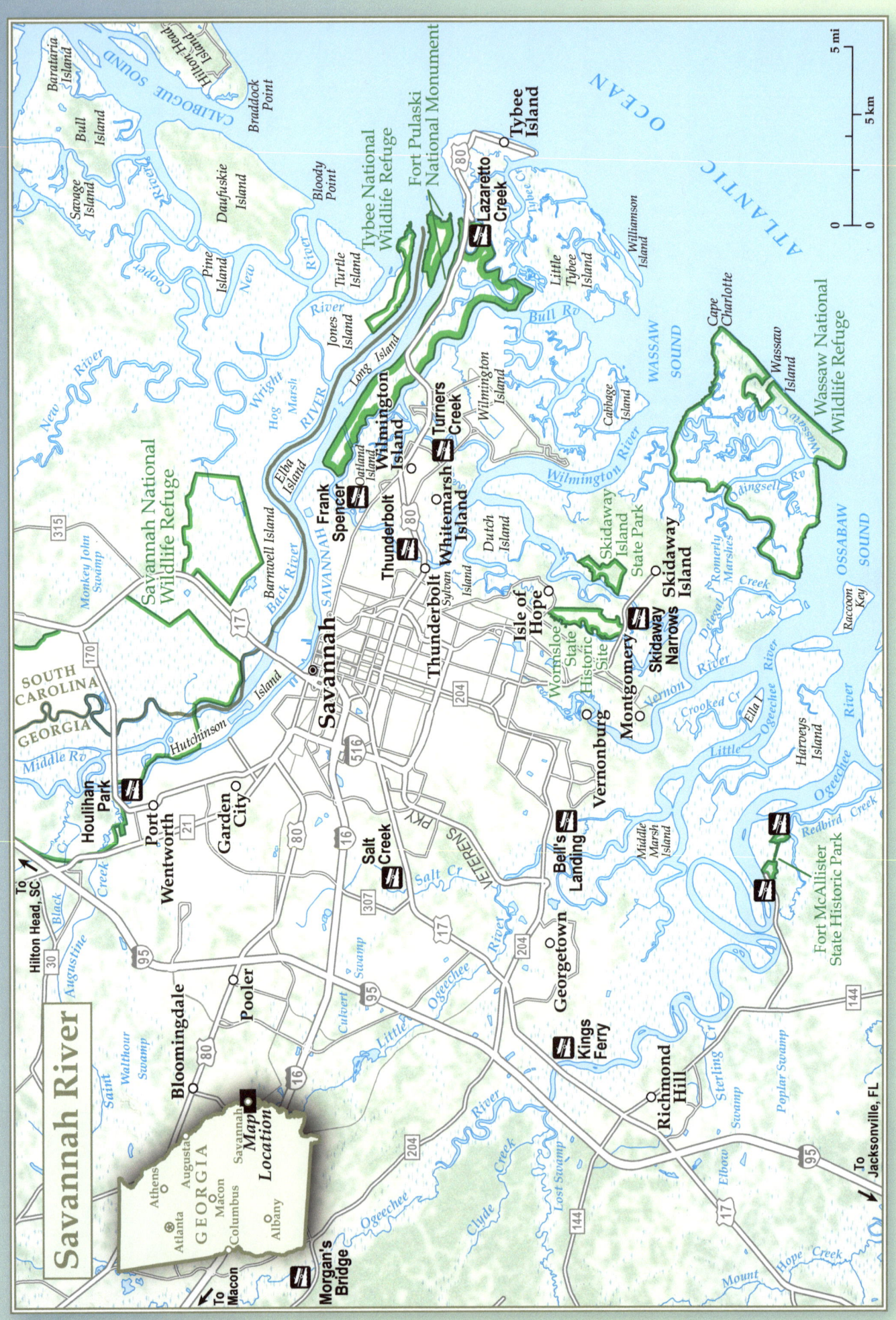

13 · Savannah River

▶ **Location:** Savannah, Georgia, is located at the intersection of Interstates 16 and 95, just 45 minutes from Beaufort and Hilton Head Island, South Carolina; it is 1 1/2 hours from Charleston, South Carolina, 2 hours from Jacksonville, Florida, and hours from Atlanta, Georgia, and Charlotte, North Carolina. Commercial flights are flown daily at Savannah / Hilton Head International Airport on Delta, United, JetBlue, and US Airways / American Airlines.

Savannah, Georgia, is Georgia's oldest city and its historical district is the most popular tourist attraction in the state. The town has hosted such historical figures as John Wesley, George Washington, Robert E. Lee, William T. Sherman, and Juliette Gordon Low. The town is located adjacent to the Savannah River, which serves as the major artery for the economy and the fishery alike.

The Savannah River is an alluvial river, which serves as one of the region's largest drainages. (An alluvial river is one that is formed and re-shaped by the size and frequency of floods, which erode, move and deposit sediment.) The river begins in the Blue Ridge Mountains and trickles through a series of dammed reservoirs to the fall line in Augusta, where it meets its last barrier, the Savannah Lock and Dam. Below the lock and dam, the river begins to retain its shape as it meanders down toward Savannah, dividing the Georgia-South Carolina border. Once the river reaches Savannah, the nation's fourth busiest port, the fishery is urban and brackish, transitioning into salt water as it flows into the Atlantic Ocean just east of town.

The fishing surrounding Savannah, Georgia, begins in the Savannah River, sprouting into myriad smaller rivers and tidal creeks that wind their way through the vast marsh and empty into numerous sounds and, ultimately, the Atlantic. Savannah boasts a year-round fishery for resident species such as redfish, speckled trout (also known as a spotted seatrout), flounder, sheepshead, and mullet, while also enjoying a seasonal fishery for striped bass, tripletail, jack crevalle, amberjack, cobia, sharks, and tarpon.

The key, as in all coastal fisheries, is to fish the tides, and the Savannah area is no exception. Many resident species,

Brendan with a tailing redfish taken from a Spartina Grass flat. Ben Austin

such as redfish and speckled trout, move and feed in direct correlation to the tide. As the water moves in on an incoming tide, the fish begin to work their way up into the shallow areas of flats and creeks, into the grass, and over oyster bars. Often these fish stage at the mouth of creeks, awaiting the water's return. The reason for this is twofold: to follow the bait and escape predation from dolphins and sharks. As the tide begins to fall, the fish begin to ease out of the creeks and off of the flats, so as not to be "a fish out of water." That speaks to the angler as well—keep a close eye on falling tides, as many

Cockspur Island Lighthouse marks the south entrance into the Savannah River. Ben Austin

Looking for tailing redfish in a sea of flooded Spartina grass at high tide. Ben Austin

anglers have been caught off guard and left stuck, helplessly waiting for hours for the incoming tide.

Savannah is best known for its redfish fishery, and this is a year-round pursuit, with the peaks of spring and fall, which boast the renowned flood tides. The challenge and reward is sight-fishing for these fish in the creeks, mud flats, jetties, oyster rakes, and the grass on flood tides. Anglers should look for tailing fish, pushes, wakes, muds, and nervous water. The water is murky the majority of the year, due to the heavy silt content in the Savannah River (combined with mud bottoms and large tides), so seeing the fish can be a challenge. Differentiating between baitfish and smaller redfish can take some adjustment, but once you get the hang of it, it'll be clear as day.

These fish are technically termed "puppy drum," as they have yet to reach sexual maturity, are under five years of age, and weigh (on average) 4–6 pounds, with fish up to 10 pounds not being uncommon. At five years of age, these fish reach sexual maturity and move offshore, returning inshore only to spawn or occasionally feed off of tidal bars, beaches, and the mouth of sounds. Shrimp, crab, and baitfish imitations in sizes 1/0–2 tied with weedguards are preferred, with 9- to 12-foot, 12- to 20-pound leaders, and 8-weight rods. Popular areas to fish for redfish, as well as trout, are Bull River, Savannah River jetties, Oyster Creek, Ossabaw Sound, and Wassaw Sound.

Fishing is most effectively accessed by boat, as wading can be difficult with soft mud bottoms. Wading opportunities are restricted to flood-tide fishing or surf fishing, and while less accessible than neighboring South Carolina, they do exist in various areas (the most common of which is off of U.S. 80, next to Fort Pulaski and Lazaretto Creek).

Seasonal fish, such as striped bass, may be fished for with baitfish imitations on the Savannah River throughout and above town by rock piles and bridges on overcast days and at dusk and dawn. The fish are best pursued with 9- to 10-weight rods and sinking lines, though some topwater action does occur at twilight. Cobia, amberjack, jack crevalle, and tripletail can be sight-fished on towers and buoys offshore in the spring

Georgia Mae and Chad enjoying some nice redfishing near Savannah Georgia. Ben Austin

Watching for tailers along the edge of the spartina grass. Ben Austin

and summer months, with shrimp and baitfish imitations and the occasional popper on 10- to 12-weight rods and floating lines.

The flora and fauna of the area comprises some of the most storied in the south. Ancient gnarled live oaks are draped in Spanish moss, intermixing with palm trees, magnolias, dogwoods, and azaleas lining the historic streets with natural canopies. Palms, pines, and oaks provide sheltered natural hammocks in the marsh and on barrier islands for wild hogs, deer, raccoons, and alligators. Loggerhead sea turtles and dolphins use the Savannah estuary as a spawning ground and are seen routinely. Pelicans, terns, oyster catchers, seagulls, sand pipers, herons, egrets, ibis, hawks, osprey, eagles, and a plethora of other birds are all common and active aviators in the sea breeze.

Whether dodging container ships in the Savannah River, winding your way through a tidal creek, wading in the grass, scraping an occasional oyster bar, or poling one of the expansive mud flats in the area, anglers are bound to have a memorable day on the water.

➤ **Regulations:**
- Redfish (all year)—Daily limit is 5; minimum length is 14 inches; maximum length is 23 inches
- Spotted seatrout (all year)—Daily limit is 15; minimum length is 13 inches
- Cobia (all year)—Daily limit is 2; minimum length is 13 inches
- Striped bass (all year, Savannah River)—Daily limit is 2; minimum length is 22 inches

- Striped bass (all year, saltwater)—Daily limit is 2; minimum length is 27 inches

▶ **Tackle:**

Redfish/Speckled Trout
- 9-foot, 7-, 8-, and 9-weight rods with floating weight-forward line with leaders 9- to 12-feet tapered to 10–20 pounds
- If wading, flats booties are recommended (watch your step!)
- Shrimp, crab, and baitfish flies are recommended

Striped Bass
- 9-foot, 9- or 10-weight rods with floating, sink tip, intermediate, full-sink lines with 4- to 9-foot leaders tapered to 20 pounds
- Baitfish flies

Cobia/Amberjacks
- 9-foot, 10- to 12-weight fly rods with floating lines and 9-foot leaders tapered to 20 pounds
- Baitfish and popper flies

Pelicans at rest along the Savannah shipping channel. Ben Austin

CLOSEST FLY SHOPS

Rivers & Glen Trading Company
Surrey Shopping Center
387 Highland Ave.
Augusta, GA 30909
www.riversandglen.com
706-738-4536

Baystreet Outfitters
825 Bay St.
Beaufort, SC 29902
843-524-5250
www.baystreetoutfitters.com

Southern Drawl Outfitters
1533 Fording Island Rd., Ste. 316
Hilton Head Island, SC 29926
843-705-6010
www.southerndrawloutfitters.com

CLOSEST GUIDES AND OUTFITTERS

Capt. Scott Wagner
912-308-3700
savannahfly@msn.com
www.savannahfly.com

Baystreet Outfitters
825 Bay St.
Beaufort, SC 29902
843-524-5250
www.baystreetoutfitters.com

Southern Drawl Outfitters
1533 Fording Island Rd., Ste. 316
Hilton Head Island, SC 29926
843-705-6010
www.southerndrawloutfitters.com

CLOSEST LODGING

The Marshall House
123 E. Broughton St.
Savannah, GA 31401
912-644-7896
www.marshallhouse.com

Bohemian Hotel Savannah Riverfront
102 W. Bay St.
Savannah, GA 31401
912-721-3800
www.bohemianhotelsavannah.com

Hampton Inn & Suites Savannah Historic District
603 W. Oglethorpe Ave.
Savannah, GA 31401
912-721-1600

Skidaway Island State Park
52 Diamond Cswy.
Savannah, GA 31411
912-598-2300
www.gastateparks.org/SkidawayIsland

River's End Campground
5 Fort Ave.
Tybee Island, GA 31328
912-786-5518
info@riversendcampground.com
www.riversendcampground.com

CLOSEST RESTAURANTS

Desposito's Seafood Restaurant
3501 Marye St.
Savannah, GA 31410
912-897-9963

Tybee Island Fish Camp
106 S. Campbell Ave.
Tybee Island, GA 31328
(912) 662-3474
www.tybeeislandfishcamp.com

Elizabeth on 37th
105 E. 37th St.
Savannah, GA 31401
912-236-5547
www.elizabethon37th.net

Tybee Island Social Club
1311 Butler Ave.
Tybee Island, GA 31328
912-472-4044
info@tybeeislandsocialclub.com
www.tybeeislandsocialclub.com

The Olde Pink House
23 Abercorn St.
Savannah, GA 31401
912-232-4286
theoldepinkhouse@bellsouth.net
www.plantersinnsavannah.com
/the-olde-pink-house

Tubby's Tank House
2909 River Dr.
Thunderbolt, GA 31404
912-354-9040

CLOSEST HOSPITALS OR URGENT CARE

Memorial Medical Associates
4425 Paulsen St., A1
Savannah, GA 31405
912-350-6000
www.memorialhealth.com

St. Joseph's Candler Hospital
5353 Reynolds St.
Savannah, GA 31405
912-819-6000
www.sjchs.org

CLOSEST BOAT RAMPS

For general information about boat ramps, see: http://parks.chathamcounty.org/Parks/Boat-Ramps-and-Fishing-Piers

Bells Landing
Apache Ave.
Savannah, GA 31406

Frank Downing Fishing Pier
Diamond Causeway
Savannah, GA 31406

Frank W. Spencer
Island Expressway
Savannah, GA 31404

Kings Ferry
Georgia 17
South Savannah, GA 31419

Lazaretto Creek
Georgia 80
Savannah, GA 31410

Rodney J Hall
25 Diamond Causeway
Savannah, GA 31406

Salt Creek
Georgia 17 South at Salt Creek Rd
Savannah, GA 31419

Thunderbolt
Macco Dr.
Savannah, GA 31404

Turner Creek
Johnny Mercer Blvd.
Savannah, GA 31404

Tybee Island Fishing Pier and Pavilion
Tybee Island
Tybee Island, GA 31328

BEN AUSTIN is an Emeritus guide, fly shop rat, blogger, captain, fly shop manager, casual consultant, collaborator, and full-time sales rep. He is a fly-fishing industry journeyman who unknowingly began his career while attending college at the University of Montana. He resides in Thunderbolt, Georgia, with his hot wife, Margaret, and their brawny chocolate Lab, Finch.

Ben Austin

Searching for redfish on the oyster racks at sunset. Ben Austin

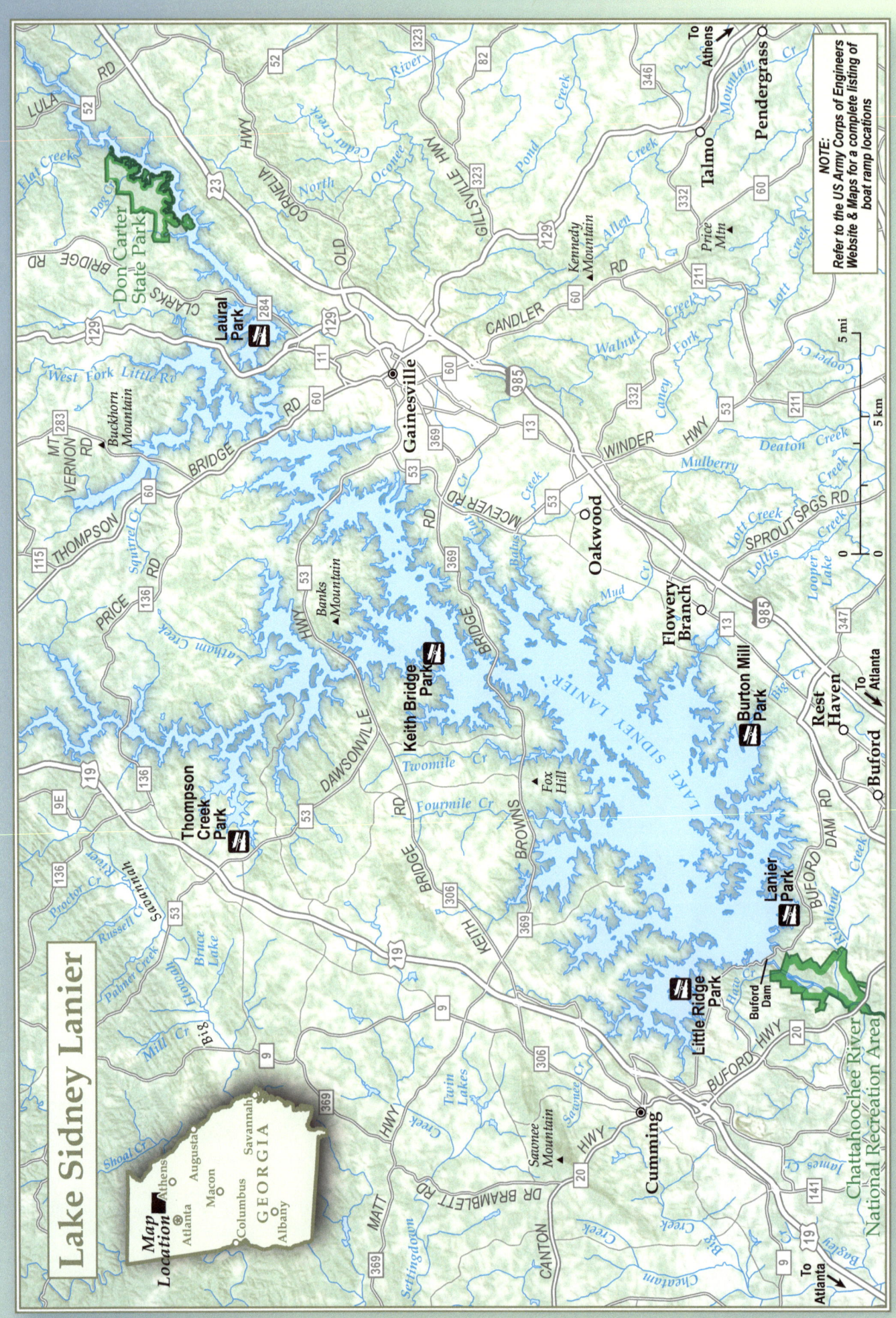

14 · Lake Sidney Lanier

➤ **Location:** Lake Sidney Lanier is located in Cumming, Georgia, to Gainesville, Georgia, from Buford Dam Road to Clarks Bridge Road, and everywhere in between. It is about 40 miles north of Atlanta.

Lake Sidney Lanier is a man-made impoundment that dates back to the 1950s when the Army Corps of Engineers dammed the Chattahoochee River in Cumming, thus forming the lake. This 38,000-acre impoundment is located a short 40 miles north of Atlanta. Its 650-plus miles of shoreline and 72 boat ramps allow for easy access to some of the best freshwater fishing east of the Mississippi. Lake Lanier is known for having three highly prized targeted species of fish: largemouth bass, Kentucky spotted bass, and striped bass. The lake is also home to some less popular species, including carp, white bass, bluegill, catfish, crappie, and walleye.

For anglers looking to fish the fly rod, this freshwater fishery is tough to beat. Lake Sidney Lanier is considered to be one of the best lakes in the entire Southeast for landlocked striped bass, and it has a world-class reputation for its Kentucky spotted bass fishery. At any time, an angler can go out and catch a Lanier slam, which involves landing a largemouth bass, Kentucky spotted bass, and highly prized striped bass all in the same day. However, it is the striped bass fishery that gets most of the attention from anglers looking to catch a saltwater gamefish many miles from the ocean. This fishery has a distinctiveness about it that has anglers feeling as if they were fishing in salt water.

➤ **Largemouth Bass:** At one time, Largemouth bass were the most sought-after of the three species on Lake Sidney Lanier. Bass hunters prize this impoundment, as largemouths in excess of 17 pounds have been taken from this lake. Tournament anglers regularly catch fish in excess of 5 pounds, and fish up to 8 pounds are not that uncommon. In order to target a big Lanier bucket mouth, it is advised that anglers fish the north end of the lake as these fish tend to frequent the shallow reaches of the more stained waters found up north.

➤ **Kentucky Spotted Bass:** Kentucky spotted bass are probably the most frequently caught fish of the big three. They tend to have similar features to that of a largemouth but have the aggressiveness and fight of a smallmouth. Kentucky spotted bass (also known as spots) can be found in approximately 30-plus states across the United States. The average size of a spot found in most lakes and rivers around the country is anywhere from 1- to 1 1/2 -pounds. A 3-pound spot would be considered a giant in most ecosystems. Not on Lake Lanier! While there are many similarly small fish caught on Lanier, the average spot found on this lake easily pushes 2–3 pounds, with fish up to 5 pounds considered common. Every year, we

Cornell and guide Henry Cowan displaying a striper. Henry Cowan

see fish being caught in the 6- to 7-pound class. For trophy hunters, this lake is considered to be one of the top three Kentucky spotted bass fisheries in the country. Lanier currently holds two of the seven IGFA (International Game Fish Association) line-class world records.

Early morning striper fishing on lake Lanier. Photo Credit Jim Klug

▶ **Striped Bass:** Striped bass, while not an indigenous species to Lake Lanier, is certainly the most talked about of the bunch. Back in the early 1970s, Georgia Department of Natural Resources (DNR) started stocking 1-inch-long fingerling striped bass to help control the abundance of threadfin shad that had taken over the lake. This was a copied plan that started back in the 1950s in South Carolina's Santee Cooper Lakes (Lake Marion and Lake Moultrie). The Georgia DNR stocks approximately ten fish per acre in Lanier. Every year, close to 400,000 little stripers are stocked in eight to ten staging areas around the lake. Two years later, we start to see these fish show up in anglers' catches. They are usually around 2–3 pounds at that time. After that, these juvenile stripers go on an eating tear and put on about 3–4 pounds a year. A five-year-old fish will weigh about 10–14 pounds! For anglers, these are hard-fighting, tackle-busting fish, and they will head straight for deeper depths and dog it all the way back to the boat once hooked. The average Lanier-caught striped bass weighs about 8–10 pounds. For fly enthusiasts, there is no better challenge than catching one of our striped demons. Lanier has the feel of a saltwater fishery, even though it is located hundreds of miles inland of any salt water. During certain times of the year, you can see terns and gulls diving to pick up fleeing bait while Lanier's striper population is creating a melee of churning whitewater on the surface. It looks like a mini blitz that one would usually associate with places such as Montauk, New York, Watch Hill, Rhode Island, or Sandy Hook, New Jersey!

Lake Sidney Lanier is an all-year fishery. We can target all three species (largemouth, spotted bass, and striped bass) all year long. However, there are certain times of the year that allow anglers the opportunity to run up big numbers of fish. In my opinion, spring and late fall are the best times to catch big numbers of fish.

For anglers targeting all three species in order to catch a Lanier slam, March and April offer the best opportunities. March and the first half of April is the time of year that the fish begin to move shallow and into the backs of the coves in search of both small threadfin shad and blueback herring. Flies such as small gray-white Clouser Minnow or a Somethin' Else are your best bet. Coyotes tied in either gray-white or blue-chartreuse-white are also a good choice. Matching the hatch is critical on this lake when fish are feeding on small baitfish!

From the end of April through all of May, Lanier anglers look for the shad spawn to take place during both the new and full moon phases, which means topwater activity can be awesome. This is the time when tossing Crease flies, Pole Dancers, or Wiggle Minnows for whippy stickers is at its peak.

June and July are not the best months for stripers or largemouth, but can be fantastic for schooling spotted bass. You will see plenty of single fish coming to the surface and keying in on a small fleeing shad or herring before heading back to the comfort of their brushpiles. A small Somethin' Else fly on an intermediate line or a Wiggle Minnow on a floating line is all that is required.

August through early October has the striped bass still hovering deep in the thermocline to find the cool oxygenated water. I tend to leave the stripers alone at this time of year as many fish pulled up through the heated water above the thermocline will stress out and die. Spotted bass can be found hanging around the brushpiles that are 15–25 feet under water. A midafternoon topwater bite can be found on the south end of the lake at this time of year. Small poppers, Wiggle Minnows, and Pole Dancer flies are your best bet.

From the end of October until mid-January, all three species can be caught (and released) all over the lake. Once again, a topwater bite occurs as the water temperatures cool down from the mid-80s to the mid-60s. At times, fish can be seen by the hundreds on the surface on the south end of Lake Lanier, tearing through schools of both small threadfin shad

Jim Klug with a Lake Lanier winter-time striped bass. Henry Cowan

Matching your fly to the bait size and shape can be critical for a successful trip. Henry Cowan.

and blueback herring. While a topwater fly is certainly effective this time of year, anglers tossing intermediate lines while fishing baitfish patterns will get the most bites. By November, the gulls and terns migrate back to the lake and can help locate schooling fish. It is at this time of year that fly fishermen see some bigger fish (up to 20 pounds) chasing bait up onto the surface. A terrific nighttime fishery also occurs on sandy beaches, as well as on lit dock lights (similar to snook fishing in Florida). Anglers tossing any streamer-type pattern will find these fish to be most agreeable when fishing dock lights.

Starting at the end of February, anglers will have the opportunity to catch the fish of a lifetime. This is typically when stripers in the 20- to 30-pound class are caught. Spotted bass in the 5- to 7-pound range can also be had. Largemouth will also be fairly aggressive at this time of year.

There are also a host of qualified guides (probably more than 50 listed) to take you out fishing "on the pond," but only one or two specialize in fly fishing.

One of the advantages to fishing Lanier is because it is a mountain lake sitting in the valley, the water is rarely rough. You will not have to deal with a rocking boat as you do on the ocean. For those with bad knees, it is the perfect remedy for having the feel of a saltwater fishing experience without the discomfort sometimes associated with saltwater fishing.

Lanier is a beautiful lake located in the heart of Georgia's Blue Ridge Mountains. It offers and ideal vacation spot for the whole family as well as the dedicated angler. In addition to short winters, friendly people, and great BBQ, you can experience world-class striper fishing without getting beat up in the ocean.

➤ **Regulations:** A nonresident license is $45 annually, or $20 for a three-day license.

➤ **Tackle:** Appropriate gear for Lake Lanier includes a 7- to 9-weight saltwater setup with multiple lines, in order to fish from the surface down to 20–25 feet. I recommend floating, intermediate, and sink-tip integrated shooting heads.

Useful fly patterns include Cowen's Coyote, Clouser Minnow, Cowen's Baitfish, Cowen's Somethin' Else, Boyer's Wiggle Minnow, Bisharat Pole Dancer, Blados Crease fly, and Chocklett's Game Changer. The best colors are gray-white or olive-white.

There are some necessary accessories for fishing on Lake Sidney Lanier, including a boat with an electric trolling motor and fish finder, polarized sunglasses, snacks or a packed lunch, drinking water, extra clothing (including a rain jacket for the occasional windy day), sunscreen, and a hat.

If you're looking for helpful books and maps, I suggest *Fly Fishing Georgia*, by David Cannon, and Kingfisher Maps, which can be reached at 800-326-0257 and www.kfmaps.com.

Henry Cowen with a Laker Lanier striper. Henry Cowen

HENRY COWEN has been pursuing striped bass for over 30 years in both salt water and fresh water. He is currently guiding in fresh water on Lake Sidney Lanier, Lake Allatoona, and the Chattahoochee River in Atlanta for stripers, hybrids, spotted bass, and carp. He is an accomplished fly designer for Umpqua Feather Merchants. Henry's name appears on the masthead of American Angler magazine as a contributing writer/editor, and he has written for many national fly-fishing publications. Henry has appeared as the personality on a number of nationally televised outdoor shows has been featured on the video titled Fly Fishing for Landlocked Stripers. Visit his website at www.henrycowenflyfishing.com.s.

CLOSEST GUIDES AND OUTFITTERS

Hammond's Fishing Center
4235 Browns Ridge Rd.
Cumming, GA 30041
770-888-6898
www.hammondsfishing.com

The Fish Hawk
3095 Peachtree Rd. NE
Atlanta, GA 30305
404-237-3473
www.thefishhawk.com

Orvis
3275 Peachtree Rd.
Buckhead Sq., Ste. 210
Atlanta, GA 30305
404-841-0093

Unicoi Outfitters
7280 S. Main St.
Helen, GA 30545
706-878-3083
www.unicoioutfitters.com

Henry Cowen
Quality Flies & Guide Service
678-513-1934
www.henrycowenflyfishing.com

CLOSEST LODGING

Comfort Suites (south end of the lake)
905 Buford Rd.
Cumming, GA 30041
770-889-4141

Quality Inn & Suites (north end of the lake)
127 Beartooth Pkwy.
Dawsonville, GA 30534
706-216-1900

CLOSEST RESTAURANTS

Marie's Italian Deli
580 Atlanta Rd.
Cumming, GA 30040
770-886-0084
www.mariesitaliandeli.com

Fagan's Biscuit Barn
1530 Peachtree Pkwy.
Cumming, GA 30041
678-455-5670
www.fagansbiscuitbarn.com

Big D's BBQ
6566 Georgia 53 E.
Dawsonville, GA 30534
706-216-6706
www.mybigdsbbq.com

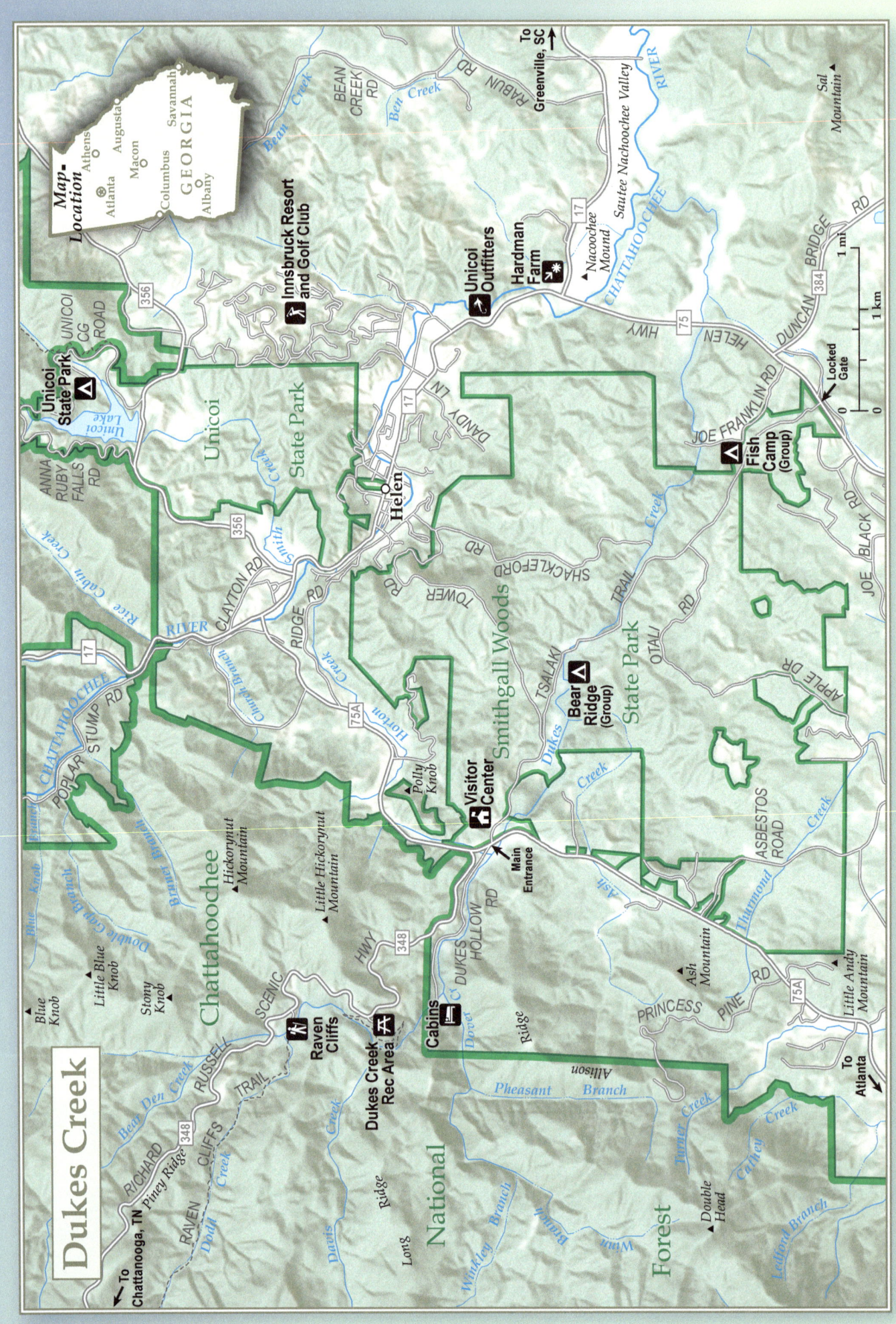

15 · Dukes Creek

▶ **Location:** The section of Dukes Creek that flows through Smithgall Woods State Park is located in Northeast Georgia near the town of Helen. It's about 85 miles from downtown Atlanta, 99 miles from Greenville, South Carolina, and 130 miles from Chattanooga, Tennessee.

When Northeast Georgia media entrepreneur and philanthropist Charles Smithgall began acquiring southern Appalachian mountain property, his ultimate goal wasn't apparent to most folks outside his immediate family. To the general public, it was obvious that he didn't want to own all of Northern Georgia, just that part that joined the land he already owned. Over time, Smithgall accumulated a tract of some 5,600 acres of second-growth forest, which just happened to be bisected by more than five miles of one of the region's most pristine trout streams, Dukes Creek. If you look at the history of what is now known as Smithgall Woods State Park, you'll wonder at the amazing odds of it becoming one of the premier natural areas in the entire country.

Originally part of the Cherokee Nation, the area was subject to the most egregious assault imaginable when gold was discovered in the valley in 1829. By the 1850s, the Trail of Tears was history, European settlers had taken over the land, and hydraulic mining was literally washing the mountains downstream in an effort to find that mother lode of gold. Hydraulic mining became illegal in the late 1880s, and the land began to heal, but the recovery was short-lived as a growing country demanded more lumber to build cities. A narrow gauge railroad was laid to the local community of Helen to service a sawmill fed by the virgin forests of the formerly remote mountainous area.

Surprisingly, over the next 75 years, the mountains survived massive clear-cutting, chestnut blight, Dutch elm disease, and moonshine wars, all while providing a meager life to its residents. It wasn't until the late 1960s, when more roads were built across the region, that it was "discovered" by Atlanta and the final assault began on these steep slopes as vacation homes sprang up in just about every holler. All the while, Charles Smithgall was tending to his growing hideaway like a mother hen guarding her chicks. Invasive nonnative vegetation was meticulously removed, streamside vegetation was restored, and farmland was allowed to revert to natural growth. And Dukes Creek ran clean, cold, and clear once again after almost 175 years of abuse.

In 1994, Smithgall surprised a lot of people by agreeing to sell his property to the state for 50 percent of its appraised value, which at the time was more than $20 million. Brilliantly,

Nymphing a run on Duke's Creek. Jimmy Harris

he conditioned the purchase on several caveats to protect the property and its resources, including the fishery. As a result, Georgia Department of Natural Resources intensively manages Dukes Creek for a quality angling experience. Reservations are required, and only 15 anglers are allowed on the stream at any one time. It's all catch-and-release fishing with artificial lures and flies only. Also, there is a strict barbless hook man-

Releasing a 22-inch winter time rainbow on Duke's Creek. Jimmy Harris

numerous stream structures to increase trout habitat, and the results have been dramatic. Interestingly,

- Section 3 drops through what was once an intensive gold mining area, complete with the now overgrown pockmarked landscape, an abandoned gold mine, and a 100-yard section of creek that was dynamited to divert water to the huge hydraulic guns used to wash away the hillsides in hopes of finding a few ounces of gold.

Among the most successful Dukes Creek regulars, there are some proven methods worthy of remembering.

- Landon Williams, Unicoi Outfitters: "I fish to the water conditions versus my historical success. I go where the fewest anglers are, and I'm constantly changing my dropper length so I'm getting the fly down to the fish. At times, it seems angling pressure will make the fish spooky to an attractor fly so I'll switch to a 'French Nymphing' technique using 12- to 15-foot leaders with a greased sighter and two nymphs."
- Jake Darling, Unicoi Outfitters Guide: "First, I like to fish the chop. I look for rougher water in the heads of runs and pools. The fish in these areas are a little more willing to eat. I also prefer to fish when it's cold. I have found that my best season is October through April, with February being tops."
- Jeff Durniak, Regional Fisheries Supervisor, Georgia DNR: "I like to fish Dukes Creek after a rain, when the water is off-color. Fish that have become super spooky in low, clear water suddenly feed with abandon when visibility drops to 1–2 feet. The watershed is well protected by national forest lands, and the

date that applies to every fly in the angler's possession while onstream. Fishing is allowed only on Wednesdays, Fridays, and Saturdays unless you are staying in one of the on-site cabins. When renting a cabin at Smithgall Woods, you are allowed to fish the upper section of the creek any day of the week.

For management purposes, Dukes Creek is divided into four sections, but anglers are not assigned "beats." They are free to fish any section of the creek they want. The uppermost section, Section 1, is accessible to foot traffic only, but Sections 2, 3, and 4 may be accessed by a DNR-operated shuttle bus. Each section has its own distinct personality:

- Sections 1 and 4 are a typical mountain stream with tumbling pocketwater and deep runs.
- Section 2 is reclaimed bottom farmland with a much shallower gradient. Georgia DNR has installed

An early season rainbow. Jimmy Harris

High-water nymphing on Duke's Creek in early March. Jimmy Harris

stream doesn't stay muddy for long, but a good rain will cloud things up for several hours. A lot of anglers make the mistake of going home when this happens, but they miss the easiest conditions for stalking and hooking big fish. Just watch the USGS river gauge for the Chattahoochee River in Helen to get an idea of what's happening on Dukes. Just after the crest passes, a San Juan Worm on 3X tippet can work impressively well. This is also the best time to take new anglers on their first quest for a trophy trout."

▶ **Hatches:** Dukes Creek, like many southern Appalachian streams, does not have massive insect hatches, so technique can mean the difference between success and failure. Dukes Creek regulars all agree in principle that some configuration of a dry/dropper rig with a long dropper (up to 6 inches) is their most productive technique. Attractor dry flies, such as Stimulators or a bushy Elk-hair Caddis with enough bulk to float with a heavy nymph dropper, will generally outperform a strike indicator and nymph rig.

Fall brown trout. Jimmy Harris

The high gradient on Duke's Creek provides nice plunge pools for nymphing. Jimmy Harris

Fishing in a rhododendron tunnel can prove challenging on the back cast. Jimmy Harris

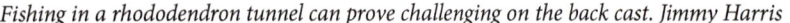

➤ **Tackle** While some anglers have developed a passion for fishing Dukes Creek with their own specialty gear, it can be fished with just about any rod designed for trout fishing. What I would not recommend are typical small-stream rods for bushwhacking blue-line streams. There are plenty of monster-size browns and rainbows in Dukes Creek to make toothpicks out of a 6-foot 2-weight. Plus, it's just not fair for the fish to go in under-gunned. Rods that are 4-, 5-, and 6-weights, from 7 1/2 to 11 feet are all used successfully on Dukes Creek.

When it comes to fly selection, keep it natural. The stream has a good population of stoneflies and hellgrammites as well as small mayflies, caddis, and aquatic worms. Look in the fly boxes of successful Dukes Creek anglers, and you'll most likely find some of the following (all barbless, of course!):

- Size 16 and size 18 Micro Mayfly in brown
- Size 16 and size 18 Mighty May Baetis
- #16–20 Pheasant-tail Nymphs (no bead)
- Size 18 and size 20 WD-40 in brown
- Size 16 and size 18 soft-hackle Pheasant Tail
- #14–18 Hare's Ear (no bead)

Jimmy Harris. David Cannon

JIMMY HARRIS is one of the owners of Unicoi Outfitters, an Orvis Endorsed Outfitter and retail fly shop located 90 miles northeast of Atlanta, Georgia, near the southern Appalachian town of Helen. Jimmy purchased 50 percent interest in Unicoi Outfitters in 1998, after wading Georgia trout streams the previous 25 years and guiding on them for four. His fly-fishing passions run the gamut from small, rhododendron covered wild-trout streams to the cold tailwaters of the southeast.

CLOSEST FLY SHOPS

Unicoi Outfitters
7280 S. Main St.
Helen, GA 30545
706-878-3083
www.unicoioutfitters.com

The Fish Hawk
3095 Peachtree Rd. NE
Atlanta, GA 30305
404-237-3473
www.thefishhawk.com

Orvis
3275 Peachtree Rd.
Buckhead Sq., Ste. 210
Atlanta, GA 30305
404-841-0093

CLOSEST LODGING

Smithgall Woods State Park
61 Tsalaki Trl.
Helen, GA 30545
706-878-3087
www.georgiastateparks.org/smithgallwoods

Creekwood Resort
5730 Georgia 356
Sautee, GA 30571
706-878-2164
www.creekwoodresort.com

Historic Habersham Mill
Habersham Mill Complex
Demorest, GA 30535
http://alltherooms.com/demorest--ga/historic-habersham-mills-shed-space-3fc4c1f8

CLOSEST RESTAURANTS

Nacoochee Village Tavern & Pizzeria
7275 S. Main St.
Helen, GA 30545
706-878-0199
www.villagetavernpizza.com

Mully's Nacoochee Grill
7277 S. Main St.
Helen, GA 30545
706-878-1020
www.mullysnacoocheegrill.com

North Georgia Barbeque
663 Edelweiss Strasse
Helen, GA 30545
706-878-5753

Bigg Daddys Restaurant & Tavern
807 Edelweiss Strasse
Helen, GA 30545
706-878-BREW
contactus@biggdaddys.com
www.biggdaddys.com

CLOSEST HOSPITALS OR URGENT CARE

Habersham Medical Center
541 Historic Hwy. 441
Demorest, GA 30535

16 · Toccoa River

▶ **Location:** The Toccoa River flows forms high in the Blue Ridge Mountains and flows down the western side of the continental divide for about 60 miles through the mountains, entering Tennessee near the town of McCaysville where it is renamed the Ocoee River. Blue Ridge Lake is located about halfway between the Toccoa River's origin and its exit point from Georgia. The section of the river above Blue Ridge Lake is known as the Upper Toccoa, and the remaining portion below Blue Ridge Dam is called the Lower Toccoa.

The wild headwaters of the Upper Toccoa are fed by many large streams, including Cooper Creek, Rock Creek, and Noontootla Creek, and the system of waterways provides a productive haven for trout. The Delayed Harvest section is about two miles in length, starting at Toccoa River Sandy Bottoms Recreation Area and ending about 200 yards above the old metal Shallow Ford Bridge on Aska Road in Blue Ridge, Georgia. To reach the bridge from Blue Ridge, follow Aska Road for about ten miles and then turn to head across Shallow Ford Bridge. After crossing the bridge, turn right and head upstream for about 100–200 yards. This is the beginning of the Delayed Harvest section and should be fishable for about 1 1/2 to 2 miles heading upstream to Sandy Bottom Canoe Launch.

The Lower Toccoa is a tailwater flowing from the Blue Ridge Dam. This section of the river has earned the reputation of being the best trout water in Georgia. The flows in this 15-mile stretch of water are regulated by the Tennessee Valley Authority for both power generation and flood management. Anglers should use extreme caution when fishing any tailwater especially the Toccoa. Water releases are subject to change without notice. For the water release schedule on Blue Ridge Dam, call 800-238-2264. Press 5 for the Ocoee and 23 for the Toccoa River. You can also download the free TVA Lake Info app on your phone for the latest water release schedule.

The Lower Toccoa offers plenty of good trout habit all the way to the Tennessee line. Even though trout can be found anywhere in the river, anglers will want to focus their fishing efforts on some type of structure, such as woody debris, rock outcroppings, riffles, deeper bend holes, or undercut banks. There are only five access points over the entire 15-mile tailwater:

Foggy mormning tight loop on the Toccoa. Daniel Peeples

Powerhouse River Access
Tammen Park
TVA River access at Curtis Switch
Horseshoe Bend Park
Toccoa River Park (McCaysville boat ramp)

While some wade fishing can be found on the Toccoa, float fishing is the most effective way to fish the Lower Toccoa because the vast majority of land adjacent to the river is private. Every state's property laws are different. Remember, just because you may have been granted access to the river by the state, you do not have the right to be on surrounding private land. Please consult local and state laws before crossing or entering upon private property. Also keep in mind that it is someone's home. Would you want all of those people doing their business on your property without your permission?

Wade anglers will only be able to access the river at one of the five points mentioned above. With so little access for wade anglers, access points can become extremely crowded especially on pretty weekends and holidays. Those looking for a more solitary fishing experience avoid the holidays and weekends and choose to float the river instead of wading.

In addition to the great trout fishing, anglers will also encounter largemouth, smallmouth, and spotted bass, as well as assorted panfish, including yellow perch. While these species are not that common, they will liven up the day when they take off screaming down the river. The Kentucky spotted bass

Daniel Peeples with a Toccoa River brown. Daniel Peeples

is an invasive species and are threatening the health of the smallmouth bass population. Therefore, anglers are encouraged to harvest their limit of spotted bass.

➤ **Hatches:**
- Midges (Year-round)
  Drys—#18–24 Griffith's Gnat
  Nymphs—#18–24 Zebra Midge, Brassie, Disco Midge
  Emergers—#18–24 WD-40, Adams, Top Secret Midge

- Caddisflies (Spring, summer, and winter)
  Drys—#14–18 Elk-hair Caddis, tan and gray (spring and summer), black (winter)
  Nymphs—#16–20 Caddis Larvae, Peeking Caddis, Z-wing Caddis
  Emergers—#16–20 Graphic Caddis, Lafontaine Caddis, Olive soft-hackle

- Mayflies (Spring and summer)
  Drys—#18–22 Parachute Blue-winged Olive, Parachute Sulphur, Purple Haze, Parachute Adams
  Nymphs—#16–20 Pheasant Tail, Split Case (Sulphur or Blue-winged Olive), Hare's Ear, soft-hackle
  Emergers—#16–20 Blue-winged Olive Emerger, Sulphur Emerger, soft-hackle

- Stoneflies (Winter and spring)
  Drys—#14–18 Stimulator, Chubby Chernobyl
  Nymphs—#12–16 Prince Nymph, Pat's Rubber Legs, Kaufmann's Stone
  Emergers—#12–16 soft-hackle Pheasant Tail, soft-hackle Hare's Ear

- Streamers (Year-round)
  #6–8 Double Bunny, Zonker
  #8–14 Wooly Bugger, Slumpbuster

- Terrestrials (Mid- to late summer and early fall)
  Drys—#12–16 Foam Beetle, Foam Hopper, Parachute Ant

➤ **Registration:**
- Trout season is open year-round.
- There is no minimum length, and the daily limit for all species is eight.
- The exceptions to the general rule are at the upper Toccoa Delayed Harvest areas from 0.4 miles above Shallow Ford Bridge upstream to a point 450 feet upstream of the Sandy Bottom Canoe Access. The Delayed Harvest is enforced November 1 to May 14 annually. Anglers must release all trout immediately and use and possess only artificial lures with a single hook per lure. The use of additional "dropper" lures on one line is permitted as long as each lure contains a single hook.
- The restrictions do not apply from May 15 to October 31 of each year.

➤ **Tackle:**
- 9-foot, 5- to 6-weight rods with floating weight-forward line
- Leaders 9–12 feet, tapered to 6X
- Waders are recommended in the fall and winter months

Wanda Taylor and Chase Pritchett netting a Toccoa River trout. Daniel Peeples

Toccoa brook trout. Daniel Peeples

Toccoa River rainbow. Daniel Peeples

Wanda Taylor in search of an early morning striper bite on Lake Lanier. Henry Cowan

WANDA TAYLOR was the first woman to be certified as a Master Casting Instructor by the International Federation of Fly Fishers. She was awarded the 2005 SE IFFF Woman of the Year and the 2008 SE IFFF Council Award of Excellence, and she is an advisory staff member of www.tforods.com. In addition, Wanda is an ambassador of Georgia Women Fly Fishers, as well as casting for recovery, and casting Carolinas. She is the owner Wanda Taylor Fly Fishing.

CLOSEST FLY SHOPS

Blue Ridge Fly Fishing
490 E. Main St.
Blue Ridge, GA 30513
706-258-4080
www.blueridgeflyfishing.com

Southern Highroads Outfitters
253 Georgia 515 E., Building 1-C
Blairsville, GA 30512
706-781-1414
www.southernhighroadsoutfitters.com

CLOSEST GUIDES AND OUTFITTERS

Blue Ridge Fly Fishing
490 E. Main St.
Blue Ridge, GA 30513
706-258-4080

Dry Flyer Outfitters
Capt. Gary Taylor
706-537-3254
gary@dryflyeroutfitters.com

Fly Fishing North Georgia Guide Services
706-833-1083
flyfishingnorthgeorgia@gmail.com
http://flyfishingnorthgeorgia.com/

Oyster Fine Bamboo Fly Rods
494 E. Main St.
Blue Ridge, GA 30513
706-374-4239
shannen@oysterbamboo.com
www.oysterbamboo.com

CLOSEST LODGING

The Oyster Cast and Blast
494 E. Main St.
Blue Ridge, GA 30513
706-374-4239
http://oysterbamboo.com/cast-and-blast-inn-blue-ridge-georgia-rooms.html

Escape to Blue Ridge
Alpharetta, GA
866-618-2521
http://escapetoblueridge.com/

Mountain Top Cabin Rentals
44 Boardtown Rd.
Blue Ridge, GA 30513
706-258-6220

Reid Ridge Lodge
30 Overview Dr.
Blue Ridge, GA 30513
706-632-4444
http://reidridgelodge.com/

Comfort Inn Suites
83 Blue Ridge Overlook
Blue Ridge, GA 30513
706-946-3333

Days Inn
4970 Appalachian Hwy.
Blue Ridge, GA 30513
706-632-2100

Toccoa Valley Campground
11481 Aska Rd.
Blue Ridge, GA 30513
706-838-4317

Camp Morganton
236 Camp Morganton Rd.
Blue Ridge, GA 30513
706-632-8385

Blue Ridge Mineral Springs RV Park
803 Mineral Springs Rd.
Blue Ridge, GA 30513
706-632-5010
http://www.blueridgemineralspringsrvpark-kandtentcamping.com/

CLOSEST RESTAURANTS

Harvest on Main
Blue Ridge Mountain Mall
576 E. Main St.
Blue Ridge, GA 30513
706-946-6164
www.harvestonmain.com/

Black Sheep Restaurant Bar & Patio
480 W. Main St.
Blue Ridge, GA 30513
706-946-3663
www.blacksheepblueridge.com

Toccoa Riverside Restaurant
8055 Aska Rd.
Blue Ridge, GA 30513
706-632-7891
toccoariversiderestaurant.com

Black Bear Bier Garten
500 E. Main St., #205
Blue Ridge, GA 30513
706-946-4440

Fightingtown Tavern
511 E. Main St.
Blue Ridge, GA 30513
706-946-2006

Blue Ridge Brewery
187 Depot St.
Blue Ridge, GA 30513
706-632-6611
blueridgebrewery.com/

Fannin Brewing Company
3758 E. First St.
Blue Ridge, GA 30513
706-258-2762
www.fanninbrewingcompany.com

Grumpy Old Men Brewing
1315 E. Main St.
Blue Ridge, GA 30513
770-331-8870
www.grumpyoldmenbrewing.com/

CLOSEST HOSPITALS OR URGENT CARE

Fannin Regional Hospital
2855 Old Hwy. 5 N.
Blue Ridge, GA 30513
706-632-3711
www.fanninregionalhospital.com

SOUTH CAROLINA

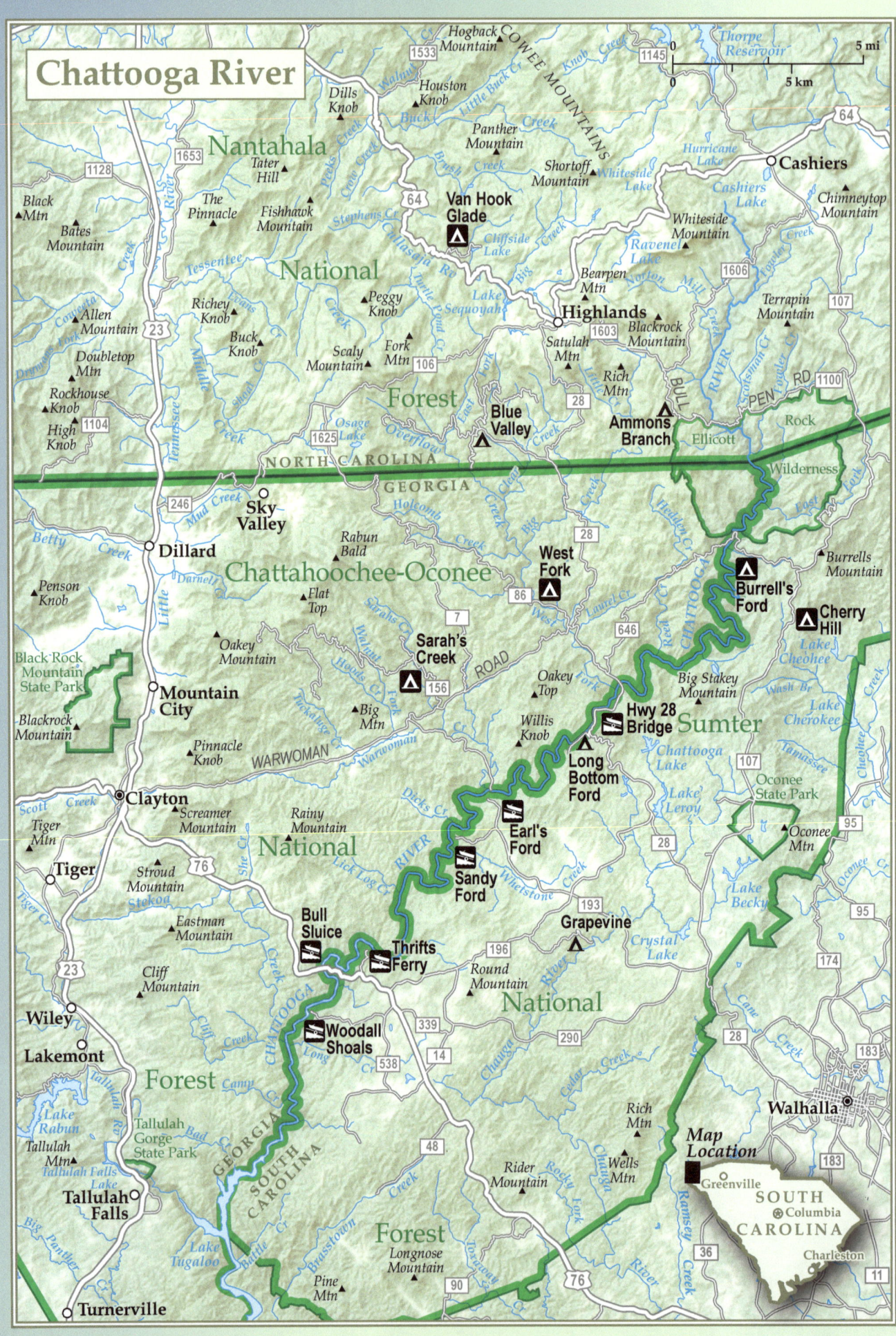

17 · Chattooga River

➤ **Location:** The Chattooga River, the "crown jewel of the Southeast," flows through South Carolina and Georgia. In South Carolina, anglers can fly in and out of Greenville, with a drive time to the river of one hour. Coming from the Georgia side, anglers can find all amenities in Clayton, Georgia, just ten minutes away. Atlanta is two hours away.

Through my late teens and twenties, I spent many summers and long winter days kayaking and fishing through the remote sections of the Chattooga River from Section 00 to the famed whitewater of Section 4. Flowing through the rhododendron tunnels of Cashiers, North Carolina, the Chattooga River spills off the steep escarpment (a sheer cliff or steep slope that is created by erosion) finally helping fill Tugaloo Lake in South Carolina.

Boasting Class I through Class V whitewater, the Chattooga also has great stocked trout waters above the Highway 28 Bridge, listed as of now as a Delayed Harvest fishery.

Along with the Delayed Harvest regulations, you will also find wild rainbow trout, brown trout, redeye bass, Coosa bass, sunfish, bream (bluegill), and the occasional largemouth bass.

The tributaries of the Chattooga can have wild brook trout—anglers will just have to walk the extra few hundred yards.

The Chattooga River rests under a Wild & Scenic River category, allowing limited road access and development. With this Wild & Scenic River category, the Chattooga has some very remote access to the river. You might even find Burt Reynolds or Ned Beatty from the movie *Deliverance*.

Starting at Bullpen Road access in Cashiers, North Carolina, you can wade-fish upstream to the narrows, a section of the upper Chattooga that has boulder-hopping access, and loads of eager wild trout that will take a dry-dropper rig. Flies such as an Elk-hair Caddis size 12, with a Tungsten Pheasant Tail size 16. Fly patterns will vary on water conditions and temperatures. The South Carolina side of the Chattooga hosts sections for access wading and limited floating. Keep in mind you will have to walk any watercraft 1/4 mile to the river, because no trailer access is available. Canoes and rafts are the main mode of floating transportation. I do not advise any inexperienced boaters to try. The Chattooga is a true jewel, and we all hope it will stay that way for kayaking, boating, hiking, and fishing.

Wade access can be found in a number of suggested sections:

➤ **Burrells Ford:** Burrells Ford has the old-school upstate characteristics. It's heavily wooded and natural, with miles

Shoals on the Chattooga River. Walker Parrott

of gravel roads that can take you deep into the wilderness of the Chattooga. Driving 2.9 miles on gravel roads, anglers will find a large pull-off on the left, along with gated access to lower Burrells Ford. Hiking away from the parking lot 1/4 mile down a sandy trail, anglers will find a larger river bottom and inviting green pools. For the quick and hurried angler who can't wait, access can be found around the bridge

Walker Parrott prepares to release a beautiful Chattooga rainbow. Kevin Howell

on both sides of the river. Anglers who want fishing all to themselves should take the trails upstream and downstream. Walking a few minutes away from the parking lot will guarantee privacy and solitude. Fishing a 7-foot, 5-inch rod will be great for the angler who wants to fish pocketwaters with a dry, and a 9-foot rod will work for the angler who wants to fish longer leaders and heavier nymph rigs. Typically, the Chattooga flows crystal clear, but after heavy rains, the levels will jump up and the clarity will be a bit stained. During these higher levels, anglers can find larger fish with larger Nymphs and Streamers.

▶ **28 Bridge to Reed Creek**: Taking Highway 28 toward Highlands, North Carolina, from Highway107 South, you will find parking access on the South Carolina side of the river. This Delayed Harvest section is in the Sumter National Forest. Anglers will find long, slow pools and river-wide riffles. The Delayed Harvest regulations will fall under catch-and-release fishing from November 1 to May 14. Stocking will be done from truck access and, at times, helicopter due to the remoteness of the Chattooga. With the Delayed Harvest regulation in mind, anglers could find a few crowds on the weekends.

As the Chattooga flows south, gradient will pick up, forming ledges and more of a boulder-type river. Having large, green, deep pools and tight riffles is not a bad thing. This part of the river can be some of the prettiest waters anyone will fish in the country.

Walking the worn-out paths above and below the 28 Bridge, you will find fewer anglers and more water to enjoy. Sometimes you just need to walk a few hundred yards. As the riverbed gets larger, 8-foot, 5-inch rods and 9-foot rods will be better due to the larger runs and bottomless pools. Dry-dropper rigs will work in the larger riffles, and midges and soft hackles in the shallow runs. Nine-foot rods or longer can reach the larger pools and deeper runs with heavily tied nymphs or Tungsten flies. Caddis hatches, along with Yellow Drake hatches during the early spring and early fall, can provide great dry-fly fishing. Winter can produce pretty decent Blue-winged Olive and midge hatches.

▶ **Earls Ford Access:** Earls Ford Access is downstream from the 28 Bridge Access. If you are looking for lunch and a break with a cold beverage, stop by the Tunnel Town Express Mountain Rest on South Carolina 28. Packed full with chips, hot sausages, rooster tails, beer, water, crickets, and a few locally tied flies in a Mustad box for only $1. Don't miss the Boiled Peanuts. Driving down Chattooga Ridge Road from South Carolina 28, Earls Ford will show you the true South Carolina mountain country. Turn onto Earls Ford Road

Walker Parrott with a beautiful fall brown. Kevin Howell

(gravel) and follow it to where it dead ends at a gate. Walk 1/4 mile to the Chattooga. You will have most of the river to yourself. Nine-foot rods will make the fishing easier for redeye bass, bream, sunfish, and maybe a few trout that have washed down from the stocking upstream. From the South Carolina 28 bridge upstream is managed for trout. The water downstream of the bridge is not managed.

As you walk downstream, you'll be targeting Coosa bass and sunfish. Poppers and sliders should produce a few nice fish. If the fish aren't paying attention to the surface action, try a nymph rig. Nymph fishing with a tight line or indicator will produce the unexpected. Hellgrammite and crayfish patterns work well with split-shot needed.

Float fishing can be done here. Kayaking, canoeing, and rafting anglers can enjoy this section with a few large ledges and some whitewater. Whitewater experience is recommended and needed.

▶ **South Carolina 76 Bridge and Bull Sluice:** Everybody should go see "the Bull" if you're in the area fishing. When you pull into the Bull Sluice Access, you will find commercial rafters enjoying this river ledge waterfall. Rafters and kayakers will have access here for the lower Chattooga's Class I through Class IV rapids. With names such as Seven Foot Falls, Raven Chute, Shoulder Bone, and the legendary Sock-em Dog, this section of whitewater is not for timid boaters. The Bull can provide great access at the rapid Bull Sluice downstream to the South Carolina 76 Bridge. There are walking trails on the Georgia side and the South Carolina side. With easy access to South Carolina 76, the Bull Access will be a zoo on weekends and during summer months. Commercial raft companies run this rapid all season from May to September.

Anglers can find access above and below the South Carolina 76 Bridge by taking the commercial rafter footpaths and wildlife trails. Heading upstream of the Bull Access, you will find long broken rapids with endless pockets in which Coosa bass hide. The larger pools can be accessed for better dry-fly fishing with poppers.

▶ **Tackle:**
- Rods—7-foot, 5-inch, 3-weight; 9-foot or 10-foot, 5- to 6-weight
- Floating lines, 150-grain sinking lines for deeper pools
- Trout dry flies
    Fat Alberts, sizes 4-12
    Chubby Chernobyls, sizes 10-16
    Yellow Drakes, sizes 10-18
    Ants, sizes 14-18
    Beetles, sizes 12-18

Coose bass are the primary game fish on the lower sections of the Chattooga. Kevin Howell

    Parachute Adams, sizes 14-18
    Elk-hair Caddis, 12-20
    Yellow Sallies, sizes 12-18
    Trudes, sizes 12-18
    Cahills, sizes 12-18
    Blue-winged Olives, sizes 14-20
    Jim Charlies

- Trout nymphs
    Sassi's Solution, sizes 16-20
    Pheasant Tails, sizes 16-20
    Trip Saver, sizes 14-18
    Eggs, sizes 10
    Swing Caddis, sizes 14-18
    Ole Hellgy
    Bitch Creek, sizes 4-8
    Girdle Bugs, sizes 6-12
    Squirmy Worms, sizes 12-16
    Golden Stones, sizes 12-20
    Larger Nymphs sizes 4–8, Nymphs sizes 14–20, Midges sizes 18–24

- Streamers
    Foxy Red, sizes 4-6
    Sparkle Minnow, sizes 4-6
    Woolly Bugger, sizes 4-6
    Madonna, sizes 4-6
    Zoo Cougar, sizes 1-6
    Clouser Minnow, sizes 1-6
    Walker's Wiggler, sizes 2-6
    Big Nasty, size 6

- Warm water
    Bitch Creek, sizes 4-6
    Superfly, sizes 4-6
    Walker's Wiggler, sizes 1-6
    Big Nasty, sizes 4-6
    Sparkle Minnow, sizes 4-6
    Wooly Buggers
    JJ Special, sizes 4-8
    Clousers, sizes 1-6
    Boogle Bugs, sizes 4-6
    Hoppers, sizes 10-18
    Fat Alberts, sizes 1–6

- Leaders, lines, and tippets
    Bass (warm water)—9-foot, 2X–4X leaders
    Trout—9-foot, 3X–6X; 7 1/2-foot, 3X–7X; mono and fluorocarbon tippet, 2X–7X
    Floating—3- to 6-weight
    Intermediate lines and 150-grain sinking lines for high water

Chattooga in early fall. Walker Parrott

Entrance sign to upper Chattooga River and Walhalla State Fish Hatchery. Walker Parrott

Walker Parrott with a Madison River brown trout. Kevin Howell

Growing up on the South Carolina coast, WALKER PARROTT was introduced to fishing as a child, catching redfish, trout, jacks, and other inshore species. While completing high school in Sandpoint, Idaho, Walker was introduced to mountain trout fishing. He wanted to stay in the mountains, but live in the Southeast. After completing Brevard College with a bachelor's degree in experimental education, Walker settled in Brevard, North Carolina where he could fish the streams and rivers for trout and bass. After college, Walker took a job with an environmental engineering firm, which he soon left to pursue his passion of fishing, landing at Davidson River Outfitters. Now, too many years later, Walker is managing Davidson River Outfitters guide service and guiding and hosting anglers to Andros Bahamas, Argentina, and Montana. Between working with a great staff in the shop and guiding trout, smallmouth, and musky trips, he has the perfect balance. While trout are the staple, Walker likes to float for smallmouth bass and musky in Tennessee, North Carolina, and Virginia. When Walker is not guiding or pacing the fly shop, Walker can be found mountain biking, kayaking, taking long walks on the beach, fishing, and hanging out with his wife vNicole, and dogs, Mojo, Mia, Cassidy, and Catch 'em.

CLOSEST GUIDES AND OUTFITTERS

Chattooga River Fly Shop
6832A Highlands Hwy.
Mountain Rest, SC 29664
(864) 638-2806
chattoogariverflyshop@yahoo.comwww.chattoogariverflyshop.com

Davidson River Outfitters
95 Pisgah Hwy.
Pisgah Forest, NC 28768
888-861-0111
info@davidsonflyfishing.com
www.davidsonflyfishing.com

CLOSEST RESTAURANTS

Tunnel Town Express
6254 Highlands Hwy.
Mountain Rest, SC 29664
864-638-0092

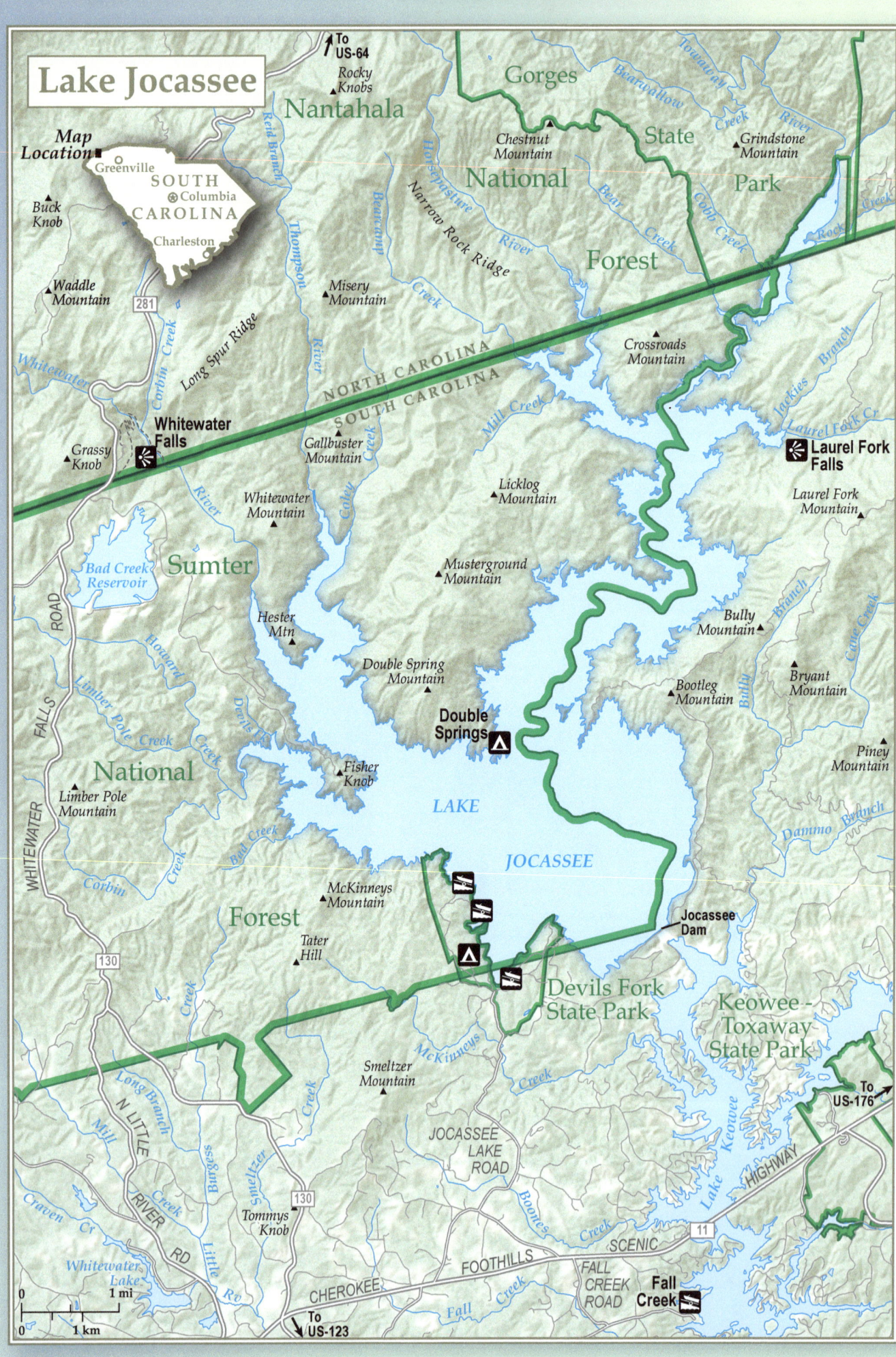

18 · Lake Jocassee

➤ **Location:** Lake Jocassee is located in the northwest corner of South Carolina and straddles the border into North Carolina. Travel time to Devils Fork State Park is about 2 1/2 hours northeast of Atlanta, Georgia, or 1 1/2 hours southwest of Asheville, North Carolina. Anglers can fly into Asheville Regional Airport or Greenville-Spartanburg International.

Lake Jocassee sets on the edge of the eastern escarpment on the North Carolina and South Carolina line. The only access to the lake is though Devils Fork State Park in South Carolina. Jocassee Dam was finished in 1973 and Duke Power began filling the lake. Jocassee Dam operates as a pumped-storage facility hydroelectric generator, producing 610 megawatts of electricity.

Like so much of the area in the southern Appalachians, the land that is now covered by Jocassee was once part of the Cherokee Nation. Keowee Town, near the confluence of the Toxaway River, was a major hub of the Cherokee Nation for all of the trading the Cherokee did with the European settlers near the town of Charleston. Jocassee even derives its name from a Cherokee maiden and means "place of the lost one."

A rare wildflower, the Oconee bell (*Shortia galacifolia*), native to only a few counties in the Blue Ridge area, was discovered in the area in 1788 by French botanist André Michaux. The creation of Lake Jocassee is said to have caused the destruction of the heart of the species' range. More recently, biologists have documented the occurrence of a number of rare, threatened, and endangered species. the Eastatoe Creek Heritage Preserve was transferred from Duke Power Company to the South Carolina Department of Natural Resources in 1979, due to the extremely diverse flora occurring there.

In 1999, another step was taken to preserve this beautiful region. In a public/private partnership, 10,000 acres were purchased from Duke Power on the north and northeast side of the lake and Gorges State Park was created. Gorges State Park encompasses the escarpment; in just four miles, there is a 2,000-foot elevation change. This unique geology makes the park home to temperate rain forest that receives more than 80 inches of rainfall annually. This setting makes the park home to numerous waterfalls, sheer rock bluffs, and some of the most remote river gorges on the East Coast.

Jocassee has also been home to several motion pictures. The Mount Carmel Baptist Cemetery, now buried under 130 feet of water, was the setting for a scene from Burt Reynolds's and John Voight's 1972 film, *Deliverance*. To this day, you can still hear banjo music when fishing in the area of the ceme-

Early morning sun lights up the abundant structure on Jacassee's shoreline. Kevin Howell

tery. In 2012, part of *The Hunger Games* was filmed on the lake as well.

Because most of the lands around the lake are in state parks or forest, Jocassee is sparsely populated. Due to the lack of development, the lake boasts some of the clearest water you will ever find in a lake. Jocassee is fed by four major rivers:

Thompson River
Whitewater River
Horsepasture River
Toxaway River

Walker Parrott displays a Lake Jocassee bass that took a Howell's herring. Kevin Howell

This makes Jocassee one of the few reservoirs in South Carolina with a fishable population of mountain trout.

Jocassee currently holds the South Carolina state records for brown trout, rainbow trout, Kentucky spotted bass, redeye bass (Coosa), and smallmouth bass. It is also home to what is believed to be the world record redeye bass, at just over 5 pounds (although it has not been confirmed due to changes in bass identification between shoal bass and redeye bass).

Anglers will need a boat to fish Jocassee, as bank access is highly limited. While a canoe or kayak is plausible, I would highly recommend that anglers use at least a 15-foot boat with a reliable motor to navigate the lake. Due to its placement on the escarpment, the orthographic lifting of hot air from the Piedmont against the cold air of the mountains can change the weather on the lake in minutes. It is not uncommon for anglers to encounter 5- to 6-foot swells in the main part of the lake because of approaching thunderstorms.

Jocassee's shoreline is an angler's paradise and offers all types of structure to anglers. However, due to the mountainous nature of the lake, the bank drops off fast, and it is not uncommon for anglers to be a good castoff of the bank and the boat to be over 30–40 feet of water. A lot of the timber was harvested before the lake was filled; however, most of the stumps were left, which provides a lot of structure for the fish. In addition to the stumps, there is a constant influx of timber falling off the banks into the lake during storms and high winds. If that were not enough for anglers who get to fish the lake during a fall drawdown, they will be amazed at the number of rock ledges, caves, and shelves. Fly anglers at times will need to fish flies with heavy lead eyes on sinking lines with short leaders, allowing for a more vertical presentation.

During the late spring and again in mid-autumn, fly anglers will find largemouth bass, redeye bass, Kentucky spotted bass, and smallmouth bass cruising the banks and willing to eat a well-presented fly on a floating or intermediate line. However, fly anglers should always arrive at the lake with a full selection of fly lines, from floating all the way to a type 6 full-sinking line. As water is generated throughout the day, it will change the location of the fish drastically.

The Cane Breaks on Lake Jocassee. Kevin Howell

During the late winter and early spring, anglers can find trout schooled up at the mouths of the rivers and creeks. However, once the summer heat rolls in, the majority of the fish in the lake (other than panfish and a few small bass) head out into the depths of the lake and suspend over humps, ditches, and ledges anywhere from 30 to 60 feet deep, and trout can even be deeper.

Most fly anglers will want to concentrate their efforts up one of the four river arms, as the main part of the lake will prove frustrating for anglers who are not accustomed to fishing sinking lines over structure that may be anywhere from 30 to 50 feet below the lake surface.

For a side trip, anglers can find a lot of good fishing in the feeder creeks and four rivers that feed the lake. The Horsepasture and Toxaway Rivers offer smallmouth bass, redeye bass, and trout on the lower end and become more dominated by trout as anglers get farther away from the lake. Anglers fishing up the Toxaway can also turn up the Little Toxaway Creek. Bearwallow Creek also offers another side trip for anglers. While the Whitewater and Thompson both hold fish, they are very rough and almost inaccessible once anglers leave the lake (due the tremendous waterfalls on the face of the escarpment) and until you reach the North Carolina state line on the top of the escarpment.

Above. Kevin Howell fishing Lake Jocassee. Walker Parrott

Left. Jocassee Coossa Bass that struck a Walker's Wiggler. Kevin Howell

➤ **Regulations:** Anglers should consult the current South Carolina DNR for current regulation and advisories at www.dnr.sc.gov/fishregs/freshwaterregs.html.

➤ **Tackle:** For fly fishing the lake, anglers will want a 7- to 9-weight fly rod. Leaders should be tapered to somewhere between 12- and 6-pound test. Lighter tippets will result in more strikes but also more lost fish in trees and rock ledges. Flies will vary as for target species. For bass, use Clouser Minnows tied with kinky fiber, Near 'Nuff Crayfish (size 2), Game Changers in 1/0 in gray with a black back, and large kinky fiber streamers, such as Cowen's Baitfish or Howell's Herring. For surface patterns, Dahlberg Divers and Pencil-style poppers will work well, as well as Boogle Bugs in moss or black. The same flies will work up the creek for bass. For trout in the lake, anglers will find success with black and olive Woolly Buggers in sizes 4–8 and kinky fiber Clousers in colors that will match the blueback herring in the lake. For anglers targeting trout up the creeks, your standard trout flies like an Elk-hair Caddis will fool most local residents.

Kevin Howell with a fine Argentinian Brown. Gonzalo Flego

KEVIN HOWELL—Kevin Howell is the owner of Davidson River Outfitters; he also is an author, lecturer, fly-fishing instructor, and guide. Kevin is a Signature fly Designer for Montana Fly Company. A 2018 inductee to the Fly Fishing Museum of the Southern Appalachians Hall of Fame and a 2018 inductee to the Legends of the Fly Hall of Fame as well. Kevin has been guiding the waters of North Carolina, South Carolina, and East Tennessee for 25 years. When not guiding he can be found fishing with his wife Mellissa, and sons David and Andrew.

CLOSEST FLY SHOPS

Brookings Cashiers Village Anglers
49 Pillar Dr.
Cashiers, NC 28717
828-743-3768
www.brookingsonline.com

Davidson River Outfitters
49 Pisgah Hwy., Ste. 6
Pisgah Forest, NC 28768
888-861-0111
www.davidsonflyfishing.com

CLOSEST GUIDES AND OUTFITTERS

Davidson River Outfitters
49 Pisgah Hwy., Ste. 6
Pisgah Forest, NC 28768
888-861-0111

CLOSEST LODGING

Devils Fork State Park
161 Holcombe Cir.
Salem, SC 29676
864-944-2639

Best Western Executive Inn
511 Bypass Hwy. 123
Seneca, SC 29678
864-886-9646

Hampton Inn and Suites
1011 E. North First St.
Seneca, SC 29678
864-482-2900

CLOSEST RESTAURANTS

There are no restaurants on or near the lake and anglers will have to travel to Seneca SC for the closest restaurants.

Black's Smokehouse
1528 Blue Ridge Blvd.
Seneca, SC 29672
864-280-2577
www.blackssmokehouse.com

FATZ
1615 Sandifer Blvd.
Seneca, SC 29678
864-888-1009

Joe's New York Pizza
685 Bypass 123, Suite D
Seneca, SC 29678
864-888-0009

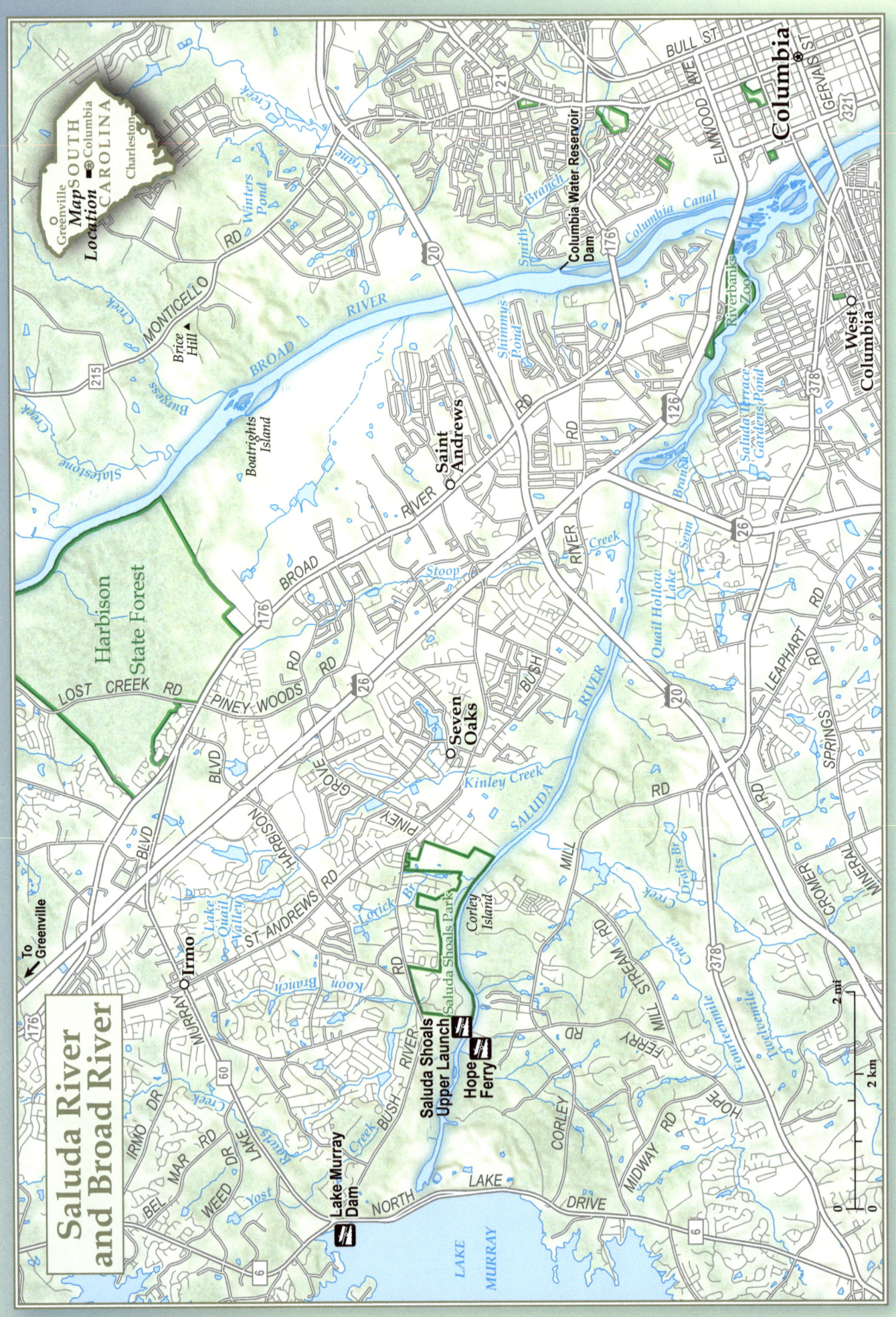

19 · Saluda River and Broad River

▶ **Location:** The Saluda River and the Broad River are located in South Carolina, mostly running between Greenville and Columbia. You can fly commercially to either river through Columbia, South Carolina; Greenville, South Carolina; Charlotte, North Carolina; or Augusta, Georgia. All four airports are between 1 and 1 1/2 hours from Columbia, South Carolina.

Both the Saluda River and the Broad River are part of the Santee River basin in South Carolina. The Broad River originates in the Blue Ridge Mountains of North Carolina and runs 150 miles southeast through South Carolina. In North Carolina, the river is dammed to form Lake Lure; in South Carolina, it passes through the Sumter National Forest and the communities of Cherokee Falls and Lockhart before joining the Saluda River to form the Congaree River in the city of Columbia.

The Saluda River is formed in the Blue Ridge Mountains just outside of Greenville. Its north and south forks meet the middle fork in Greenville County, where the Saluda then runs a general southeasterly direction where it is dammed a number of times for industry and reservoir needs. The lower Saluda then joins the Broad River, forming the Congaree River in Columbia, South Carolina.

The lower Saluda River begins its ten-mile journey just below Lake Murray Dam, and in May 1991, it was designated a state scenic river by the South Carolina legislature. The Lake Murray Dam is regulated by SCE&G and generates electricity for the surrounding areas. No public generation schedules are available, but sirens along the upper stretch are in place to warn of water release downstream. If you plan on fishing regularly, there is also a hotline available that will send mobile alerts and e-mails in the event of generation. The water can rise quite quickly, so it is imperative that all anglers and boaters are prepared to exit the river in under ten minutes of the initial warning. While larger releases affect short-term fishing, smaller releases can have little negative effect.

The lower Saluda's cold water creates a great environment for trout and striped bass. This, combined with the surrounding topography and rock outcrops similar to mountain streams and the heavily wooded landscape, make the lower Saluda River corridor an outstanding natural resource within the urban environment of metropolitan Columbia. Trout are generally stocked around the beginning of December, and the fishing stays consistent through spring. In the spring, landlocked striped bass run up the Saluda in search of spawning grounds as well as feed on the population of trout. Although the trout population becomes thinned out, some make it through the summer and grow to become trophy fish.

Accessing the upper stretches of the lower Saluda River can be done by kayak, canoe, or small johnboat from either the east or west sides of the river. Wading is possible, but access is very limited. From the west side from Interstate 20, take Corley Mill Road north to Hope Ferry Road, where a public boat ramp is available. From the east side of the river on Interstate 20, take Bush River Road to Saluda Shoals Park,

Anglers will also encounter sub species like Yellow Perch while fishing the Saluda. Walker Parrott

where you can access the river for a small fee. Three and a half miles downstream of Saluda Shoals, anglers can access the east bank of the river just before the Interstate 20 Bridge at Gardendale via Bush River Road. There is no boat ramp, so you must carry any watercraft to and from the parking lot. Below Gardendale, there is no public access for another 3 1/2 miles until you reach Riverbanks Zoo. Use caution, as there

With limited access on the Saluda, anglers will find rafts and canoes the best method for fishing the river. Walker Hopkins

are multiple rapids between Gardendale and Riverbanks Zoo. Depending on water levels, these rapids can be a Class III or higher. The final rapid is Mill Race Rapids, by far the most dangerous on the river, meeting a Class V rating a certain water levels. Mill Race Rapids should be portaged—walk around it! A portage trail begins in a power line right-of-way just upstream of Mill Race Rapids on the right bank (west side) of the river. Takeout is just below the rapids on the west bank, just above Riverbanks Zoo.

Anglers will find that a nymph and indicator rig is the most productive technique when fishing faster moving water near shoals. Caddis and Baetis nymphs, along with hellgrammites, Woolly Buggers, and leeches are all effective patterns. Streamers are the most effective technique for the slower-moving stretches between shoals, but occasionally you will find rising fish, generally feeding on small caddis, Blue-winged Olives, and mayflies. I recommend a 9-foot, 4X leader with a 4- to 6-weight rod for general use for trout, although later in the spring wary fish may require 5X fluorocarbon. It is also important to remember that the upper stretch of the lower Saluda (above I-20 Bridge) is where the South Carolina DNR stocking program mostly focuses, and access is available in this section. Below the Interstate 20 Bridge, the waters can and do hold fish, yet a dedicated full day is required and hiring a guide is highly recommended. Stripers show up around April, and move upstream through June. Six- to eight-weight rods with 12- to 20-pound fluorocarbon leaders are necessary. Any baitfish pattern is usable, although either a chartreuse and white size 2 Clouser or Puglisi Peanut Butter is a good choice. Although quite rare, stripers weighing more than 30 pounds have been caught on the Saluda.

The Broad River is widely regarded as a top smallmouth river, although access is very difficult. There are many access points above Parr Shoals Reservoir, two of which are recommended floats on which to concentrate:

Bowens Creek to South Carolina 29
Neal Shoals to Sandy River

To reach Bowens Creek from Interstate 85 (exit 96), head north on South Carolina 18. After crossing Broad River, take the first left onto S-11-98 and drive until you cross Bowens

Broad river near Columbia, South Carolina. Tom Caskey

Debbie Gillespie releasing a rainbow trout on the Saluda River. Kevin Howell.

Above. Walker Parrott nets a Saluda River trout for Debbie Gillespie. Kevin Howell

Facing. Debbie Gillespie with a Saluda River brown trout. Kevin Howell

Creek. The access is on the left. This 4 1/2-mile float is suitable for a canoe or kayak and is dominated by shoals. Take-out is an access area off Ford Road from South Carolina 29. Below Neal Shoals to Sandy River is a 7.3-mile float suitable for a canoe, kayak, or small boat. This float is also dominated by shoals, and constant navigation is required. Private land dominates from Parr Shoals Reservoir downstream to the Congaree River, yet fishing the shoals in this stretch can be very productive. There is a boat ramp at Parr Shoals Reservoir for kayaks and canoes. It is about 17 miles between the boat ramp and the Interstate 20 Bridge, so a day float is a very hard accomplishment. The majority of both sides of the river are private, as well as the islands, and camping is not allowed. Floating this section is very productive, yet very hard to accomplish.

I recommend 5- to 7-weight rods for smallmouths with 10-pound leaders. Baitfish patterns and poppers dominate with nymph/indicator rigs being a solid backup technique. My favorite patterns are Walker's Wigglers, Todd's Wiggle Minnows, Sparkle Minnows, Game Changers, Puglisi Minnows, and Clousers. Dead-drifting Girdle Bugs, the Big Nasty, black Woolly Buggers, and large Prince Nymphs under indicators are also very effective. The best times to target smallies are from spring until fall. In general, the larger males move up in shallow water as the water temperature rises in search of areas for the females to lay eggs, called redds. As soon as the timing is right, females will come into the area and begin the spawning process. Later in the season, smallies can hold in water very similar to trout. Look for riffles, braids, and structure for the best results.

Above. Saluda River near Saluda Shoals. Kevin Howell

Inset. Saluda River brown trout. Kevin Howell

Facing page. Walker Hopkins with a nice rainbow trout. Walker Hopkins.

Walker Hopkins with a Saluda rainbow. Walker Hopkins

WALKER HOPKINS is a Thomson, Georgia, native who, from a very early age, began enjoying hunting and fishing on the family farm. Walker attended the University of Georgia and Augusta State University during his pursuit in education and continued his love for fly fishing during weekends (and some weekdays) during college. After purchasing Rivers & Glen Trading Company in 2010, the local waters around Augusta became his new focus. Quickly, he fell in love with the Saluda River and its wily trophy fish.

CLOSEST FLY SHOPS

Barron's Outfitters
1725 Harden St.
Columbia, SC 29204
803-254-5537
www.barronsoutfitters.com

Rivers & Glen Trading Company
Surrey Center
387 Highland Ave.
Augusta, GA 30907
706-738-4536
www.riversandglen.com

CLOSEST LODGING

Wingate by Windham
108 Saluda Pointe Ct.
Lexington, SC 29072
803-957-5000

CLOSEST RESTAURANTS

Tako Sushi
210 The Alley
Aiken, SC 29801
803-642-8899

Pawleys Front Porch
827 Harden St.
Columbia, SC 29205
803-771-8001

Pearlz Oyster Bar
936 Gervais Street
Columbia, SC 29201
803-661-7741
pearlzvista@hghosp.com
www.pearlzoysterbar.com/

Real Mexico
2421 Bush River Rd.
Columbia, SC 29210
803-750-8990

20 · Hilton Head Island

➤ **Location:** Hilton Head Island is one of the most southern barrier islands of South Carolina. Just two hours south of Charleston, 45 minutes north of Savannah, and two hours southeast of Columbia, Hilton Head is an easy trip for most East Coasters. Hilton Head Island is known to be a great family destination, with endless outdoor activities and over 100 restaurants, and it is also a great place to fly fish year-round. About 80 percent of our fly fishing around Hilton Head is sight casting. Whether it's a large school of winter redfish over the mud flats, tailing redfish in the flooded spartina grass (cord grass), openwater schools of giant jack crevalle, topwater cruising cobia, or even sharks on a sand flat, sight casting can be very productive. The other 20 percent of our fly-fishing opportunities are spent blind casting around structure for speckled trout, ladyfish, Spanish mackerel, bluefish, and whatever else is willing to suck down baitfish and shrimp patterns.

Redfish are our primary target here in Hilton Head, because they are available year-round and are typically cooperative with well-placed flies. During the fall and winter, for a few hours on each side of low tide, redfish stage up on shell bars, mud and sand flats, and small creeks. Anywhere from one to more than 100 fish can be sight casted or blind casted to in these areas.

Larger schools of redfish are not any easier to feed than the smaller schools, but they sure do get our adrenaline pumping as 100 fish come barreling down the flat, creating wakes and muds along the way. These cooler seasons are very productive, due to better water visibility and the migrations of shrimp and baitfish, which keep the redfish in feeding mode. Typical casts are 30–80 feet, and the more accurate the better. Shrimp patterns work wonders through the fall and winter, as well as Clouser Minnows, small crab patterns, Dupree's Spoons, and baitfish patterns, such as the EP Minnows. Seven- to nine-weight rods with floating lines are best for redfish any time of year.

Spring and summer are exciting times to fly fish in Hilton Head, with more and more fish entering our waters. Targeting tailing redfish is the most popular form of fly fishing for redfish in South Carolina. (The term "tailing redfish" comes from the fish actually waving its tail above the surface as it combs the bottoms of the flats for its prey.) Around an hour on each side of our larger spring tides, when the sun, moon, and earth are aligned, the warmer spartina grass flats flood and come alive. These flats are home to over a million small fiddler crabs per acre, along with snails, birds, and of course, the mud minnows that bite at your feet if you decide to chase them down on foot. Redfish in the 20- to 30-inch range swim onto these flats in search of crabs, shrimp, mud minnows, and finger mullet. These flooded grass flats are the most challenging, exciting, and rewarding places to fly fish for redfish. Catching one redfish in the grass is worth five or even ten fish in any other redfishing scenario.

Walker Parrott with a nice black drum near Hilton Head. Kevin Howell

Typical casts to tailing redfish on the grass flats are anywhere from 10 to 50 feet. Stealth is the name of the game on the flats, so keep the splashing to a minimum and try to land your fly quietly ahead of your target. Heavier crab and shrimp patterns work well, as they are able to sink quickly into the

Walker Parrott battling a redfish outside of Bluffton. Kevin Howell

grass. The Kung-Fu Crab, gold Mylar crab, Razzmatazz, and Dupree's Spoons are great choices for tailing redfish.

The warmer months around Hilton Head Island offer some exciting fly fishing in the Port Royal Sound and Calibogue Sound, as well as offshore. With schools of menhaden, mullet, threadfins, and glass minnows in abundance, finding something to throw flies at is usually not a problem. Looking for diving birds is a great way to find Spanish mackerel, ladyfish, bluefish, and medium-size jack crevalle. Smaller flies that resemble glass minnows such as the Gummy Minnow, white and silver Clouser Minnows, and small EP Baitfish are seldom refused when the action is on the surface. Driving around on the beachfront on a calm summer day and chasing down baitfish blitz after blitz is an absolute blast with a fly rod. Six- to eight-weight fly rods work well on calmer days, and 9-weight rods make shooting line into the wind a bit easier. Floating lines or floating/intermediate lines are great for the surface action, and sink-tip lines work great over structure when the birds are no help.

Summer is also a great time to fly fish for giant jack crevalle in both Port Royal and Calibogue Sounds. Large schools of at least 50–100 fish in the 30-pound range arrive in May and frequent the waters until early fall, or until the first significant weather event that drops the water temperature. Hunting big jack crevalle on a fly rod takes patience and time, as this is strictly sight casting for fish that never seem to stop swimming. Locating these fish requires calm winds and other favorable conditions like higher tides and the presence of menhaden pushing into the sounds. There are days when the schools are daisy chaining in tight, oily circles, happy to take a fly, and there are many days when locating jack crevalle is nearly impossible. Big popper flies such as the Umpqua

Above. Speckled trout. Kevin Howell

Below. Gonzalo Flego with his very first redfish. Caught near Hilton Head Island. Walker Parrott

Jack Popper work great in yellow, white, blue, and green. Large streamers seem to work just as well and can be easier to cast. Flashtail Whistlers, EP Baitfish, and Half & Halfs are also good choices in white, orange, yellow, and green. When choosing a rod to tackle these yellow-tailed freight trains, I recommend 10- to 12-weight rod/reels spooled with a 200-plus yards of backing. It might seem strange to break out the tarpon gear for a 30-pound fish, but feeding a giant jack with your redfish outfit is a mistake you'll only make once.

➤ **Regulations:**
Redfish—3 per person; 15–23 inches long
Speckled trout—10 per person; 14-inch minimum
Spanish mackerel—15 per person; 12-inch minimum

Capt. Kai Williams with a lowcountry redfish. Kevin Howell

CAPT. KAI WILLIAMS has been fishing all his life and guiding fishermen for half of it. Having been fortunate enough to grow up on Hilton Head Island, Kai learned the ins and outs of redfishing at a young age and began saltwater fly fishing at age 14. Capt. Kai dedicates himself to exploring every nook and cranny of the low-country salt marshes, searching for unique fly-fishing opportunities. For such a young and enthusiastic guide, Kai has logged many days on the poling platform of his flats skiff and in front of the vise. If you're searching for your next saltwater fly guide in South Carolina, be sure to give Kai a call.

CLOSEST FLY SHOPS

Southern Drawl Outfitters
1533 Fording Island Rd., Ste. 316
Hilton Head Island, SC 29926
843-705-6010
www.southerndrawloutfitters.com

Bay Street Outfitters
825 Bay St.
Beaufort, SC 29902
843-524-5250
www.baystreetoutfitters.com

Rivers & Glen Trading Company
24 Drayton St.
Savannah, GA 31401
912-349-2352
www.riversandglen.com

CLOSEST LODGING

The Westin Savannah Harbor Golf Resort and Spa
1 Resort Dr.
Savannah, GA 31421
912-201-2000
www.westinsavannah.com/

Hilton Garden Inn Savannah Historic District
321 W. Bay St.
Savannah, GA 31401
912-721-5000

Marriott Barony Beach Club
5 Grasslawn Ave.
Hilton Head Island, SC 29928
843-342-1608
www.marriott.com/hotels
/travel/hhhbb-marriotts-barony
-beach-club/

CLOSEST RESTAURANTS

Neo
1533 Fording Island Rd., #326
Hilton Head Island, SC 29926
843-837-5111
www.neohhi.com

Skull Creek Boat House
397 Squire Pope Rd.
Hilton Head Island, SC 29926
843-681-3663
www.skullcreekboathouse.com/

CQ's Restaurant
140 Lighthouse Rd.
Hilton Head Island, SC 29928
843-671-2779

Marker 13 Buoy Bar
397 Squire Pope Rd.
Hilton Head Island, SC 29926
843-681-3663
www.facebook.com/pages/Marker
-13-Buoy-Bar/160442900693356

Hudson's Seafood House on the Docks
1 Hudson Rd
Hilton Head Island, SC 29926
www.hudsonsonthedock.com

Big Bamboo
1 N. Forest Beach Dr.
Hilton Head Island, SC 29928
843-686-3443
http://m.mainstreethub.com
/bigbamboocafe

Old Town Dispensary
15 Captains Cove
Bluffton, SC 29910
843-837-1893
www.otdbluffton.com

21 · Charleston Low Country

➤ **Location:** There are countless locations for every angler within minutes of downtown Charleston, South Carolina.

Fly-rod opportunities abound in historic and beautiful Charleston. The offering ranges from our tidal rivers and estuaries to nearshore wrecks off the beach. Redfish (also known as spot-tail bass or red drum) are the most sought after inshore species. Spotted sea trout and flounder are often caught effectively with the fly rod in the same areas that redfish are found.

Seasonally, our nearshore fishery offers cobia, Spanish mackerel, false albacore, and amberjack. All these fish love to eat a fly. The springtime nearshore cobia run has become an outstanding fishery that more than a few inshore charter captains have figured out, much to the delight of the avid fly rodder looking for a real challenge.

The following pages will touch on the areas in Charleston that are popular for fly rodding, the best opportunities based on the low-country season, available bait species and favorite fly imitations, and guides for the visiting fly angler to contact and enjoy.

A separate section will cover kayak fishing opportunities. We see more and more paddlers fly fishing and so the kayak section should provide a bit of helpful information.

➤ **Rivers that form Charleston Harbor (Ashley, Cooper and Wando)**

The Charleston fishery can be broken down into several areas that you may consider for your next excursion. Charleston has a 5- to 7-foot tide range that should be remembered when fishing shallow-water flats. Many an afternoon and evening have been spent by anglers stuck on a flat, out of cold beverages, waiting for the tide to come in to refloat their boat.

The Ashley, Wando, and Cooper Rivers join around the peninsula of Charleston to form Charleston Harbor. The Ashley River originates near Summerville, South Carolina, as a blackwater river supporting bream, largemouth, and striped bass. Salinity increases as the river flows toward Charleston Harbor, and the river offers excellent areas to target redfish and speckled trout. There are good flats near the Citadel campus and between Elliot Cut and the mouth of James Island Creek.

The Cooper River is the primary source of fresh water into the Charleston Harbor. The Cooper has been developed industrially over the years and so is not as scenic as the Ashley or Wando Rivers. That said, there are excellent areas to fish for redfish, but more importantly, the Cooper is well-known for great numbers of speckled trout and flounder. Drum Island, Castle Pinckney, and the mouth of Clouter Creek are easily accessed spots that offer good speckled trout fishing. Farther up the Cooper, there are areas that are off-limits to fishing because of the security around the Naval Weapons Station.

Capt. JR Waits with a hightide tailing Charleston redfish. Capt. JR Waits

The Wando River has the most diverse ecology and has the least development compared to the Ashley and Cooper Rivers. Redfish, speckled trout, and flounder are very abundant in the Wando. Horlbeck Creek and the surrounding flats are good areas for reds and trout. North of South Carolina 41 Bridge is smaller water, and Guerin Creek offers opportunities for trout and redfish. Tailing flats abound north of the

A tailing redfish finds the hook and heads for open water. Tucker Blythe

bridge. I strongly recommend tapping into local knowledge for chasing tailing redfish. Paying a guide or having a buddy show you good tailing flats will be the difference between getting multiple shots at tailers and poling your boat for two or three hours through a seemingly barren marsh.

➤ **Isle of Palms (Grey Bay, Hamilin Sound, Copahee Sound, and Bullyard Sound)**

The best-known area for chasing redfish and trout is the inshore marshes behind Isle of Palms. This area is adjacent to Mount Pleasant, just east of the Charleston peninsula. This is arguably the most pressured area in Charleston. Grey Bay is most easily accessed from Wild Dunes Marina and offers excellent flats fishing for redfish. Hamlin Sound and Copahee Sound are farther east and likewise have outstanding schools of redfish. The Bullyard Sound is immediately adjacent to the Intracoastal Waterway and is the easiest access for new boaters.

➤ **Stono River/Kiawah River:** The Kiawah and Stono Rivers join just behind Stono Inlet on the south end of Folly Beach. This area is lightly developed and offers some of the most pristine coastal ecology close to Charleston. Good areas to target include Bass Creek just inside the inlet. There are good mudflats on either side of the Stono around Bass Creek. There is a great hard sand flat (good for wade fishing) just behind Bird Key or, if you are looking on Google Maps, immediately to the south of Cole Island. One other good area for reds on the flats is located near Bryans Creek, directly across from the boat docks on Kiawah Island.

➤ **Kayak fishing in Charleston:** Low tide flats around Charleston are primarily soft "pluff mud" bottoms that make wading difficult or impossible. Many fly rodders have gone to kayaks for reaching and fishing the mud flats. For anglers looking for tailing redfish, a kayak is a very efficient way of moving across flooded spartina grass flats. Here are some suggestions for good areas that have put-ins for kayaks and reasonable paddles to the good flats:

- Wild Dunes Marina— This put-in offers access to Gray Bay and Hamlin Sound.
- South Carolina 41 Bridge—This boat landing offers access to the upper Wando River.

Greater amberjacks will test the durability of tackle and angler. Michael Bruner

- Gadsdenville Public Ramp—This ramp offers access to Copahee Sound.
- Folly Beach boat ramp (along South Carolina 171)—This put-in offers access to the Folly River and Stono Inlet.
- Sol Legre (off Folly Road, South Carolina 171)—This public boat landing offers access to the Stono River.
- Northbridge Park (South Carolina 7, Sam Rittenberg Road)—This put-in offers access to the Ashley River.

▶ **Peak Fishing Times:** Charleston has a year-round fishery for both redfish and speckled trout. There are several peak periods to come to Charleston for redfish and trout. The two key periods for redfish are May through July and October through early December. Wintertime sight fishing can also be rewarding but is less reliable because of variable weather conditions.

May through September offers flood tides for tailing redfish. While you can find tailing reds every day during the summer months, most anglers will identify the bigger high tides that occur just before and just after the full- and new-moon periods each month. The best tailing tides will occur in the morning or in the late afternoon. Charter captains know this and book these dates well in advance of the tailing tides. Speckled trout can also be caught during this period, but higher water temperatures and reduced water clarity makes for tougher fishing.

Additionally, early morning topwater fishing can be very productive for redfish and trout if you are in the area waiting for your tailing tide. Fishing during incoming or outgoing tides with poppers early before the sun is on the water is a great option while you wait for the afternoon tailing tides. Slack tides can produce, but both trout and redfish will not feed as aggressively as the tide goes slack.

Ladyfish are very plentiful during the mid- and late-summer months and can provide some spectacular action when fishing topwater flies for speckled trout.

The other peak period for redfish and speckled trout runs from October to early December. During the fall, as water temperatures cool to the 70s and high 60s, bait species begin to migrate out of the shallow bays and creeks into deeper wa-

Tucker Blythe with a spinner shark he landed just off the coast of Charleston. Tucker Blythe

ter. Shrimp and mullet are the two key bait items that redfish and trout target during the fall. Menhaden can be a factor for speckled trout in early fall.

Shrimp begin to move to deeper water and during this period, redfish will begin to group up and physically run shrimp on the Charleston mud flats. Many times, redfish can be found under diving birds as they run shrimp over mud flats. This is possibly the most exciting and productive time for lots of hook-ups while throwing shrimp flies. Redfish are very aggressive and just about any fly placed in front of a school of reds running shrimp can result in hook-ups. Attractor patterns can be devastating.

Speckled trout can also be found at creek mouths and other spots that effectively funnel current and shrimp. Many times, trout will force shrimp to the surface and seagulls will flock over a school of trout that are working a creek mouth, oyster rake, or funneling area. Sinking flies combined with sink-tip lines that get down 2–8 feet will be very effective, and poppers will get topwater strikes as well. One warning: while throwing poppers when birds are working, you may have to take your fly away from the birds! Trout are sight feeders and are influenced by water clarity. Many of the best trout tides will occur on the smallest tides. Generally, small tides occur when the moon is half full. These tides have smaller volumes of water moving and so less turbulence occurs during the tides.

➤ **Winter-time Sight Fishing for Redfish:** Wintertime (late November through February) can offer the best sight-fishing opportunities in the Charleston area. When water temperatures drop into the low 60s down to the mid to low 50s, redfish will group in schools and will move into shallow water. As temperatures drop, suspended algae will die off and water clarity improves, allowing for good sight fishing. The downside during the period is that reds will feed less and will become much less active.

Tactics for wintertime reds include downsizing your flies and using small worm, crab, or mud minnow imitations. Very slow retrieves will often be required to get fish to eat your flies when water temperatures are at the seasonal low point.

Wintertime sight fishing can be very rewarding if you are looking for a challenge of accurate presentation, delicate retrieves, and repeated refusal by sluggish reds traveling in groups from 10 to 100 fish.

High fall flood tides offer great opportunities for tailing redfish in the Charleston area. Michael Bruner

Below. Mark Phelps with Spadefish. Mark Phelps

► Bait Fish Species and Flies to Imitate each Specie

Throughout the year, Charleston's baitfish species vary considerably and should be watched when planning a trip. Following, you can find a table that lists common baitfish, when they are abundant and targeted by our inshore species and flies that imitate these baitfish.

► Near Shore Species and Fly Rod Opportunities

During the year in Charleston, several nearshore species make an appearance and offer a chance for the adventurous fly angler to test his or her openwater fishing skills. Beginning in April and May, cobia will migrate north along the South Carolina coast in a spawning run that ends in numerous large estuaries. Spring will also have nearshore runs of Spanish mackerel and false albacore. As water temperatures increase, more Spanish appear, and in deep water, amberjack become very active.

Each year, we see more and more fly rodders target sharks during the summer months. A regular scenario for sharks is to find local shrimp boats and fish behind them, either when the boats are trolling or when catches are sorted and bycatch is discarded overboard.

There are a number of guides who run both flats skiffs and larger center consoles that make nearshore trips comfortable and exciting. Spanish and false albacore can be caught on the same equipment used for redfish, while cobia and amberjack require 10- to 12-weight rods and reels. Much of this nearshore fishing is done with sink-tip or full-sinking fly lines.

RANDY HAMILTON moved to the low country years ago to pursue the many inshore species of the low country of South Carolina. Leaving the bug rich fresh waters of Pennsylvania, Randy can be found fishing inshore with his two boys. Whether he's fishing farm ponds, inshore or offshore, Randy can catch 'em. He works for St.Croix Rods as the Southeast territory manager. Randy has the life.

Facing. Randy Hamilton with a healthy redfish. Tucker Blythe

CLOSEST GUIDES AND OUTFITTERS

Capt. Mike Able Jr.
Able-Minded Charters
740 Veron Pl.
Mt. Pleasant, SC 29464
843-475-7696
captmike@haddrellspoint.com
www.ablemindedcharters.com

Capt. Scotty Davis
843-709-0307
scottydalaska@yahoo.com

Capt. Michael Bruner
Fins and Flies Charters
843-860-6536
captmichaelbruner@finsandflies.com
www.finsandflies.com

Capt. Peter Brown
Saltwater Charters
843-830-0448
phbrown08@comcast.com
www.saltcharters.com

Capt. J. R. Waits
111 Bass Alley
Wando, SC 29492
843-509-7337
jrwaits@fishcall.com
www.fishcall.com

Capt. Hunter Allen
Lighter Breeze Charters
2408 Fulford Ct.
Mt. Pleasant, SC 29466
843-371-2049
lighterbreeze@gmail.com
www.charlestoninshoreguide.com
/captainhunterallen

Capt. Ben Floyd
Charleston Fish Finder
75 Forest Trl.
Isle of Palms, SC 29451
843-670-3123
ben@charlestonfishfinder.com
www.charlestonfishfinder.com

Capt. Jamie Hough
843-442-5033
hough12@aol.com

Capt. Mark Phelps
Shore Thang Charters
843-475-1274
shorethangcharter@hotmail.com
www.shorethangcharters.com

Capt. Tucker Blythe
Grey Ghost Charters
1518 Lynton St.
Charleston, SC 29412
843-670-8629
tuckblythe@hotmail.com
www.greyghostcharters.com

Capt. John Ward
Affinity Charters
1771 Clarks Hill Cir.
John's Island, SC 29455
843-693-2460
captainjohnward@gmail.com
www.affinitycharters.com

Capt. John Irwin
Fly Right Charters
1114 Oakcrest Dr.
Charleston, SC 29412
843-860-4231
john@flyrightcharters.com
www.flyrightcharters.com

CLOSEST LODGING

Embassy Suites
337 Meeting St.
Charleston, SC 29403
843-723-6900

Belmond Charleston Place
205 Meeting St.
Charleston, SC 29401
843-722-4900
info.cph@belmond.com
www.belmond.com/charleston-place

Holiday Inn Historic Downtown
425 Meeting St.
Charleston, SC 29403
843-718-2327

CLOSEST RESTAURANTS

Sticky Fingers
235 Meeting St.
Charleston, SC 29403
843-853-7427
www.stickyfingers.com

California Dreaming
1 Ashley Point Dr.
Charleston, SC 29407
843-766-1644
www.californiadreaming.co

Halls Chophouse
434 King St.
Charleston, SC 29403
843-727-0090
www.hallschophouse.com

NORTH CAROLINA

22 · Harkers Island

➤ **Location:** Harkers Island is situated behind lower Core Banks and the Cape Lookout National Seashore, and it is a part of North Carolina's Crystal Coast. It is approximately three hours from Raleigh, North Carolina. You will need to fly into Raleigh-Durham International Airport.

Made famous as a port of call for false albacore fishing, Harkers Island and the greater Crystal Coast area offers fly anglers a wide variety of opportunities for many saltwater species. Inshore, near coastal, and offshore species can be targeted.

False albacore are officially known as "little tunny." These fish propelled the sleepy fishing village of Harkers Island into the fly-angling spotlight through fantastic fall runs off the beaches of Core and Shackleford Banks and Atlantic Beach. Much has been written about this fishery, and it has been visited by the who's who of fly anglers over the years. Although the number of anglers visiting the area during the fall run has decreased a bit over the years, the fishing remains just as exciting. Peak season for albacore is October through November. As cold fronts approach the area, vast shoals of baitfish exit from Beaufort and Barden Inlets, pulling the fish from offshore waters close to the beach. Due to the geography of the barrier islands, the cool fall winds from the north to northeast flatten and clear the near coastal waters, providing ideal conditions to fly fish for these fish. Most of the fishing is done by boat, although there are small opportunities to cast to a fish from the beaches of Cape Lookout. Bay boats

Mark Geever with a nice Harkers Island albacore. Capt Gary Dubiel

and small center consoles are ideal fly-fishing platforms, and typically the boat handler needs to position the angler to cast into breaking fish. Much of this is a run-and-gun experience, and the fly caster needs to be quick and accurate to be successful.

Fly rodders need to carry 9- or 10-weight outfits with high-quality reels with 200 or so yards of 20- to 30-pound backing. Anticipate the fly line and many yards of backing to clear the deck and the reel in seconds. The fight can be long and powerful, and a reasonable amount of pressure needs to be put on the fish to ensure a successful release. False albacore are not good table fare and should be released alive.

Albacore will eat a variety of finfish, like bay anchovies and silver sides; therefore, flies should be tied to imitate those small baitfish. Clouser Deep Minnows, Ultra Clousers, Finesse Flies, Surf Candies (as described in *Pop Fleyes* by Bob Popovic), and the like are all good choices. Anglers should take note of the size of bait the fish seem to be feeding on and choose a pattern more to the size and less in line with color.

More important than the fly pattern is getting the fly to the fish quickly and into his line of sight. Casting can do part of that, but clear sink-tip or intermediate sinking fly lines will help sink the fly a bit more quickly than a floater and can result in more hook-ups. Anglers should not focus on gen-

Albacore love the area near the bite despite the crowded waters. Capt. Gary Dubiel

Once you are hooked up to an albie, the work is just begining. Capt Gary Dubiel

erating fly retrieve speed but rather getting the line tight and pausing the fly, especially after placing it in front of breaking fish. Anglers who have not fished for albacore before should seriously consider hiring a guide. Boat handling can be difficult on your own and a challenge for the inexperienced. It is also a big ocean and time limitations are well served with an experienced captain.

In addition to the fall false albacore fishing, there is a small spring run of fish. Atlantic bonito also move through the area in April and May. Bluefish and Spanish mackerel will move into the area in those months as well, with more Spanish arriving in May and June. Spanish, bluefish, a variety of small jacks, and even small albacore can frequent these same near-coastal waters all summer and even remain right into early fall at the start of the albacore run. Eight-weight outfits are perfect to target bonito, blues, and Spanish. Many of the same fly patterns will be productive. Floating, intermediate, and even fast-sinking lines all have their place and a well-prepared fly angler should be ready to change lines to get the fly to the fish.

Big-game opportunities are available as well. Cobia move through Crystal Coast waters in May and June and can be found swimming around buoys, bait balls, tides lines, and near turtles and rays. A number of shark species can also be found around baits and commercial vessels culling bycatch. Sharks will readily take a fly, especially when feeding behind shrimpers. The peak season for sharks is June into October.

Amberjack will hold on near coastal wrecks during these same months and can challenge any fly rodder with serious power. Twelve-weight-plus fly rods are required for these big fish, and outfits should be rigged with sinking lines. Many large baitfish patterns are productive. Large redfish and king mackerel can also be found cruising near coast waters and fall victim to the long rod.

Offshore enthusiasts can also get into the fly-fishing scene, especially by targeting dolphinfish. School dolphinfish can be easy to target and catch, but big bulls will also fall for the fly. Calm summer days are helpful in locating these fish along any offshore structure, including grass lines and debris. Both baitfish and squid imitations are productive and fish well from 10-weight outfits.

The inshore waters near Harkers and along the Crystal Coast hold plenty of redfish. Reds can be found in the flooded marsh around Harkers, the North and Newport Rivers, Core and Bogue Sounds, Middle and Newport Marshes, and Core Creek from April into November (and even December). Look for redfish waking, pushing, and tailing. Seven- and eight-weight outfits with floating lines are ideal. Redfish will eat a variety of fly patterns, and as a rule of thumb, flies with browns, tan, gold, and copper are all productive. Spotted seatrout and flounder can also be found in the same areas and eat the same flies.

▶ **Regulations:** Consult North Carolina Depart of Motor Vehicles' website or regulations book. Anglers will need a North Carolina coast fishing license.

Regardless of size, albacore can challege the skills of any fly angler. Capt. Gary Dubiel

▶ **Tackle:** For Albacore, I recommend a 9-foot, 9- or 10-weight saltwater rod with large arbor fly reel packed with 30-pound backing. For lines, the best would be weight-forward floating, clear-tip intermediate, or full-clear intermediate and 300- to 400-grain sinking lines. I suggest leaders of 20-pound mono from 4 to 9 feet.

For Spanish mackerel, bluefish, redfish, and other inshore species, I recommend a 9-foot, 7- and 8-weight saltwater rod with large arbor fly reel packed with 20 pound backing. Good lines are weight-forward floating, clear-tip intermediate, or full-clear intermediate and 250- to 350-grain sinking lines. I recommend leaders of 20-pound mono from 4–9 feet. Consider 40- to 60-pound bit tippets for blues and Spanish mackerel.

For amberjack and shark, I suggest a 9-foot, 12-weight saltwater rod with large arbor fly reel packed with 30-pound backing. Try weight-forward floating, clear-tip intermediate, or full-clear intermediate and 300- to 500-grain sinking lines. I recommend leaders of 20-pound mono from 4 to 9 feet and steel leader for sharks and king mackerel.

Capt. Gary Dubiel.

CAPT. GARY DUBIEL runs Spec Fever Guide Service in Oriental, North Carolina, fishing the Neuse River, Pamlico Sound, and the Crystal Coast. He is on the Temple Forks Outfitters Advisory Staff as well as a number of pro-staffs. He has appeared in TV shows, magazines, and books and speaks at numerous events and seminars. He is an IGFA fly-rod world record holder.

CLOSEST FLY SHOPS

Cape Lookout Fly Shop
601 Atlantic Beach Cswy., #H
Atlantic Beach, NC 28512
252-240-1427

CLOSEST GUIDES AND OUTFITTERS

Capt. Gary Dubiel
Spec Fever Guide Service
100 Midyette St.
Oriental, NC 28571
252-249-1520
captgary@specfever.com
www.specfever.com

Capt. Joe Shute
Cape Lookout Fly Shop
601-1 Atlantic Beach Cswy.
Atlantic Beach, NC 28512
252-240-2744
captjoesinfo@yahoo.com
www.captjoes.com

Capt. George Beckwith
Down East Guide Service
1907 Paulette Rd.
Morehead City, NC 28557
252-671-3474
info@DownEastGuideService.com
www.pamlicoguide.com

Capt. Rob Pasfield
Last Cast Charters
(sailing from Harkers Island Fishing Center)
1002 Island Rd.
Harkers Island, NC 28531
252-728-3907

CLOSEST LODGING

Inlet Inn
601 Front St.
Beaufort, NC 28516
252-728-3600
www.inlet-inn.com

Beaufort Inn
101 Ann St.
Beaufort, NC 28516
252-728-2600

Holiday Inn Express
5063 Executive Dr.
Morehead City, NC 28557
252-247-5001

CLOSEST HOSPITALS OR URGENT CARE

Carteret General Hospital
3500 Arendell St.
Morehead City, NC 28557
252-252-808-6000

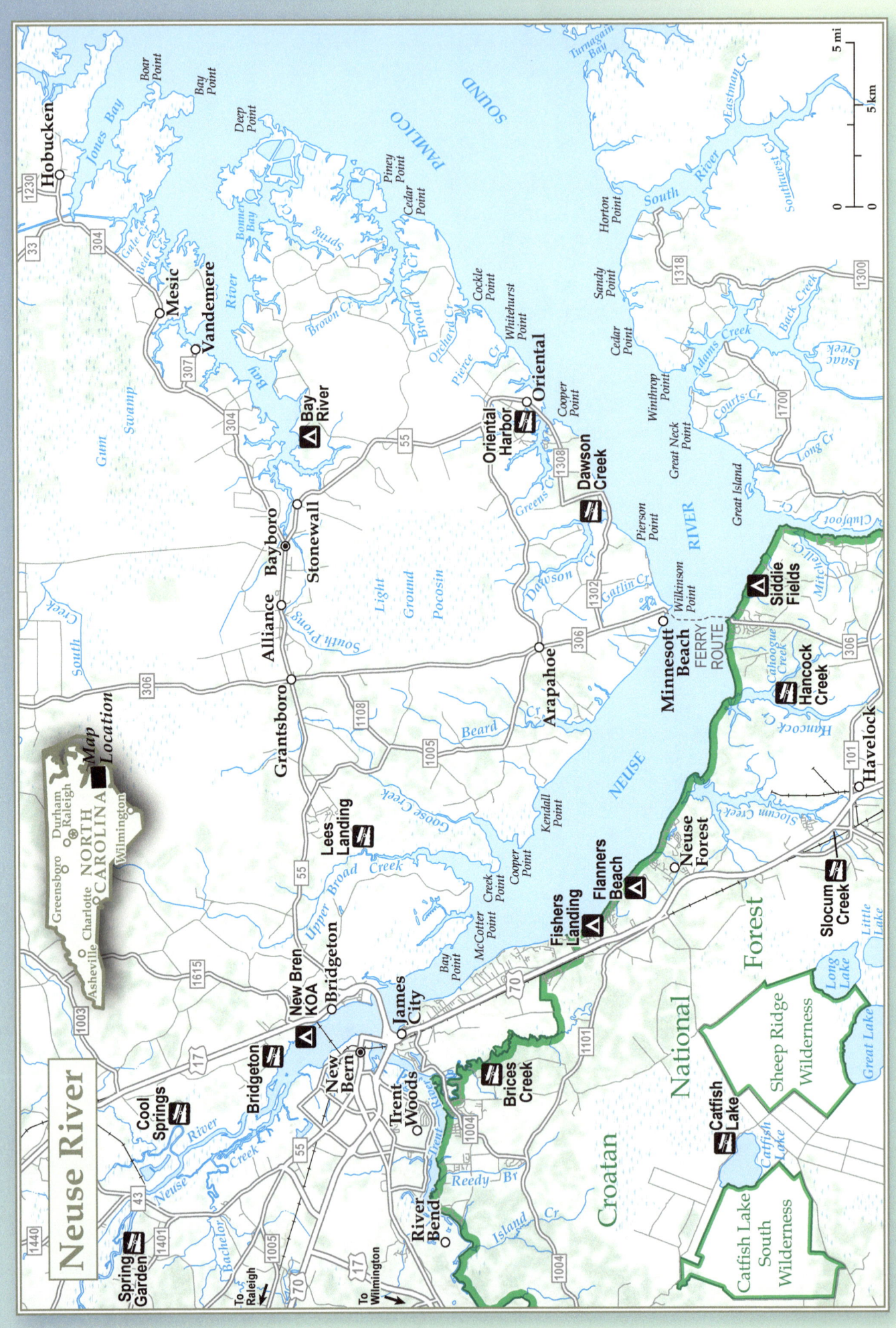

23 · Neuse River

➤ **Location:** The Neuse River is just over two hours southeast of Raleigh, North Carolina, and just under two hours north of Wilmington, North Carolina. The closest airport is Coastal Carolina Regional Airport. If you need an international airport, choose to fly into Raleigh International Airport or Wilmington International Airport.

The Neuse River, just upstream of New Bern, is narrow, deep, and lined with cypress trees. It has a distinct channel edge and can be influenced by river flow coming downstream from Raleigh. During periods on low rainfall, salinity can rise and saltwater species can migrate upstream several miles above the New Bern city limits. Unlike those stretches of river above New Bern, downstream of the city to Oriental and the Pamlico Sound, water depths are no greater than 22 feet. There is no river flow, and the river widens to an average of three to four miles. Cypress shorelines give way to pine and live oak with a mix of salt marsh that turns exclusively to salt marsh at the mouth. Saltwater fish are the mainstay.

The entire lower Neuse River and western Pamlico Sound has wind-dominated water levels, and the area has no lunar influence. Wind speed and direction contribute more to current, water color, and salinity than does rainfall. As a general rule of thumb, winds from the north and east push water upriver and winds from the south and west push water out. Heavier northeasterly breezes can raise water levels by several feet and, similar to high tides, can push baitfish and their predators tight to the bank. Quite the opposite, hard west winds can lower levels by feet, scatter bait and fish, and make fishing difficult.

The Neuse is a massive river system that stretches over 30 miles, from New Bern to the sound, and it is 7 ½ miles wide at that location. There are also numerous tributaries from New Bern to the sound. These large tributaries or "creeks" are located on either side of the Neuse and add a different dimension to the area's fishing.

A variety of gamefish call the Neuse River home. Redfish can be found from above New Bern to the Pamlico Sound and can be categorized in two different groups: juvenile fish (or those less than 32 inches) and the adults (a migratory group that ranges from 36 inches to more than 60 inches). Spotted seatrout are available year-round. Striped bass are available seasonally as they migrate between spawning grounds up river and in the ocean. Additionally, one can find flounder, weakfish, bluefish, Spanish mackerel, black drum, and tarpon, as well as freshwater species that include largemouth bass, white and yellow perch, crappie, bream, pickerel, and gar and more transient species such as American and hickory shad.

Breaking down the river system into sections can help you locate different species at different time of the year.

➤ **Neuse River (Above the Railway Trestle at New Bern)**
This part of the Neuse has a freshwater feel. Many branches of the main river will hold freshwater species, such as bass, pickerel, and panfish. Excellent popper fishing can be found

Stuart Creighton with a blue fish near Oriental, North Carolina. Capt Gary Dubiel

Early morning redfishing on the Nuese River. Capt. Gary Dubiel

during warmer months, while fall through spring, schools of very large white perch and crappie can be found around points, ledges, and logs. Striped bass frequently hold along this stretch of the river in the winter and early spring, often holding on the hard break line in 8–20 feet of water. The current is typically slow moving and 250-grain sink-tip lines will get your choice of weighted fly to the fish. Both hickory and American shad spawn on the Neuse. They will pass through this area in February and March. Smaller rods with sink-tip lines work best. Look for shad to hold in areas of the river with current breaks. Peak season for a great mix of shad, stripers, and panfish will be in late February and March.

➤ **The Trent River :** The Trent River will have shore and-bottom structure similar to the Neuse above New Bern. The Trent has a mix of freshwater and saltwater fish, as well. Peak fishing here is in November and December, when many saltwater fish move upstream from the Neuse. Stripers and specks will dominate your species list, but redfish, flounder, bass, crappie, white perch, and pickerel can also be abundant. All the fish are eating a variety of baitfish and all will take the same flies. Anglers should carry 7- to 9-weight rods with a mix of lines that include floating, intermediate, and 250-grain sink tips.

➤ **The Creeks:** The set of creeks closer to New Bern have deep sections to them, with channels reaching to more than 20 feet. With this additional depth, they can hold fish much of the winter. Specks, reds, and stripers are the primary species. Although deep, all these creeks have shallow shorelines and bays that warm quickly in the spring and productive shallow-water fishing can occur in them as early as late February and early March. Fall can also be outstanding, with numerous forage fish moving into the creeks. Cooler waters require slow-sinking and intermediate lines, but warmer water temps can lead to great topwater fishing, especially in areas of the creek that have eroded banks full of old cypress stumps and fallen trees.

Similar to the creeks closer to New Bern, the tributaries closer to Oriental fish very well in the fall and early winter and again in the spring. Ideal water depths to target fish here will be 3–4 feet. Reds, specks, and flounder are again the principal species. Floating and intermediate lines work well here. Each creek is well protected by trees, which can provide a break during breezy days.

▶ **Main River Shorelines:** The north side of the Neuse River has creeks with miles of wooded shorelines. On days with north to northeast winds, water levels will rise, flooding the timber and pushing bait, stripers, reds, and specks into the banks. Floating lines and large poppers fished on 8- and 9-weights are perfect combos to take all three species. The peak of this action occurs from May into early November. The area also has a number of hard structures including two trestles, two bridges, and an artificial reef, which will hold fish.

The main river near Oriental faces east to west. During dominate south-southwest summer winds, that south side of the river fishes well. Much of this area is marsh with protective trees. Specks, reds, and flounder thrive here during the summer and early fall. I recommend using 7- and 8-weights rigged with both floating and intermediate lines.

Near the mouth of the river are three large bays: Turnagain Bay, West Bay, and Long Bay. They house excellent summer fishing, as well. These areas are more open marsh.

August and September are prime months for the redfish of a lifetime on the Neuse. Adult red drum move up the river to spawn during this time frame. The river has many shoals where water depths can change from 3 to 18 feet, and it is these hard breaks the fish move along. Unlike other saltwater locations, sight-casting opportunities to these large fish are rare. Locating large schools of baitfish and casting Dubiel's Pop-N-Fly rig will generate noise to draw the fish to the suspending fly, resulting in a battle not soon forgotten. The rig is fished from a 10-weight rod with floating lines.

▶ **Regulations:** Anglers will need both a North Carolina saltwater and freshwater license to fish many areas of the Neuse River and its tributaries, and they should consult both North Carolina Division of Marine Fishers and North Carolina Wildlife Resources Commission for the latest regulations on limits and season for each species.

Double spotted redfish on the Nuese River. Capt Gary Dubiel.

Battling a redfish on a stormy summer afternoon. Capt Gary Dubiel

Sea trout are also very common on the Nuese River and Pamlico Sound. Capt Gary Dubiel.

The Nuese River and Pamlico Sound are known for monster redfish. Capt. Gary Dubiel

CAPT. GARY DUBIEL runs Spec Fever Guide Service in Oriental, North Carolina, fishing the Neuse River, Pamlico Sound, and the Crystal Coast. He is on the Temple Forks Outfitters Advisory Staff as well as a number of pro-staffs. He has appeared in TV shows, magazines, and books and speaks at numerous events and seminars. He is an IGFA fly-rod world record holder.

Capt. Gary Dubiel.

CLOSEST FLY SHOPS

Cape Lookout Fly Shop
601 Atlantic Beach Cswy., #H
Atlantic Beach, NC 28512
252-240-1427

CLOSEST GUIDES OR OUTFITTERS

Capt. Gary Dubiel
Spec Fever Guide Service
100 Midyette St.
Oriental, NC 28571
252-249-1520
captgary@specfever.com
www.specfever.com

Capt. Joe Ward
Down East Guide Service
1907 Paulette Rd.
Morehead City, NC 28557
252-671-3474
info@DownEastGuideService.com
www.pamlicoguide.com

CLOSEST LODGING

New Bern KOA Campground
1565 B St.
New Bern, NC 28560
800-562-3341
www.koa.com/campgrounds/new-bern

Courtyard by Marriot
218 E. Front St.
New Bern, NC 28560
252-636-0022

DoubleTree by Hilton
100 Middle St.
New Bern, NC 28560
252-638-3585

BridgePointe Hotel
101 Howell Rd.
New Bern, NC 28562
877-283-7713
frontdesk@bridgepointe.com
www.bridgepointe.com

Comfort Suites
1006 Old Cherry Pt.
New Bern, NC 28560
252-649-1717

Oriental Marina & Inn
103 Wall St.
Oriental, NC 28571
252-249-1818
www.orientalmarina.com

River Neuse Suites
201 Mildred St.
Oriental, NC 28571
252-249-1404
www.riverneuserentals.com

River Dunes
465 E. Harborside Rd.
Oriental, NC 28571
800-975-9565
www.riverdunes.com

Bay River Campground
682 Weaver Camp Rd.
Merritt, NC 28556
252-745-4879

CLOSEST RESTAURANTS

Persimmons Waterfront Restaurant
100 Pollock St.
New Bern, NC 28560
252-514-0033
www.persimmonsrestaurant.com

MJ's Raw Bar and Grille
216 Middle St.
New Bern, NC 28560
252-635-6890
www.mjsrawbar.com

Captain Ratty's Seafood and Steakhouse
202 Middle St.
New Bern, NC 28560
252-633-2088
www.captainrattys.com

The Chelsea
335 Middle St.
New Bern, NC 28560
252-637-5469
www.thechelsea.com

Toucan Grill and Fresh Bar
103 Wall St.
Oriental, NC 28571
252-249-2204
info@toucangrill.com
www.toucangrill.com

M&M's
205 S. Water St.
Oriental, NC 28571
252-249-2000

Brantley's Village Restaurant
900 Broad St.
Oriental, NC 28571
252-249-3509

CLOSEST HOSPITALS OR URGENT CARE

CarolinaEast Medical Center
2000 Neuse Blvd.
New Bern, NC 28561
252-633-8817
www.carolinaeasthealth.com

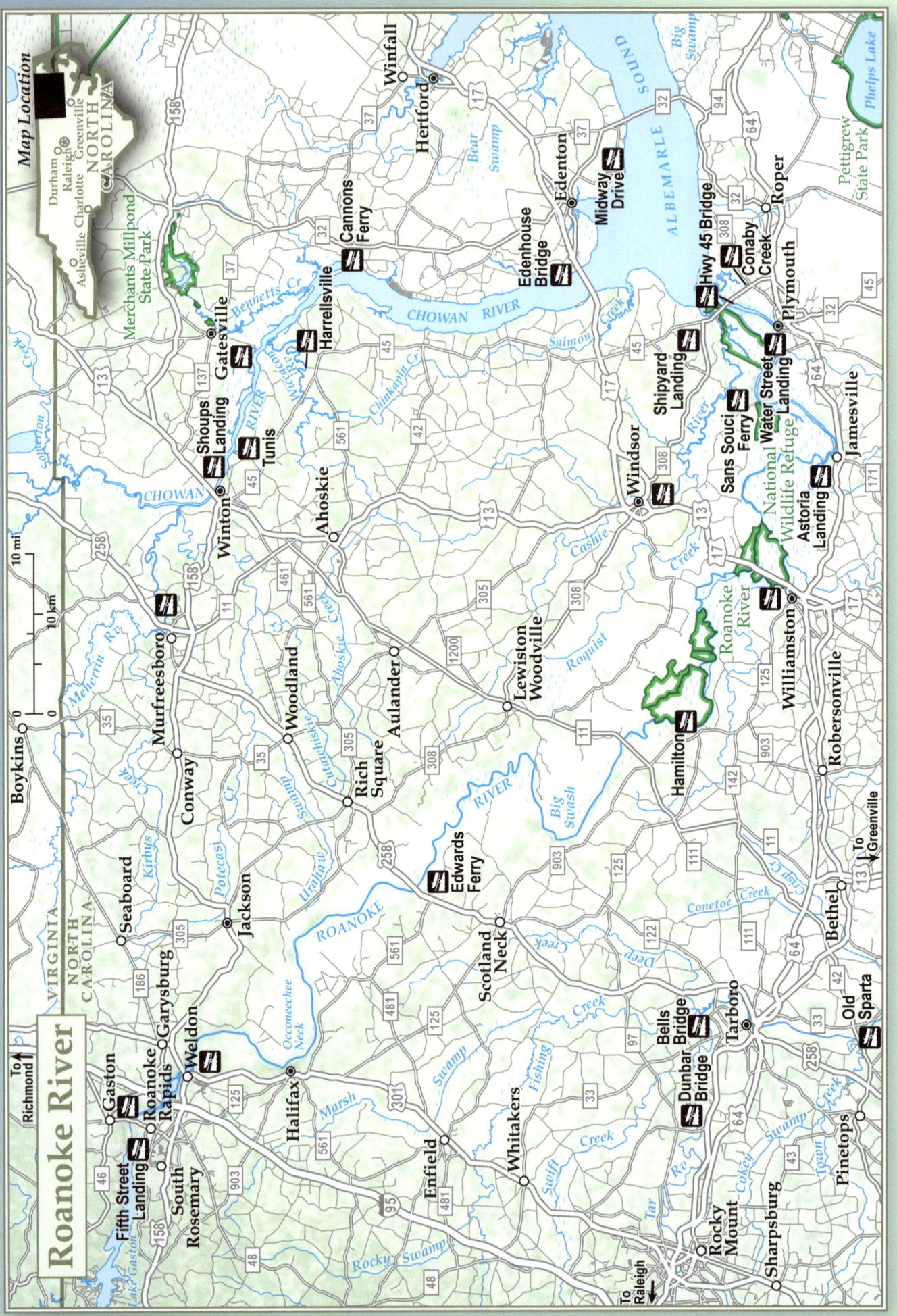

24 · Roanoke River

➤ **Location:** The Roanoke River is located just outside of Weldon, North Carolina. You can fly into either Greenville, North Carolina, or Richmond, Virginia.

The Roanoke River's claim to fame is its spring striped bass spawning run. The fishing is centered on North Carolina's public boat landing in the town of Weldon, the self-proclaimed "Rockfish Capital of the World." The area attracts thousands of fishermen each March, April, and May. Although the spring fishing is the most popular, the Roanoke offers a fantastic winter fishery for stripers and an earlier spring shad fishery that is as good as it gets.

The Roanoke River has its origins in Virginia, but a series of dams stops its natural flow to the Albemarle Sound until it reaches Roanoke Rapids, North Carolina. The final dam is a hydroelectric facility, and the lake itself supplies water to the Virginia Beach area. River flow can vary based on rainfall as well as for the needs of water and electricity. Variations in water flow can significantly change the fishing, and anglers should take note of river flow. High water flows can allow stripers and shad to move well above the fall line at Weldon during the spawning runs. This stretch of the river can be very hazardous, with many submerged rocks and boulders. During more normal flow, stripers and shad will congregate downstream of the Weldon ramp, an area of the river with few hazards.

The striped bass that migrate up the Roanoke River are part of the Albemarle Sound population of fish and have little to no contribution to ocean stocks of fish. These estuarine stripers are, for the most part, a separate group of fish from other North Carolina river systems that also have their own population of estuarine fish. River fish should not be compared to oceanic giants, and fly anglers can count on great numbers but seldom will land fish in excess of 10 pounds. The numbers of fish can be amazing, though, and in good years, fly anglers can land 25–100 stripers in a day.

Fly fishing for stripers from Weldon is typically done with 8- and 9-weight rods. Sinking lines are essential as anglers will need to get the fly 10–20 feet in swift current. In lower flow years, 300-grain sinking heads work just fine but moving to 400 grains may be necessary on years with higher flow. Fly patterns can be simple, and it's hard to beat the Clouser Deep Minnow.

Few anglers take advantage of the pre- and post-spawn movement of striped bass on the Roanoke and fewer still the excellent winter fishing. Access to miles of river can be found through the towns of Plymouth, Jamesville, and Williamston. Concentrations of fish can be found near the lower Roanoke River, the Cashie River, and into the upper Albemarle Sound in December, January, and February. There are many turns, deep ledges, and tributaries in the area that will fill with stripers, and they can provide hours of successful fly fishing. Seven- and eight-weights work great here, as the flow is often a touch slower than the upper reaches of the

April and May are the peak of the striper run on the Roanoke River. John Smolko

river. Likewise, the stretches of the Roanoke between Plymouth and Weldon will see the massive pre- and post-spawn fish move through them. Anglers can adjust their launch locations to get into the action. The North Carolina Wildlife

Sunrise on the Roanoke means a great striper bite. John Smolko

Resources Commission (NCWRC) keeps a close watch on fish movements and frequently updates their website with migration locations and fishing reports.

Both hickory and American shad migrate from the ocean and up the Roanoke River to spawn. Hickory shad will be the predominant species. Fly anglers can expect huge numbers, sometimes into the hundreds of shad strikes on a day's trip. Peak fishing occurs in March. Four-, five-, and six-weight rod and sink-tip lines are perfect for shad fishing. Bright, flashy flies tied with some weight on size 4 and size 6 hooks will be productive. Anglers who have not shad fished should give it a try. These small, 1- to 3-pound fish pull hard and jump frequently and they are a blast on the long rod.

North Carolina Wildlife Resources and private boating access locations for the Roanoke River include the following:

- North Carolina 45 Access Area (NCWRC)—Located near Plymouth on North Carolina Highway 45, about three miles north of U.S. Route 64
- Conaby Creek Access Area (NCWRC)—Located near Plymouth off North Carolina 45, approximately two miles north of U.S. Route 64
- Water Street Access Area (NCWRC)—Located in downtown Plymouth on the west end of Water Street
- Shipyard Landing Campground (fee)—Located on Cashoke Creek (Cashie River) off North Carolina 45, about five miles north of U.S. Route 64
- Sans Souci Access Area (NCWRC)—Located on Cashie River, at the end of Woodard Road, about 12 miles from Windsor off U.S. Route 13 and North Carolina 17

- River's Edge Restaurant (fee)—Located in Jamesville off U.S. Route 64 and Stewart Street
- Astoria Landing Access Area (NCWRC)—Located on Astoria Road in Jamesville off U.S. Route 64
- Gardner's Creek Marina (fee)—Located on Route 64 about one mile west of Jamesville
- Williamston Access Area (NCWRC)—Located at the U.S. Route 13 and North Carolina 17 Bridge, just north of Williamston
- Hamilton Access Area (NCWRC)—Located in Hamilton just off North Carolina 903 at the end of East Main Street
- Edward's Ferry Access Area (NCWRC)—Located at the Route 258 Bridge, north of Scotland Neck
- Weldon Access Area (NCWRC)—Located off Route 158/301, just downstream of the U.S. Route 301 Bridge
- Gaston Access Area (NCWRC)—Located off North Carolina 48, just across the river from Roanoke Rapids in the town of Gaston

➤ **Tackle:**

- 9-foot, 8- or 9-weight fly rods with 330- to 400-grain sinking-head fly lines for stripers
- 9-foot, 4- to 6-weight fly rods with type 3 sink tip lines for shad

Fishing for rockfish near Weldon, North Carolina. John Smolko

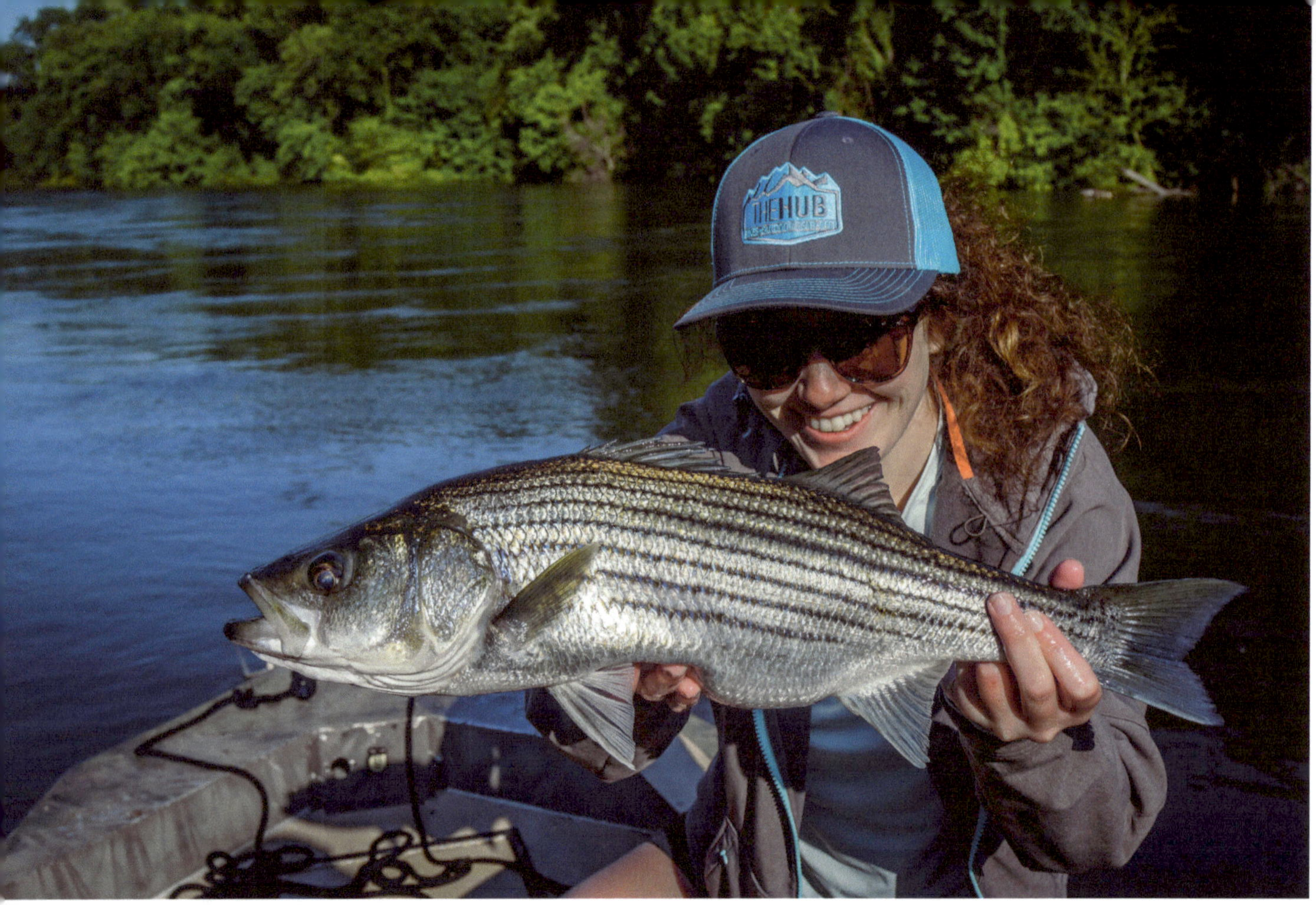
THE HUB

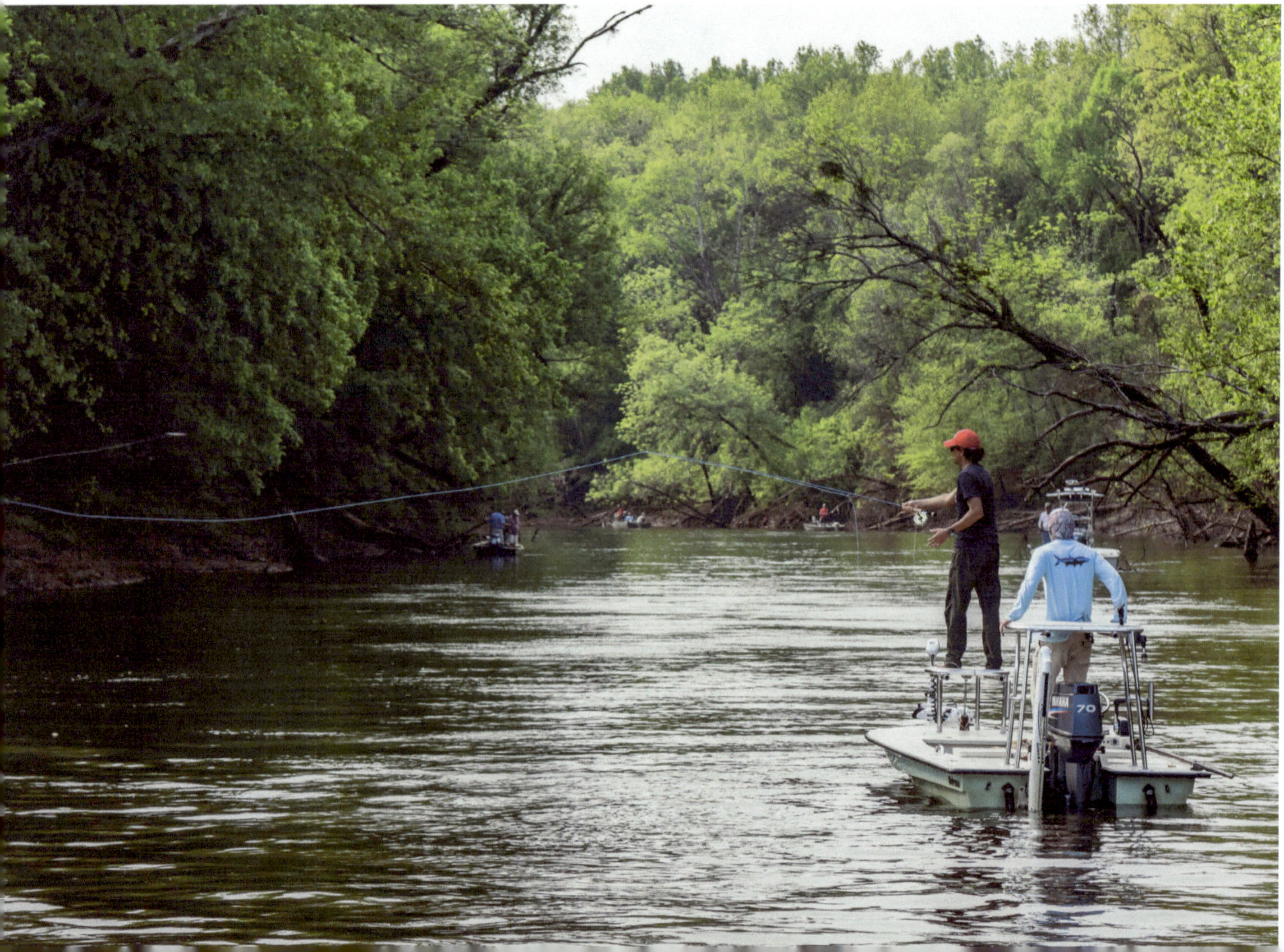
70

Facing top. The vast majority of stripers caught on the Roanoke range from 3-8 pounds. John Smolko

Facing bottom. The Roanoke can get crowded at times, but most anglers are tolerant especially when the shad or stripers are running. John Smolko

Below. Releasing a striper.

Capt. Gary Dubiel.

CAPT. GARY DUBIEL runs Spec Fever Guide Service in Oriental, North Carolina, fishing the Neuse River, Pamlico Sound, and the Crystal Coast. He is on the Temple Forks Outfitters Advisory Staff as well as a number of pro-staffs. He has appeared in TV shows, magazines, and books and speaks at numerous events and seminars. He is an IGFA fly-rod world record holder.

CLOSEST FLY SHOPS

Bobby Colston's Tackle Box
232 Roanoke Rapids Rd.
Gaston, NC 27832
252-537-6485

CLOSEST GUIDES AND OUTFITTERS

Capt. Richard Andrews
Tar-Pam Guide Service
252-945-9715
richard@tarpamguide.com
http://tarpamguide.com

Capt. Mitch Blake
FishIBX.com (Inner Banks Charters)
412 Victoria Dr.
Chocowinity, NC 27817
252-495-1803
mitch@fishibx.com
www.easternncfishingguide.com

Capt. Greg Voliva
Four Seasons Guide Service
1303 Kimberly Rd.
New Bern, NC 28562
252-514-5086
fourseasonsgs@gmail.com
www.fourseasonsgs.com

CLOSEST LODGING

There are numerous places to stay along Interstate 95 near Weldon and Roanoke Rapids, as well as several hotels in Williamston, Plymouth, and Jamesville.

Hampton Inn Roanoke Rapids
85 Hampton Blvd.
Roanoke Rapids, NC 27870
844-649-9654

Hampton Inn-Williamston
1099 Hampton Ct.
Williamston, NC 27892
252-809-1100

CLOSEST RESTAURANTS

Ralph's BBQ
1400 Julian R. Allsbrook Hwy.
Weldon, NC 27890
252-536-2102
www.ralphsbbq.com

David's Restaurant
1011 Roanoke Ave.
Roanoke Rapids, NC 27870-3701
252-537-3262

Hitchin Post
1981 U.S. Route 17
Williamston, NC
252-792-0088

Jamesville Chuck Wagon
2200 Main St.
Jamesville, NC 27846
252-792-1278

Closest Hospitals or Urgent Care

Halifax Regional Medical Center
250 Smith Church Rd.
Roanoke Rapids, NC 27870
252-535-8011
info@halifaxrmc.org
www.halifaxmedicalcenter.org

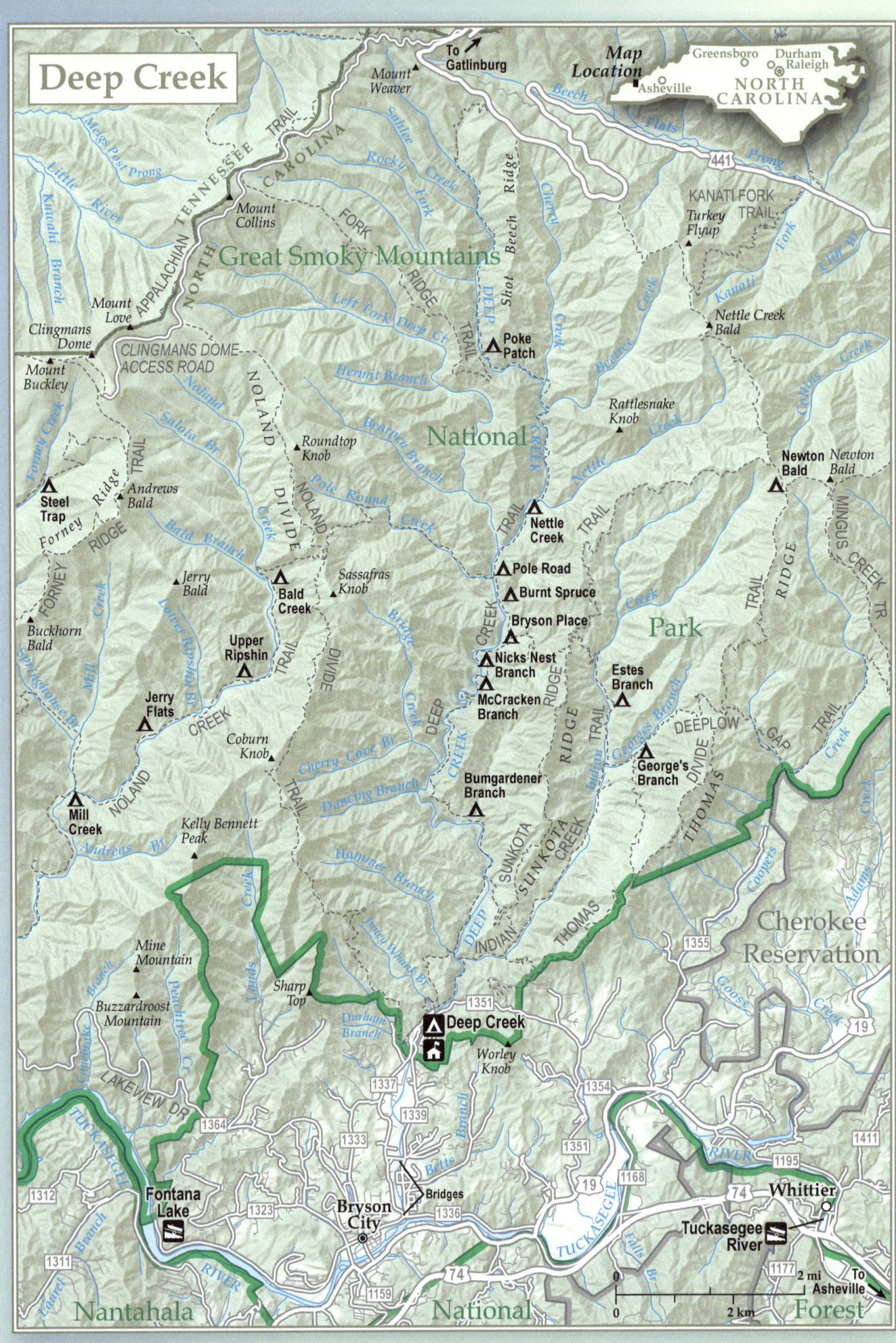

25 · Deep Creek

➤ **Location:** Deep Creek is located inside Great Smoky Mountains National Park, just outside the town of Bryson City, North Carolina, and approximately one hour and ten minutes west-southwest of Asheville, North Carolina.

Deep Creek is one of the more heavily used drainages in Great Smoky Mountains National Park. Each year, the Deep Creek trail system sees thousands of visitors, and the stream itself sees almost as many users during the warmer months. Fortunately for fly anglers, most of these river users are swimmers and tubers that are confined to the extreme lower reaches of the creek. There is some fly-fishing pressure on Deep Creek, as well, but most of these anglers stay within an easy walk of the lower trailhead, and most of those are summer tourists or weekend warriors. This leaves miles of pristine wild-trout water for those anglers who like to hike and little competition for those fortunate enough to have a flexible schedule.

Deep Creek can be broken down into four distinct fishing sections, and for the purposes of this book, we will refer to them as follows: Hatchery Supported, Picnic Area, Day Hike, and Backcountry. The Hatchery Supported section is actually not inside the national park. This stretch reaches downstream from the park boundary all the way to where Deep Creek enters the Tuckasegee River in the town of Bryson City. Access in this stretch is limited, as most of the land the creek runs through is private property. There is some access around the two bridges that cross the stream and on weekdays at the Deep Creek Baptist Church in Bryson City. Fishing in this stretch can be good for the nymphing crowd, and despite the Hatchery Supported designation, there are plenty of holdovers and wild fish to be caught.

The next section of Deep Creek is the one that flows from the No Tubing sign at the confluence of Indian Creek and Deep Creek through the National Park Service picnic area and campground. The trout in this stretch see heavy pressure from both anglers and swimmers during peak tourist season, making this stretch a better wintertime Smokies option. There are deep pools in which to nymph and plenty of small pockets for dry-fly fishing. This stretch is a top spot for local Bryson City anglers looking for a quick fish, so anglers should not expect solitude when fishing here.

J.E.B. Hall fishing at Toms Branch Falls. J.E.B. Hall

The Day Hike section of Deep Creek can be defined as the stretch that begins at the aforementioned No Tubing sign and continues all the way up to the first backcountry campsites at the bottom of Bumgardner Mountain. This section does receive moderate angling pressure, but like most any other river, this occurs on weekends and holidays. While walking into this stretch can be done in waders and boots, I do not recommend it. A pair of sneakers for the walk-in, coupled with a small backpack in which to carry wading gear, will make for happier feet at the end of the day.

Deep Creek's best fishing is reserved for anglers who like long walks in the woods, sleeping under the stars, and close

Above. The tube hatch can be an interruption on the lower end of Deep Creek near the main campground. J.E.B. Hall

encounters with black bears. The Backcountry section of Deep Creek is home to famous Smokies fishing locations, such as Poke Patch and Bryson Place. Perfect pocketwater, stunning wild browns and rainbows, and the ability to fish entire days with only basic dry flies make fishing the interior of the Deep Creek valley nothing short of legendary. Successful fishing in these remote areas requires an overnight stay to allow time for adequately covering the water. All camping in the park requires a backcountry permit, and some of the more famous fishing campsites fill up quickly during the summer months. Being "bear aware" is critical in the Smokies. Anglers should not only hang up food and cooking supplies at night but also any gear that has come into contact with fish during the day.

▶ **Hatches:** Streams in the Smokies do not experience huge hatches of aquatic insects by Western and New England standards. However, there are insects present all times of the year. Spring brings mayflies of all varieties, with quills and March Browns showing up around the third week in March. Caddisflies are ever present, even in the winter months. Stoneflies that can be found in Deep Creek include Giant Dark Stones, Golden Stones, both Yellow and Green Sallies, and Small Dark Stones in winter.

▶ **Tackle:** Fly rods ranging from 3-weight to 5-weight in lengths of 8 feet, 6 inches to 9 feet are ideal for Deep Creek. Leaders should be at least 9 feet long, ending in tippets no greater than 4X. Most anglers find fishing tippets of 5–6X will yield the best results. Fly selections for Deep Creek should include basic drys such as Elk-hair Caddis, Stimulators, and Parachute Adams. Add to the drys a collection of beadhead nymphs ranging from size 6 Stoneflies down to size 20 Zebra Midges, and a few medium-size streamers for high-water days.

Top left. Like most southern trout streams, Deep Dreek offers plenty of shade and overhanging rhododenron. J.E.B. Hall

Bottom left: J.E.B. Hall prepares to fish a nice run on Deep Creek. J.E.B. Hall

J.E.B. HALL is a full-time fly-fishing guide and instructor in western North Carolina and East Tennessee for Davidson River Outfitters. In addition to guiding in the Southeast, J.E.B. has spent numerous summers guiding in Southwest Alaska for Alaska West and is a former operations manager for the Andros South Bonefish Lodge on South Andros Island in the Bahamas. J.E.B. is also the author of *The Southern Appalachian Fly Guide* and occasionally dabbles in photography.

J.E.B. Hall.

CLOSEST FLY SHOPS

Davidson River Outfitters
49 Pisgah Highway Suite 6
Pisgah Forest NC 28768
888-861-0111
www.davidsonflyfishing.com
info@davidsonflyfishing.com

Brookings Cashiers Village Anglers
49 Pillar Dr.
Cashiers, NC 28717
828-743-3768
www.brookingsonline.com

828-Rivers Edge Outfitters
1235 Seven Clans Ln.
Whittier, NC 28789
828-497-9300
www.wncfishing.com

CLOSEST GUIDE AND OUTFITTERS

Smoky Mountain Adventures
P.O. Box 995
Bryson City, NC 28715
828-736-7501
steve@steveclaxton.com
www.steveclaxton.com

Davidson River Outfitters
49 Pisgah Highway Suite 6
Pisgah Forest NC 28768
888-861-0111
www.davidsonflyfishing.com
info@davidsonflyfishing.com

Brookings Cashiers Village Anglers
49 Pillar Dr.
Cashiers, NC 28717
828-743-3768
www.brookingsonline.com
828-

CLOSEST LODGING

Scenic View Motel
1000 North Carolina 19 S.
Bryson City, NC 28713
828-488-3378

Sleep Inn
500 Veterans Blvd.
Bryson City, NC 28713
828-488-0326
www.sleepinnbrysoncitync.com

Great Smoky Mountains National Park Service Campground
877-444-6777
www.nps.gov/grsm/planyourvisit/frontcountry-camping.htm

CLOSEST RESTAURANTS

Naber's Drive In
1245 Main St.
Bryson City, NC 28713
828-488-2877

Anthony's Italian Restaurant
15 Depot St.
Bryson City, NC 28713
828-488-8898
www.anthonysbrysoncity.com

The Cork and Bean
16 Everett St.
Bryson City, NC 28713
828-488-1934
www.brysoncitycorkandbean.com

Pasqualino's Italian Restaurant
25 Everett St.
Bryson City, NC 28713
828-488-9555

Guayabito's Mexican Restaurant
236 North Carolina 19 S.
Bryson City, NC 28713
828-488-1336

Nantahala Brewing Company
61 Depot St.
Bryson City, NC 28713
828-488-2337
www.nantahalabrewing.com

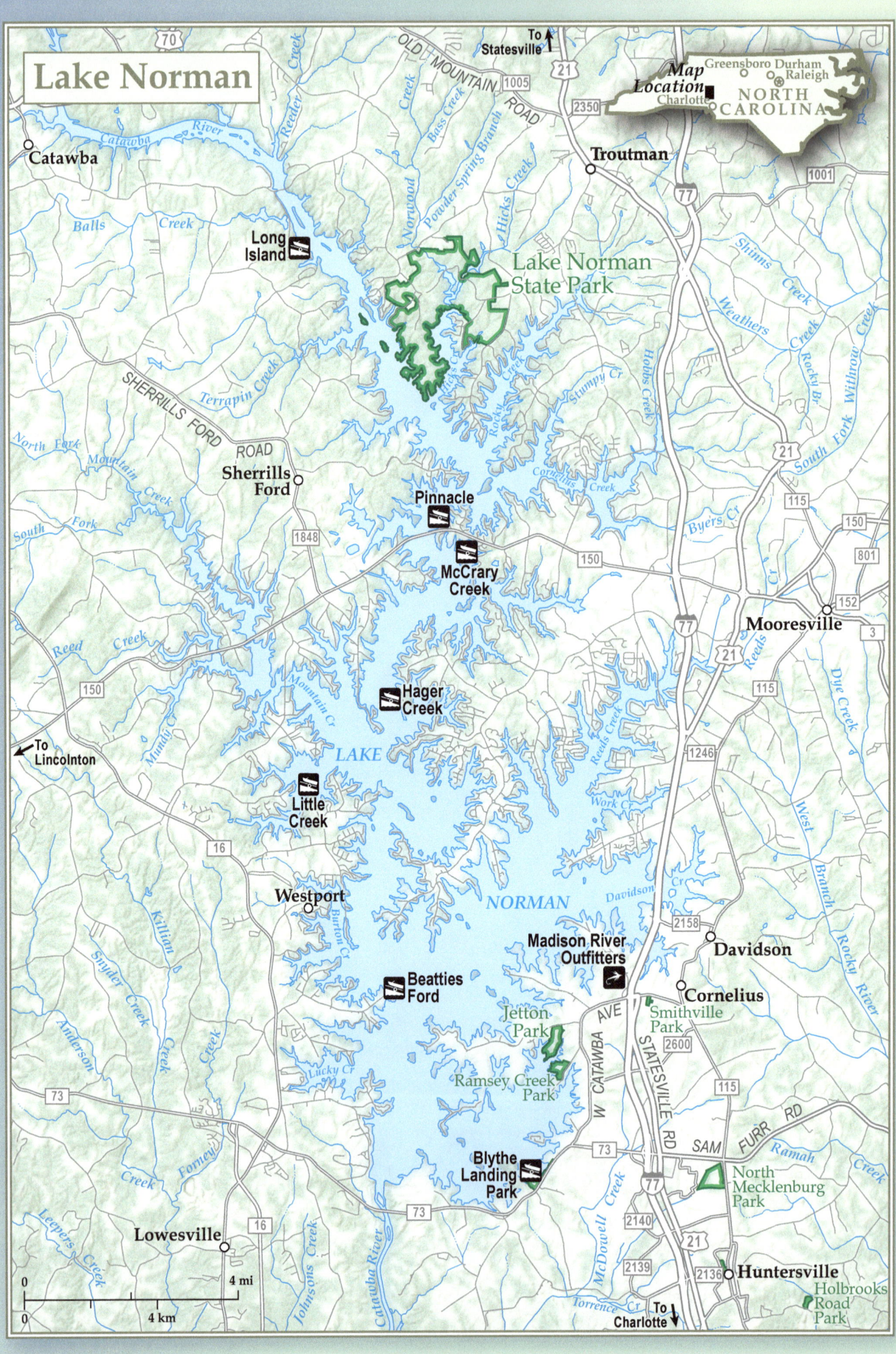

26 · Lake Norman

➤ **Location:** Lake Norman is located 45 minutes north of Charlotte, North Carolina. You can fly into Charlotte/Douglas International Airport.

With the completion of the dam at Cowans Ford (now called the Cowans Ford Hydroelectric Station) in 1963, the largest man-made body of fresh water was formed in North Carolina. At 32,500 acres, the lake is home to two power plants that provide water and electricity for the Piedmont Carolinas. Traveling north on Interstate 77 from Charlotte, one cannot escape the lake's first impression as being "urban," with traffic, development, large homes, and shoreline docks. With a large array of activities, such as restaurants, NASCAR, high-end shopping opportunities, and family entertainment, great fly fishing may not come to mind. Digging deeper, though, the smaller surrounding communities of Davidson, Cornelius, and Huntersville (and a little time on the water) can easily change one's first impression.

The lake is managed by Duke Power, allowing for plentiful and easy public access at any number of launch sites. These areas can provide limited wading opportunities, but I highly recommend a watercraft.

The lake offers excellent fly fishing for spotted and largemouth bass, common carp, grass carp, crappie, sunfish, and channel catfish. The striper fishing on the fly has declined significantly, but the hybrid bass fishing is coming on strong. Recently stocked hybrids are now in the 14-inch range and are increasingly becoming available on the fly.

With its immense size, it is best to break the lake into smaller sections, using a major creek as a starting point. You can spend an entire day in one or two of the lake's largest creeks. North Carolina 150 is considered a good mid-lake marker and dividing point between upper and lower lake sections. The upper section is more river-like and has less development. The Pinnacle launch is convenient and allows one to fish this section's numerous finger coves and its four large creeks. The lake does stay clear, but the upper section can get stained with heavy rainfall. For spotted bass action, focus your efforts on submerged structures that are visible; for carp, find the shallowest water you can get into in the backs of creeks and coves.

The lower section of the lake is much wider and deeper with multiple creeks and large points, both primary and secondary. You will quickly notice boat docks of all shapes and sizes dotting riprapped shorelines. The Beatty Ford Access is convenient and just off the main lake channel, which is noticeably marked. Using the channel as a guide, anglers can find shoals and points acting as transition areas for finding fish. Marker M1 is just one example to emulate in your search.

Finding schools of bait in these zones will result in topwater and small streamer action for spotted bass. The fish

Carp offer the ultimate challenge in fresh water. Capt. Paul Rose

Charlotte, North Carolina carp. Capt. Paul Rose

Schooling spotted bass are a common occurancy on lake Norman. Capt. Paul Rose

will be seen either working the surface in open water or back in the creeks relating to structure, such as natural rock. Carping is best here on any point you can find with a foot of water or less. Any flat between boat docks is also a top location. The water is very clear and good polarized glasses can aid in seeing both muds and tails from a distance. Once spotted, a quiet approach can be planned, so as not to spook these wary fish. If the fish remains in a feeding position, a pinpoint cast in front of the target will result in eats. Both common carp and grass carp are present in good numbers and sizes. The lower section does have significant boat traffic, so fish main lake areas very early and move to secondary areas in creek endpoints and coves where traffic remains light. The far back of Mountain Creek is an example of an area worth exploring midday.

▶ **Regulations:** Most anglers are required to have a basic or sportsman license. For children under age 16, no license is required. The bass limit is five fish with only two allowed less than 14 inches. Carp do not have size or creel limits. Crappie must be 8 inches, and 25 fish is the limit.

▶ **Tackle:** 9-foot, 5- to 7-weight rods will work well for bass and smaller common carp rigged with weight-forward lines. I suggest using 9- to 12-foot leaders tapered to 1–3X. Leaders for bass and other species are not critical, but for carp, longer and lighter tippets might be needed if you are getting repeated refusals. Small white and gray marabou or white chenille streamer patterns to match shad forage will work as your go-to fly choice. They are deadly for most species, including the lake's growing hybrid population. The carp can be more

Selecting the right carp fly. Capt. Paul Rose

Winter time schooling spotted bass near Mcguire Steam Plant outflow. Capt. Paul Rose

selective (yet opportunistic at the same time), so a variety of Hex nymphs, crayfish imitations, standard trout nymphs, aquatic worms, and even terrestrials should be carried. Fly colors of brown, black, and burnt orange are best in varying sink rates and in sizes from 8 to 12. At times, a regular size 10 Woolly Bugger works just fine, and other days you need to throw the whole box at them. Nelson's RLD and Roughfisher Carp Crack patterns are two other choices. Seed and vegetation patterns take grass carp, along with smaller bonefish flies.

CAPT. PAUL ROSE owns and operates www.carolinabonefishing.com in Belmont, North Carolina. Having fly fished for over 30 years, he is equally at home guiding coldwater, warmwater, and saltwater venues. Paul is well published and active member of the Southeast Press Association. He also is a Federation of Fly Fishers casting instructor and a Federation of Fly Fishers guide member.

CLOSEST FLY SHOPS

Carolina Mountain Sports
123 W. Broad St.
Statesville, NC 28677
704-871-1444
www.carolinamountainsports.com

Great Outdoors Provision
Park Road Shopping Center
4275 Park Rd.
Charlotte, NC 28209
704-523-1089
greatoutdoorprovision.com
http://greatoutdoorprovision.com/locations/charlotte

Jesse Brown's Outdoors
4732 Sharon Rd., #2M
Charlotte, NC 28210
704-556-0020
www.jessebrowns.com

Madison River Fly Fishing Outfitters
20910 Torrence Chapel Rd.
Cornelius, NC 28031
704-896-3676
www.carolinaflyfishing.com

Orvis
6800 Phillips Pl. Ct.
Charlotte, NC 28210
704-571-6100

CLOSEST OUTFITTERS

Carolina Bonefishing
Capt. Paul Rose
704-616-6662
captpaulrose@gmail.com
www.carolinabonefishing.com

CLOSEST LODGING

Visit Lake Norman
704-987-3300
visitorcenter@lakenorman.org
www.visitlakenorman.org

CLOSEST RESTAURANTS

The Landing Restaurant
(at Lake Norman Hotel)
4491 Slanting Bridge Rd.
Sherrills Ford, NC 28673
828-478-5944
info@landingatthelake.com
http://www.landingatthelake.com/

Rusty Rudder
20210 Henderson Rd.
Cornelius, NC 28031
704-892-9195
http://lakenorman.therustyrudder.net

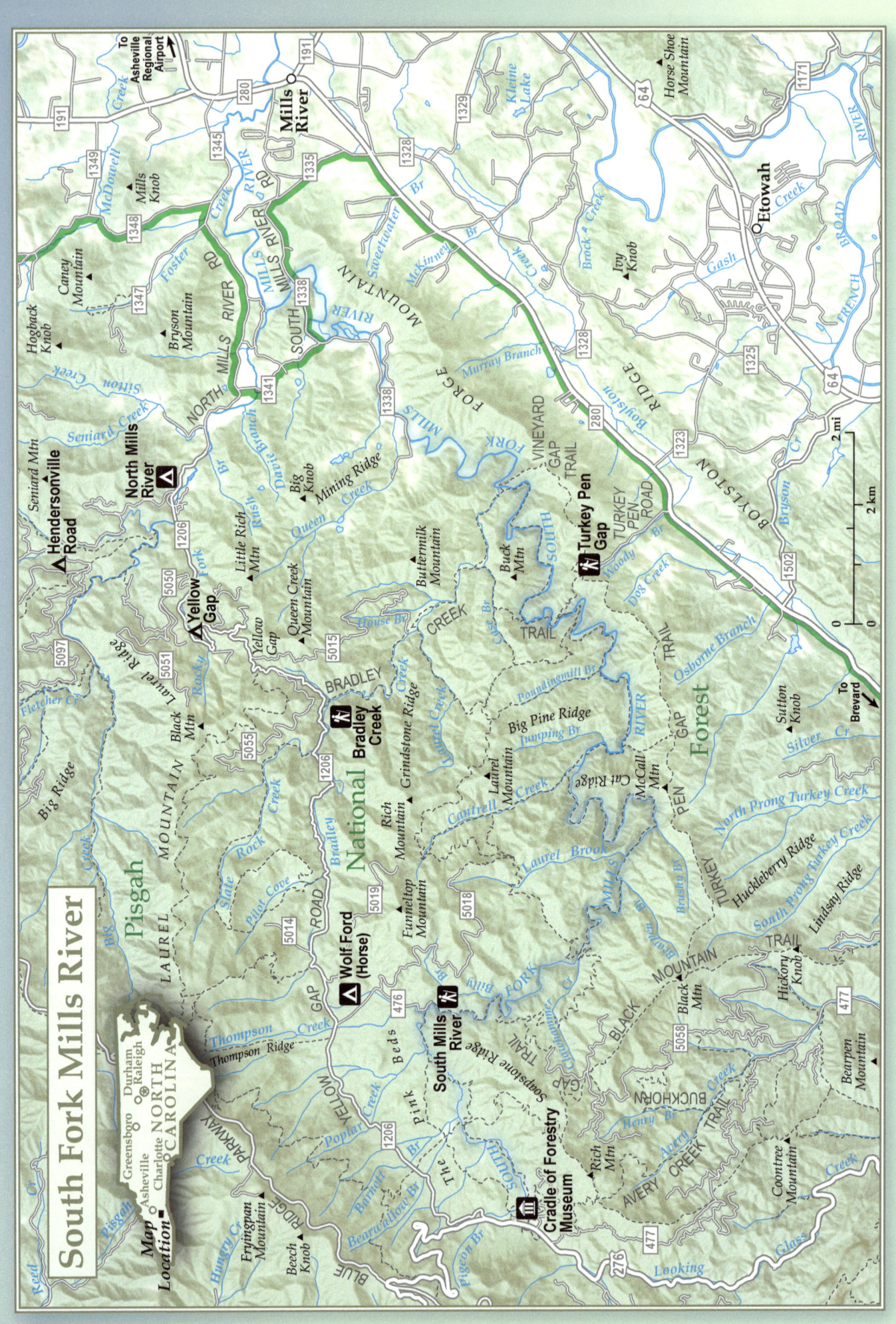

27 · South Mills River

▶ **Location:** The South Mills River is located in Western North Carolina, flowing from a south-facing slope off the Blue Ridge Parkway, between Routes 280 and 276 in Transylvania County. It is about 30 minutes from Asheville. You can fly into Asheville Regional Airport.

If you have ever fished the Davidson and thought to yourself, or said aloud to your buddies, "You know, this is a great river, but how nice would it be if it was in the middle of nowhere instead of right next to the road," well, then, this may very well be the river for you. The South Mills is a sister drainage to the Davidson, and the two have many similarities, as well as a few key differences. The first and most glaring difference is that to fish the South Mills, or at least the river proper, will require a minimum of a mile hike, and to get to the "good water," it will require a few more miles and a bit more effort.

The South Mills begins as small headwater streams on the south-facing, rhododendron-choked slopes off the Blue Ridge Parkway. These small streams, such as the Thompson River and Slate Rock Creek, gather at the foot of the slope in the Yellow Gap between Wagon Road Ridge and Thompson Ridge. While the streams begin around 4,500 feet, they quickly drop to an elevation of around 3,400 feet in the Yellow Gap/Pink Beds area and begin to slow and meander through boggy seeping stands of hardwoods, pines, and "rhodo hells," where the river takes on a tannic stain and picks up a large amount of nutrients from the swamp.

These small tannic rivulets eventually gather near the USGS gauging station and culminate into what is commonly known as the South Mills River Proper. At this point, the river widens and begins to descend in more dramatic fashion than the bog upstream and more closely resembles what one would imagine as a southern Appalachian trout stream. Access to this area is via the South Mills River Road off Yellow Gap Road (F.S. 1206). From this point downstream, there are no more access points via roadway until the Turkey Pen area. The distance between the USGS gauging station and the Turkey Pen access is approximately 12 miles.

The Turkey Pen Access is located off U.S. Route 280, near the hamlet of Boylston, between the towns of Pisgah Forest and Mills River, North Carolina. Turkey Pen Road is a private and poorly maintained road that eventually connects with a fairly well maintained Forest Service road. At the end of the Forest Service road is a large parking area with sections designated for vehicle and horse trailer parking. Be sure to park in the proper area, as the Forest Service will enforce the regulation.

From this parking area, access is via foot trail or a closed Forest Service road, and the river is just less than a mile from the parking area. This area is frequently used by hikers, mountain bikers, horseback riders, and a few fishermen. The foot trail from Turkey Pen meets up with the river near the swinging bridge. The closed roadbed meets the river at a ford just downstream of the bridge. The trail following the

South Mills USGS Benchmark. Heath Cartee

river is located on the north side and is accessed by fording the river or crossing the bridge. From these points, public access to the river continues down river for a short distance before ending on private property, and it continues up river for about 12 miles to the USGS gauging station and the Yellow Gap/Pink Beds area.

The South Mills is a wonderful and beautifully scenic trout stream of many different personalities. It can be both magical and humbling when it comes to the fishing, and these characteristics of the river can vary from day to day and from season to season. The fish are wild and range from perfect for a pan to perfect for a photo opportunity. This river is Wild & Scenic, and is very special.

South Mills wwinging bridge. Heath Cartee

Facing top. South Mills River from the first swinging bridge. Heath Cartee

Facing bottom. South Mills rainbow. Heath Cartee

▶ **Hatches:** The full gamut of hatches, from midges to mayflies, can be found on the South Mills. Because it is a sister drainage to the Davidson, South Mills follows nearly the same pattern and rhythm when it comes to seasons, times, and insects. It should be noted, however, that the South Mills has an abnormally gentle gradient for a trout stream in an area known as the "Land of Waterfalls." For this reason, silt and sand tend to dominate the river bottom in the boggy upper portion and are quite common on the insides of bends between the runs and riffles in the lower portions.

The discerning angler should be able to draw his or her own conclusions about certain hatches when considering the aforementioned information concerning the gradient and character of the stream bottom.

▶ **Tackle:** Anything from a 9-foot, 6-weight to a 6-foot, 2-weight would be perfect, depending on which section of the river one is fishing. In the lower sections, and the river proper, a heavier and longer rod would be great for nymph and streamer fishing, as well as dry-fly fishing during hatches of some of the larger mayflies. For general purposes, an 8-foot or 8 1/2-foot, 4- or 5-weight rod will fish well for most of the stream. Anglers may want to fish smaller, lighter rods if they decide to tackle some of the smaller feeder streams flowing from the parkway to Yellow Gap Road.

179

South Mills near Wolf Ford. Heath Cartee

CLOSEST FLY SHOPS

Davidson River Outfitters
49 Pisgah Highway Suite 6
Pisgah Forest, NC 28768
888-861-0111
www.davidsonflyfishing.com
info@davidsonflyfishing.com

One Fly Outfitters, LTD
112 Cherry St.
P.O. Box 591
Black Mountain, NC 28711
828-669-6939
www.oneflyoutfitters.com

Hunter Banks
29 Montford Ave.
Asheville, NC 28801
828-252-3005
www.hunterbanks.com

CLOSEST LODGING

The Sunset Motel
523 S. Broad St.
Brevard, NC 28712
828-884-9106
owner@thesunsetmotel.com
www.thesunsetmotel.com

Hampton Inn
275 Forest Gate Dr.
Pisgah Forest, NC 28768
828-883-4800

Holiday Inn Express
2228 Asheville Hwy.
Brevard, NC 28712
828-862-8900
www.hiexbrevard.com

Hemlock Hideaways
740 Williamson Creek Rd.
Pisgah Forest, NC 28768
828-577-9363
www.vrbo.com/460883

Heath Cartee.

HEATH CARTEE has been fishing and guiding the waters in and around North Carolina for the last ten years. Small streams and backcountry waters are his favorites. He lives in Pisgah Forest, North Carolina, with his wife and daughter, and any stray dog, cat, or fishing bum that might wander through.

Ash Grove Mountain Cabins & Camping
749 E. Fork
Brevard, NC 28712
828-885-7216
www.ash-grove.com

Mountains and Meadows
350 Generation Pass
Pisgah Forest, NC 28768
828-329-8430
info@mountainmeadownc.com
www.mountainmeadownc.com

Davidson River Campground
1 Davidson River Cir.
Pisgah Forest, NC 28768
828-877-3265

Cascade Lake Recreation Area & Campground
1679 Little River Campground Rd.
Pisgah Forest, NC 28768
828-877-4475
www.cascadelakerecreationarea.com

CLOSEST RESTAURANTS
The Square Root
33 Times Arcade Aly.
Brevard, NC 28712
828-884-6171
squarerootrestaurant@gmail.com
www.squarerootrestaurant.com

Jordan Street Cafe
48 W. Jordan St.
Brevard, NC 28712
828-883-2558
jordanstreetcafe30@gmail.com
www.thejordanstreetcafe.com

Big Mike's
12 S. Gaston St.
Brevard, NC 28712
828-884-3663
www.bigmikesnc.com

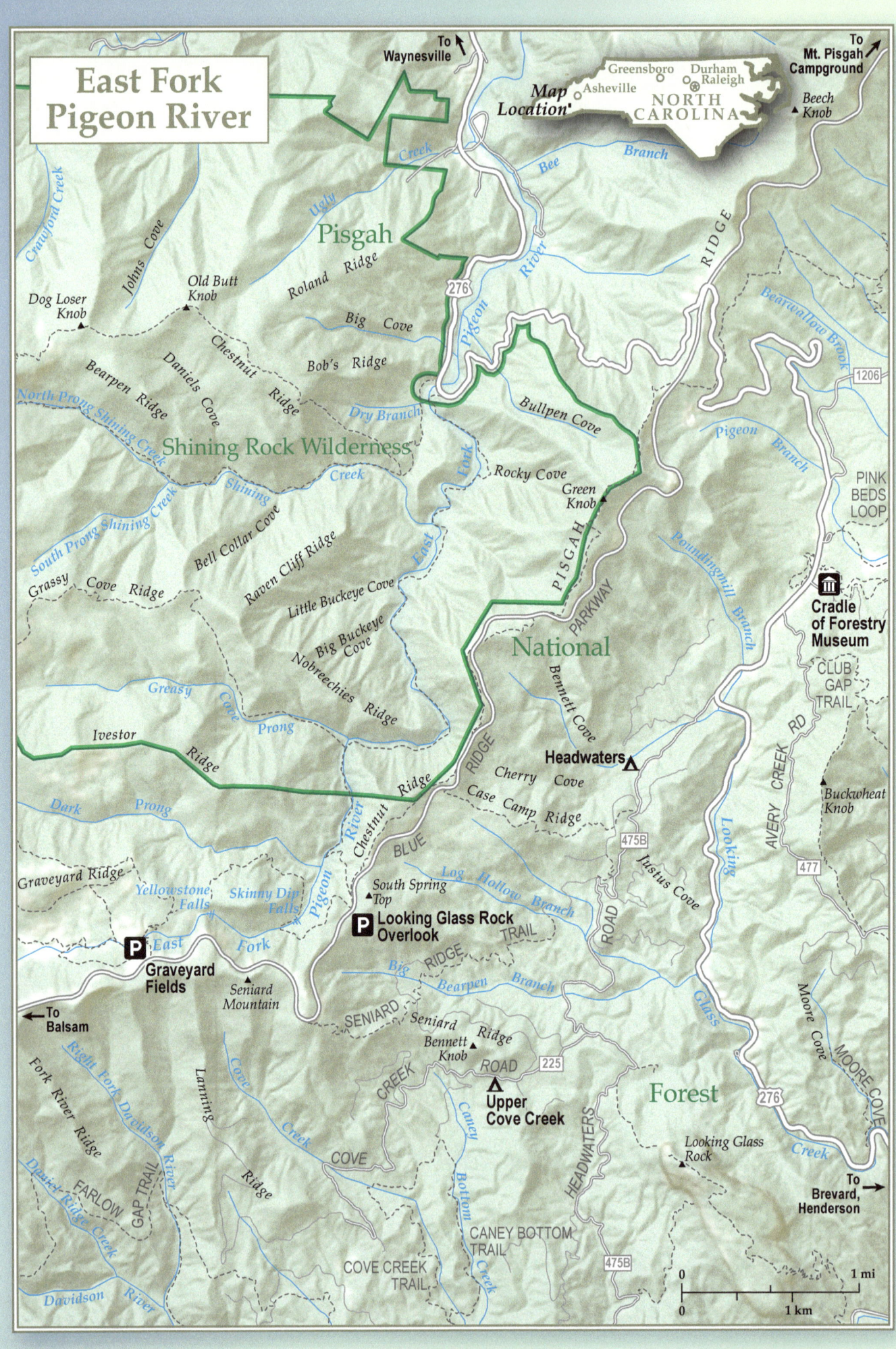

28 · Big East Fork of the Pigeon River

▶ **Location:** The Big East Fork of the Pigeon River is located in western North Carolina, about 35 minutes from Brevard, North Carolina, and about an hour from Asheville, North Carolina, via Interstates 40 and 215, or via Blue Ridge Parkway.

The Big East Fork of the Pigeon River rises out of the Balsam Mountains and flows through the Shining Rock Wilderness in Haywood County, Western North Carolina. It begins its journey at a popular hiking, camping, fishing, and sightseeing area known as the Graveyard Fields, a boggy valley of rhododendron and other low-growing shrubs at an elevation of around 5,000 feet and surrounded by peaks in excess of 6,000 feet. No one is quite sure where the name, "Graveyard Fields," originated. Some locals believe that it is from stumps being left in the area after heavy logging at the turn of the twentieth century. Others contend that a massive storm overturned a bunch of spruce trees and that their root balls resembled gravestones in the common early morning fog. Regardless of the origin of the name, the area is revered as a sacred place by the native Cherokee Indians.

Graveyard Fields experienced catastrophic fires in the last century, once in 1925 and again in the early 1940s. These fires swept through the area, destroying the stumps and scorching the soil enough to render it sterile. Today, few signs of this fiery heritage are visible, a testament to nature's ability to heal itself and to create beauty from devastation. Populous plants include mountain laurel and rhododendron, as well as many wildflowers, such as bluet, galax, aster, and honeysuckle. In summer and fall, hikers can enjoy blackberries, gooseberries, and blueberries scattered throughout Graveyard Fields. The berries also attract a variety of wildlife, including a large number of white-tailed deer.

Flowing from the Graveyard Fields, the river is made up of small headwater rivulets that flow smoothly (and relatively slow, when compared to the rest of the river) over yellowish rock and pea gravel before dropping over Yellowstone Falls and beginning its plummet down through the gorge, picking up speed and volume from feeder creeks and a quick drop in elevation. The Graveyard Fields area can be accessed from a large parking area off Blue Ridge Parkway at milepost 418.8.

After spilling over Yellow Stone Falls and leaving Graveyard Fields, the river begins to resemble a typical freestone stream with large granite boulders and plunge pools. It flows

Upper Falls on Yellowstone Prong and surrounding Graveyard Fields. Kevin Howell

through a dense, temperate deciduous rainforest, and the amount of rain that this drainage can receive at one time is evident by the contrast between the volume of flowing water present and the size of the streambed. Flash flooding can occur on high gradient streams like the Big East Fork, and water levels and force can rise very quickly, making wading or crossing difficult, dangerous, or life threatening. Fishermen should take care to observe the expected weather forecasts, their surroundings, and their proximity to trails and exits

Big East Fork trailhead. Heath Cartee

should they be caught in inclement weather or a powerful and sudden thunderstorm, which can pop up quickly in the mountainous terrain of the area. The river is easily fishable at normal flows, and this area is one where the Appalachian trout slam of brook, brown, and rainbow can be sometimes accomplished in the span of one or two pools.

The next section downstream begins at a popular area known as Skinny Dip Falls. This is a swimming hole located off the Blue Ridge Parkway, and it's very popular with tourists and locals during the summer months. Good fishing is to be had just downstream of Skinny Dip Falls, but the swimming area is usually much too crowded with other user groups for the kind of fishing most backcountry anglers would enjoy. The Skinny Dip swimming hole and the river upstream and downstream can be accessed via a trail from the Looking Glass Overlook off the Blue Ridge Parkway at milepost 417. The trail leading downstream brings you deeper into the gorge and farther from crowds. This trail also will bring the angler to the smaller feeder streams of the Big East Fork for a cozier fishing experience.

Downstream of the Skinny Dip area, the river becomes larger and more open with an even greater ratio of streambed to water volume. The forest and banks are a good distance from the stream for this area, and longer rods are easily fishable through this section of the gorge. This section is the most remote of an already fairly remote area. The river here is characterized by very large boulders and drops, making scrambling and climbing between holes the order for the day. This area just upstream and downstream of Little Buckeye Cove is a favorite of mine. The river is big, the going is tough, the water is clear, and the fish are spooky and of good size for an Appalachian mountain stream.

The lower reaches of the river from U.S. Route 276 upstream to Shining Creek. Little Buckeye Cove can also be accessed via the Big East Fork trailhead located off U.S. Route 276 between Brevard and Waynesville, North Carolina. The trail system in this area from top to bottom can be a tricky one. The entire area is located inside the Shining Rock Wilderness and so trails tend to be rugged, unmarked, and unmaintained. Any angler venturing into this area should bring both a map and a compass, and the knowledge of how to use them.

The vast majority of the Big East Fork watershed lies in the Shining Rock Wilderness area. Shining Rock was designated as a Wilderness Area in September 1963 and encompasses over 18,000 acres. The wilderness area changes in elevation

Anglers have to concetrate their fishing on the plunge pools in the well-scoured upper reaches of the Big East Fork. Patrick Williams

Plunge pool fishing on the Big East Fork. Patrick Williams

Above. Early fall fishing in the Balsam Mountains means beautifully colored brook trout. Patrick Williams

Inset. Releasing a spectacularly colored fall brookie on the Big East Fork. Notice the disporportionate head due to malnutrition. Patrick Williams

Below left. Beautiful Big East Fork brookie. Patrick Williams

from 3300 feet at its lowest point to more than 6,000 at its highest. Because the Wilderness designation trails are not blazed nor maintained, anglers will need to be experienced in orienteering to navigate in the wilderness area. Groups are limited to ten or fewer. Campfires are strictly prohibited. For current regulations, be sure to check in at the Pisgah Ranger Station for current closures due to weather, bears, and other bans that might be in effect.

➤ **Hatches:** The Big East Fork is a typical North Carolina freestone stream with a large variety of hatches throughout the spring and transitioning over to terrestrials in the summer months. It flows on a north-facing slope, and due to this, the hatches tend to be a week or two behind what one would find just over the ridge on the south-facing Brevard side of the mountain. The Quill Gordons and Blue Quills are usually the first mayflies of the season to show and normally happen around mid- to late March. From March through early June, the river follows a typical hatch chart of the area. Any angler fishing this stream should keep stonefly patterns, both nymph and dry, on his or her person at all times. From June into the height of the summer, the river remains cold throughout most of its drainage, and terrestrial patterns such as ants, inch worms, and beetles produce good fish. As fall sets in, a good hatch of the Autumn Sedges begin around early October and last through the end of November. It would be difficult to classify this stream as a winter fishery—but some still give it a go, seeking more solitude and beauty than actual fishing, and manage a few here and there on tiny winter stonefly patterns and the occasional Blue-winged Olive hatch.

➤ **Tackle:** Most of the river from U.S. Route 276 upstream can be fished comfortably with an 8- or 9-foot rod due to the nature of the streambed. An 8-foot, 3- or 4-weight seems to be about perfect for the majority of the river, unless one is fishing Graveyard Fields where a 7-foot, 2- or 3-weight rod may be more appropriate. The water is clear and the fish are spooky, so 5X and 6X leaders tend to be standard when dry-fly fishing, combined with a careful approach and a clean and proper presentation. Much of this river (especially the lower sections with deep, clear plunge pools) would be more appropriately described as "trout hunting" rather than fishing, as care in wading and approach is essential to success.

Summertime on the Big East Fork. Patrick Williams

Graveyard Fields overlook BEF access Yellow Stone Prong. Heath Cartee

Big East Fork brook trout. Robbie Robertson

HEATH CARTEE has been fishing and guiding the waters in and around North Carolina for the last ten years. Small streams and backcountry waters are his favorites. He lives in Pisgah Forest, North Carolina, with his wife and daughter, and any stray dog, cat, or fishing bum that might wander through.

Heath Cartee.

CLOSEST FLY SHOPS

Davidson River Outfitters
49 Pisgah Highway Suite 6
Pisgah Forest, NC 28768
888-861-0111
www.davidsonflyfishing.com
info@davidsonflyfishing.com

Brookings Cashiers Village Anglers
49 Pillar Dr.
Cashiers, NC 28717
828-743-3768
www.brookingsonline.com

828-Hunter Banks
29 Montford Ave.
Asheville, NC 28801
828-252-3005
www.hunterbanks.com

CLOSEST LODGING

The Sunset Motel
523 S. Broad St.
Brevard, NC 28712
828-884-9106
owner@thesunsetmotel.com
www.thesunsetmotel.com

Hampton Inn
275 Forest Gate Dr.
Pisgah Forest, NC 28768
828-883-4800

Holiday Inn Express
2228 Asheville Hwy.
Brevard, NC 28712
828-862-8900
www.hiexbrevard.com

Hemlock Hideaways
740 Williamson Creek Rd.
Pisgah Forest, NC 28768
828-577-9363
www.vrbo.com/460883

Ash Grove Mountain Cabins & Camping
749 E. Fork
Brevard, NC 28712
828-885-7216
www.ash-grove.com

Mountains and Meadows
350 Generation Pass
Pisgah Forest, NC 28768
828-329-8430
 info@mountainmeadownc.com
www.mountainmeadownc.com

Davidson River Campground
1 Davidson River Cir.
Pisgah Forest, NC 28768
828-877-3265

CLOSEST RESTAURANTS
The Square Root
33 Times Arcade Aly.
Brevard, NC 28712
828-884-6171
squarerootrestaurant@gmail.com
www.squarerootrestaurant.com

Jordan Street Cafe
48 W. Jordan St.
Brevard, NC 28712
828-883-2558
jordanstreetcafe30@gmail.com
www.thejordanstreetcafe.com

Big Mike's
12 S. Gaston St.
Brevard, NC 28712
828-884-3663
www.bigmikesnc.com

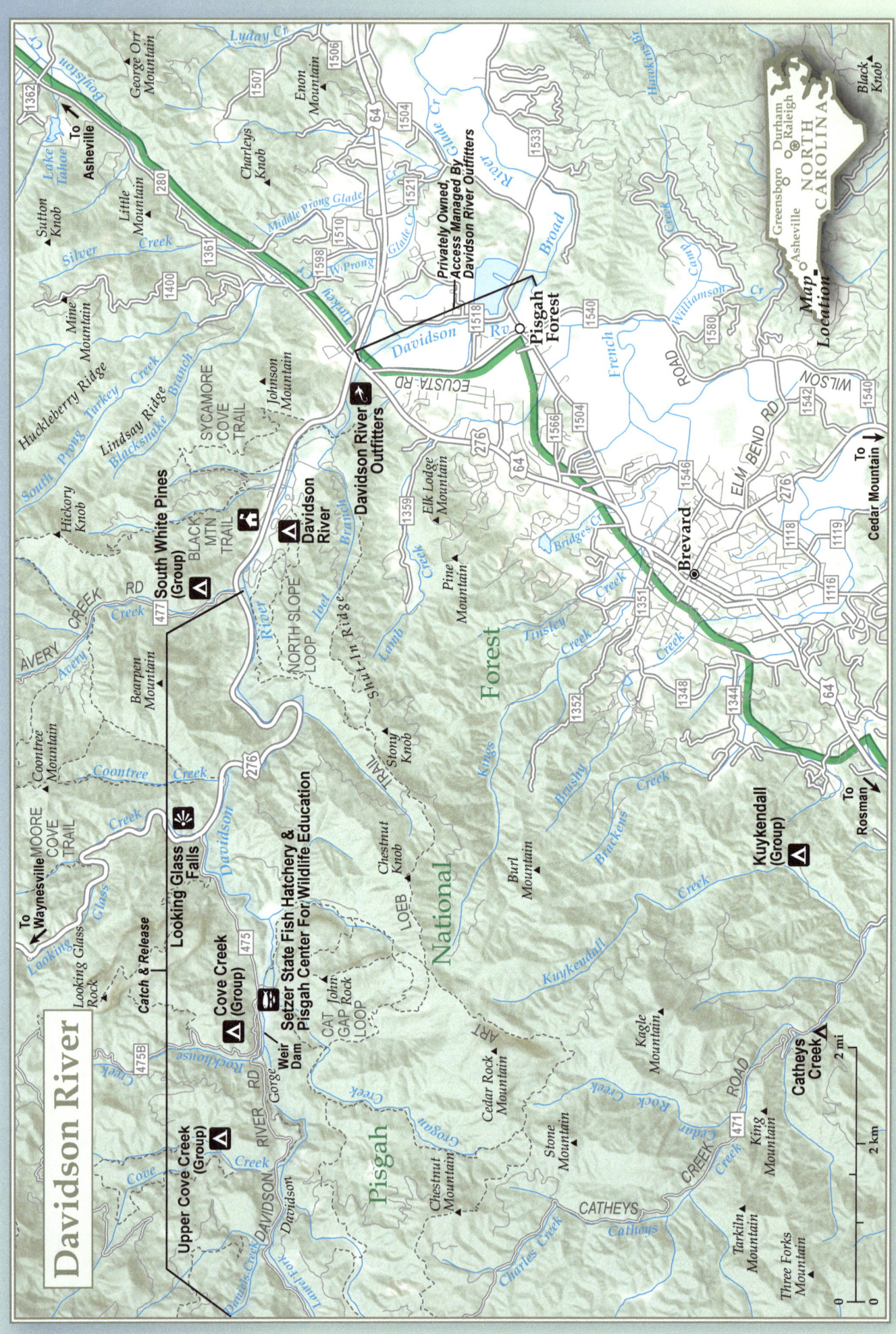

29 · Davidson River

▶ **Location:** The Davidson River is located in Pisgah National Forest near Brevard, North Carolina, 30 minutes southwest of Asheville, North Carolina; about three hours northwest of Charlotte, North Carolina; and about three hours northeast of Atlanta, Georgia. Access to the Davidson is via Route 276 North and F.S. 475.

The Davidson River begins life high in the Balsam Mountains at the confluence of Laurel Prong and Daniels Creek. From the confluence, the Davidson flows approximately 16 miles until its confluence with the French Broad River in the town of Pisgah Forest, North Carolina. For 13 miles, the Davidson flows through Pisgah National Forest, which was once all part of George Vanderbilt's Biltmore Estate. The last three miles of the river flow through what was once the Ecusta paper mill and are privately owned. Davidson River Outfitters currently manages the private section of the river, and you can gain access to the private stretch through a daily rod fee.

The 13 miles of the river that flow through Pisgah National Forest are commonly divided into four sections:

- The section from the confluence of Daniels Creek and Laurel Prong downstream to the Weir Dam at the NCWRC Pisgah Fish Hatchery is referred to as the Gorge or Upper Section.
- The section from the Weir Dam downstream to the confluence of Grogran Creek is the Hatchery Section.
- The section from the confluence of Grogran Creek to the confluence of Avery Creek is referred to as the Lower Section.
- From Avery Creek downstream to the United States Forest Service (USFS) boundary is referred to as the Campground Section.

The Davidson was the first river in North Carolina to be designated catch-and-release fly fishing only by the NCWRC in the mid-1980s. It is consistently ranked as one of the top 100 trout streams in the United States by Trout Unlimited. The downside to the Davidson is that 65 percent of the nation can drive to it in a days' time. The river is currently undergoing a transition with the demise of the Carolina hemlocks. These large trees, some of which are over 150 years old, are being killed by the woolly adelgid. While there is a cure to treat the trees, the cost far exceeds the capability to treat all the hemlocks. As the trees are dying, they are falling into the river, creating sweepers and massive logjams.

The two-mile long section of the Davidson from the confluence of Daniels Creek and Laurel Branch to the Weir Dam at the NCWRC Fish Hatchery is a classic mountain plunge pool trout water. The stream ranges from 20 to 35 feet wide.

Mellissa Howell fishing on the Davidson. Kevin Howell

(It is one of the few sections of the Davidson where you can escape some of the crowds.) The water stays cool in the summer, and the wild rainbow and brown trout in this section will readily take a well-presented dry fly or a dry with a small nymph dropper. Access to this section is via F.S. 475 or the Davidson River Trail.

The 5/8-mile-long section from the Weir Dam to Grogan Creek is the most pressured section on the river. Half of the water flow from the Davidson gets diverted through the Bobby N. Setzer Hatchery. As the water returns to the river, it is full of midge larvae and undigested trout pellets and other affluent from the hatchery. Not only can the anglers see the

Linda Michael streamer fishing on the Davidson. Kevin Howell

large fish, but they also have a constant chum slick to fish in. In this section, anglers must try to figure out what the angler in front of them was using and try something different. This is also the section where manners and good ethics are often set by the wayside. Don't be surprised if another angler walks within 30 feet of you and starts fishing. If you do not do well in crowds, then this is not the section for you to fish. When fishing in this section, you will need a 9- to12-foot leader and will need to fish a lot of midge patterns in the size 20–26 range.

By the time Grogran Creek enters the Davidson, the river has, for the most part, reached the valley floor and maintains a width of about 40–45 feet. From here to its confluence with the French Broad, the river is characterized by long, deep, flat pools that are divided by small shoals of fast water. These long pools provide for some spectacular hatches from March to early June and again in late September and early October. During the summer months, the fish will readily come to a well-presented terrestrial. You must be careful when wading the long slicks—errant casts and sloppy wading will result in

Linda Michael with a beautiful Davidson River 'bow. Kevin Howell

spooky fish that make for tough fishing. The lower end of this section can be plagued by the "rubber hatch" (inner tubes) between Memorial Day and Labor Day; when hooked in the ear, a passing tuber can be challenging to land on light tippet.

The section from Avery Creek down to the USFS boundary is the only section of hatchery-supported water on the river and is open to any type of lure or bait. (Anglers may

Kevin Howell with a Davidson River brown. Walker Parrot

keep seven fish of any size.) It is also the only part of the river that is stocked by the NCWRC. While you will primarily catch stocked fish in this section, you will also encounter some very large resident brown trout in its holes. This section of the river sees the most nonfishing traffic in the summertime. From swimmers to dog walkers and tubers, all are present from Memorial Day to Labor Day. However, by late September the river has cleared out and you can fish in peace until Memorial Day the following year.

The Davidson is one of the most nutrient-rich streams that flow out of the Balsams. It is well-known for good hatches of Quill Gordons, Cahills, Little Yellow Sallies, caddis and tons of other insects. From mid-May all the way until the first frost, terrestrials play a large role on this stream. The ever-present green inch worms hanging from the rhododendron and other streamside vegetation offer a high-protein, easily captured meal for the trout. Anglers fishing the Hatchery Section will need a varied selection of midges, the smaller the better. Black, red, or white Zebra Midges always seem to produce a few fish in this section.

Gene Reeder's Davidson River trophy brown trout caught while fishing with Davidson River Outfitters. Heath Cartee

White squirrels are a welcome sight in Brevard and on the lower Davidson River. Kevin Howell

The Davidson is a year-round fishery; however, the fishing is best from mid-September to mid-July. Late July to early September can be great if it is a rainy summer; however, if the water becomes low in the midsummer months, then the fishing will definitely slow as the water warms and fish become spooky.

Anglers should note that the Davidson River is part of the Balsam Mountain range, which is classified as a deciduous rainforest. It receives 80-plus inches of rainfall annually. Anglers should always be cognizant of stream levels. A cloudburst that occurs on the head of Daniels Creek some 16 miles away can easily send a 24-inch wall of water surging down the river and catch unsuspecting anglers off guard.

Due to the mountainous terrain, do not rely on cell phones because you might have service on one side of the mountain and not on the other side. Also, if you do not have service, be sure to turn you phone off. Otherwise, it will drain your battery, and when you do reach cell service, your phone will be dead.

▶ **Regulations:** The Davidson has three different sets of regulations on the river. Anglers should consult the current North Carolina fishing regulations at www.ncwildlife.org or a local tackle shop about the current regulations and the boundaries in which those regulations pertain. Currently, the upper 13 miles of the river from Avery Creek upstream are classified as fly fishing only and catch-and-release only.

▶ **Tackle:** Anglers will want an 8 1/2- to 9-foot, 4- to 5-weight fly rod for most of the fishing on the Davidson. Leaders will need to be 9–12 feet in length and taper to 5–6X tippet for most conditions. During higher water flows and winter months, anglers can get by with 4X tippet, while summer low water may necessitate 7X tippet.

KEVIN HOWELL—Kevin Howell is the owner of Davidson River Outfitters; he also is an author, lecturer, fly-fishing instructor, and guide. Kevin is a Signature fly Designer for Montana Fly Company. A 2018 inductee to the Fly Fishing Museum of the Southern Appalachians Hall of Fame and a 2018 inductee to the Legends of the Fly Hall of Fame as well. Kevin has been guiding the waters of North Carolina, South Carolina, and East Tennessee for 25 years. When not guiding he can be found fishing with his wife Mellissa, and sons David and Andrew.

Kevin Howell with a fine Argentinian Brown. Gonzalo Flego

CLOSEST FLY SHOPS

Davidson River Outfitters
49 Pisgah Highway, Suite 6
Pisgah Forest, NC 28768
888-861-0111
www.davidsonflyfishing.com
info@davidsonflyfishing.com

Brookings Cashiers Village Anglers
49 Pillar Dr.
Cashiers, NC 28717
828-743-3768
www.brookingsonline.com

828-One Fly Outfitters
112 Cherry St,
Black Mountain, NC 28711
828-669-6939
www.oneflyoutfitters.com

CLOSEST LODGING

The Sunset Motel
523 S. Broad St.
Brevard, NC 28712
828-884-9106
owner@thesunsetmotel.com
www.thesunsetmotel.com

Hampton Inn
275 Forest Gate Dr.
Pisgah Forest, NC 28768
828-883-4800

Holiday Inn Express
2228 Asheville Hwy.
Brevard, NC 28712
828-862-8900
www.hiexbrevard.com

Hemlock Hideaways
740 Williamson Creek Rd.
Pisgah Forest, NC 28768
828-577-9363
www.vrbo.com/460883

Ash Grove Mountain Cabins & Camping
749 E. Fork
Brevard, NC 28712
828-885-7216
www.ash-grove.com

Mountains and Meadows
350 Generation Pass
Pisgah Forest, NC 28768
828-329-8430
 info@mountainmeadownc.com
www.mountainmeadownc.com

Davidson River Campground
1 Davidson River Cir.
Pisgah Forest, NC 28768
828-877-3265

CLOSEST RESTAURANTS

The Square Root
33 Times Arcade Aly.
Brevard, NC 28712
828-884-6171
squarerootrestaurant@gmail.com
www.squarerootrestaurant.com

Jordan Street Cafe
48 W. Jordan St.
Brevard, NC 28712
828-883-2558
jordanstreetcafe30@gmail.com
www.thejordanstreetcafe.com

Big Mike's
12 S. Gaston St.
Brevard, NC 28712
828-884-3663
www.bigmikesnc.com

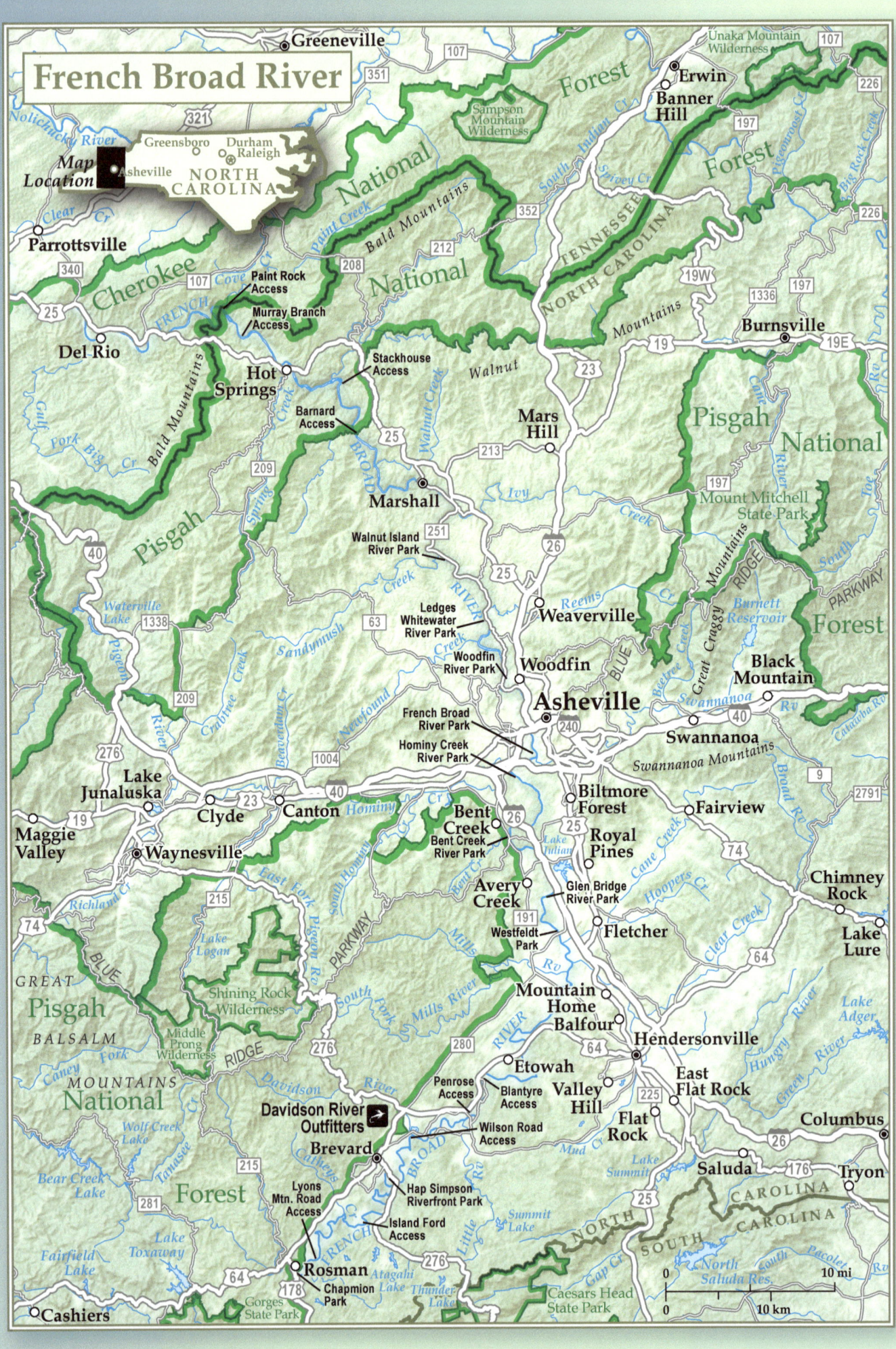

30 · French Broad River

▶ **Location:** The French Broad River originates in the small mountain town of Rosman, North Carolina (about an hour from Asheville, North Carolina), flowing downstream to Cocke County, Tennessee. It starts as a small stream in North Carolina with many tributaries. The French Broad grows in size, water flow, and gradient as the river takes a northern direction, flowing through Western North Carolina and eventually Tennessee.

The French Broad River gains speed from the main tributaries of the North Fork, West Fork, East Fork, and the Middle Fork. Forming the French Broad River in Rosman, these tributaries help support rainbow, brown, brook trout, smallmouth, musky, redeye, and an overwhelming population of redhorse suckers and warpaint shiners, the Smoky Mountain cutthroat. Flowing about 213 miles from Rosman to its terminus at Lake Douglas, Tennessee, the French Broad has an extremely wide array of angling opportunities. Wade access for trout is easy to find in the town of Rosman. Parking at Champion Park in downtown Rosman, anglers will have wade access downstream and upstream toward the forks of the river. In Rosman, the fishing regulations are hatchery supported, allowing anglers to keep a few fish for the grill. Fly anglers can expect to catch a few fish on drys and droppers. This section has great Yellow Drake and caddis hatches that will entertain any dry-fly fisherman toward the late hours of spring and fall evenings.

Rosman is the headwaters of the French Broad, with cooler water temperatures helping trout survive through the year with natural reproduction. As the French Broad flows north toward Asheville, water temperatures rise, and the French Broad starts to pick up water volume with the help of many tributaries. Smallmouth and musky roam these waters with a few trout caught as far as Asheville during cooler months.

Floating from Hap Simpson Riverfront Park to Wilson Road can provide anglers with great musky fishing and a few smallmouths. Musky can be tough, so pack an intermediate line and a stiff 10-weight, with a few large streamers dressed in dark colors. Carrying a 7-weight, anglers can fish for smallmouth with minnow patterns and floating lines. Oh yeah, a lot of patience and ice for your sore casting arm will help. Musky like to haunt anglers' dreams until the next time they get a follow.

Smallmouth fishing can be great from Bent Creek to Hominy Creek. Floating through the Biltmore Estate, anglers will have the chance to catch smallmouth bass on crease flies with floating lines, streamer fishing with intermediate lines with minnow, and crayfish patterns. Rig a musky rod for these lower sections, as well. Focus on the large pools and deeper runs. Wading can be tough in this section, with limited road access and private property. Floating in a canoe will be the best way to access this six-mile float. With the

Andrew Howell with a lower French Broad River smallmouth, the numerous rock ledges in the background provide prime habitat for smallies. Kevin Howell

Great Blue Heron are a common site along the banks of the French Broad River. Credit Kevin Howell

Always be aware of the regulations. Walker Parrott

growing popularity of Asheville, this float can be congested with tubers and recreation boaters. Fishing can be better on the weekdays, but the weekends will definitely give you some entertainment during slow periods of fishing.

Traveling downstream on North Carolina 251 toward Marshall, North Carolina, you will find many pull-off points for wade access. Alexander Park, Ledges Park, and Ivy River will give wade anglers easy access to large shoals, deep holes, and ledges. Smallmouths should be the target in this section. Floating can be great with a canoe or lightweight raft, but most access is not riverfront, so be prepared to carry or drag your desired watercraft to and from the river.

During summer's low-water flows, smallmouths will take Clousers and crayfish patterns on a floating line. Topwater flies with a floating line can find larger fish during summer cicada hatches in July. Water levels will drastically fluctuate in these lower sections, due to the many tributaries that flow into the French Broad. Watch the weather and stream gauges for wade access and floating.

Downstream of Marshall, in the town of Hot Springs, the French Broad becomes wider and gradient starts to fall, creating a few Class III and Class IV rapids. This is Section 9 of the French Broad, starting in Barnard and finishing in the town of Hot Springs. Running rapids like Pillow, Frank Bell's, and Kayaker's Ledge, anglers will need rowing and paddling skills to access this all-day float. Section 9 has many commercial rafting outfitters that can provide shuttle services with verbal permission. The small river town of Hot Springs has a few places to eat, and one great gas station right in front of Hot Springs Campground, which serves a well-deserved cold beer after a long day on the river. For the multi-day angler, Hot Springs Campground will have riverfront camping spots

Guide Kevin Howell nets an upper French Broad River smallie for Bob Clouser. Linda Heller

(or stay in one of the cabins they rent per night). With the slow pools and never-ending shoals, smallmouths will take topwater flies and small minnow patterns. Muskies will hang out in the deeper, slower pools. In the late spring, anglers can have a shot at a few white bass and walleye, depending on water flows and temperatures.

Just a few miles of gravel roads on river, right downstream of Hot Springs, Paint Creek Access will be the end of the road for fishing the French Broad in North Carolina. Road access will travel away from the river, creating a wilderness-type setting. Floating to Del Rio, Tennessee, from Paint Creek will be a long day with huge views of the river's gorge and wide ledges. Shuttling and access to civilization will be tough, as this section is extremely remote. Below Del Rio, the French Broad joins the Pigeon River and Nolichucky River to form Douglas Lake, finally spilling into the Holston River in Knoxville, Tennessee.

Many river advocates have helped the French Broad heal from the polluted past, and it remains one of the greatest waterways in the Southeast. In its lower reaches, in the valleys of Tennessee, the French Broad rests under many hydroelectric switches and flows at the mercy of the Tennessee Valley Authority. The French Broad is a great river to explore for the day or on a multi-day float-and-fish trip. River camping can be preselected for the public through the Western North Carolina Alliance's Paddle Trail. For directions and river access, look at the French Broad River Paddle Trail.

Enjoy this great river and dynamic fishery.

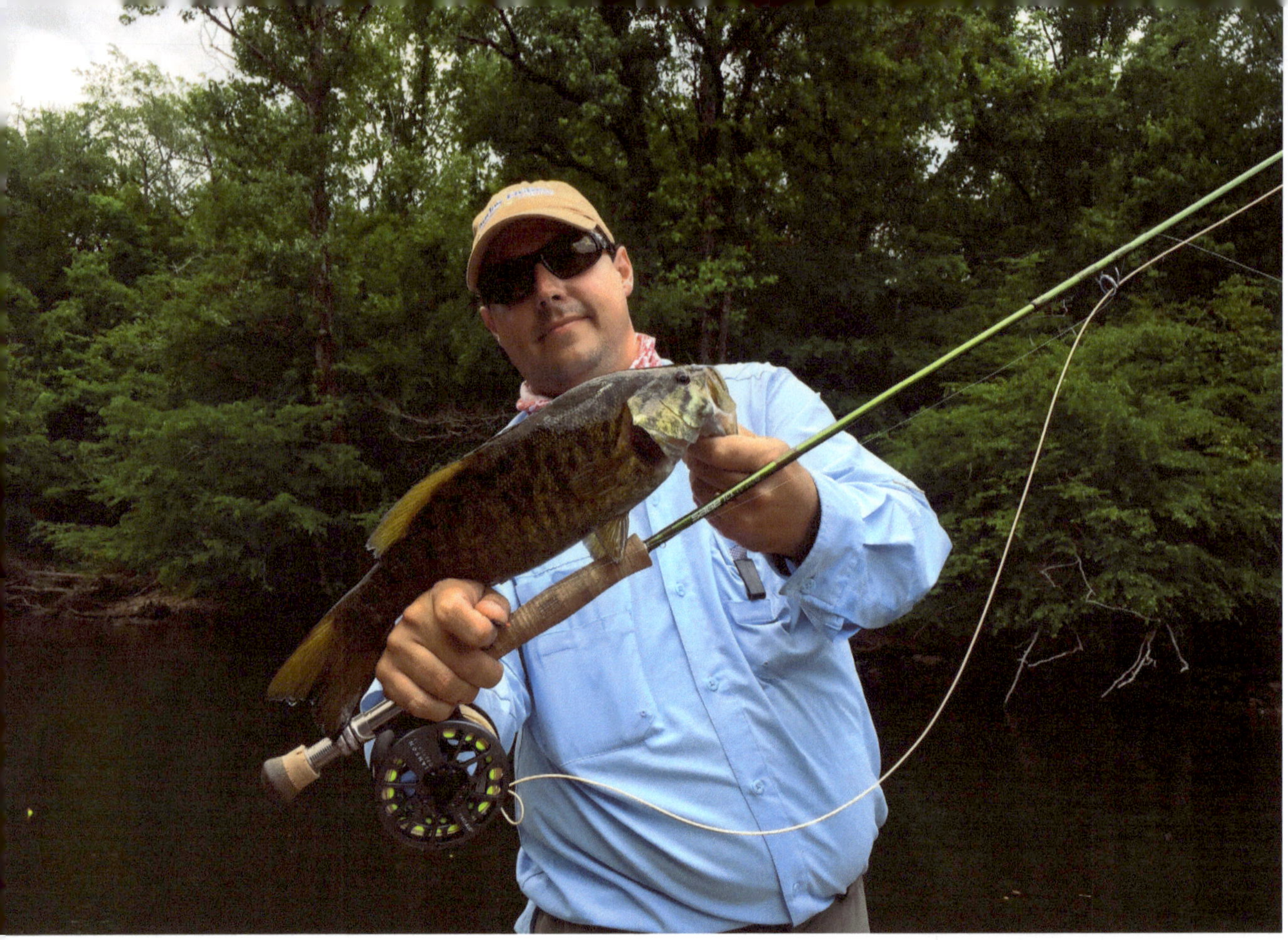

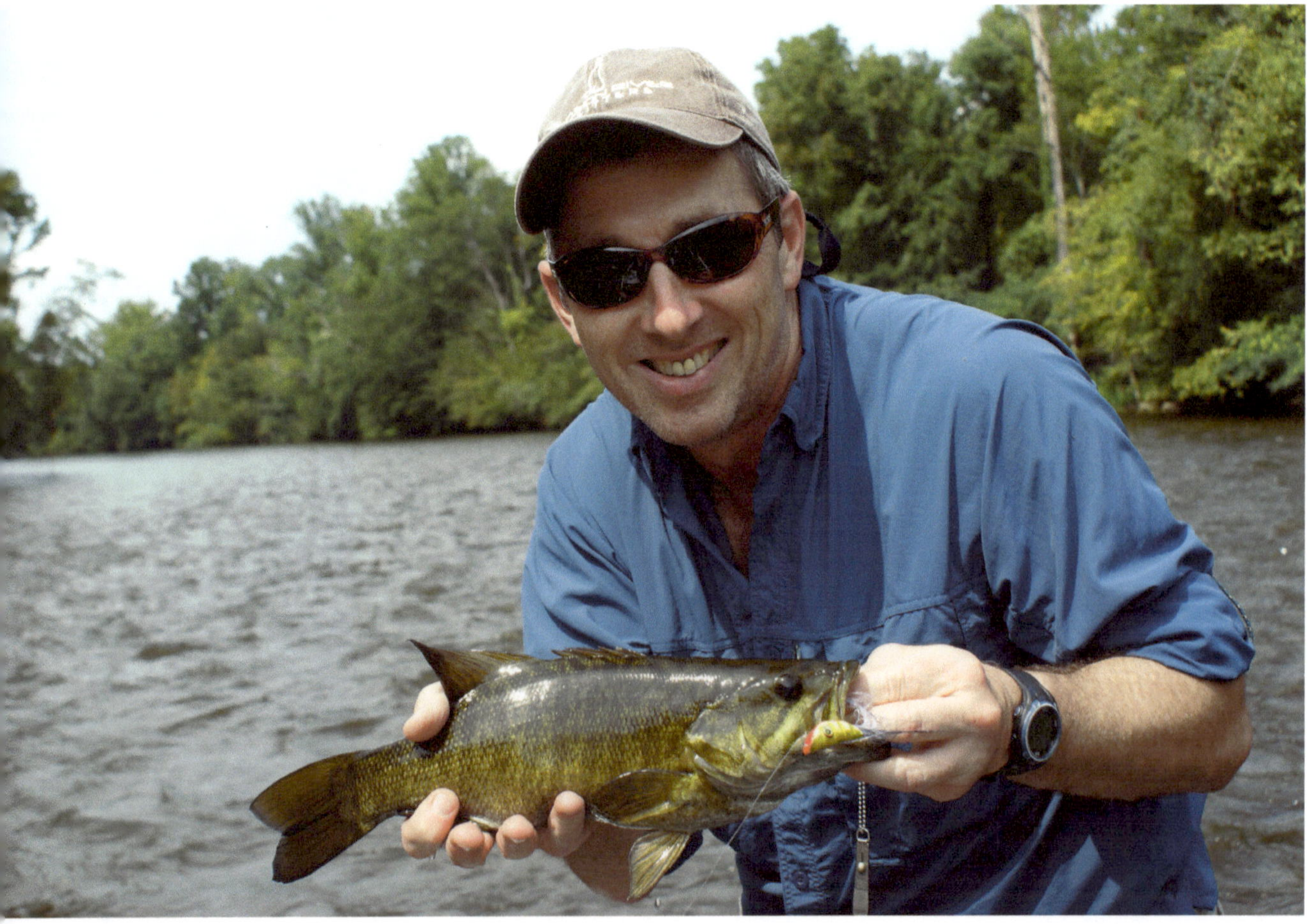

Above. Linda Michael with a French Broad River smallmouth. Kevin Howell

Facing top. Gustavo Hiebaum from Argentina with his first ever smallmouth bass caught on the lower French Broad River on a sparkle minnow. Kevin Howell

Facing bottom. Dr. Mal Lawrence with a lower French Broad River smallmouth.

➤ **Tackle:**

Flies
- **Trout Dry Flies**
    - Yellow Drake, sizes12-20
    - Green Drake, sizes 12-18
    - Caddisfly (black, tan, and yellow), sizes 12-18
    - Ants and beetles, sizes 14-20
    - Kevin's Caterpillar, size 10
    - Yellow Trudes, sizes 14-18
    - Blue-winged Olives, sizes 16-20
    - Parachute Adams, sizes 16-20
    - Royal Wulff, sizes16-20
- **Trout Nymphs**
    - Pheasant Tail, sizes 14-22
    - Girdle Bug, sizes 6-10
    - Squirmy Wormie, sizes 12-16
    - Red Fox Squirrel Nymph, sizes 12-18
    - Lightning Bug, sizes 12-18
    - Soft Hackle, sizes 14-20
    - Sucker Spawn, size 10
    - Eggs, sizes10-18
- **Trout Streamers**
    - Woolly Bugger, sizes 4-10
    - Weir Sculpin, sizes 4-8
    - Slump buster
    - Madonna, sizes 4-8
    - Zoo Cougar, size 4
    - Catch 'Em All, sizes 4-8
    - Meat Whistle, sizes 4-6
    - Walkers Wigglers sizes 1/0-4
- **Bass Flies**
    - Boogle Bug, sizes 4
    - Walker's Wiggler, sizes 1/0-4
    - Clouser Minnow, sizes 1-8
    - Scorpions, sizes 4-6
    - Grub fly, sizes 4-6
    - Bitch Creek, sizes 4-8
    - Big Nasty, sizes 6
    - Gummy Minnow, sizes 4-8
    - Sneaky Pete, sizes 6-8
- **Musky Flies**
    - Half and Half, sizes 1/0-5/0
    - Clouser Minnow, sizes 1/0-5/0
    - T-Bone, sizes 1/0-5/0
    - Dahlberg Diver (6- to 9-inch)

Walker Parrott with musky.

Leaders
- **Trout**
    - 9-12 foot leaders
    - 35X tippet
- **Smallmouth, Largemouth, White Bass, and Walleye**
    - 9-foot leaders
    - 1–4X leaders
    - 2–4X tippet
- **Musky**
    - 7-foot leader
    - 60–80X bite leader

Rods
- **Trout Rods**
    - 7-foot, 5-inch to 9-foot moderate to fast action
- **Smallmouth Rods**
    - 9-foot, 5- to 8-weight fast action
- **Musky**
    - 9- to 10-weight fast rods

Fly Lines
- **Floating, intermediate, full-sink, mini-sink tips**
    - Watercraft
    - (float tubes or belly boats are not recommended)
    - Drift boats
    - Canoes
    - Fishing kayaks
    - Rafts

Growing up on the South Carolina coast, **Walker Parrott** was introduced to fishing as a child, catching redfish, trout, jacks, and other inshore species. While completing high school in Sandpoint, Idaho, Walker was introduced to mountain trout fishing. He wanted to stay in the mountains, but live in the Southeast. After completing Brevard College with a bachelor's degree in experimental education, Walker settled in Brevard, North Carolina where he could fish the streams and rivers for trout and bass. After college, Walker took a job with an environmental engineering firm, which he soon left to pursue his passion of fishing, landing at Davidson River Outfitters. Now, too many years later, Walker is managing Davidson River Outfitters guide service and guiding and hosting anglers to Andros Bahamas, Argentina, and Montana. Between working with a great staff in the shop and guiding trout, smallmouth, and musky trips, he has the perfect balance. While trout are the staple, Walker likes to float for smallmouth bass and musky in Tennessee, North Carolina, and Virginia. When Walker is not guiding or pacing the fly shop, Walker can be found mountain biking, kayaking, taking long walks on the beach, fishing, and hanging out with his wife Nicole, and dogs, Mojo, Mia, Cassidy, and Catch 'em.

CLOSEST FLY SHOPS

Davidson River Outfitters
49 Pisgah Highway Suite 6
Pisgah Forest, NC 28768
888-861-0111
www.davidsonflyfishing.com
info@davidsonflyfishing.com

Hunter Banks
29 Montford Ave.
Asheville, NC 28801
828-252-3005
www.hunterbanks.com

CLOSEST GUIDES AND OUTFITTERS

Davidson River Outfitters
49 Pisgah Highway Suite 6
Pisgah Forest, NC 28768
888-861-0111
www.davidsonflyfishing.com
info@davidsonflyfishing.com

Western North Carolina Alliance
29 N. Market St., Ste. 610
Asheville, NC 28801
828-258-8737

3 Rivers Angler
5113 Kingston Pike
Knoxville, TN 37919
865-200-5271
info@3riversangler.com
www.3riversangler.com

CLOSEST LODGING

The Sunset Motel
523 S. Broad St.
Brevard, NC 28712
828-884-9106
owner@thesunsetmotel.com
www.thesunsetmotel.com

Hampton Inn
275 Forest Gate Dr.
Pisgah Forest, NC 28768
828-883-4800

Holiday Inn Express
2228 Asheville Hwy.
Brevard, NC 28712
828-862-8900
www.hiexbrevard.com

Hemlock Hideaways
740 Williamson Creek Rd.
Pisgah Forest, NC 28768
828-577-9363
740Williamson@gmail.com
http://www.vrbo.com/460883

Ash Grove Mountain Cabins & Camping
749 E. Fork
Brevard, NC 28712
828-885-7216
www.ash-grove.com

Mountains and Meadows
350 Generation Pass
Pisgah Forest, NC 28768
828-329-8430
info@mountainmeadownc.com
www.mountainmeadownc.com

Davidson River Campground
1 Davidson River Cir.
Pisgah Forest, NC 28768
828-877-3265

Cascade Lake Recreation Area & Campground
1679 Little River Campground Rd.
Pisgah Forest, NC 28768
828-877-4475
www.cascadelakerecreationarea.com

CLOSEST RESTAURANTS

The Square Root
33 Times Arcade Aly.
Brevard, NC 28712
828-884-6171
squarerootrestaurant@gmail.com
www.squarerootrestaurant.com

Jordan Street Cafe
48 W. Jordan St.
Brevard, NC 28712
828-883-2558
jordanstreetcafe30@gmail.com
www.thejordanstreetcafe.com

Big Mike's
12 S. Gaston St.
Brevard, NC 28712
828-884-3663
www.bigmikesnc.com

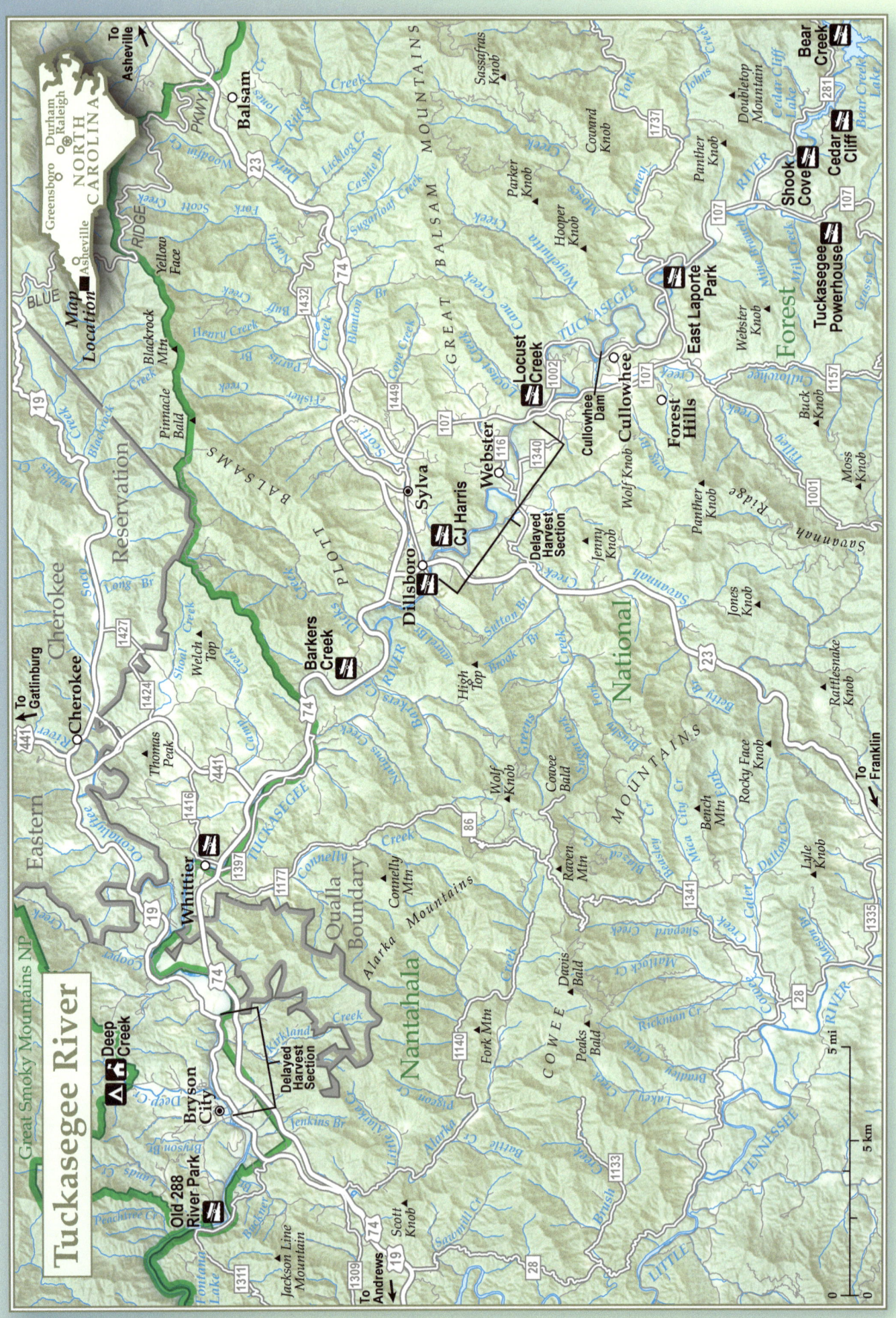

31 · Tuckasegee River

➤ **Location:** "The Tuck" flows north just outside of Glenville, North Carolina, close to the resort towns of Cashiers and Highlands. It is about 1 1/2 hours from Asheville, North Carolina. You can fly into either the Asheville Regional Airport, or Greenville Spartanburg International Airport in South Carolina.

It is controlled by two dams, Cedar Cliff Dam in the East Fork and Thorpe Dam in the West Fork. The Tuck is not a tailwater in the respect that the outflow does not come from the bottom of the lake. Instead, the Tuck is a topwater release. Water temps and water flows will fluctuate as both the weather and need for power changes. The water release schedule from Duke Energy can at times be inaccurate. With the provided water release info, always take into account the recent ten-day forecast before traveling. The Tuck can run cloudy after just a few late afternoon thunderstorms. (To see Duke Energy water release schedules for North Carolina, visit www.duke-energy.com/north-carolina.asp.)

When the water levels agree, anglers can have great fishing for rainbow, brown, and brook trout and smallmouth bass. Spilling into Lake Fontana in Bryson City, North Carolina, the Tuck has road and float access throughout the 50-plus miles. Fishing regulations will vary throughout the river, from Delayed Harvest to Hatchery Supported. I recommend calling local shops for weekly fishing reports, water levels, and regulations.

With more than 50 miles of river to choose from, use the sections covered in this chapter to help narrow your focus. While wade fishing and float fishing are good ways to access the fishery, anglers will find more wade access than floating. Guides and float anglers tend to float the Delayed Harvest section from Locust Creek Access to C. J. Harris Access. Wade anglers can access the river through many pull-offs and state-maintained boat ramps.

➤ **East Laporte Access to Cullowhee Dam Access**

East Laporte Access to Cullowhee Dam Access provides access to wade anglers with and without power generations. Floaters with oar rigs will find larger pools and long riffles.

This section can provide wild trout and stocked trout, with a shot of catching some smallmouths. Typically, this

Foggy morning float on the Tuck. Walker Parrott

John Popowski with a lower Tuck brown. Kevin Howell

section fishes better in the spring and winter months, with cooler temps being better for trout. Summer fishing can be a great time for smallmouth. Poppers and sliders on a floating line fished in the larger pools will provide a good topwater bite. When smallmouth don't want to look up, try the reels with an indicator and a crayfish or hellgrammite fly.

Spring and winter months can provide anglers with a good mix of wild and stocked trout. Nymph fishing the deeper pools and riffles will require indicators, or tight lining will produce some great fish. Dry-fly fishing can be productive with long leaders and caddis patterns or Blue-winged Olives.

With access to Western Carolina University close by, tubers and recreation floaters can make fishing hard on the weekends, and on any pretty summer day.

▶ **Locust Creek to C.J. Harris:** Locust Creek to C. J. Harris is the most popular and heavily fished section. The East Fork Dam provides a great level for wade and float anglers. This section is heavily stocked for Delayed Harvest, meaning the river is under a catch-and-release, single-hook-artificial regulation from the first Saturday in October to the first Saturday in June. During these months, anglers can fish 9-foot leaders with a double-nymph rig and an indicator. The ledge-filled and deep-run features of this section can provide plenty of holding-runs for fish and easy access for anglers.

When Duke Power is running "two pipes," the West Fork and the East Fork water levels can be pretty tough for wade anglers. I suggest floating in a drift boat or an oar rig for transportation. Target the larger pools and longer slicks with a 12-inch leader or longer and plenty of split-shot. Sinking

Fish on! Kevin Howell

lines with a 6-weight will help produce larger fish. At this level, wading is not recommended.

This Delayed Harvest section of the Tuck has great road access on North River Road and South River Road downstream to Dillsboro, North Carolina. (With easy road access and Delayed Harvest, this section can be crowded.)

► **Dillsboro Bridge Access to Barkers Creek Access (The Gorge)**

Dillsboro Bridge Access to Barkers Creek Access, known as "the Gorge," has great fishing for trout, smallmouth, bluegill, and redeye bass. This section falls under Hatchery Supported regulation, meaning it is closed the month of March and opens the first Saturday in April. Wading access is limited due to private property. Wade fishing the Gorge can provide some excellent fishing and fewer crowds than you find elsewhere on the river. All other access can be made with an oar rig.

This section can be low and scrappy during lower natural flows. With one generator and healthy natural flows, anglers will enjoy deeper pools and some Class II rapids. With both generators, just enjoy the rapids. The Gorge has some whitewater and is not recommended for inexperienced rowers.

► **Tackle:**

Flies
- **Drys**
    October Caddis, sizes 12-18
    Parachute Adams, sizes 12-18
    Fat Alberts, sizes 4-12

Facing. Fishing with a friend on the Tuck. Walker Parrott

Above. Ancient Cherokee Indian weir on the Tuckaseegee. Walker Parrott

    Chubby Chernobyl, sizes 6-12
    Jim Charlies, sizes 14-20
    Texas Piss Ant, sizes 12-16
    Lime Trude, sizes 12-16
- **Nymphs**
    Girdle Bug (brown/black), sizes 4-8
    Eggs (in assorted colors), sizes 10
    Squirmy Worms (in assorted colors), sizes 12-16
    Tungsten Pheasant Tails, sizes 12-20
    Sassi's Solution, sizes 12-20
    Trip Saver, sizes 10-16
    Peacock Soft Hackle, sizes 12-18
    San Juan Pink, sizes 12-18
    Lightning Bug, sizes 12-18
    Surveyor, sizes 14-20
    Zebra Midge, sizes 12-22
- **Streamers**
    Sheila Sculpin, sizes 4-6
    Woolly Bugger (black and white), sizes 4-12
    Zonkers, sizes 4-6
    Crystal Minnows, sizes 4-8
- **Rods and Lines**
    8 ½-foot, 4-weight and 5-weight rods during low water levels
    9-foot, 6-weight rods during high water levels

Fall fishing on the Tuck. Walker Parrott

Growing up on the South Carolina coast, **Walker Parrott** was introduced to fishing as a child, catching redfish, trout, jacks, and other inshore species. While completing high school in Sandpoint, Idaho, Walker was introduced to mountain trout fishing. He wanted to stay in the mountains, but live in the Southeast. After completing Brevard College with a bachelor's degree in experimental education, Walker settled in Brevard, North Carolina where he could fish the streams and rivers for trout and bass. After college, Walker took a job with an environmental engineering firm, which he soon left to pursue his passion of fishing, landing at Davidson River Outfitters. Now, too many years later, Walker is managing Davidson River Outfitters guide service and guiding and hosting anglers to Andros Bahamas, Argentina, and Montana. Between working with a great staff in the shop and guiding trout, smallmouth, and musky trips, he has the perfect balance. While trout are the staple, Walker likes to float for smallmouth bass and musky in Tennessee, North Carolina, and Virginia. When Walker is not guiding or pacing the fly shop, Walker can be found mountain biking, kayaking, taking long walks on the beach, fishing, and hanging out with his wife Nicole, and dogs, Mojo, Mia, Cassidy, and Catch 'em.

Guide Walker Parrott displays a Tuck rainbow for a happy client. Walker Parrott

CLOSEST GUIDES AND OUTFITTERS

Davidson River Outfitters
49 Pisgah Hwy., Ste. 6
Pisgah Forest, NC 28768
888-861-0111
www.davidsonflyfishing.com

Tuckasegee Fly Shop
3 Depot Street
Bryson City, NC 28713
828 488 333
www.tuckflyshop.com

Hunter Banks
29 Montford Ave.
Asheville, NC 28801
828-252-3005
www.hunterbanks.com

CLOSEST LODGING

Dillsboro Inn
146 N. River Rd.
Dillsboro, NC 28725
866-586-3898
info@dillsboroinn.com
www.dillsboroinn.com

The Jarrett House
100 Haywood Rd.
Dillsboro, NC 28725
800-972-5623
jarretthouse.dillsboronc@gmail.com
www.jarretthouse.com

CLOSEST RESTAURANTS

Haywood Smokehouse
403 Haywood Rd.
Dillsboro, NC 28725
828-631-9797
info@haywoodsmokehouse.com
www.haywoodsmokehouse.com

Kostas Family Restaurant
489 Haywood Rd.
Dillsboro, NC 28779
828-631-0777
www.kostasdillsboro.com

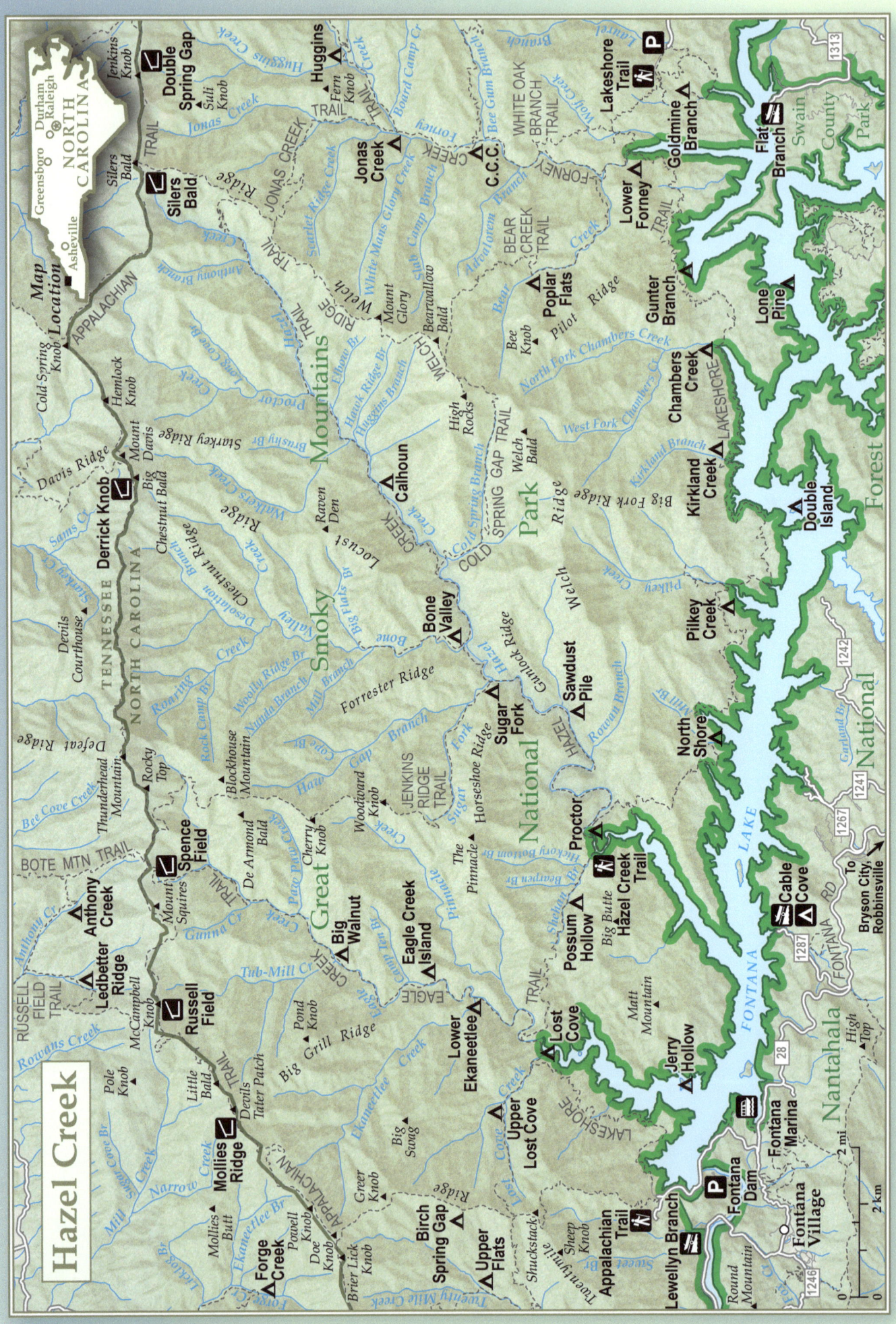

32 · Hazel Creek

▶ **Location:** Hazel Creek is nestled in western North Carolina, inside Great Smoky Mountains National Park. Only accessible by boat, horseback, or on foot, the trail heads and boat launches are almost two hours from Asheville, North Carolina. The nearest small towns from which anglers can base themselves are Bryson City and Robbinsville.

Hazel Creek is arguably the most famous of all the streams in Great Smoky Mountains National Park. Beyond its healthy population of rainbows and browns, Hazel Creek is home to the remnants of the pre-park logging town of Proctor, making a walk up the stream a walk through history. Visitors should take time not only to fish but to explore some of the ruins and cemeteries that can be found throughout the drainage.

Hazel Creek is also remote. A visit to the creek requires anglers to put forth more effort than most trout streams in the southeastern United States. Only accessible by a long hike, boat ride, or horseback, Hazel Creek is not for those who don't want to commit at least a full day to fishing. Most visitors choose to camp in one of the many primitive campsites located along the stream. All campers must register for individual sites with the National Park Service before their trips, and popular sites—such as Bone Valley—get booked fairly quickly.

For the majority of anglers who visit Hazel Creek, a trip starts out at either the Lakeshore Trail trailhead at Fontana Dam or at the Fontana Village Boat Dock. The hike in from the dam is for those who like hiking as much as fishing. If walking in mountainous terrain for several hours does not appeal to you, then look into boat shuttles from the Fontana Village Boat Dock. The boat shuttles from the marina run on a regular schedule spring through fall and, during peak season, may require a reservation. For those who have their own watercraft, an easier lake crossing can be made from the Cable Cove boat ramp located almost directly across the lake from Hazel Creek. A small motorboat makes the lake crossing an easy endeavor; however, canoe and kayak enthusiasts make the crossing on a regular basis. Paddlers and boaters alike should be advised that the lower end of Fontana Lake can get rough in windy conditions, and the water depth in the main channel approaches 400 feet. A capsized boat here would mean a long swim to shore in deep water. Wearing personal floatation devices while crossing the lake is a must.

There are other ways to access Hazel Creek, as well. The first of these alternatives is to hike from Clingmans Dome, out the Appalachian Trail, and then down into Hazel Creek. Again, this is for folks who like to hike as much as fish, and this trip involves at least two nights of primitive camping to effectively fish.

The second alternative is to ride in on horseback. This approach is only recommended for anglers who own horses and have significant trail riding experience.

Hazel Creek is a large stream in comparison to most of the creeks that drain into the north shore of Fontana Lake. Its width, combined with its boulder-strewn pocketwater, gives Hazel almost twice the holding water of her sister streams,

Hazel Creek near Proctor, North Carolina. J.E.B. Hall

Kevin Howell re-rigging on the rhododendron lined banks of Hazel Creek. Mellissa Howell

Facing. David Howell enjoying a fall afternoon on Hazel Creek, low clear water in the fall can make the fish especially spooky. Kevin Howell

such as Eagle Creek or Twentymile Creek. As one would expect, more holding water means more fish. Most pockets with any depth to them—and almost all pools—hold fish—sometimes, even surprisingly large fish.

Large is a relative term in the Smokies. Sixteen inches is a large Smokies fish. An 18-inch fish is the fish of the year. Twenty inches is the fish of a lifetime. There are certainly some very large fish hiding in the deep pools, but fly anglers will probably never encounter them in a hooked-up scenario. Stories of fish landed that are longer than 25 inches are common, but should be taken very lightly.

Despite the lack of trophy trout, Hazel Creek still has lots of nice wild trout, and even some nice native brook trout in the higher elevation reaches of the watershed. In the fall, there are even a few fish that enter the stream from Fontana Lake to spawn. This isn't a huge run of fish that can be predicted, but it is something that can be enjoyed if one happens to be on the stream when it occurs.

From a technical standpoint, fishing on Hazel Creek is not difficult. Basic drys with or without droppers are all that are needed. Drift over pattern is the rule in the Smokies. As long as you can make a good drift, it doesn't really matter what pattern you are fishing. Conversely, anglers can have the most technical fly patterns, but if they can't effectively make dead drifts in pocketwater, they won't catch fish. There are certain fly patterns that work at certain times of year but none that are specific to the stream. No matter what flies anglers you choose to fish, staying mobile is critical. Three to four good drifts to a pocket or run will tell if there is an active fish present. If there is no interest, it is time to move to the next pocket. Standing in one pool all day on Hazel Creek will greatly reduce your chances for success.

▶ **Hatches:** The streams of the Smokies don't have the huge hatches that are found in other parts of the world. There are hatches but on a smaller scale. Spring hatches include quills, March Browns, caddisflies of all colors, Cahills, Yellow and Green Sallies, and a few drakes of one type, or another. Summer will see nightly stonefly hatches right at dark. Fall will bring caddisflies back on the menu, and as colder weather sets in, Blue-winged Olives and midges also appear.

▶ **Tackle:** Fly rods appropriate for Hazel Creek include 8 ½- to 9-foot fly rods that are 3- to 5-weight. The stream is wide enough that short sticks will hinder rather than help. Leaders should be in the 9- to 12-foot range and ending in

tippets no heavier than 4X. Fluorocarbon that is 5X is just about perfect for most applications. Fly patterns can be kept simple for Hazel Creek and most Smoky Mountain streams. Elk-hair Caddis, Parachute Adams, Palmers, and Stimulators are solid choices for dry flies. Pheasant Tails, Hare's Ears, and Copper Johns are good nymphs. Classic Smokies patterns, such as Thunderheads and Tellico Nymphs, work well, too. Throw in a few dark streamers for post-rain situations and your Hazel Creek fly box is complete.

Left. Vanessa Rollins displaying an average size Hazel Creek rainbow trout for the camera. Kevin Howell

Below. J.E.B. Hall fishing lower Hazel Creek. J.E.B. Hall

J.E.B. HALL is a full-time fly-fishing guide and instructor in Western North Carolina and East Tennessee for Davidson River Outfitters. In addition to guiding in the Southeast, J.E.B. has spent numerous summers guiding in Southwest Alaska for Alaska West and is a former operations manager for the Andros South Bonefish Lodge on South Andros Island in the Bahamas. J.E.B. is also the author of *The Southern Appalachian Fly Guide* and occasionally dabbles in photography.

J.E.B. Hall in NYC. J.E.B. Hall

CLOSEST FLY SHOPS

Tuckasegee Fly Shop
3 Depot Street
Bryson City, NC 28713
828 488 333
www.tuckflyshop.com

Brookings Cashiers Village Anglers
49 Pillar Dr.
Cashiers, NC 28717
828-743-3768
www.brookingsonline.com

Davidson River Outfitters
49 Pisgah Highway Suite 6
Pisgah Forest NC 28768
888-861-0111
www.davidsonflyfishing.com
info@davidsonflyfishing.com

CLOSEST GUIDES AND OUTFITTERS

Smoky Mountain Adventures
P.O. Box 995
Bryson City, NC 28715
828-736-7501
steve@steveclaxton.com
www.steveclaxton.com

Mac Brown
779 W. Deep Creek
Bryson City, NC 28713
macbrownflyfishing.com
macbrownflyfishing@gmail.com

CLOSEST LODGING

The Hike Inn
3204 Fontana Rd.
Fontana Dam, NC 28733
828-479-3677
hikeinn@graham.main.nc.us
www.thehikeinn.com

Fontana Village Resort
300 Woods Rd.
Fontana Dam, NC 28733
828-849-2258
info@fontanavillage.com
www.fontanavillage.com

Phillips Motel
290 Main St.
Robbinsville, NC 28771
828-479-3370
www.phillipsmotelonline.com

CLOSEST RESTAURANTS

Stecoah Diner
1751 North Carolina 28
Robbinsville, NC 28771
828-479-8430

Guayabitos Mexican Restaurant
236 North Carolina 19 S.
Bryson City, NC 28713
828-488-1336

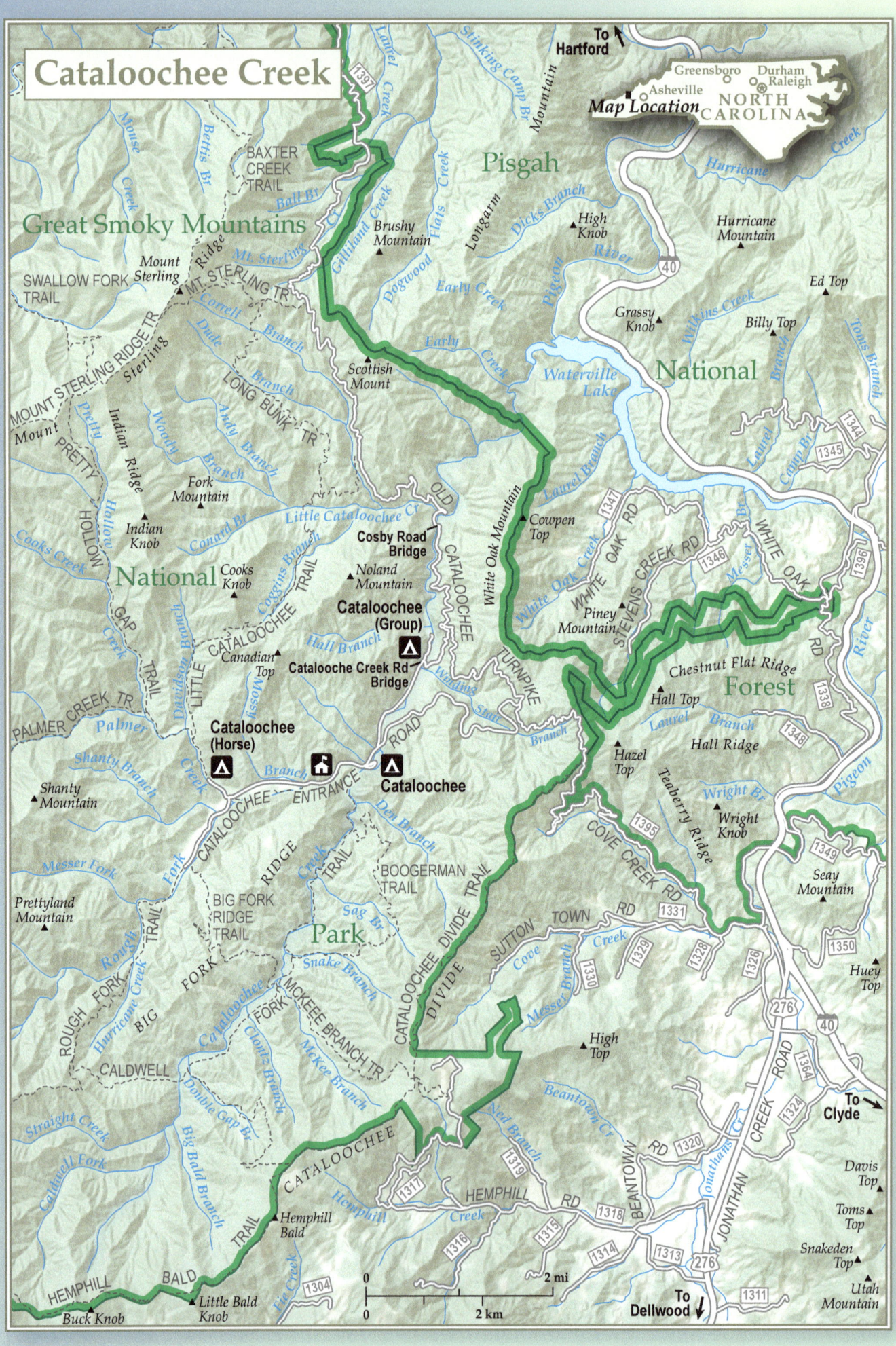

33 · Cataloochee Creek

➤ **Location:** Access to the Cataloochee Creek and the Cataloochee Valley is via Cove Creek Road and Old Cataloochee Turnpike Road (one and the same). Anglers should allow 45 minutes to make the 12-mile journey from Interstate 40 to the valley floor. Be very cautious because you will encounter large trucks towing horse trailers or campers coming out of the valley on a gravel road that is slightly better than a Sherpa path with blind curves, shear drop-offs, and steep grades. Travel time to the Cove Creek Road is about 30 minutes from Asheville, North Carolina, and 1 1/2 hours from Knoxville, Tennessee. For anglers flying into the area, the closest airport is Asheville Regional Airport.

The Cataloochee Valley is one of the most beautiful and remote areas in Great Smoky Mountains National Park. The valley is surrounded by the 5,000- to 6,000-foot-tall peaks of the Balsam Mountains to the east and Mt. Sterling to the west.

The valley was once the summer hunting and fishing grounds for the Cherokee Nation. The first settlers in the valley came to graze cattle and livestock on the grassy balds of the surrounding mountains and the valley floor. The valley offered abundant wildlife as well as farming opportunities and quickly grew into a thriving southern Appalachian community. By the beginning of the 20th century, the valley had grown to a population of nearly 750 people. Due to its remoteness, and later its induction into Great Smoky Mountain National Park, it did not suffer the logging and deforestation that was so rampant in the southern mountains in the late nineteenth and early twentieth centuries.

Cataloochee Creek is formed by Rough Fork, Palmer Creek, and Caldwell Fork (the latter two were named after the early settlers who lived in the area). Cataloochee Creek is approximately 7 1/2 miles long from the confluence of Rough Fork and Palmer Creek to its mouth at Waterville Lake. Cataloochee Creek can be divided into basically three sections:

- the lower section from Waterville Lake to the bridge on Old Cataloochee Turnpike (Cosby Road);
- the middle section from Old Cataloochee Turnpike Bridge upstream to the bridge on Cataloochee Creek Road adjacent to the Cataloochee Group Camp area
- The upper section (sometimes referred to as the meadows section), from Cataloochee Creek Road Bridge upstream to the confluence of Rough Fork and Palmer Creek

Upper Cataloochee Creek. Kevin Howell

A beautiful upper Cataloochee rainbow. Kevin Howell

Rainbow trout are the predominate fish in Cataloochee, along with some brown and a few brook trout. Anglers should expect the average fish to be in the 8- to 12-inch range with large fish in the 15- to 18-inch range. The exception is found on the lower end of the creek, where in the fall, anglers might encounter some larger trout that have traveled up the creek from Waterville Lake to spawn. These migratory fish rarely travel more than one mile or so upstream from the lake. The tributaries Rough Fork, Caldwell Fork, Palmer Creek, and Little Cataloochee Creek all offer excellent fishing for the angler who wants to take a 7-foot, 3-weight and a small dry fly out for a fun day on the water.

The lower section of the river, from Waterville Lake to North Carolina Highway 284 is the least pressured section of the entire river. Little Cataloochee Creek enters the main river about 500 feet downstream of the bridge, and beyond that point there are no trails and no access to the river other than bushwhacking your way through the rhododendron. This section is also populated with smallmouth bass in addition to trout. For the angler who has the desire to get away from the crowd, this is the place to do it.

The section from Cosby Road Bridge upstream to the Cataloochee Group Camp area is also extremely remote and tough to access. There are no trails, and the creek flows through a narrow gorge in this section. Anglers will have to fish through the entire two-mile length of stream, or they will have to bushwhack their way back down the edge of the river. There is no need to even try to scale the surrounding ridges, as you will spend hours (if not days) crawling through copperheads and poison ivy. Anglers will do better to utilize a friend, and leave one vehicle at the Group Camp Area and then drive a second vehicle around to the North Carolina Highway 284 Bridge and fish upstream to the group camp area. Be sure to allow a full day to fish through this section, as there is no other way to access the stream, and I would not recommend a cold night on the side of the stream in the Smokies.

The upper section from the Cataloochee Group Camp area upstream to the confluence of Rough Fork and Palmer Creek is the most heavily fished section on the creek. The creek flows through meadow pasture settings reminiscent of a western spring creek. Here, the first angler on the water will do well, and the following anglers will have to figure out what the first angler was not using in order to get a strike. In the summer, the meadows offer a great habitat for grasshoppers, crickets, and other terrestrials.

For its entire length, Cataloochee Creek is one of the clearest streams that most anglers will ever step into. Anglers

Above. Kevin Howell fishing Cataloochee Creek. Mellissa Howell
Inset. Cataloochee rainbow fooled by a caddis. David Knap

will be forced to fish 9- to 12-foot leaders tapered to at least 5X (if not 6X) tippet. While every good looking spot harbors several fish, anglers will often only catch one or two fish per decent hole, due to the spooky nature of the fish in the crystal clear water.

Anglers should note that the Cataloochee Valley is part of the Balsam Mountain range, which is classified as a deciduous rainforest and receives 80-plus inches of rainfall annually. Anglers should always be cognizant of stream levels. A cloudburst that occurs on the head of Palmer Creek some 20 miles away can easily send a 24-inch wall of water surging down Cataloochee Creek.

Due to the mountainous terrain, do not rely on cell phones, because you might have service on one side of the mountain and not on the other side. Also keep in mind if you do not have service, be sure to turn your phone off—otherwise, it will drain your battery, and when you do reach cell service, your phone will be dead.

There are no restaurants or lodging available inside the park boundary, other than Cataloochee Group Camp. If anglers are planning on camping, they need to make reservations well in advance and plan accordingly, as there is nothing simple about getting into or out of the Cataloochee Valley.

➤ **Hatches:** The spring (March through mid-June) offers the best fishing in Cataloochee Creek, as the higher water flows, combined with decent insect hatches, make for less spooky fish and easier fishing conditions. The fall also offers a spectacular time to fish Cataloochee. While the fish can be spooky because of low water, the changing leaves make for a spectacular vista. Summer in the meadows can be good with

Kevin Howell places a cast under overhanging rhododendron. Mellissa Howell

small hoppers and other terrestrial patterns; however, this is the most commonly fished section of the river, and you will also encounter people playing in the river in the meadow section, so go early and stay ahead of the crowd.

▶ **Regulations:** Park regulations state that anglers may have a five-fish aggregate limit of smallmouth bass, rainbow, brook, or brown trout. All fishing is artificial-lure, single-hook only. Minimum size on trout is 7 inches. Anglers should consult the current regulations at www.nps.gov/grsm/planyourvisit/fishing.htm prior to fishing for any current closures or regulation changes.

▶ **Tackle:** Cataloochee anglers will want a 4- to 5-weight fly rod for the main stem and a 2- to 4-weight fly rod for the smaller tributaries. Leaders should be at least 9 feet in length and taper to a 5–6X tippet. Hatches are sporadic, as the creek has a fairly high acidic level, which makes the trout very opportunistic feeders. A good presentation and accurate casting will catch more fish than the correct fly. Higher water levels will provide better fishing than the low water of midsummer. Anglers will find that most all of their regular trout flies will produce fish out of Cataloochee; however, anglers should always be sure they have a Green Weenie (#10–12), Texas Piss Ant (#12–16), and a Howell's Trip Saver handy when fishing on Cataloochee Creek.

*Right. Cataloochee brown trout.
Jeb Hall*

*Below. Caldwell Fork in the Fall.
David Knapp*

Bugling Cataloochee bull elk. David Knapp

KEVIN HOWELL—Kevin Howell is the owner of Davidson River Outfitters; he also is an author, lecturer, fly-fishing instructor, and guide. Kevin is a Signature fly Designer for Montana Fly Company. A 2018 inductee to the Fly Fishing Museum of the Southern Appalachians Hall of Fame and a 2018 inductee to the Legends of the Fly Hall of Fame as well. Kevin has been guiding the waters of North Carolina, South Carolina, and East Tennessee for 25 years. When not guiding he can be found fishing with his wife Mellissa, and sons David and Andrew.

Author Kevin Howell with an Argentina Brown Trout. Gonzalo Flego

CLOSEST FLY SHOPS

Davidson River Outfitters
49 Pisgah Hwy., Ste. 6
Pisgah Forest, NC 28768
888-861-0111
www.davidsonflyfishing.com

Hunter Banks
29 Montford Ave.
Asheville, NC 28801
828-252-3005
www.hunterbanks.com

CLOSEST GUIDES AND OUTFITTERS

Davidson River Outfitters
49 Pisgah Hwy., Ste. 6
Pisgah Forest, NC 28768
888-861-0111
www.davidsonflyfishing.com

Brookings Cashiers Village Anglers
49 Pillar Dr.
Cashiers, NC 28717
828-743-3768
www.brookingsonline.com

CLOSEST LODGING

Pisgah Inn
Milepost 408.6 Blue Ridge Pkwy.
Brevard, NC 28712
828-235-8228
info@pisgahinn.com
www.pisgahinn.com

Best Western Smoky Mountain Inn
130 Shiloh Trail
Waynesville, NC 28786
828-456-4402
www.bwsmokymountaininn.com

Cataloochee Campground, National Park Service
3576 Ranger Station Rd
Waynesville, NC 37876
828-497-9270

CLOSEST RESTAURANTS

Pisgah Inn
Milepost 408.6 Blue Ridge Pkwy.
Brevard, NC 28712
828-235-8228
info@pisgahinn.com
www.pisgahinn.com

Clyde's Restaurant
2107 S. Main St.
Waynesville, NC 28786
828-456-9135

Haywood Smokehouse
79 Elysinia Ave.
Waynesville, NC 28786
828-456-7275
info@haywoodsmokehouse.com
www.haywoodsmokehouse.com

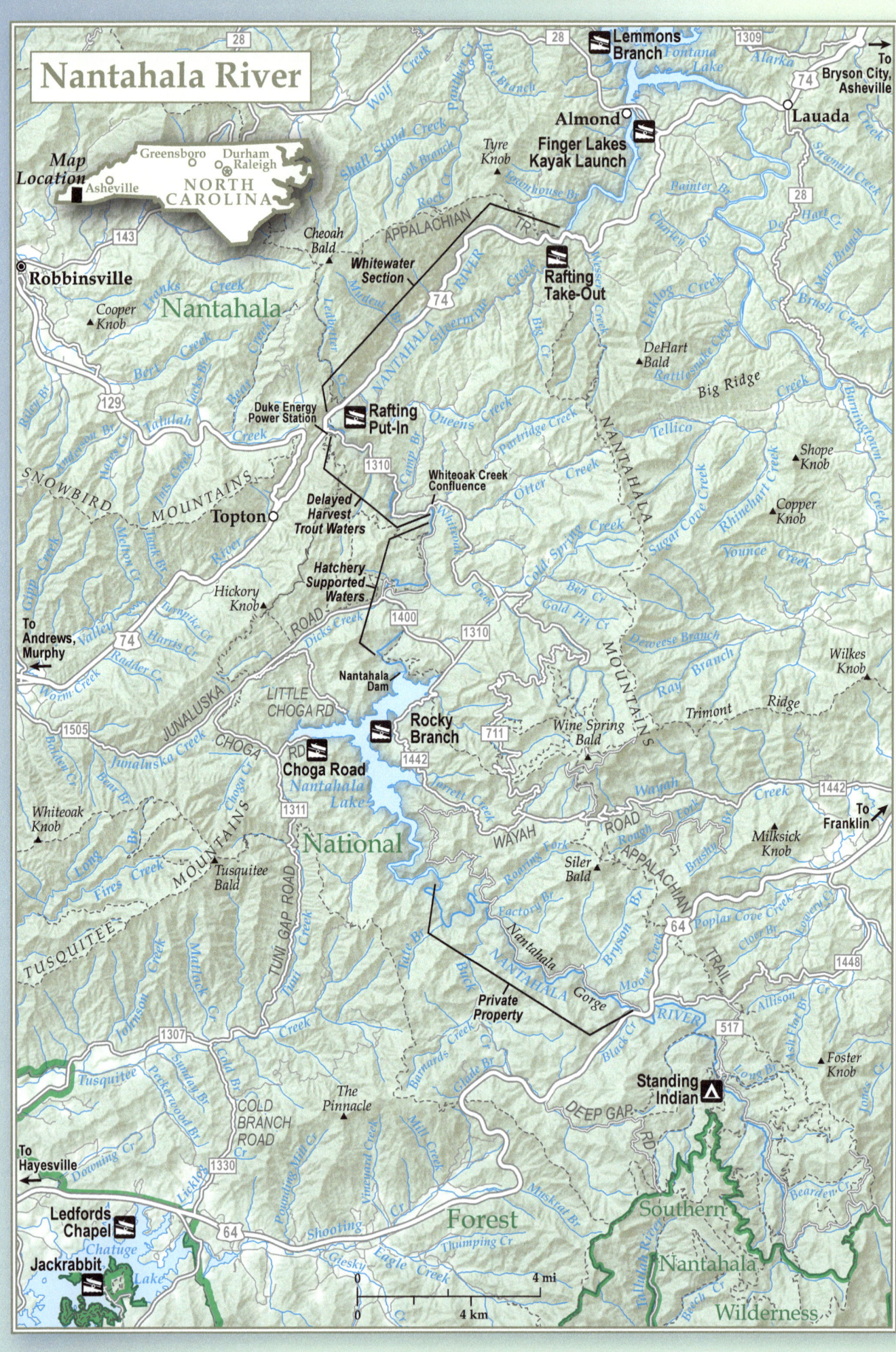

34 · Nantahala River

➤ **Location:** The Nantahala River is located in Western North Carolina, 15 minutes west of the town of Bryson City and about 1 1/2 hours west from the city of Asheville, North Carolina.

The Nantahala River is a unique Appalachian trout stream that features both tailwater and freestone trout fishing and can be thought of as having three distinct fisheries. The first of these stretches is found in the Standing Indian area upstream of North Carolina 64, between Franklin and Hayesville, North Carolina. This stretch is a wild-trout fishery on a small pocketwater-style stream. The fish here are relatively small but take flies readily. Anglers can also conveniently base themselves out of the Standing Indian Campground (located streamside). Between North Carolina 64 and Nantahala Lake, the stream is private and uninvited anglers should not attempt to access the river.

Below the lake, the river enters a deep gorge. The Nantahala Gorge is known as "the Land of the Noonday Sun," due to the lack of sunlight directly reaching the river during the day. The water here can be very cold, but in the lower eight miles of the stream, the low water temperature is not due to the lack of sun. This section of the Nantahala is a tailwater, and its source is the aforementioned Nantahala Lake, from which the water is piped out from deep in the reservoir and then sent through a penstock to a powerhouse. Water temperatures below the powerhouse stay between 49°F and 52°F throughout the year. The consistently cold water produces some fine year-round trout fishing and allows for excellent natural reproduction of the rainbows that live in the stream. There are also brown trout here of legendary proportions, and the Nantahala has been home to several state records.

Fishing in the tailwater is good whether the water is up from power generation or low when the generators are off, and it is one of two trout streams in North Carolina that can fished at night. (Wading during power generation is limited, and caution should be used when entering the river.) There are also numerous whitewater rafters and kayakers that utilize the section below the powerhouse for recreation. While it might seem as though their presence would harm the fishing, the trout don't seem to mind and can even be seen rising among the rafts during hatches.

When the water is low, the Nantahala can be safely waded almost anywhere, but the fish require a stealthier approach. Access points for the tailwater stretch can be found along North Carolina 74, from where the river enters Fontana Lake all the way up to the powerhouse.

Wade fishing the river requires no extra permitting beyond a valid North Carolina fishing license, but float anglers must obtain a U.S. Forest Service river permit. This permit

Fishing the upper Nantahala River. J.E.B. Hall

comes in the form of a wristband that can be attached to personal flotation devices or hats. Floating the river also comes with its own set of rules. The Forest Service requires all passengers in boats to wear their personal flotation devices at all times. They do check and they do ticket. The river itself requires those rowing it to have competent Class II through Class III river-running skills to navigate the many rapids found during times of power generation. The Nantahala is not floatable when there is no release from the powerhouse.

Above the powerhouse, there is another section of the Nantahala that is a semi-freestone fishery. The *semi-* comes from the fact that it is regulated by the dam that feeds the

Jeb Hall with an upper Nantahala trophy rainbow. J.E.B. Hall

tailwater section below, but its flow is mainly dependent on rain-fed tributaries throughout the watershed below the dam. It also happens to be the first Delayed Harvest stream designated in North Carolina. Since the early '90s, anglers from all over the South have flocked to this section of the Nantahala from October until June to enjoy the well-stocked catch-and-release fishing found here. The North Carolina Wildlife Resources Commission stocks in October, November, March, April, and May. The fish they put in are mix of rainbows, browns, and brook trout, with some of the fish stocked being more than photo worthy.

The streambed in this section is rough wading, and the upper reaches of the Delayed Harvest stretch are found in a deep gorge that contains Class V whitewater rapids after rain events. Fishing through this short gorge should only be attempted during times of low water. If the water looks high, anglers should stick to other stretches of the Delayed Harvest section.

▶ **Hatches:** The Nantahala has some excellent hatches. The tailwater section sees most of the insect activity, with the most significant hatches occurring in spring. Quills, March Browns, Hendricksons, caddisflies of all varieties, Yellow Sallies, Golden Stones, and even Giant Eastern Salmonflies can be found hatching in spring. These hatches are often best midday while the water is flowing from the powerhouse and the whitewater rafters are out on the river. Evening hatches can be good in summer, with Yellow Sallies being the staple insect. Fall brings caddisflies, both tan and black, along with the return of the Blue-winged Olives. As colder weather comes on, the Blue-winged Olives dominate the menu, especially on overcast days with a little precipitation.

▶ **Tackle:** A 9-foot, 4-weight or 5-weight fly rod is good for the Nantahala. Czech Nymph anglers prefer a 10-foot rod. Short fly rods make fishing the large tailwater portion almost impossible, but they do have a place on the Delayed

Harvest section and in the wild-trout waters above Standing Indian area. Tailwater fish require 6–7X fluorocarbon tippets when the water is low and long leaders of at least 10 feet in length. Streamers should be fished on tippets no lighter than 4X. Sinking poly leaders will also help during times of power generation. Delayed Harvest fish are less picky, and anglers can get away with shorter leaders and heavier tippets. Fly boxes for the tailwater section should include a variety of small beadhead nymphs, as well as more technical dry flies and a variety of midges. Anglers looking to chase large brown trout should bring large streamers, especially patterns that imitate small rainbow trout and sculpins. Delayed Harvest boxes should comprise basic drys, flashy nymphs, and egg patterns.

Left. Upper Nantahala. J.E.B. Hall

Below. Guide Walker Parrott shows a lower Nantahala brown for Wes Humphries. Amanda Bushon

Above. Walker Parrott with a Nantahala brown. Amanda Bushon

Left. Jeb Hall highsticks a run on the upper Nantahala. J.E.B. Hall

J.E.B. HALL is a full-time fly-fishing guide and instructor in Western North Carolina and East Tennessee for Davidson River Outfitters. In addition to guiding in the Southeast, J.E.B. has spent numerous summers guiding in Southwest Alaska for Alaska West and is a former operations manager for the Andros South Bonefish Lodge on South Andros Island in the Bahamas. J.E.B. is also the author of *The Southern Appalachian Fly Guide* and occasionally dabbles in photography.

J.E.B. Hall in NYC. Jeb Hall

CLOSEST FLY SHOPS

Tuckaseegee Fly Shop
3 Depot Street
Bryson City, NC 28713
828-488-3333
www.tuckflyshop.com
tuckriverclub@gmail.com

Hunter Banks
29 Montford Ave.
Asheville, NC 28801
828-252-3005
www.hunterbanks.com

CLOSEST GUIDES AND OUTFITTERS

Smoky Mountain Adventures
P.O. Box 995
Bryson City, NC 28715
828-736-7501
steve@steveclaxton.com
www.steveclaxton.com

Mac Brown
779 W. Deep Creek
Bryson City, NC 28713
828-736-1469
macbrownflyfish@gmail.com
www.macbrownflyfish.com

Davidson River Outfitters
49 Pisgah Hwy., Ste. 6
Pisgah Forest, NC 28768
888-861-0111
www.davidsonflyfishing.com

CLOSEST LODGING

Nantahala Outdoor Center
13077 W. North Carolina 19
Bryson City, North Carolina 28713
828- 785-4840
www.noc.com

CLOSEST RESTAURANTS

River's End Restaurant at Nantahala Outdoor Center
13077 W. North Carolina 19
Bryson City, NC 28713
828- 488-7172
www.noc.com/places/restaurants/rivers-end-restaurant

Big Wesser BBQ & Brew at Nantahala Outdoor Center
(open May–September)
13077 W. North Carolina 19
Bryson City, NC 28713
828- 488-7174
www.noc.com/places/restaurants/big-wesser-bbq-brew

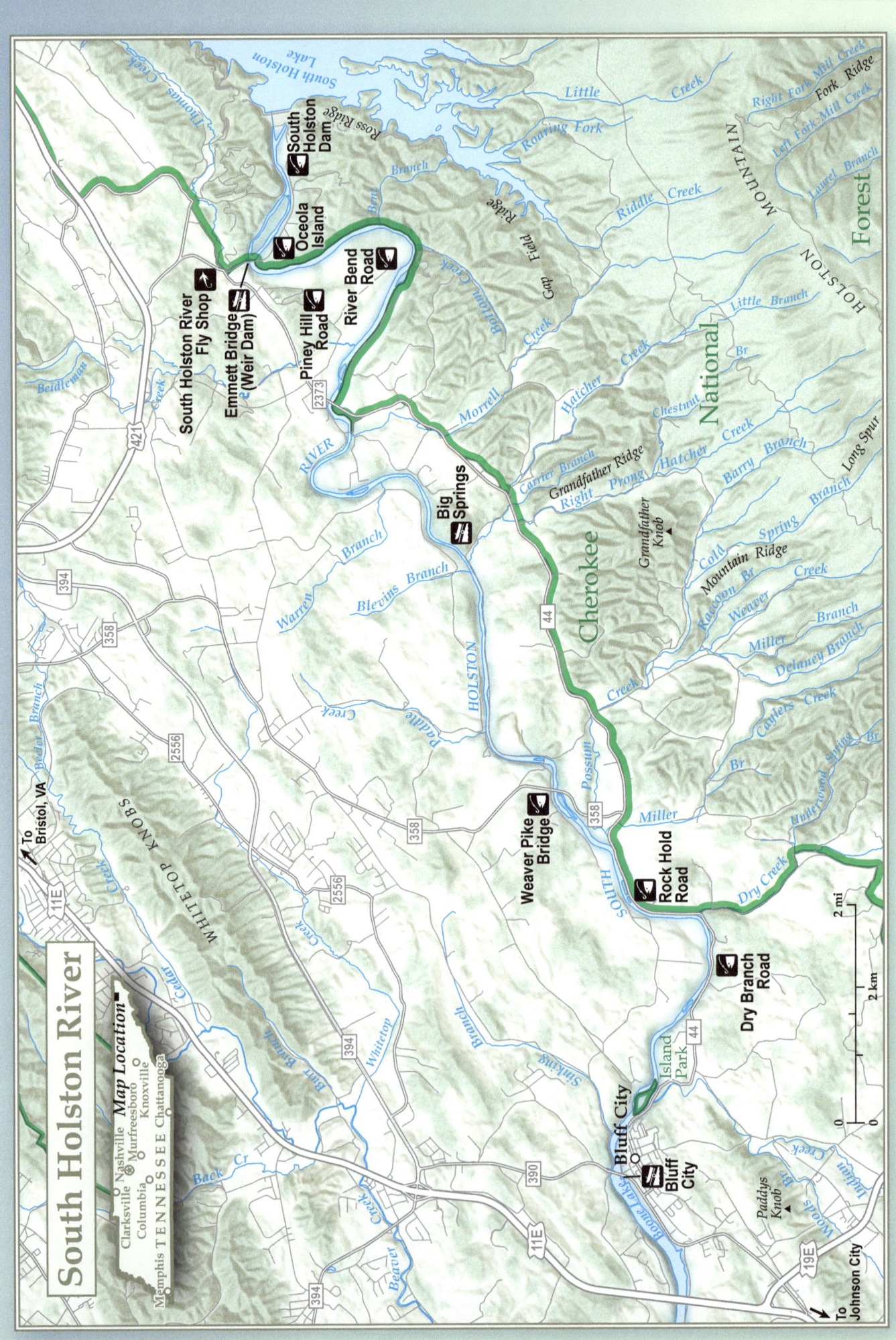

35 · South Holston River

➤ **Location:** The South Holston River flows from South Holston Lake west to Boone Lake near Bluff City, Tennessee, approximately 30 minutes northeast of Johnson City, Tennessee.

Affectionately referred to as "the SoHo," the South Holston River might possibly be the most famous of all southern trout streams. Known for its mayfly hatches and large resident brown trout, the South Holston offers local anglers a taste of out west-style trout fishing. The first thing visiting anglers will notice about the South Holston is its size. The river is wide in most places and trout can be observed feeding from bank to bank during the lower water periods between power generations. There are several access points from which to enter the river along the road, from Bluff City up to the South Holston Dam. The more popular ones, such as the "Cul-de-sac" and the "Powerlines," are managed by the Tennessee Wildlife Resources Agency (TWRA) and have dedicated parking spaces for anglers. Others are merely unmarked gravel pull-outs. Most of the river flows through private property and all no-trespassing signs should be heeded.

While most of this large tailwater river is wadable at low water, a release from the powerhouse makes it only fishable by boat. Wade anglers should be sure to check the latest TVA generation schedules before visiting the SoHo and stay vigilant for any changes in water levels while fishing. Wade fishers should also use caution when walking on the limestone bedrock ledges. The slick nature of the rocks themselves, combined with the slimy algae that covers them, has led to even sure-footed anglers taking an impromptu swim.

Floating the SoHo might be the most romantic way to see the river. A release from the dam turns the riverbed into a fast-flowing sheet of clear water and makes for an easy row in a drift boat or raft. There are even some sections that are fishable by motorboat, but poor etiquette has caused some powerboat anglers to make enemies among the driftboat crowd.

There are a few access points on the river for launching watercraft. The public ramps are located just below the labyrinth weir (a "folded" manmade structure that alters water flow by adding oxygen to the water) at the top of the tailwater and at the bottom where the river enters Boone Lake in Bluff City. There are a few other private ramps that are

Anglers often use their boats to navigate between wading locations on the South Holston. Josh Pfeiffer

accessible for a fee at other points along the river. These private ramps make for shorter floats and help anglers avoid areas closed for brown trout spawning in winter.

For trout anglers who like a little more adventure, the SoHo has a nocturnal treat that isn't for the faint of heart. It so happens that the brown trout here love to take mouse patterns fished at night. As glamorous as it seems, night fishing requires deft wading, solid boat handling, and a sixth sense to predict the take. If you don't mind losing a night's sleep for the chance of landing a giant brown, night mousing the South Holston is certainly worth the effort.

➤ **Hatches:** What makes the SoHo so unique is the aquatic insect life that it breeds. In mid- to late spring, Sulphur mayflies begin to hatch on the river. Anglers will notice that some of the insects have an orange-yellow tint, while others have a light greenish yellow coloring. The color variation comes from the fact that all of these "Sulphurs" are actually two different species of mayflies. Some days, the greenish Pale Evening Duns are hatching, while other days the orange Sulphurs are hatching, and there are times when both can be found on the river.

The trout here receive enough pressure that fly color matters, and during hatches they will often lock into feeding on one color over the other. More importantly, anglers should focus on fishing patterns that imitate the mayflies at the life cycle stage on which the trout are currently feeding. While

Facing, Wading fishing offers great dry fly fishing on the South Holston. J.E.B. Hall

Above. Landing a winter time rainbow on the SoHo. J.E.B. Hall

there may be numerous adult Sulphurs in the air, the trout might only eat an emerger or a cripple pattern tied with the proper shade of yellow dubbing. Drys should be properly tied, as well.

The mayflies here seem to have wings that are larger than their body size. In the air, they can appear to be size 14 or size 16, but when captured and stretched out on a hook shank, the insects' bodies are a hook size smaller. This slight variation in pattern sizing can make all the difference.

In addition to Sulphurs, the SoHo also has solid Blue-winged Olive hatches during the colder months, crane flies in summer, and an ever-present midge population that hatches throughout the year. The Blue-winged Olives are similar to the Sulphurs in that their imitations should match the real thing perfectly for successful fishing. Scuds are also present in large numbers in the South Holston and are a major food source for the trout that live there. No SoHo fly box would be complete without a few scud patterns tied in smaller sizes.

➤ **Tackle** Due to the open nature of the SoHo, anglers should come armed with rods in lengths from 8 1/2 to 10 feet. Rod weights can vary from 2 to 6, depending on the situation, but 4-weight and 5-weight rods will handle most situations. Leaders should be at least 9 feet in length, but 10- to 12-foot leaders aren't out of the question at low water. Due to the pressured nature of the river, tippets for fishing drys and nymphs should be no heavier than 5X, with 6X fluorocarbon being preferable.

Above. Beautiful SoHo brown. J.E.B. Hall

Right. Chunky South Holston rainbow. Josh Pfeiffer

J.E.B. HALL is a full-time fly-fishing guide and instructor in western North Carolina and East Tennessee for Davidson River Outfitters. In addition to guiding in the Southeast, J.E.B. has spent numerous summers guiding in Southwest Alaska for Alaska West and is a former operations manager for the Andros South Bonefish Lodge on South Andros Island in the Bahamas. J.E.B. is also the author of *The Southern Appalachian Fly Guide* and occasionally dabbles in photography.

J.E.B. Hall in NYC. J.E.B. Hall

CLOSEST FLY SHOPS

Eastern Fly Outfitters
6209 Bristol Hwy.
Piney Flats, TN 37686
423- 538-3007
efo@easternflyoutfitters.com
www.easternflyoutfitters.com

Virginia Creeper Fly Shop
16501 Jeb Stuart Hwy.
Abingdon, VA 24211
276- 628-3826
vcflyshop@embarqmail.com
www.vcflyshop.com

Mahoney's
830 Sunset Dr.
Johnson City, TN 37604
423- 282-5413
www.mahoneysports.com

CLOSEST GUIDES AND OUTFITTERS

Davidson River Outfitters
49 Pisgah Highway Suite 6
Pisgah Forest, NC 28768
888-861-0111
www.davidsonflyfishing.com
info@davidsonflyfishing.com

Altamont Anglers
828- 698-5250
www.altamontanglers.com

Mike Adams Fly Fishing Outfitters
2914 Watauga Rd., #304
Johnson City, TN 37601
423- 741-4789
adamsflyfishing@gmail.com
www.adamsflyfishing.com

CLOSEST LODGING

South Holston River Lodge
1509 Bullock Hollow Rd.
Bristol, TN 37620
877- 767-7875
www.southholstonriverlodge.com

Hampton Inn
340 Commerce Dr.
Abingdon, VA 24211
276- 619-4600

Hampton Inn
508 North State of Franklin Rd.
Johnson City, TN 37604
423- 929-8000
www.hamptoninnjohnsoncity.com

CLOSEST RESTAURANTS

Bonefire Smokehouse
260 W. Main St.
Abingdon, VA 24210
276- 623-0037

Cootie Brown's
2715 N. Roan St.
Johnson City, TN 37601
423- 283-4723

Cheddar's Casual Cafe
3000 Franklin Ter.
Johnson City, TN 37604
423- 262-0087

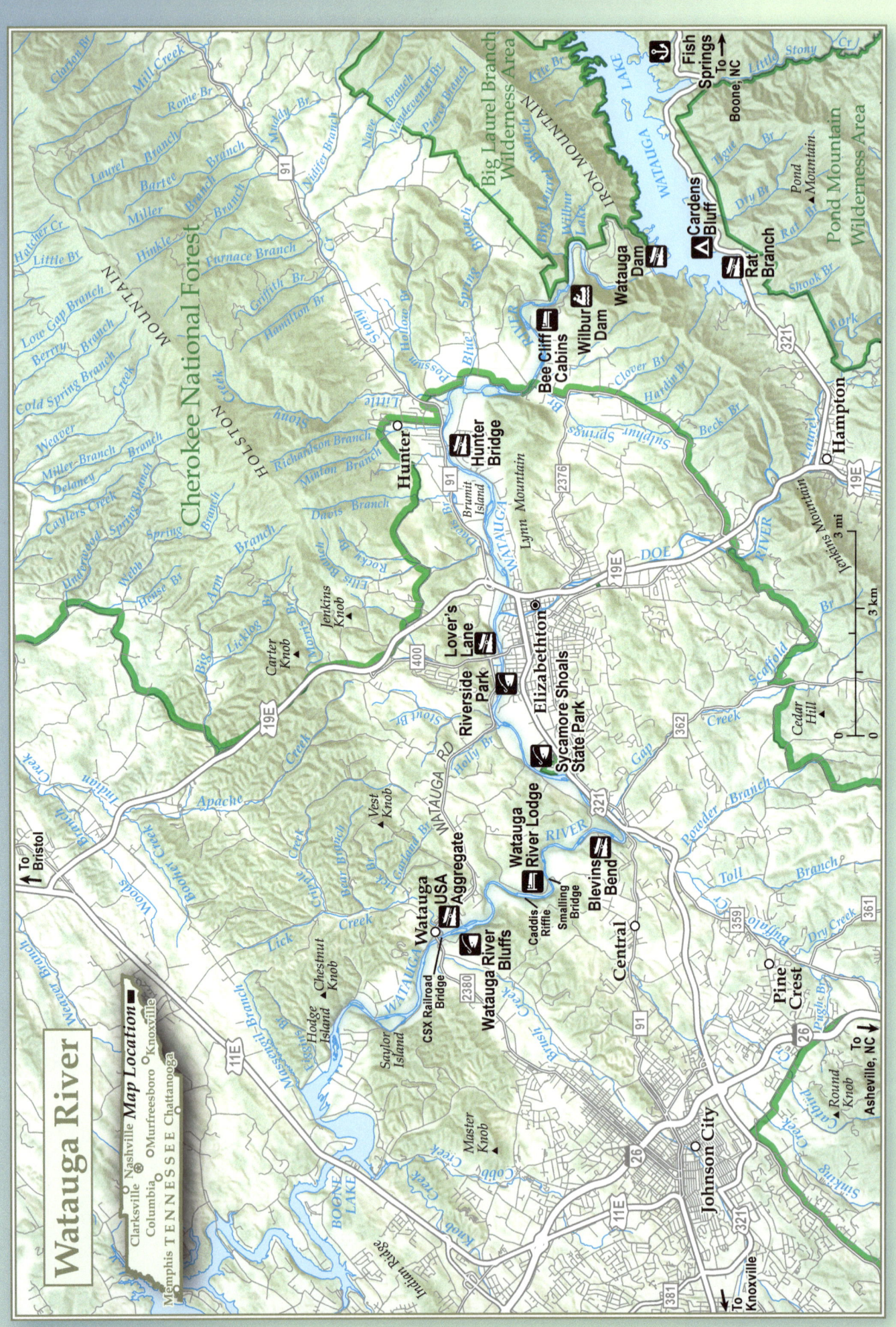

36 · Watauga River

➤ **Location:** The Watauga is located near Boone, North Carolina, and flows to Elizabethton, Tennessee. Travel time is two to three hours from Charlotte, North Carolina, about 1 hour from Asheville, North Carolina, and two to three hours from Knoxville, Tennessee. Anglers can fly via commercial flights into Asheville, North Carolina, or Tri-Cities Regional Airport in Tennessee.

The Watauga begins life high in the Blue Ridge Mountains, under the Blue Ridge Parkway. On its run to Boone Lake, outside Johnson City, Tennessee, the river undergoes several transitions. From Boone Fork down the mountain and to the valley town of Valle Crucis, North Carolina, the river is predominately a trout fishery. Once on the valley floor, the river warms primarily due to its agricultural surroundings and small riparian buffer. From Valle Crucis downstream to Watauga Lake, the river is predominately a warmwater fishery for rock bass (redeye bass or goggle eyes), smallmouth bass, carp, and similar species. As the river leaves Watauga Lake, it spills directly into Wilbur Lake, which has a low water discharge forming the tailwater section of the Watauga River.

While the North Carolina section of the river offers good fishing for trout and bass, anglers will find that a lot of the river is privately owned and access can be an issue. Therefore, most anglers focus on fishing the Tennessee side of the river.

The discharge of Wilbur Dam is regulated by the TVA and they maintain a minimal flow release throughout the summer. This flow, combined with the deepwater release, provides a mean summertime water temperature of 51–54°F. for the entire length of the tailwater, from Wilbur Dam to the mouth of Boone Lake. In addition to the minimal flow, additional discharge is driven by power demand, rain events, and maintenance issues. A large summer rain event or heavy thunderstorm on the head of the Doe River can muddy the river downstream of Elizabethton for a couple of days. If the TVA is generating water, anglers can float upstream of Elizabethton.

The vast majority of land surrounding the Watauga is private, effectively eliminating wade fishing on most of the river outside of the TWRA access areas. The only public wade access locations are at the Sycamore Shoals State Park, the TWRA access points. For those anglers staying at the Ledges

The view from the bow. Nick Roberts

Lodge, Watauga River Lodge, and Bee Cliff Cabins, some of the campgrounds offer limited wading access—any other access will require landowners' permission.

The Watauga is characterized by long, deep, flat pools and small shoals and riffles. In the long pools, anglers can usually find pods of trout rising to small midges, Blue-winged Olives, or Sulphurs. While small nymphs, like a Howell's Memory Maker or Split Case Nymph in size 16, will usually produce fish, larger trout can be taken on streamers (especially in times of high water or when the river is under generation). However, anglers who are streamer fishing in

Zach Smith with a Watagua River brown. Kevin Howell

the summertime need to be prepared for the fight of their lives because striped bass from Boone Lake will push upriver as far as the Blevins Road TWRA Access during the summer months. A large striper (25–40 pounds) that engulfs a white streamer being fished on a 6-weight will test the nerves and skills of even the best angler.

The Watauga has several launch sites. The most common launch site is the Blevins Road TWRA Access, which offers a float downstream to the TWRA access on Wagner Road (an old steam plant) or down to Boone Lake. However, the takeout at Boone Lake is through a private campground, and anglers will need to secure permission to take out prior to launch. Above Blevins Road, anglers can launch at the TWRA access at Wilbur Dam, at Lynn Valley Bridge and Lover's Lane under the North Carolina 37 bridge. However, the river above Blevins Road is difficult to float unless the river is under generation.

▶ **Hatches:** The Watauga, like most tailwaters, has some great hatches. Small mayflies, like Sulphurs and Blue-winged Olives, are the most prominent insects, with caddisflies following closely behind. Anglers will want a good selection of nymphs in sizes 16–22 and drys ranging in the same size. During the summer months, terrestrials will also produce a lot of fish. During times of generation, the river will turn a slightly milky color, and anglers can use larger nymphs in sizes ranging from 12 to 16, as well as heavier tippets in the 3–5X range.

▶ **Regulations:** For any combination of trout species, the daily limit is seven fish. There is no minimum length. The exceptions to this are that only two trout in a creel can be lake trout and that the minimum length of brook trout is 6 inches.

Watauga River (Quality Trout Fishing Area; Smallings Bridge downstream to CSX railroad bridges)—14-inch minimum length, two trout creel limit. Use or possession of any bait is prohibited. Trout less than 14 inches may not be in possession.

Above. Linda Michael fishing the famed caddis riffle on the Watauga. Kevin Howell

▶ **Tackle:** A 9-foot, 4- to 5-weight rod is the most common selection for the Watauga. Anglers should match a good floating fly line with a 9- to 12-foot leader. Lighter tippets, in the 6–7X range, will generate more strikes but will also usually end up in more lost fish and flies. Most fishermen carry two rods—one rigged with a double-nymph rig 3–7 feet under an indicator, with the second rod rigged with a small dry fly to match the current hatch. Anglers that are streamer fishing may want to use a 6- to 7-weight rod (especially during the summer months), in the event that they encounter striped bass. Streamer fishermen should also carry a 250- to 300-grain sinking line in addition to a floating fly line.. Because the water is quite cold, waders are highly recommended.

Rainbows this size can make any angler happy. Kevin Howell

Above. Kate Wagonlander nymphing a run. Kevin Howell

Below. The Watauga produces happy fish and anglers. Kevin Howell.

The Watauga is full of prime trout habitat like this riffle loaded with broken rocks and wood debris. Kevin Howell

KEVIN HOWELL—Kevin Howell is the owner of Davidson River Outfitters; he also is an author, lecturer, fly-fishing instructor, and guide. Kevin is a Signature fly Designer for Montana Fly Company. A 2018 inductee to the Fly Fishing Museum of the Southern Appalachians Hall of Fame and a 2018 inductee to the Legends of the Fly Hall of Fame as well. Kevin has been guiding the waters of North Carolina, South Carolina, and East Tennessee for 25 years. When not guiding he can be found fishing with his wife Mellissa, and sons David and Andrew.

Kevin Howell with a nice Argentinian brown. Gonzalo Flego

CLOSEST FLY SHOPS

Hunter Banks
29 Montford Ave.
Asheville, NC 28801
828-252-3005
www.hunterbanks.com

Mahoney's
830 Sunset Dr.
Johnson City, TN 37604
423-282-5413
www.mahoneysports.com

CLOSEST GUIDES AND OUTFITTERS

Davidson River Outfitters
49 Pisgah Highway Suite 6
Pisgah Forest, NC 28768
888-861-0111
www.davidsonflyfishing.com
info@davidsonflyfishing.com

One Fly Outfitters
112 Cherry St,
Black Mountain, NC 28711
828-669-6939
www.oneflyoutfitters.com

Watauga River Lodge & Outfitter
643 Smalling Rd.
Watauga, TN 37694
828-208-3428
booking@wataugariverlodge.com
www.wataugariverlodge.com

CLOSEST LODGING

Watauga River Lodge & Outfitter
643 Smalling Rd.
Watauga, TN 37694
828-208-3428
booking@wataugariverlodge.com
www.wataugariverlodge.com

Bee Cliff Cabins
141 Steel Bridge Rd.
Elizabethton, TN 37643
423-542-6033
www.beecliffcabins.com

Watauga River Cabins
720 Smalling Rd.
Johnson City, TN 37601
800-334-6720
www.whiddenflyfishinglodge.com

Holiday Inn Express
2 Orr Ct.
Johnson City, TN 37615
423-328-0500

Misty Waters Bait and Camping
246 Wilbur Dam Rd.
Elizabethton, TN 37643
423-543-1702

CLOSEST RESTAURANTS

Cootie Brown's
2715 N. Roan St.
Johnson City, TN 37601
423-283-4723

Creekers BBQ
256 Tennessee 91
Elizabethton, TN 37643
423-542-2272

Beef 'O' Brady's
173 Hudson Dr.
Elizabethton, TN 37643
423-543-3399
www.beefobradys.com

CLOSEST HOSPITALS OR URGENT CARE

Wellmont Urgent Care
378 Marketplace Blvd., #5
Johnson City, TN 37601
423-282-0751
www.wellmont.org

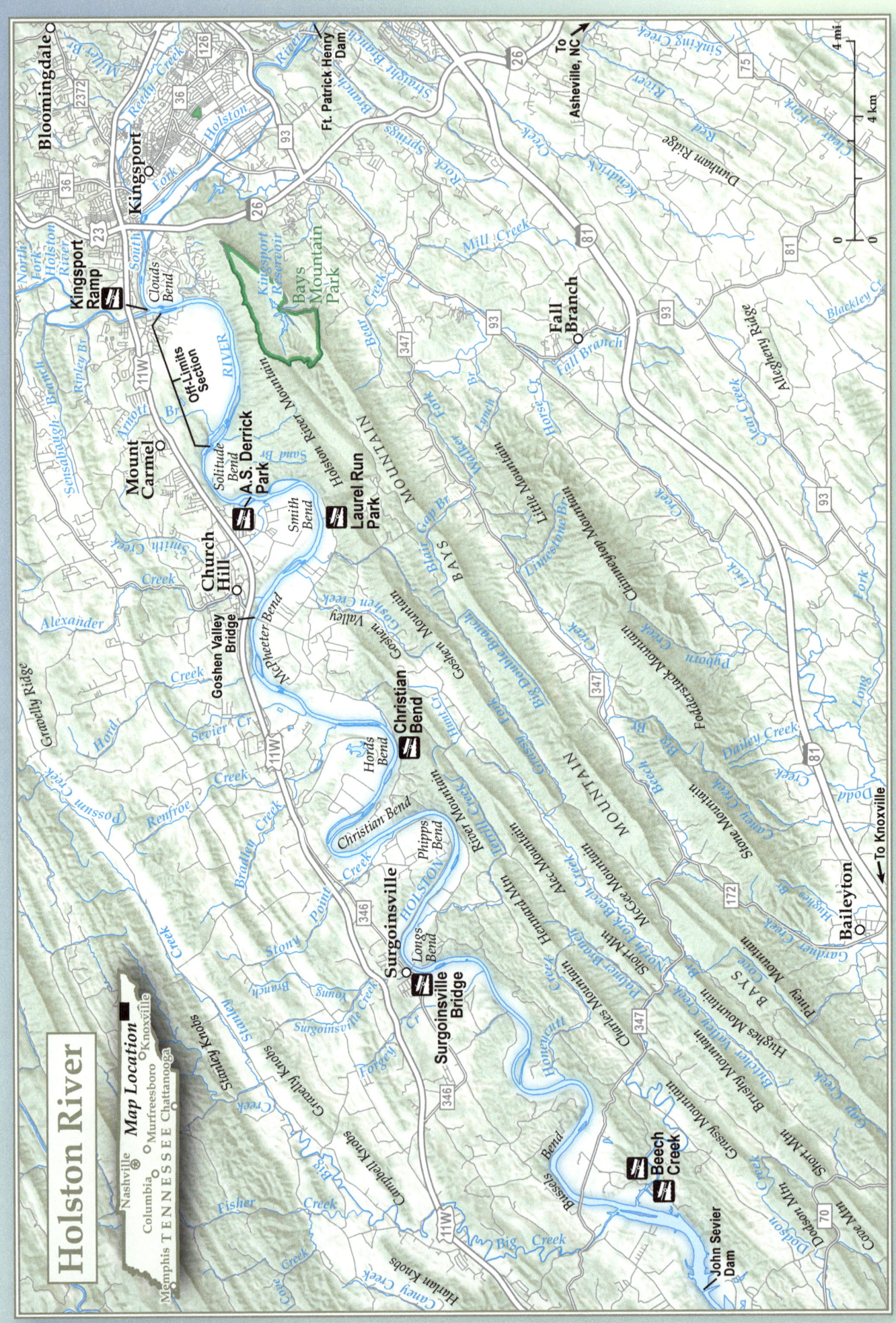

37 · Holston River

➤ **Location:** The Holston River is located in northeast Tennessee, about one hour and twenty minutes from Asheville, North Carolina, about two hours from Knoxville, Tennessee; about four hours from Charlotte, North Carolina, and six hours from Washington, D.C. You can fly in commercially or privately to fish on the Holston River via Asheville, North Carolina, or Tri-Cities Regional Airport in Tennessee.

The Holston River proper is one of the most varied rivers you will ever cast a fly line on, being considered a tailwater river with a mild influence from the free-flowing North Fork of the Holston River. It is a truly unique fishery that offers anglers year-round opportunities for smallmouth bass. The spring, summer, and fall seasons are the primary concentrations by anglers, but there are many respectable days for hooking into trophy bronzebacks throughout the winter months.

This gentle giant river gets its humble beginnings from three different locations in Southwest Virginia.

- The North Fork of the Holston runs to the southwest from Sharon Springs in Bland County.
- The Middle Fork of the Holston flows from near the western border of Wythe County and joins the South Fork of the Holston southwest of Abingdon.
- The South Fork begins near Sugar Grove in Smyth County.

The Middle and South Forks combine and flow through South Holston Lake, then on to Boone Lake and finally Fort Patrick Henry Lake before joining with the North Fork on the western end of Kingsport, Tennessee. From this confluence, the three forks flow toward the upper end of Cherokee Lake.

The flows on the Holston River are regulated by the TVA through the Fort Patrick Henry Dam. The water release schedules from the Fort Patrick Henry Dam are to keep the necessary water levels required by the various industries that draw water from the river as it flows through the city of Kingsport, Tennessee. This results in ebbing and flowing conditions on the Holston River while other undammed rivers are at the mercy of weather conditions for their water levels.

The water in the Holston River in the summer averages 70–79°F. During the winter months, the river never drops lower than the 48–55°F. range. This is made possible due to the warmwater discharges from those same industries that make the water draws from the river.

The Holston River encompasses a large drainage basin. The heavy summer storms can cause the many small creeks running through the riverside farm fields as well as the free-flowing North Fork of the Holston to deteriorate the river, making fishing conditions unfavorable. The river will usually clear after a 24- to 36-hour period of no precipitation.

The rainbows below Cherokee dam are more likely to be encountered in the shoals and more oxygenated water. Josh Pfiefer, Frontier Anglers Tennessee

Above. The Cherokee Dam anglers will find a mix of rainbow trout and smallmouth bass. Josh Pfiefer, Frontier Anglers, Tennessee

The Holston River offers anglers a wide range on how they would like to fish for smallmouth bass. When arriving riverside, anglers are always surprised at the size of this water. With a number of sections nearing 200 yards in width, it is quite possibly one of the largest smallmouth rivers in the Southeast. Because of the limited access points on the Holston River proper, anglers should be prepared for an extended day of fishing. The Holston River is best experienced from watercraft such as canoes, kayaks, fishing rafts, and drift boats. There are very limited wading opportunities available from the public access points, due to the river's depth at the areas. While floating the river, there will be areas that you can pull your craft into the shallows, then get out and enjoy a wade experience.

There are the long runs of rise-and-fall limestone shoals where you will find these river predators. They will be staged in the deeper drops or will be sunning themselves on the tops of the shoals, depending on their attitude for that day. These shoals are in two distinct sections of the river. The first grouping is just below where the float trips start at A. S. Derrick Park, a boat launching ramp and walking park run by the city of Church Hill, Tennessee. The trips start at this ramp due to the off-limits section upriver from there containing the Holston Army Ammunition Plant. These shoals continue for almost four miles, floating past Laurel Run Park. There is a county-run park and boat ramp, but the access is limited from 8:00 A.M. to dusk. (This park is well-known because the movie *The River* was filmed here in the mid '80s.)

When reaching Goshen Valley Bridge, this first grouping ends. Shoals are a prime habitat for the smallmouth bass's favorite food source, crawdads. Many times, when landing your fish, you will see their mouths filled with them, and yet they still hit your presentation. You will want to anchor up and spend considerable time in these shoal sections to effectively work them.

Once at Goshen Valley Bridge, the river takes on a slow-moving lake atmosphere. The river depths begin running from 12 to 15 feet in depth. Along the banks in this lake section, there is great bass holding habitat, mainly consisting of large rock boulders blasted into the river as they built the CSX rail line on the bluff above the river. There is also a good amount of timber interspersed among the boulders along the riverbanks that give you the opportunity to throw a topwater presentation looking for that explosive bite.

The annual growth of the grass flats starts showing up in late June to early July. The next short zone through Goshen Valley gives you the opportunity to work the undulating grasses where this mighty predator can hide and ambush its prey.

From here, the river goes back to its up-and-down shoal personality. It meanders along to the next river access ramp, which is operated by TWRA at Christian Bend. The shoals continue for ten more river miles through Phipps Bend before coming to another TWRA river access ramp at the town of Surgoinsville, Tennessee.

Smallmouth fishing on the Holston is best in the summer months but with little shade anglers have to take precautions from the sun. Josh Pfeiffer, Frontier Anglers, Tennessee

Anglers can expect to find good sized bass along the shaded banks in the woody debris.
Josh Pfiefer, Frontier Anglers Tennessee

Smallmouth trips down the Holston River proper offer great experiences for everyone, from the beginner to the hard-core bass angler.

▶ **Regulations:** On the Holston River from John Sevier Dam upstream to North Fork Holston River, the protected length range for smallmouth bass is 13–17 inches, with a creel limit of five black bass. Only one smallmouth bass in the creel is allowed to be greater than 17 inches.

▶ **Tackle:** A 9-foot 4-5 weight rod is the most common selection for the Watauga. Anglers should match a good floating fly line with a 9- to 12-foot leader. Lighter tippets in the 6-7X range will generate more strikes, but will also usually end up in more lost fish and flies. Most fishermen carry two rods:

- One rod rigged with a double nymph rig 3-8 feet under an indicator
- One rod rigged with a small dry fly to match the current hatch

Anglers who are streamer fishing might want to use a 6-7 weight rod especially during the summer months in the event that they encounter striped bass. Streamer fishermen should also carry a 250-300 grain sinking line in addition to a floating fly line. Waders are needed only during winter trips.

RANDY RATLIFF guides on the South Holston, Watauga, Holston tailwaters, and mountain streams of East Tennessee. Besides being a well-known guide, he is an accomplished fly tier. When not on the water, Randy will be at the vice, tying his proven local patterns for trout and smallmouth, as well as working on innovative new designs.

Randy Ratliff

CLOSEST FLY SHOPS

Mahoney's
830 Sunset Dr.
Johnson City, TN 37604
423-282-5413
www.mahoneysports.com

Davidson River Outfitters
95 Pisgah Hwy.
Pisgah Forest, NC 28768
888-861-0111
www.davidsonflyfishing.com

Hunter Banks
29 Montford Ave.
Asheville, NC 28801
828-252-3005
www.hunterbanks.com

CLOSEST GUIDES AND OUTFITTERS

East Tennessee on the Fly
Adam Campbell
423-220-0230
www.easttnonthefly.com

CLOSEST LODGING

Pappaw's Fishing Pad
298 Old Weaver Pike
Bluff City, TN 37625
423-534-1203
www.pappawsfishingpad.com

Bee Cliff Cabins
141 Steel Bridge Rd.
Elizabethton, TN 37643
423-542-6033
www.beecliffcabins.com

Comfort Suites
3118 Browns Mill Rd.
Johnson City, TN 37604
423-610-0010

Holiday Inn Express
2 Orr Ct.
Johnson City, TN 37615
423-328-0500

Hampton Inn
2000 Enterprise Pl.
Kingsport, TN 37660
423-247-3888

CLOSEST RESTAURANTS

Cootie Brown's
2715 N. Roan St.
Johnson City, TN 37601
423-283-4723

Ridgewood Barbecue
900 Elizabethton Hwy.
Bluff City, TN 37618
423-538-7543

Sleepy Owl Brewery
151 E. Main St.
Kingsport, TN 37660
www.sleepyowlbrewery.com

CLOSEST HOSPITALS OR URGENT CARE

Wellmont Urgent Care
111 W. Stone Dr., #110
Kingsport, TN 37660
423-224-3701
www.wellmont.org

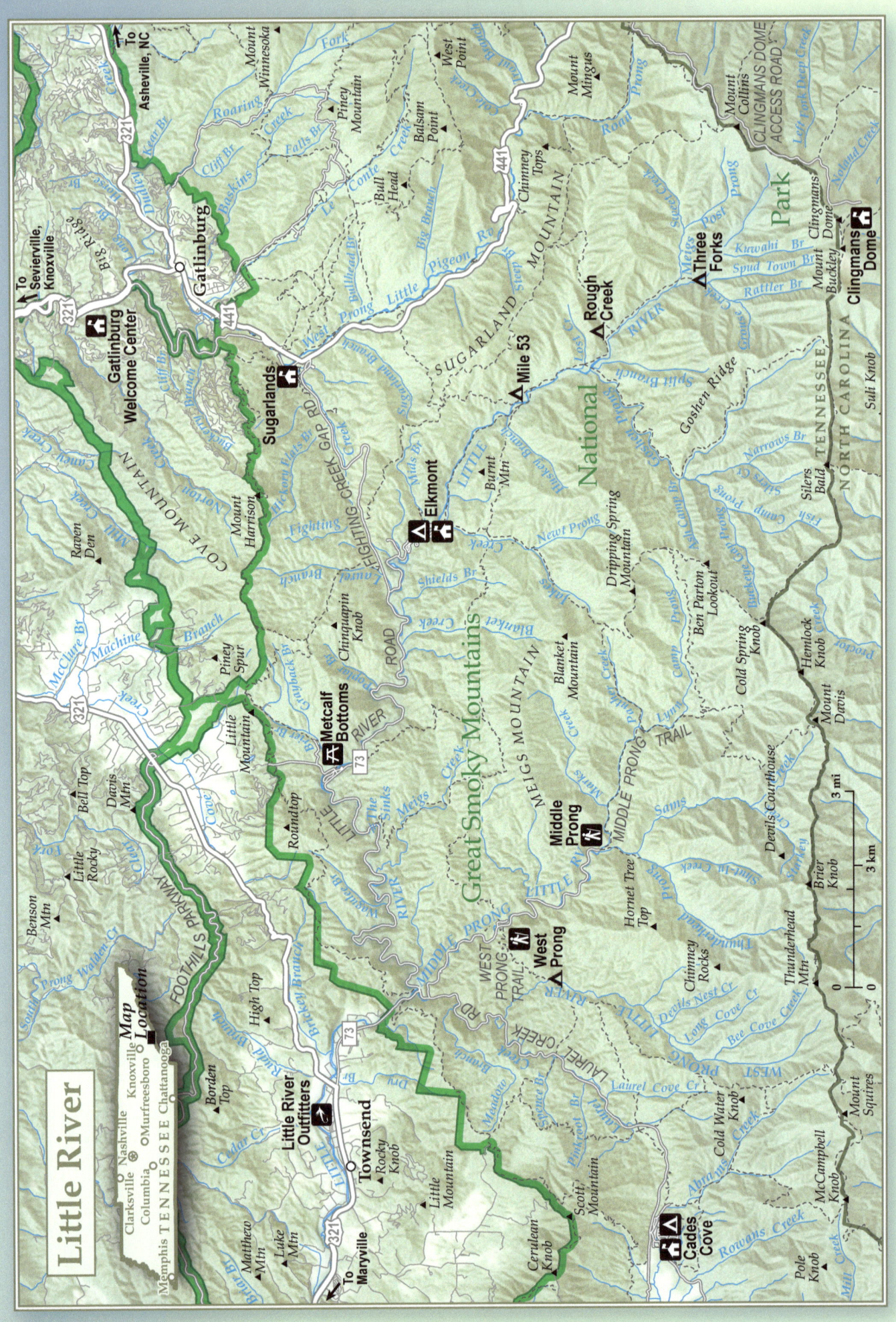

38 · Little River

▶ **Location:** The upper sections of Little River are made up of three major prongs located in Great Smoky Mountains National Park. The easiest way to access Little River in the park is through the towns of Townsend or Gatlinburg, Tennessee. Little River Road, otherwise known as Tennessee Route 73, follows the river for about 15-s inside the boundaries of the national park. Outside the park, access is close to Townsend, Walland, Maryville, Alcoa, and Knoxville, Tennessee.

The East Prong of Little River is about 50 miles long. It is formed by tributaries in Great Smoky Mountains National Park draining from near Clingmans Dome, which is the highest elevation location in Tennessee at 6,643 feet above sea level.

Eighteen miles downstream from the Elkmont Campground, Little River is joined by the Middle and West Prongs near the National Park's Townsend entrance. From there, the mountain stream becomes a lowland low-gradient river and flows 33 miles through Townsend, Walland, near Maryville and Alcoa, and eventually into the Tennessee River at Fort Loudoun Lake.

Aside from its natural beauty and high gradient character, Little River is chock-full of large, round boulders and gravel-laden pools. Little River is also a very popular fly-fishing destination. Populations of southern Appalachian brook trout inhabit the many mid- to high-elevation tributaries. The three prongs contain populations of wild rainbow and brown trout. There is no stocking of trout in Great Smoky Mountains National Park. (Stocking ceased in the early 1970s.) Smallmouth bass can be caught in the lower reaches inside the park, but most people target and catch the three species of trout.

Normally, brook trout in the tributaries are small. A 9-inch brook trout is large. A 12-incher is a trophy. The same holds true for rainbow trout. Rainbows have a short life in the Smokies, due to the harsh conditions. A three-year-old rainbow is old. Normally, rainbow trout lengths run between tiny to 12 inches. A 15-inch rainbow in Little River's wild-trout sections is a trophy. Brown trout, however, live longer. They become predators later in life, feeding on rainbow trout and other fish. A brown can live up to eight years and reach lengths up to 30 inches, though one that size is very rare.

All three prongs of the Little River have excellent access along roads for many miles, and trails in the backcountry provide miles of access minus the crowds. Backcountry campsites are available on the East Prong and West Prong of Little River. Elkmont is a large, developed campground suitable for tent, travel trailer, and motor home camping. The campground has public restrooms but no showers and no electrical or sewer hookups.

Rainbow trout are stocked during the cooler months in Townsend by Tennessee Wildlife Resources Agency. Below Townsend to the confluence of the Tennessee River, Little River becomes an excellent warmwater stream with populations of smallmouth bass, rock bass, and other panfish.

Fall is a great time to fish Little River. Rob Fightmaster

Much of the land is private. Floating in a canoe, kayak, or raft is popular for anglers in this section. Currently, one canoe rental and shuttle service operates on 14 miles of the river. There are some lowhead dams on Little River outside

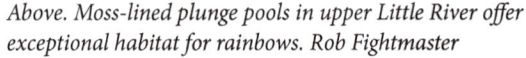

Above. Moss-lined plunge pools in upper Little River offer exceptional habitat for rainbows. Rob Fightmaster

Inset: Little River has a large population of trophy browns for the anglers that can master its clear waters. David Knapp

Below: Little River is home to the most beautiful wild rainbows in the smokies. David Knapp

the park to Fort Loudoun Lake. You should become familiar with the location of these before striking out on your own in a small craft.

Rain events can trigger flooding at times, since there is no flood-control dam on the river. Flows can vary, but typical low water is 90 to 120 cubic feet per second at the Townsend entrance to the park. One large flood in the early 1990s created a flow of over 15,000 cubic feet per second at that same gauge.

▶ **Hatches:** The park has a year-round fishing season, making it popular with visiting anglers from colder regions. Fly fishing is slow during the winter months when the water temperature drops below 40°F. Fly fishing for trout picks up when the water warms to 50°F in the spring, which can be as early as February. This kicks off the first major hatches of the year.

Aquatic insect species are diverse in Little River. You might see tiny Black Stoneflies and Blue-winged Olives during the winter, as well as daily midge hatches that can bring the trout to the surface on all but the coldest of days. When the water begins to warm, Quill Gordons and Blue Quills hatch in the early spring. Numerous stoneflies and caddisflies also show up. At times, you will see March Browns, Hendricksons, and other early spring hatches.

As we move into later spring, the mayflies are lighter. You will find Sulphurs and Light Cahills on the water. Three hatches that last all summer are the Yellow Sally Stoneflies, Golden Stoneflies, and Isonychia (or Slate Drake) mayflies. Dry versions of the first hatch work very well while anglers will generally have the most success on nymph versions of the last two. Many flies are tied to mimic the Yellow Sallies, and trout feed on them for months—therefore, yellow is a very good color for flies in the Smokies. Terrestrials such as beetles, ants, and inchworms, work very well during the summer months. When late fall and winter arrives, anglers switch to nymphs or midges and Blue-winged Olives.

▶ **Regulations:** Inside Great Smoky Mountains National Park, any combinations of trout species or other gamefish have daily limit of five and a minimum length of 7 inches.

Live bait or scented-bait fishing is not allowed in the park. Only artificial lures with single hooks are legal. No treble hooks are allowed. You may use two flies (dropper), but they must be spaced 12 inches apart.

Outside Great Smoky Mountains National Park, any legal method of fishing with a rod and reel is allowed, including baitfishing and treble hooks. The daily limit for trout is seven fish with no size limit.

▶ **Tackle:** Seven-foot to nine-foot, 4- to 6-weight fly rods are appropriate for fishing in the Smoky Mountains. If chasing smallmouth bass or trout outside the park, a 9-foot, 5- or 6-weight rod is perfect.

Waders and felt-soled boots are recommended during the cold months. Wet wading with felt-soled boots is recommended during the summer.

Hooked up to a fiesty early season Little River trout. Rob Fightmaster

Left. Broken water helps keep Little River well oxygenated even in the heat of summer. David Knapp

Below. Spawning browns. Josh Pfeiffer

BYRON BEGLEY lives in Townsend, Tennessee, a gateway to Great Smoky Mountains National Park. Little River flows through Townsend. Begley owns Little River Outfitters with his wife, Paula, and Daniel Drake. Little River Outfitters is a fly shop, fly-fishing school, and mail order company. Byron began fly fishing in 1962, and enjoys fishing for any species, in fresh or saltwater, with a fly rod.

Byron Begley.

CLOSEST FLY SHOPS

Little River Outfitters
106 Town Square Dr.
Townsend, TN 37882
865-448-9459
info@littleriveroutfitters.com
www.littleriveroutfitters.com

Orvis
136 Apple Valley Rd.
Sevierville, TN 37862
865-774-4162

Smoky Mountain Angler
469 Brookside Village Way
Gatlinburg, TN 37738
865-436-8746
www.smokymountainangler.com

CLOSEST GUIDE AND OUTFITTERS

Fightmaster Fly Fishing
Rob Fightmaster
P.O. Box 4146
Maryville, TN 37802
865-607-2886
rob@fightmasterflyfishing.com
www.fightmasterflyfishing.com

Frontier Anglers TN
Josh Pfeiffer
865-719-0227
pheasanttail12@live.com
www.frontieranglerstn.com

R&R Fly Fishing
P.O. Box 60
Townsend, TN 37882
865-448-0467
info@randrflyfishing.com
www.randrflyfishing.com

Smoky Mountain Angler
469 Brookside Village Way
Gatlinburg, TN 37738
865-436-8746
www.smokymountainangler.com

Trout Zone Anglers
David Knapp
931-261-1884
troutzoneanglers@gmail.com
www.troutzoneanglers.com

River John's Outfitters
4134 Cave Mill Rd.
Townsend, TN 37804
865-982-0793
www.riverjohns.com

CLOSEST LODGING

Holiday Inn Express
130 Associates Blvd.
Alcoa, TN 37701
877-859-5095

CLOSEST HOSPITALS OR URGENT CARE

Blount Memorial Hospital
907 E. Lamar Alexander Pkwy.
Maryville, TN 37804
865-983-7211
www.blountmemorial.org

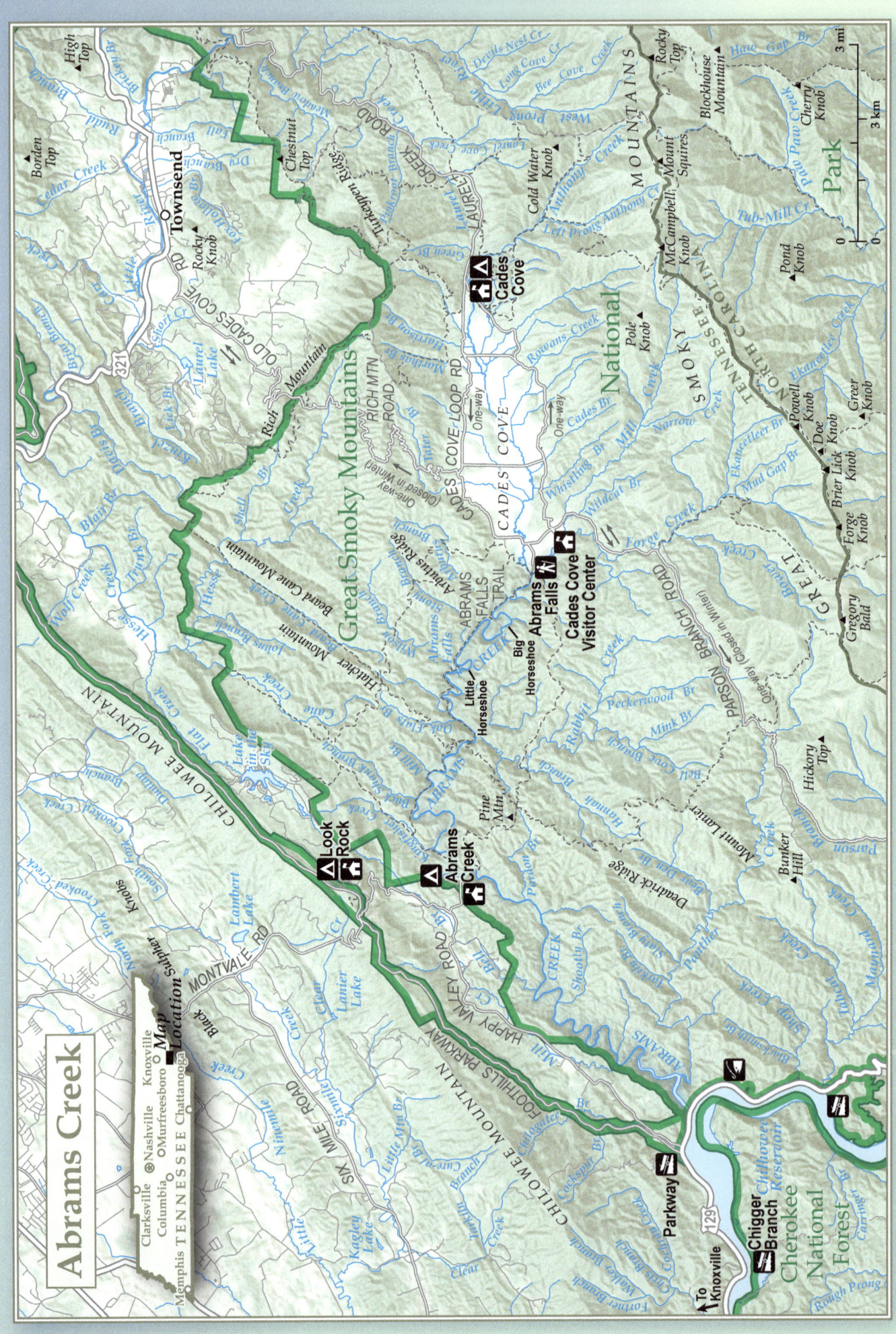

39 · Abrams Creek

➤ **Location:** Abrams Creek is located on the Tennessee side of Great Smoky Mountains National Park. Access to Abrams Creek is via the Cades Cove Loop Road and the Abrams Falls Trail or Abrams Creek Campground. Travel time from Asheville, North Carolina, is about three hours and about 1 1/2 hours from Knoxville, Tennessee.

Anglers traveling to fish Abrams Creek via the Cades Cove Loop Road should allow a minimum of 30 minutes (and up to one hour) to navigate the nearly six miles to Abrams Falls Trail trailhead. Anglers should take special care in planning a fishing trip to Abrams Creek. Loop Road opens at sunrise and closes at sunset (except on Wednesday and Saturday mornings, when Loop Road is closed to vehicle traffic until 10 a.m. to allow bicycle access to the cove).

Cades Cove was once a major thruway and hunting grounds for the Cherokee Nation on their way to the Overhill settlements. In fact, Abrams Creek derives its name from the Cherokee Chief Old Abraham. Much like the Cataloochee Valley, Cades Cove attracted early settlers because of its unique geology. It offered abundant grazing opportunities, and the limestone base of the valley offered excellent soil for subsistence farming. John Oliver was the first settler in the cove in 1818, and by 1850, the cove had a thriving population of about 671 people. Due to its population and the demand for lumber and grazing areas for the cattle, the cove suffered massive deforestation by the time of the formation of Great Smoky Mountains National Park (GSMNP). In an effort to produce a better and more dynamic sport fishery, the National Park Service, in conjunction with Alcoa and the TVA, eradicated all fish below Abrams Falls in 1957, so that they could introduce the sportier brown and rainbow trout.

Today, Abrams Creek is considered by many to be the finest trout water in Great Smoky Mountains National Park. This bold statement can easily be verified by studying the reports of Park Biologist Steve Moore, who shows Abrams has nearly double the biomass of fish than any other stream in the park.

Abrams Creek begins high in the Smokies as Anthony Creek, which flows down the mountain as it nears the valley floor and Cades Cove. Roughly 60 percent of the stream filters underground and flows through the valley via a large limestone deposit. The underground portion of the creek filters back into the stream just upstream of the confluence of Mill Creek, near the Abrams Falls Trail trailhead. The 40 percent of the stream that flows above ground through the

Abrams Falls in early Spring. David Knapp

valley flows through hundreds of acres of pastureland, where it picks up sediment and affluent from the grazing cattle and horses. This unique combination of affluent and limestone increases the stream's pH level to support one of the healthiest populations of caddisflies and other aquatic insects found in the Southeast.

Anglers will want to get to the stream early. Otherwise, when you approach the Abrams Falls Trail trailhead, you will realize that someone has dropped a people bomb directly on

Above. Working upstream in search of Great Smoky Mountain National Park trout. Kevin Howell

Inset. A split cane bamboo rod is perfect for the fiesty wild rainbows in Abrams Creek. Daniel Munger

top of it. While there are anglers in the mix, most are hikers traveling to the falls or swimmers. Anglers who walk all the way to the falls to fish need to have some bright colored flies to match the daily bikini hatch that occurs in the summer months.

The upper river above Abrams Falls is accessed via the Cades Cove Loop Road and the Abrams Falls Trail. Due to high traffic volume on the one-way loop road, it might take anglers up to one hour or longer to reach the parking area for the Abrams Falls Trail. For the top half mile or so of the Abrams Creek Trail, anglers will encounter a lot of park visitors swimming and playing in the creek.

Anglers walking down the trail toward the falls need to be aware of two horseshoe bends in the creek. The upper horseshoe is about a mile in length, and it will take most anglers the better part of a day to fish around. The lower and smaller horseshoe is about three-quarters of a miles long, and will take anglers well over half a day to fish around. Anglers should be sure of their location in the stream, so as to not get trapped late in the day and conversely locked into the cove overnight. Do not fish the horseshoe bends without adequate preparation—allow at least eight hours of fishing time, and be sure to carry water, lunch, and a light rain parka. You can get hypothermia in the Smokies if you get caught in a rain and then cold winds set in, even in the summer. Once you start around the horseshoe bends, there is no turning back, and I do not recommend trying to bushwhack your way over Arbutus Ridge to get back to the trail.

The fishing above the Abrams Falls Trail parking area is good, especially during the cooler months. With so much of the stream flowing underground through the cove, the water is usually warmer than the air and offers excellent fishing.

Abrams Creek below the falls offers very little access to fishermen—the only access is located at the Abrams Creek Campground. Anglers who are willing to hike the nearly two miles from the campground upstream to the falls will find good fishing. The section around the campground and up to the falls offers anglers one of the few places in the Smokies where you can escape the crowd. In addition to the excellent trout fishing, Abrams Creek has one of the best smallmouth bass populations in the park below Abrams Falls. It is not uncommon at all for anglers to hook a 3- to 4-pound smallmouth and think they have hooked a world record brown trout.

▶ **Regulations:** Fishing is permitted year-round in open waters. Anglers can fish in Great Smoky Mountains National Park with either a valid North Carolina or Tennessee fishing license. Fishing is allowed from a half hour before official sunrise to a half hour after official sunset.

The daily possession limit is five brook, rainbow, or brown trout, smallmouth bass, or a combination of these, each day or in possession, regardless of whether they are fresh, stored in an ice chest, or otherwise preserved. The combined total must not exceed five fish. (Twenty rock bass may be kept in addition to the above limit.) A person must stop fishing immediately after obtaining the limit.

The size limit for brook, rainbow, and brown trout is 7 inches. The size limit for smallmouth bass is also 7 inches. There is no minimum limit for rock bass.

Above. A beautiful, wild wintertime rainbow that took a big size 12 prince nymph. Michael Turbyville

Below. Deer feeding in Cades Cove. Kevin Howell

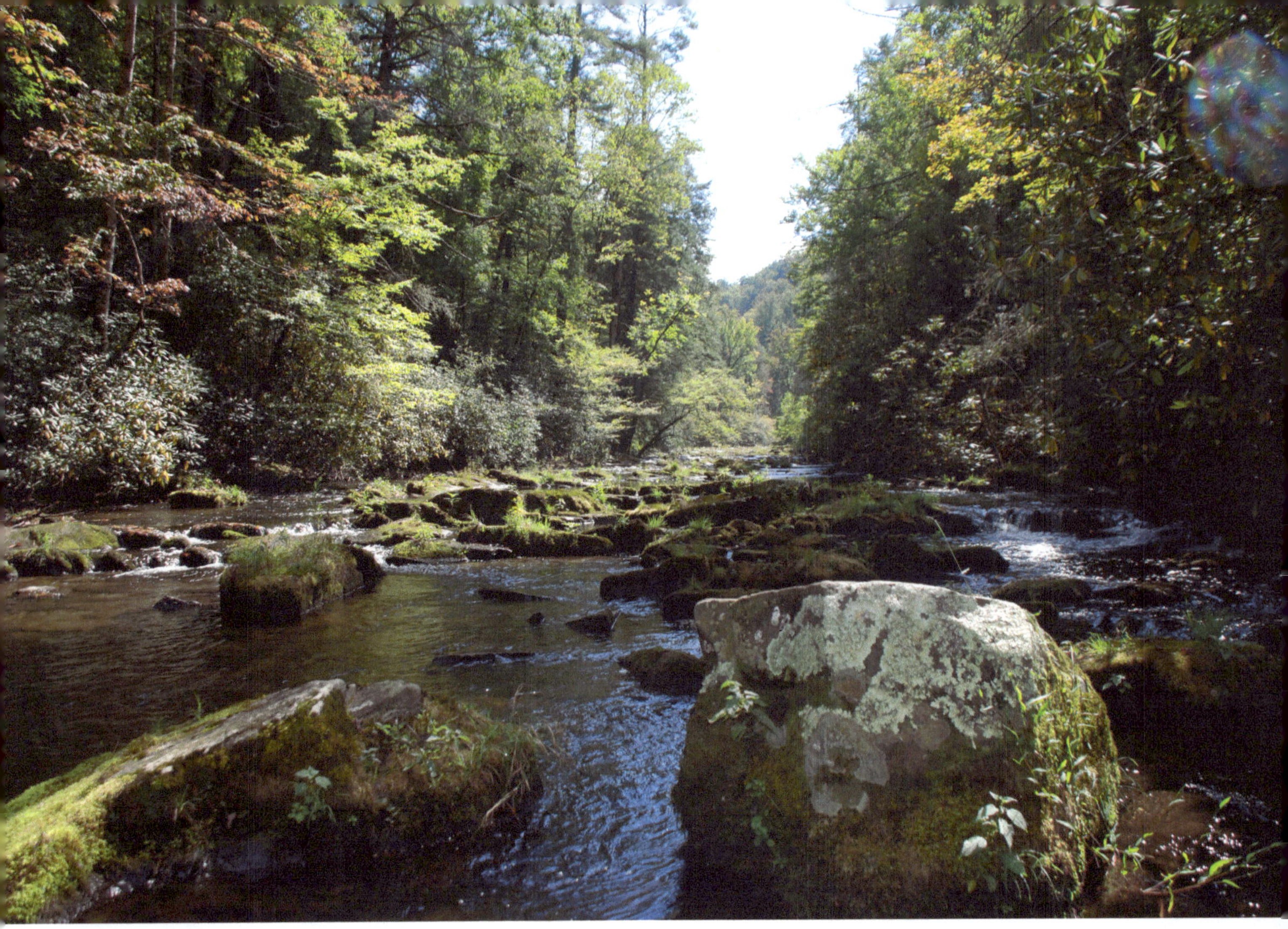

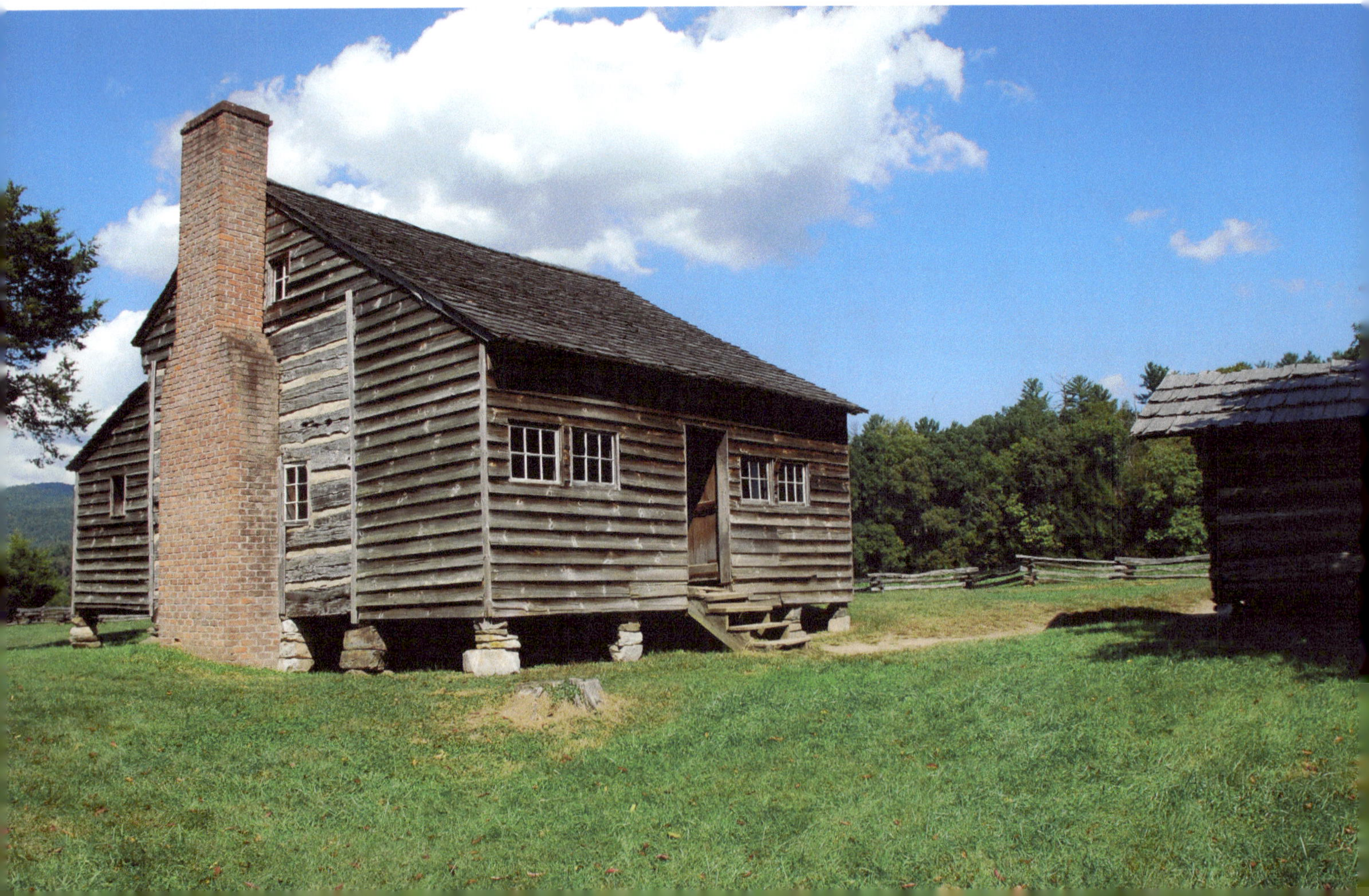

► **Tackle:** Abrams Creek offers anglers some of the best hatches found in the Smokies, especially caddisflies. While other insects are present, the overabundance of caddisflies seems to dictate that anglers always need to have some form of a caddisfly handy. Abrams can easily be fished with a 9-foot fly rod. Trout anglers will want a 4- to 5-weight rod, while bass anglers will want a 6- to 7-weight rod. Streamers and crayfish patterns will work best for the bass. Trout anglers will need to fish with a 4–6X tippet, based on the water level. Bass anglers will find that a 2–4X tippet better suits their needs.

Kevin Howell with a nice Argentinian brown. Gonzalo Flego

KEVIN HOWELL—Kevin Howell is the owner of Davidson River Outfitters; he also is an author, lecturer, fly-fishing instructor, and guide. Kevin is a Signature fly Designer for Montana Fly Company. A 2018 inductee to the Fly Fishing Museum of the Southern Appalachians Hall of Fame and a 2018 inductee to the Legends of the Fly Hall of Fame as well. Kevin has been guiding the waters of North Carolina, South Carolina, and East Tennessee for 25 years. When not guiding he can be found fishing with his wife Mellissa, and sons David and Andrew.

Facing top. Boulders in Abrams Creek. Kevin Howell

Facing bottom. Dan Lawson Cabin in Cades Cove. Kevin Howell

CLOSEST FLY SHOPS

Little River Outfitters
106 Town Square Dr.
Townsend, TN 37882
865-448-9459
info@littleriveroutfitters.com
www.littleriveroutfitters.com

3 Rivers Angler
5113 Kingston Pike
Knoxville, TN 37919
865-200-5271
info@3riversangler.com
www.3riversangler.com

Orvis
136 Apple Valley Rd.
Sevierville, TN 37862
865-774-4162

Fightmaster Fly Fishing
Rob Fightmaster
P.O. Box 4146
Maryville, TN 37802
865-607-2886
rob@fightmasterflyfishing.com
www.fightmasterflyfishing.com

Frontier Anglers TN
Josh Pfeiffer
865-719-0227
pheasanttail12@live.com
www.frontieranglerstn.com

Trout Zone Anglers
David Knapp
931-261-1884
troutzoneanglers@gmail.com
www.troutzoneanglers.com

CLOSEST LODGING

Auntie Belham's Cabin Rentals
1024 Charlotte's Ct.
Pigeon Forge, TN 37863
865-436-6618
www.auntiebelhams.com

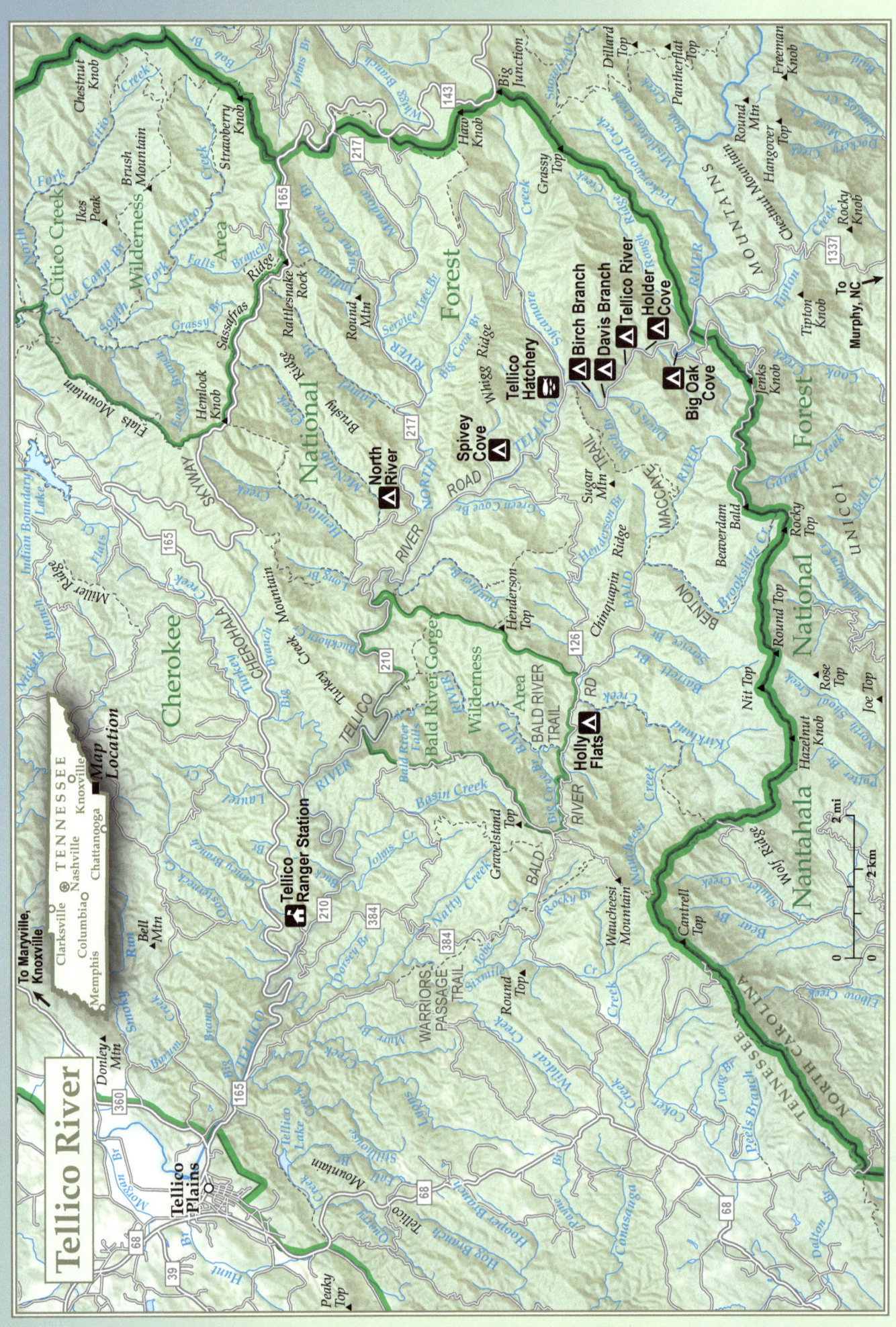

40 · Tellico River

➤ **Location:** The Tellico River is located near Tellico Plains, Tennessee, absolutely 1½ hours northeast of Chattanooga, Tennessee, and 1¼ hours southwest of Knoxville, Tennessee.

The Tellico River drainage has long been a favorite destination for fly anglers from the Southeast. The endless ledges and pools of the lower reaches of the river, combined with the classic pocketwater of the small streams that make up the headwaters of the drainage, give visiting anglers a wide variety of sections in which to fish. In addition to great fishing, the Tellico River drainage is also home to some fantastic scenery, including waterfalls that merit a visit all on their own.

While all sections of the Tellico have good fishing at various times of the year, some are better than others. The main attraction for most fly anglers is the Delayed Harvest section of the Tellico. The Delayed Harvest regulations begin on October 1 and run through mid-March each year. During this time, anglers may only fish single-hook artificial lures or flies, and all fishing is catch-and-release. As with any Delayed Harvest stream, weekend crowds can be expected, especially with the Tellico's proximity to both Knoxville and Chattanooga. Anglers who don't want to fish around others might want to cash-in a few vacation days for a midweek visit to the Tellico. Wading on the Delayed Harvest section can range from easy to hazardous. The danger comes from the handful of Class III and Class IV rapids that can be found on the river. During periods of low water, these rapids are more of a climbing obstacle than a hazard—but after a heavy rain, the consequences of wading above or below some of the drops

Fishing the Tellico in early fall. J.E.B. Hall

Abundant overhangs on the Tellico offer shade in the middle of the day. J.E.B. Hall

could be lethal. Anglers should take extra caution and check water levels when fishing the Tellico after a weather event.

Beyond the fishing in the Delayed Harvest section, the Tellico offers some of the finest put-and-take water in all of southern Appalachia. During the spring and summer months, the Tennessee Wildlife Resources Agency works hard to keep the Tellico well stocked (so well, in fact, that anglers are required to purchase a daily Tellico-Citico permit in addition to their Tennessee fishing license). While keeping fish isn't popular with most of the long rod crowd, the fishing in these sections in good enough that it shouldn't be overlooked.

Fly anglers looking for wild trout, fewer people, and smaller water should look to the headwater streams of North River and Bald River. Both streams offer excellent fishing for wild trout, and both require just enough effort to eliminate any real crowds. The North River is mostly "roadside," and its streambed is comprised of beautiful pocketwater. The lower sections of the North River are more heavily visited and, in turn, have less consistent fishing. The highest sections are small and choked with rhododendron, and only the most dedicated small-stream anglers will find this water enjoyable.

Bald River offers somewhat more open fishing than North River, with a more wilderness feel. While the top reaches are roadside and somewhat heavily fished by car campers, the section from just above Bald River Falls up to the Holly Flats Campground is only accessible to those anglers who like to hike to reach their fishing hole. The Bald River Trail runs along this section of the Bald River and can be accessed by trailheads on the Tellico River Road or just below the Holly Flats Campground.

The Tellico River is a remote fishery and has limited amenities, including limited lodging and eating options. Staying in Murphy, North Carolina, will give anglers access to the river just 20–30 minutes away.

Releasing a fall Rainbow on the Tellico. J.E.B. Hall

▶ **Hatches:** Like most streams of its size in the Southeast, the Tellico River has a good variety of insects. March will bring dark caddis hatches along with the season's first quills. April and May will see Yellow Sallies and Light Cahills in the evening hours. Summer is terrestrial time, with a few late evening hatches. Fall means Blue-winged Olives and Blue-winged Rusts or Mahoganies. Finally, winter is time for dark stoneflies, Blue-winged Olives on cloudy days, and midges in the foam lines.

▶ **Tackle:** Fly rods of at least 8 feet, 6 inches are recommended for fishing most sections of the Tellico River. A wide riverbed, deep runs, and precise drift control make fishing shorter rods feel somewhat inadequate. While most fishing can be done with a 4-weight fly line, 5- and 6-weights will handle heavier nymph rigs with ease and can double as streamer sticks when the water is up.

For the North River and the Bald River, rods ranging from 2-weight to 4-weight are more than enough stick for the small wild fish that anglers will encounter in these streams.

Leaders and tippets will vary based on where anglers are at in the drainage, but for most applications, leaders of 9 feet in length and ending in 5X tippet will do the job.

Flies for the Tellico are similar to those anglers will fish on other rivers in the South. Dry-fly selections should include a variety of parachute mayfly imitations, Elk-hair Caddis, and terrestrials both large and small. Nymph boxes composed of small beadhead mayfly and stonefly nymph patterns will serve anglers well, and one can't fish the Tellico River without bringing along a few Tellico Nymphs for the occasion. While this pattern seems dated, it will get the job done from March through July. The larger waters of the lower Tellico can make for great streamer fishing. Those who are looking to hunt trophy fish or are looking for a high-water option should try stripping their favorite baitfish imitation among the large boulders and ledges of the lower Tellico.

J.E.B. HALL is a full-time fly-fishing guide and instructor in Western North Carolina and East Tennessee for Davidson River Outfitters. In addition to guiding in the Southeast, J.E.B. has spent numerous summers guiding in Southwest Alaska for Alaska West and is a former operations manager for the Andros South Bonefish Lodge on South Andros Island in the Bahamas. J.E.B. is also the author of *The Southern Appalachian Fly Guide* and occasionally dabbles in photography.

J.E.B. Hall in New York City.

CLOSEST FLY SHOPS

There are no immediate fly shop near Tellico River.

CLOSEST GUIDES AND OUTFITTERS

Tellico Angler
739 Sawmill Rd.
Tellico Plains, TN 37385
423-519-6081
tellicoangler@gmail.com
www.tellicoangler.com

Southeastern Anglers
149 McCormick Rd. SW
Cartersville, GA 30120
423-338-7368
danelaw@southeasternanglers.com
www.southeasternanglers.com

CLOSEST LODGING

Hampton Inn
1550 Andrews Rd.
Murphy, NC 28906
828-837-1628

Best Western
1522 Andrews Rd.
Murphy, NC 28906
828-837-3060
www.bestwesternnorthcarolina.com/hotels/best-western-of-murphy

CLOSEST RESTAURANTS

Murphy's Chophouse
130 Valley River Ave.
Murphy, NC 28906
828-835-3287
www.murphyschophouse.com

Tellico Grains Bakery
105 Depot St.
Tellico Plains, TN 37385
423-253-6911

Facing. Early fall is a great time to fish the Tellico. J.E.B. Hall

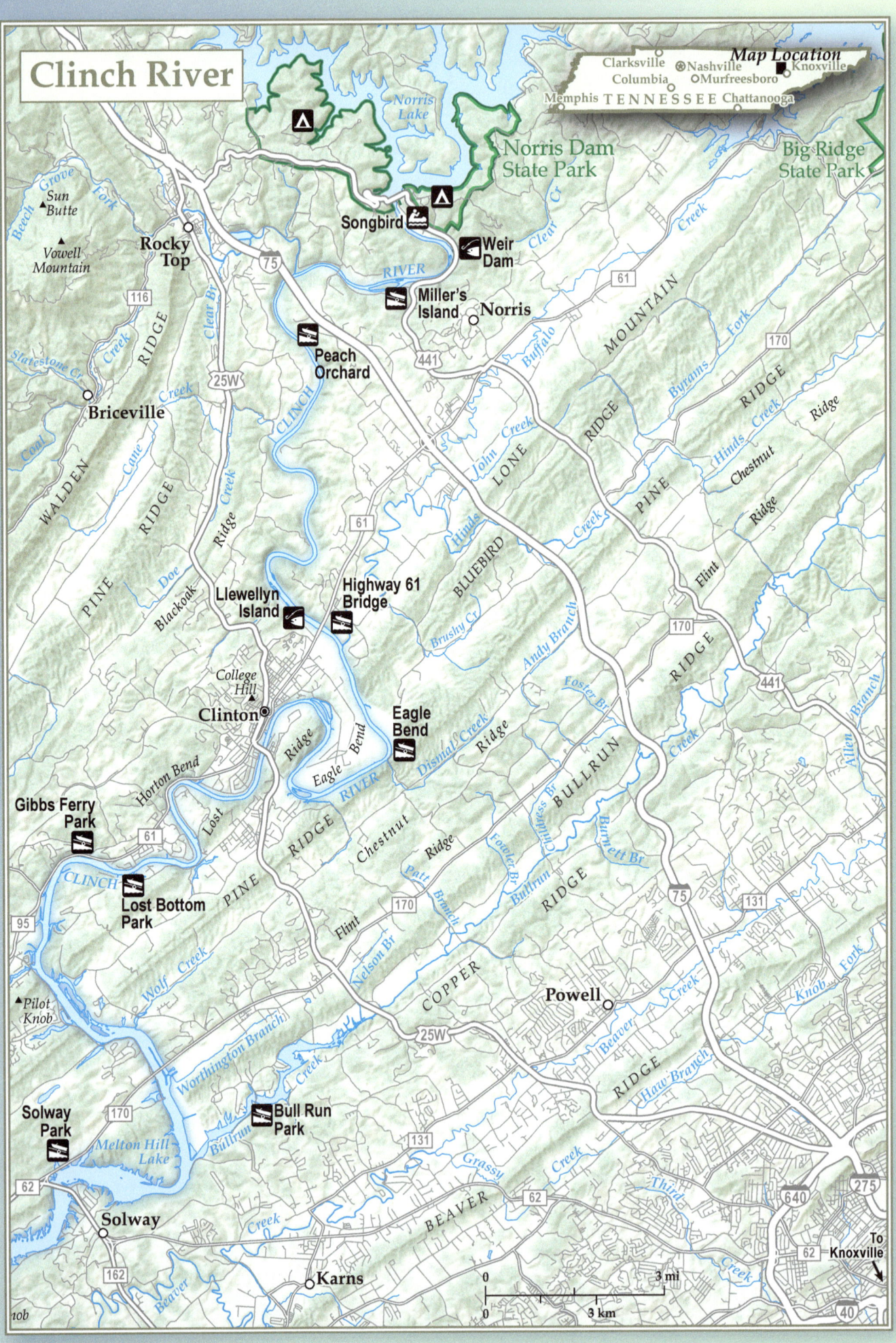

41 · Clinch River

▶ **Location:** The tailwater section of the Clinch River is located approximately 20 miles north of Knoxville, Tennessee, and is approximately two hours from Asheville, North Carolina; two and a half hours from Lexington, Kentucky; three hours from Nashville, Tennessee; and four hours from Charlotte, North Carolina. Anglers can fly commercially to the Clinch via the Knoxville McGhee Tyson Airport.

The Clinch River rises from the mountains of Southwest Virginia near Tazewell County and flows southwest through the Great Appalachian Valley before crossing the Tennessee state line near the town of Sneedville, Tennessee. From the headwaters in Virginia to its impoundment in Tennessee, the Clinch is a freestone river that supports an abundant population of smallmouth bass and other warmwater species. It is not until the tailwater portion of the river, below Norris Dam, that the river is capable of supporting trout.

Norris Dam is regulated by the Tennessee Valley Authority and impounds Norris Lake, which is the largest reservoir on any of the Tennessee River tributaries. At 265 feet in height, the dam releases cold water from the bottom of Norris Lake at a near constant 50–54°F year-round. TVA maintains a weekend recreational release schedule on the Clinch from Memorial Day until Labor Day. The recreational schedule provides aminimal flow until 10 a.m., one generator (3,400 cubic feet per second) from 10 a.m. until 2 p.m., and two or more generators (6,100–8,400 cubic feet per second) from 2 p.m. onward. This recreational schedule provides both wading and boating anglers and opportunity to fish the Clinch on both Saturdays and Sundays during the summer months. Outside of the recreational schedules, generations are determined by power demand, reservoir levels, and an indeterminable algorithm developed by the powers that be at TVA. The nature of the river changes significantly at different flows, and the methods used to fish the Clinch must be adjusted in accordance with water levels; however, the river is fishable on all flows, provided an angler has access to a boat.

It takes one generator of water approximately an hour to reach Miller Island 2¾ hours to reach Peach Orchard Access and 5½ hours to reach the Tennessee 61 Bridge. Two (or more) generators will reach Miller Island in about half an hour, Peach Orchard in about 1¾ hours, and the Tennessee 61 Bridge in about four hours. The most popular float on the Clinch is the Peach Orchard Access to the Tennessee 61 Bridge. On one generator, the river is navigable with a jet boat, and you can expect to see some boat traffic, particularly on weekends. On two generators, or approximately 8,400 cubic feet per second, the Clinch is fishable to the fly angler but should be approached with large rods and heavy sinking line.

Foggy mornings are a common site on the Clinch in the summertime. Matt Crockett

At minimal flows (no generation), the Clinch is characterized by long pools interspersed with horizontal bedrock ledges and the occasional run. Gin-clear water is the norm, provided no summer storms have passed over and filled the many feeder creeks with turbid water. As a result, long leaders and stealthy presentations are required at lower flows.

Dick Williams and a Clinch River whopper. Allen Gillespie

Abundant wading access can be found in the weir pool, which is located in the mile of river immediately below the dam. Fishing in the weir pool can be very productive but is extremely challenging, due to the weir pool's slow flow. Fishing within the pool requires a diligent angler and long, drag-free drifts. There is also significant wading access and faster water on low flows immediately below the weir dam, as well as a mile downstream at Miller Island Access. The next access point for the wading angler is ten miles downstream at the Llewellyn Island Access, near the town of Clinton.

For the boating angler, the optimal flow on the Clinch for fly fishing is one generator, which equates to approximately 3,300 cubic feet per second. While a sustained flow on the Clinch at 3,300 cubic feet per second is relatively rare, it is possible to float the lower section of the tailwater on this optimal flow, provided the recreational schedule mentioned above is in effect.

There are effectively three floats on the Clinch: the weir pool down to Miller Island Access (2 1/4 miles), Miller's Island Access down to Peach Orchard Access (3 1/2 miles), and Peach Orchard down to Highway 61 (about 7 miles). It's important to note that the upper float within the weir pool requires a raft or kayak, as trailered boats are not permitted to launch anywhere in the weir pool. Additionally, this float requires the boater to navigate the weir dam, which should only be done by experienced boaters, or paddle back upstream to the launch sites.

The Clinch is similar to other tailwaters in the region, and small dry flies and nymphs are the norm. The exception to this rule would be on high flows where larger streamers are utilized in the hopes of dredging a large brown from the depths. While the Clinch supports a large biomass, it lacks diversity within its biomass when compared to other tailwaters in the region. The principal hatches associated with the

A Clinch River behemoth brown. Allen Gillespie

Clinch are Sulphurs, midges, and, to a lesser degree, Black Caddis. In the spring, starting in April, the Clinch exhibits some truly amazing Sulphur hatches. While these hatches can occur on low water, it is not uncommon for them to be triggered by the arrival of generation from the dam. With the hatch in full swing, the fish on the Clinch become very educated, and a 12-foot, 6X leader is nearly requisite. Earlier in the season, before the crowds have arrived, 5X may be sufficient. Outside of the spring hatches, the standard Clinch rig is a beadhead Pheasant Tail (#16) with a Zebra Midge (#18–22 in a variety of colors) dropped below it. If fishing the weir pool, it is advisable to have a selection of scuds and sow bugs in your fly box. During the winter months, egg patterns have been known to be productive, particularly in the upper stretches of the river as the fish go through the motions of spawning.

▶ **Regulations:** From Norris Dam downstream to the Tennessee 61 Bridge, including tributaries, 14 to 20 inches is the protected length range on all trout. The creel limit is seven trout, and only one trout may be greater than 20 inches. All trout 14 to 20 inches should be released immediately.

▶ **Tackle:** I suggest using 9-foot, 4- or 5-weight rods with floating weight-forward lines with 5X or 6X, 9- or 12-foot leaders on low-flow wading conditions or one generator flows when nymphing or fishing dry flies.

When drifting on higher water generation and throwing streamers, 9-foot, 6-, 7-, or 8-weight rods with 200- to 250-grain sink-tip lines are best.

Above. Wade fishing the Clinch when there is no generation can provide for some great fishing. Photos by Matt Crockett

Inset. Clinch River brown trout.

Below. Clinch River rainbow.

ALLEN GILLESPIE was raised on the Tennessee River as it flows through Knoxville. After graduation from the University of Tennessee, his travels took him to some incredible places: exotic locations, like Indonesia where he worked with indigenous sperm whalers; the Amazon rainforest of Bolivia, where he spent 18 months; and Buenos Aires, Argentina, where he fished the storied waters of Patagonia as often as possible. From Patagonia, his travels took him to New Zealand, where he stalked the legendary waters of the North and South Islands. Now, back in his native land, with a lifetime of experiences to share, Allen is ready to serve those who fish the waters of East Tennessee.

Allen Gillespie holds a trophy Clinch River brown.

CLOSEST FLY SHOPS

3 Rivers Angler
5113 Kingston Pike
Knoxville, TN 37919
865-200-5271
info@3riversangler.com
www.3riversangler.com

Orvis
136 Apple Valley Rd.
Sevierville, TN 37862
865-774-4162

Little River Outfitters
106 Town Square Dr.
Townsend, TN 37882
865-448-9459
info@littleriveroutfitters.com
www.littleriveroutfitters.com

CLOSEST GUIDES AND OUTFITTERS

3 Rivers Angler
5113 Kingston Pike
Knoxville, TN 37919
865-200-5271
info@3riversangler.com
www.3riversangler.com

Rocky Top Anglers
865-388-9802
tnrockyraccoon@yahoo.com
www.rockytopanglers.com

Clinch River Outfitters 865
894 Park Ln.
Andersonville, TN 37705
865-494-0972

CLOSEST LODGING

Clinch River House
4700 Coster Rd.
Knoxville, TN 37912
865-250-9361
reservations@clinchriverhouse.com
www.clinchriverhouse.com

Norris Dam State Park Cabins
125 Village Green Cir.
Rocky Top, TN 37769
865-426-7461
www.tnstateparks.com/parks/cabins/norris-dam-standard

Clinch River Lodge
865-599-1115
lcooper@salesmanage.com
www.clinchriverlodge.com

Holiday Inn Express
495 Springridge Rd.
Clinton, MS 39056
601-708-0400

Hampton Inn
105 Hillvale Rd.
Clinton, TN 37716
865-691-8070

CLOSEST RESTAURANTS

Harrison's Grill and Bar
110 Hillvale Rd.
Clinton, TN 37716
865-463-6368
www.harrisonsgrill.com

Golden Girls Restaurant
2211 N. Charles G. Seivers Blvd.
Clinton, TN 37716
865-457-3302

Zaxby's
109 Buffalo Rd.
Clinton, TN 37716
www.zaxbys.com

CLOSEST HOSPITALS OR URGENT CARE

Physicians Regional Medical Center
900 E. Oak Hill Ave.
Knoxville, TN 37917
865-545-8000
www.tennova.com

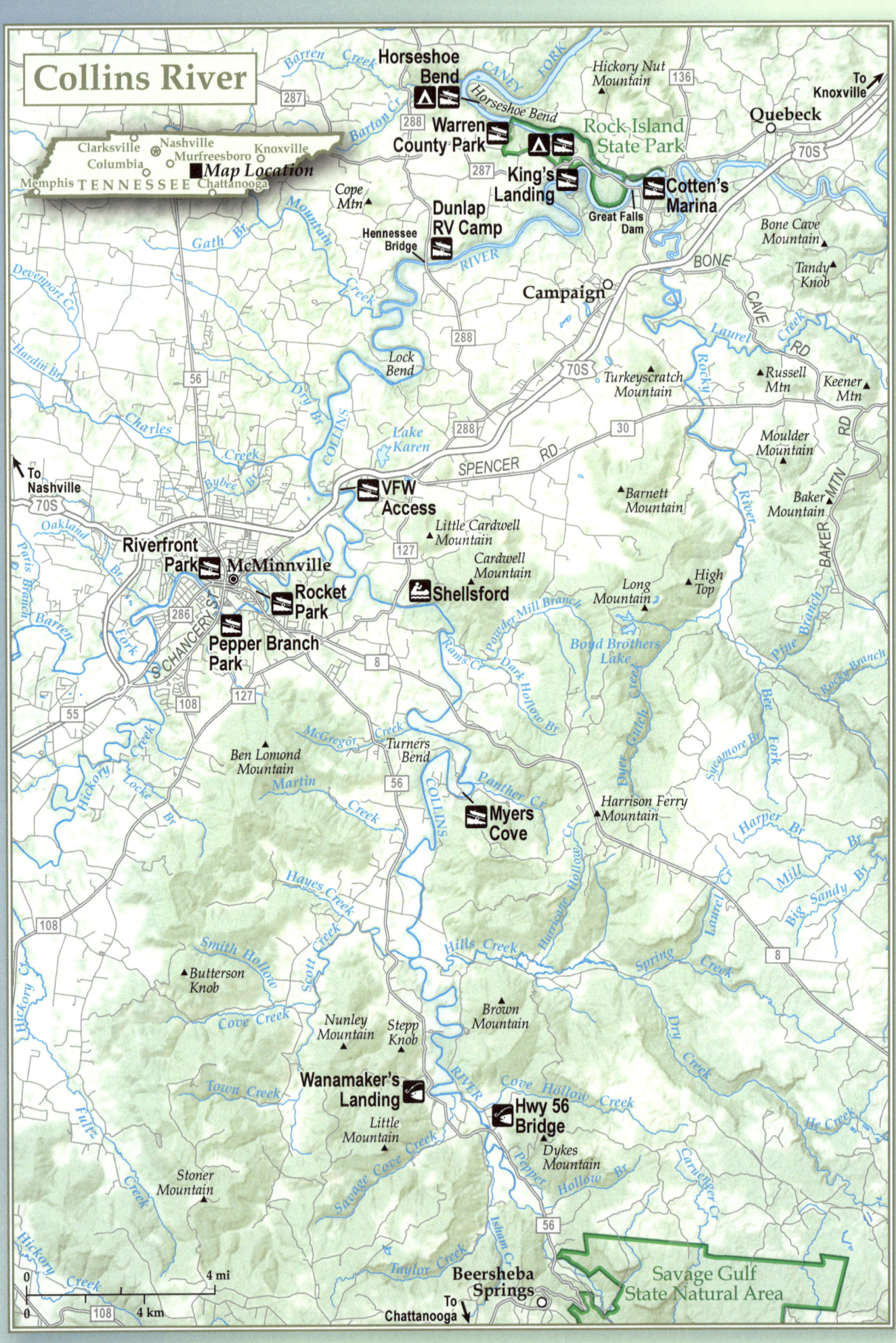

42 · Collins River

> **Location:** The Collins River is a 67-mile long tributary of the Caney Fork that flows from atop the Cumberland Plateau to its confluence with the Caney Fork above Great Falls Dam, near Rock Island in Warren County, Tennessee. The most popular put-ins and services are near McMinnville, Tennessee, which is located approximately one hour and ten minutes southeast of Nashville, one hour north of Chattanooga, and two hours west of Knoxville. Commercial air service is available through all three of these cities.

The Collins River forms as a collection of swift creeks atop the Cumberland Mountains in Grundy County before plunging off the plateau while running through the Savage Gulf Wilderness Area. From shallow, rocky riffles and slab rock to pastoral flows and, finally, a deep reservoir, the Collins provides anglers with the ability to target large musky in a variety of settings. While the musky is a native of Cumberland Plateau waters, populations were severely impacted by dam building in the first half of the twentieth century. A decades-long stocking program by the Tennessee Wildlife Resources Agency and natural reproduction has yielded musky up to 54 inches, with good numbers of fish in the 40-inch range and large smallmouth. Musky can be found all along the river's course.

The Collins is most easily divided into three sections with the upper river lying above the Myers Cover ramp, the middle river running from Myers Cove downstream to Mountain Creek, and the lower river running from Mountain Creek to Great Falls Dam.

The karst region of the upper river is riddled with caverns, and the river disappears into underground courses and reappears at several points along its route. Many stretches of the extreme upper river only flow above ground during periods of heavy rain. Anglers begin to find reliable water flow near the Warren County line where the cobblestone bottom begins to give way to limestone slab and gravel. The upper river can most easily be accessed from its downstream end at the Myers Cove put-in on Myers Cover Road off Tennessee 56, south of McMinnville. Anglers can expect anything from boney, rocky shallows that require dragging over gravel bars to easy motoring for miles upstream on higher levels to somewhat dangerous navigation during high flows due to strainers. Pools in this section are often shallower and farther apart. Shallow-running skiffs and kayaks are ideal for this section of the river.

The middle river can most easily be accessed by either the Myers Cove put-in at its upstream end or the VFW put-in, located about two-thirds down this section off Highway 70 at the McMinnville city limits. While this is the most driftboat friendly section of the river, the approximately 16 miles between these two ramps makes it very difficult to properly work cover while still getting off the river before sunset, especially in winter. Pools become deeper and closer together. As with the upper river, it is not uncommon to have to drag

Brian Porter does battle with a Collins River musky. Todd Gregory

over shallow gravel bars during periods of low flow. The only reliable wading access on the Collins can be found at the Shells Ford Access off Shells Ford Road near McMinnville. While there is no boat ramp at Shells Ford, it does provide excellent access for kayaks and canoes. Anglers should note that the Barren Fork of the Collins can be most easily accessed from the VFW ramp.

Walker Parrott navigates his skiff up the Collins River in search of musky. J.E.B. Hall

Long gliding strips often prove fatal for musky. J.E.B. Hall

The lower river is best accessed from any of the Great Falls Lake ramps, such as King's Ramp or Cotten's Marina, both in Rock Island. Once downstream of Mountain Creek, the Collins begins to slow down as it enters the deep water of Great Falls Lake. In addition to fallen trees and rock cover, flooded timber cover may be found on most river levels. This section of river will be your best bet, if you are fishing from a larger boat with plenty of prop depth, up to the Hennessee Bridge and even beyond on higher river levels. Boaters who are unfamiliar with the river should exercise caution once they near Hennessee Bridge on all water levels, as several large rocks are submerged just below the surface.

Anglers should also plan to target the main Caney Fork and its other major tributaries, such as the Calfkiller and Rocky Rivers while in the area, as all hold musky. Both rivers can be accessed from the Cotten's Marina ramp in Rock Island.

Once off the water, anglers can catch live music on most weekends at Collins River BBQ and Cafe, traditional Bluegrass at the Rocky River Community Center, or a taping of Bluegrass Underground at Cumberland Caverns (www.bluegrassunderground.com, www.cumberlandcaverns.com). The Bonnaroo Music Festival in June (www.bonnaroo.com) and the Muddy Roots Music Festival in August (www.muddyrootsrecords.com) are both nearby. Warren County also celebrates its status as "The Home of Southern Musky" with a catch-and-release fly tournament the first weekend in May.

Right. Todd Gregory.

Left. Walker Parrott works a shoreline in search of musky. J.E.B. Hall

TODD GREGORY, owner and founder of Towee Boats, now lives in Tennessee where he builds boats and sponsors the Hardly Strickly Musky tournament. Before returning to Tennessee, Todd spent years guiding and fishing the lower Florida Keys throughout the 1990s.

CLOSEST LODGING

Rock Island State Park Cabins
82 Beach Rd.
Rock Island, TN 38581
931-686-2471
www.tnstateparks.com/parks/cabins/rock-island

Best Western
809 Sparta St.
McMinnville, TN 37110
931-473-2159

Horseshoe Bend Marina
640 Webbs Camp Rd.
Walling, TN 38587
931-657-5080
horseshoebendmarina1@hotmail.com
www.horseshoebendmarina.com

CLOSEST RESTAURANTS

Collins River BBQ and Cafe
117 E. Main St.
McMinnville, TN 37110
931-507-3663

The Foglight Foodhouse
275 Powerhouse Rd.
Walling, TN 38587
931-657-2364
www.foglight-foodhouse.com

➤ **Regulations:** A valid Tennessee fishing license is required, and while a 50-inch minimum limit is in force on the Collins, catch-and-release is highly encouraged.

➤ **Tackle:** The preferred tackle for big Southern river musky are 10-weight rods with sinking or intermediate lines. Any good quality reel will fit the bill. Larger flies tied in attractor patterns and sucker imitations, along with topwater patterns, are most productive summer through winter, with somewhat smaller flies doing well in spring. Anglers should target heavy rock and wood cover, both along the banks and midstream.

While a jet outboard is certainly not required, the Collins can be tough on boats, especially during low water. Carrying an extra prop and prop wrench is highly recommended.

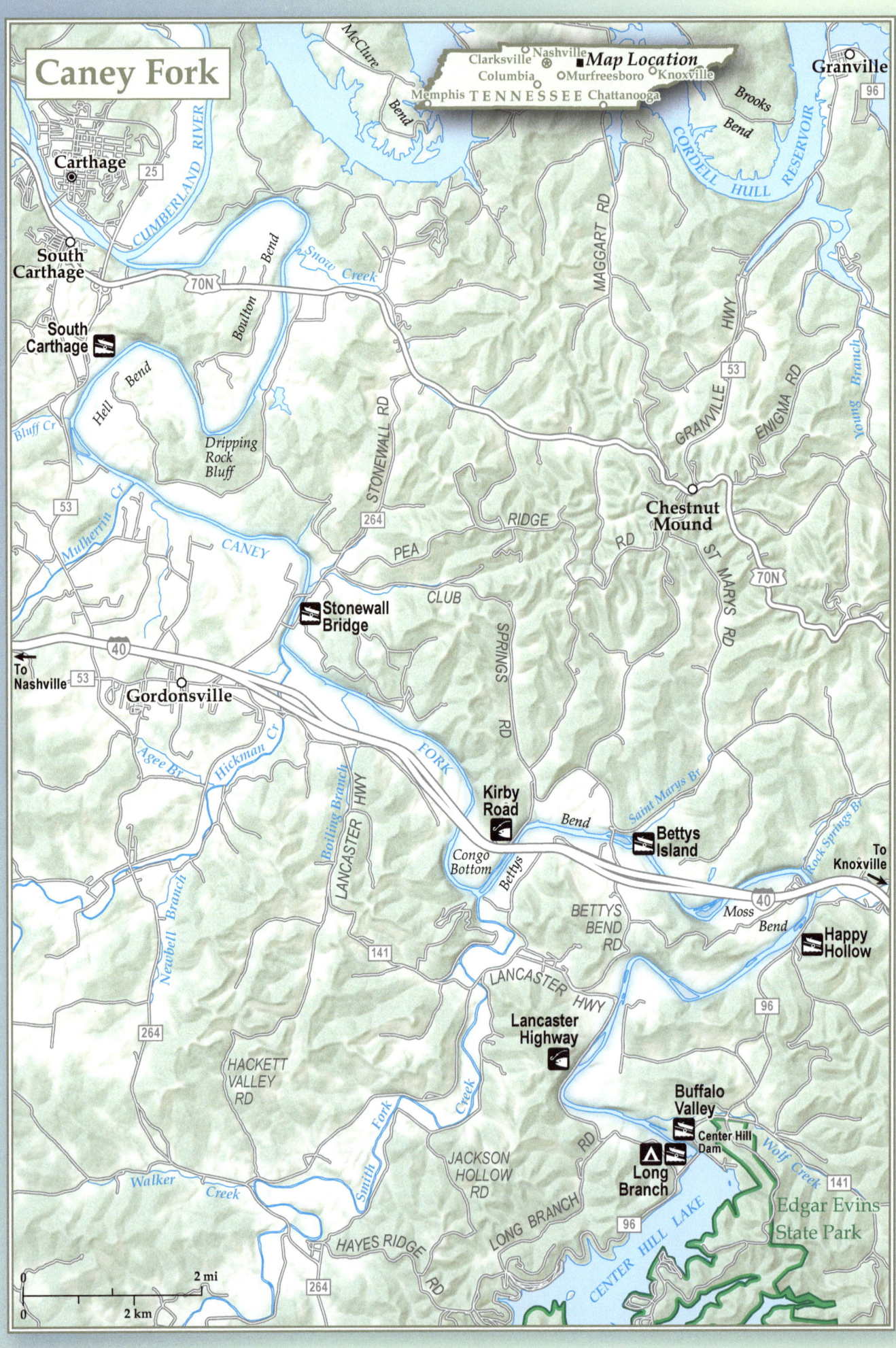

43 · Caney Fork

▶ **Location:** The Caney Fork is located in Middle Tennessee, approximately one hour east of Nashville on Interstate 40, and approximately two hours west of Knoxville on Interstate 40.

The Caney Fork is typical of southern hydroelectric tailwater, situated below Center Hill Dam, which is operated by the Army Corps of Engineers. Daily releases of cold trout-sustaining water from Center Hill Dam meander 26 miles through the gentle hills of Middle Tennessee. The river crosses under Interstate 40 five times before joining the Cumberland River near the town of Carthage, Tennessee.

The river, at first glance, is not your classic trout stream environment. The gentle riffles, runs, and deep pools of the Caney Fork lack structure and cover, which makes it a tricky river to read and a difficult environment in which to locate trout. The river also lacks the prolific mayfly hatches found in the tailwaters of East Tennessee. Crustaceans and midges dominate the food base. Do not let the lack of classic hatches fool you—anglers are pleasantly surprised by the number of quality rainbows, browns, and brook trout found throughout the river. Recent water quality improvements and trophy trout regulations continue to improve both size and quantity of fish.

The Caney Fork is a year-round fishery, and it runs at about 250 cubic feet per second when the Corps is not generating for power or releasing water through a sluice or floodgate. Water releases can reach volumes upward of 15,000 cubic feet per second. Wadable water levels are found during times of no water releases, 300 cubic feet per second and lower. The river is also very fishable during higher water with a drift boat, canoe, or other boats with motors. Most anglers prefer a water level below 5,000 cubic feet per second. The river can be a dangerous float at higher water levels. Make sure you have checked what the water release schedule is for the day; water levels can go from the top of your wading boots to over the top of your head in a matter of minutes! Release schedules are always subject to change, so be sure to check it in the morning before departure. Water release schedules can be obtained online at www.tva.gov/river/lakeinfo/index.htm.

The upper eight miles of the river (from the dam to Betty's Island) supports the majority of fish, anglers, recreational paddlers, and guides. The summer months, in this section of the river, can be very crowded. This is due to a combination of easy access, proximity of a campground, the highest number of fish per mile, and the recent proliferation of canoe and kayak liveries. The upper eight miles also has the two shortest floats on the river. So, from May through September, fishing on a weekday is a far better experience than the weekend. The middle and lower river has less traffic, but there is very little legal access other than by boat or canoe.

If you're coming to fish the Caney Fork, always have plenty of midge, blackfly, scud, and sow bug patterns in your fly box. These are the big four trout foods found on the river, top to bottom, 12 months out of the year. Sow bugs are my go-to pattern when the fish are tight-lipped—winter, spring, summer, or fall.

Long flat pools in the Caney Fork produce some nice rainbows. Jim Mauries

Above. Caney Fork brown trout. Notice the sow bugs in the vegetation above his gill plate. Jim Mauries

Inset. Releasing a Caney Fork 'bow. Jim Mauries

Facing. Thomas Mauries learning to row at a young age on the Caney. Jim Mauries

April usually kicks off the season on the Caney with caddis hatches in the middle and lower sections that can run through June some years. Scuds, sow bugs, and midges dominate the upper section. The fishing in the spring is usually fast and furious. After long periods of higher water, the fish are fat, strong, and usually not as selective. April is also when the first run of buffalo come into the river to spawn. Thousands of fish that typically run in size from 6 to over 20 pounds come up the Caney Fork, usually in two waves. They will eat a dead-drifted San Juan Worm, Super Bugger, crayfish pattern, or some days, a good old Wooly Bugger. After they enter the river, they will all spawn at the same time, and overnight, they will be gone. They leave small cream eggs everywhere on the bottom of the river, and the trout gorge themselves on the eggs for a short time after the buffalo spawn.

June through October on the Caney is midge and blackfly time of year. Long leaders and fine tippets rule the day during the summer months. The river is usually very wadable and fishes like a big spring creek this time of year. If sight-casting to feeding fish in thin, clear water is what you like, then you will love the river this time of year. The fish can be very selective about size and color. They will not move far for the fly. Fish will even move away from brightly colored strike indicators in thin water.

Summer months in Tennessee can also bring some great terrestrial fishing. Grasshoppers, crickets, beetles, and ants can always be found struggling in the surface film. October usually brings caddis back into the middle and lower river sections. One other thing to note is that middle to late summer is striper time on the Caney Fork. The Cumberland River fish move into the Caney when the summer heat sets in. Gizzard shad pour into the river, and usually starting in July, the stripers will always follow the shad. Fish over 30 pounds are very common on a fly rod this time of year.

The river during November through the end of March usually requires a boat, because this is our rainy season. It is

Caney Fork buffalo carp—a face only a mother could love. Jim Mauries

common to have no wadable water for months on end. The fishing during this time of year calls for streamers and big sink tips, and heavier 8- to 9-weight rods with 200–450 grain are the norm. The cold winter months on the Caney Fork are the big-fish time of year. When the stars align correctly, and we have just the right amount of moisture so the river doesn't blow out, and the air temperatures stay cold enough to start killing shad on the lake side of the dam, then, get ready! The shad get sucked through the generators in such massive numbers, that it creates a feeding frenzy. The shad hatch on the Caney is something every angler should experience at least once in his or her lifetime. Big trout, stripers, walleye, skipjack shad, and buffalo all get in on the buffet. Nothing beats a floating shad pattern getting crushed by a 10-pound trout or a 30-pound striper! This is our reward after months of 15-foot leaders, 8X tippet, and size 26 flies!

▶ **Hatches:** See the following hatch chart for Caney Fork.

Caney Fork Hatch Chart

	Jan	Feb	Mar	Apr	May	Jun	Jul	Aug	Sep	Oct	Nov	Dec
Midges	X	X	X	X	X	X	X	X	X	X	X	X
Black Flies	X	X	X	X	X	X	X	X	X	X	X	X
Scuds	X	X	X	X	X	X	X	X	X	X	X	X
Sowbugs	X	X	X	X	X	X	X	X	X	X	X	X
Caddises				X	X	X	X			X	X	
Light Cahills						X	X	X				
Craneflies							X	X	X			
Terrestrials						X	X	X	X			
Threadfin Shad	X	X									X	X
Gizzard Shad				X	X	X	X	X	X			
Sculpins Darters Minnows	X	X	X	X	X	X	X	X	X	X	X	X
Snails							X	X	X	X		

➤ **Regulations:** The Caney Fork is a year-round fishery with opportunities to both wade and float. Special trout regulations apply to the Caney from Center Hill Dam downstream to the Cumberland River, including tributaries. Total daily creel of all trout in combination is five fish (rainbow, brook, and brown). Rainbow trout regulations include 14- to 20-inch slot, with only one fish over 20 inches. Brook trout regulations include 14- to 20-inch slot, with only one more than 20 inches. For brown trout, the regulation is one per day, with a 24-inch minimum length limit. Anglers must purchase a Tennessee fishing license and a trout stamp. See www.twra.gov for more information.

➤ **Tackle:** Low-water rods and reels should be 9-foot, 4- and 5-weights, loaded with floating lines, leaders 9–15 feet, and fluorocarbon tippet sizes 4–8X. High-water rods should be 9-foot, 6- to 9-weights, loaded with floating lines and 30-foot, type 6 sinking tips up to 350 grains.

Jim Mauries.

JIM MAURIES owns and operates Fly South, a full-service fly shop located in Nashville, Tennessee. He has been a professional fly tier and has guided and instructed fly fishers in the mid-South for more than 25 years.

CLOSEST FLY SHOPS

Cumberland Transit
2807 West End Ave.
Nashville, TN 37203
615-321-4069
info@cumberlandtransit.com
www.cumberlandtransit.com

Fly South
115 19th Ave. S.
Nashville, TN 37203
615-341-0420
flysouth@bellsouth.net
www.flysouth.net

Caney Fork Canoe Rental at Big Rock Market
(carries a very limited supply of fly gear but is the only fly shop on the river)
1193 Wolf Creek Rd.
Silver Point, TN 38582
931-858-4585
www.caneyforkcanoerental.com

CLOSEST GUIDES AND OUTFITTERS

Fly South
115 19th Ave. S.
Nashville, TN 37203
615-341-0420
flysouth@bellsouth.net
www.flysouth.net

Rod and Gun Guide Services
3502 Amanda Ave.
Nashville, TN 37215
615-385-1116
www.rodandgunguide.com

Southeastern Fly
615-796-5143
www.southeasternfly.com

CLOSEST LODGING

Holiday Inn Express
826 S Cumberland St,
Lebanon, TN 37087
615-994-3225
https://www.ihg.com

Hampton Inn and Suites
1065 Franklin Rd,
Lebanon, TN 37090
615-444-3445

Caney Fork Canoe Rental at Big Rock Market
1193 Wolf Creek Rd.
Silver Point, TN 38582
931-858-4585
www.caneyforkcanoerental.com

Edgar Evins State Park Cabins
1630 Edgar Evins State Park Rd.
Silver Point, TN 38582
931-858-2114
www.tnstateparks.com/parks/cabins/edgar-evins

Long Branch Recreation Area
(located on the river beneath the dam)
Silver Point, TN 38582
615-548-8002

CLOSEST RESTAURANT

The Galley (open April through October)
2100 Edgar Evins State Park Rd.
Silver Point, TN 38582
931-858-2424
www.thegalleyeem.com

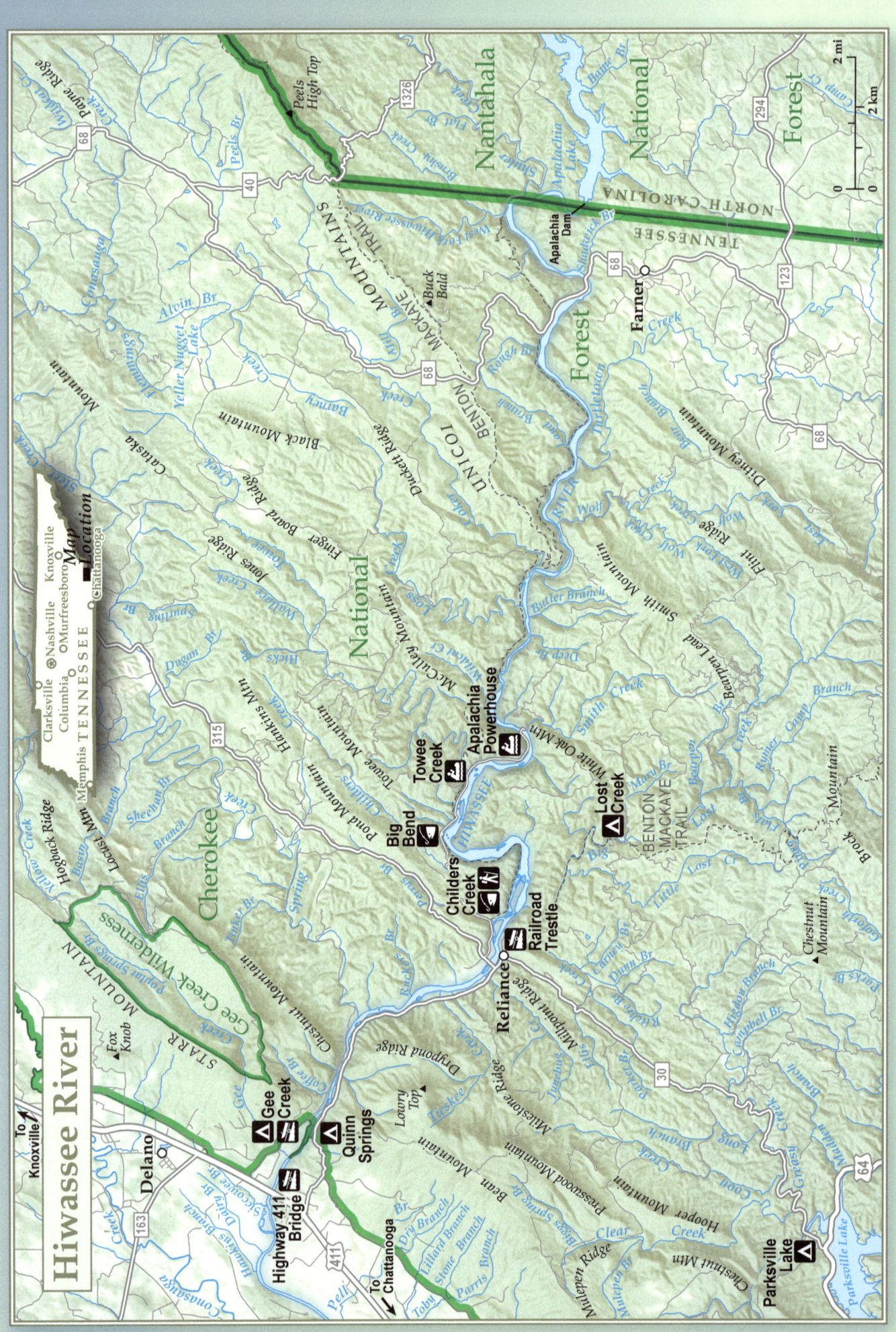

44 · Hiwassee River

▶ **Location:** To reach the headwaters of the Hiwassee River, travel Tennessee 411 north from Benton, Tennessee, taking a right onto Tennessee 30. Drive approximately six miles on this winding road that shows you views of rocky cliffs, mountain wildflowers, riverside picnic areas, and primitive campgrounds into the historic community of Reliance, Tennessee. This district was listed on the National Register of Historic Places because of its local architectural and historical significance and the fact that it represents a significant and distinguishable entity that conveys a sense of time and place. Make a left at Webb Brothers' General Store onto the bridge, crossing the Hiwassee River. At the end of the bridge, make a right onto the John Muir Trail and Forest Service Road 108. This road follows the river, traveling over the Hood Mountain overlooks view of Big Bend, the Hiwassee's mile-wide curve, with the John Muir Trail traversing below. In approximately five miles, the road ends at the Tennessee Valley Authority Apalachia Powerhouse. The Apalachia Dam is located in Cherokee County, North Carolina. The water from Apalachia Lake and Apalachia Dam travels underground 8.3 miles, where a conduit carries water from the dam's reservoir to the powerhouse located 12 miles downstream, across the state line in Polk County, Tennessee. TVA records a water flow schedule each day after 6 P.M. You can receive the information by calling 800-238-2264. Press 4 for Apalachia Dam and 22 for the Hiwassee River, or download the free TVA water release app on your phone to check the water release schedule at any given moment.

This tailwater river has three, approximately five-mile-long sections. (All three sections are stocked and are put-and-take fisheries, but an encouragingly high number of anglers practice catch-and-release.) The top section is from the Apalachia Powerhouse boat launch to the railroad trestle ramp in Reliance. The middle section is from Reliance to the Tennessee 411 bridge, where the boat ramp is under the bridge. The third section begins there and ends at the Patty Bridge ramp a few miles from Benton, Tennessee.

The uppermost section at the Apalachia Powerhouse has deep pools with limestone rock formations and should be treated with extreme caution even when the river is "off" and wadable. The powerhouse does have flashing lights and sirens alarming anglers prior to water release in this top section. Unfortunately, one mile downstream it is impossible to see or hear the alarm. Diligent awareness of the water levels around you at all times is pertinent to fishing the uppermost reaches of the Hiwassee in safety. When the river is "on" and the powerhouse is running its two generators, a watercraft is recommended. This section of the river has Class II and III rapids and is managed by the USDA Forest Service. Under the forest service's specifications, all watercraft individuals are to wear U. S. Coast Guard–approved personal flotation devices at all times. Alcohol is not allowed in this region of the Hiwassee River. With all that said, this breathtaking section of the river can and will produce good trout fishing year-round for anglers afoot or afloat.

Rainbows like the one pictured here are numerous in the Hiwassee. Bill Stranahan Hiwassee River Guides

Above. Areas like the steps provide great holding water for trout. Bill Stanahan Hiwassee River Guides.com

Inset. Early fall browns on the Hiwasse are aggresive in nature and spectacular in color. Dane Law
Southeastern Anglers

The middle section and lower sections of the Hiwassee fish very well in the early spring months and are stocked by Tennessee Wildlife Resources Agency (TWRA). The river travels deep and calm through farmland, high mountain cliffs, and private river homes on to her destination at the Tennessee River. In this region, you will have good opportunities of catching trout, bass, striper, shad, and sunfish. Many days in this area, you will be overshadowed while fishing by a glider from the Chilhowee Gliderport, an eagle, an osprey, or a kingfisher. It's also not uncommon to see the horses and buggies of the Amish farmers and families along the riverbanks of this lower section of the Hiwassee.

▶ **Hatches:** In winter, think both ends of the spectrum in terms of size. Midges, midges, midges. Employ sizes 18–24 in gray, black, olive, and red, but be on the lookout for Blue-winged Olive hatches every day, which are still small (anywhere from size 18 to sizes in the 20s). Then be ready to prospect with medium to big streamers, and yes, the old tried-and-true black or olive Woolly Buggers will work. If you happen to be there immediately after a hard freeze, fish a White Zonker, Woolly Bugger, or Bunny Fly. There can be shad killed in the upper reservoir, and they sink and come through the TVA turbines. Big fish go nuts for them.

In the spring, be prepared for a virtual tailwater smorgasbord. Mid-March into April, even all through April, be armed with March brown imitations. Size 14 is in order. Then you'll see Hendricksons, and you'll want to use size 14 again. You can even use the occasional size 14 Cahills (few in numbers, usually, but the fish will pass everything up for one.) The Blue-winged Olives will show in two, if not three, sizes and the fish will key in decidedly. Be prepared with sizes 16, 18, and even sizes in the 20s. If this is not enough, Sulphurs will begin hatching, again in two or three sizes. I've found size 16 and size 18 fit the bill, as the trout seem to ignore the big, very yellow size 14. Round this out with a good supply of size 18 black, as well as tan, caddis. It seems all fish everywhere like caddisfly pupae, too. This holds true all year as well—if you see fish feeding but can't see the hatch, try a size 18 black caddisfly. Caddisflies are virtually impossible for you to see on the water, but not so for the trout! Mid-April can bring on a short but storybook-like hatch of Grannom Caddis with green (almost lime green) body, bleached elk wing, and size 14. You'll see fish taking them even midair!

All the major hatches collide in June. It's not until July when you see the darker-colored flies diminish. The Sulphurs will hang on to some degree all month and into mid-August, providing action all day. The good news is that a fairly rare mayfly begins taking precedence. There's not even a fly shop name for it, other than the Latin name *Isonychia*! It's profuse

Floating the Hiwassee is the most popular way to fish this large river. Bill Stranahan Hiwassee River Guides

for three months during the hottest part of the summer. The *Isonychia* is big (size 14) with a dark claret body with slate gray wings. The nymph is a swimmer—a very, very fast and active one. Try fishing wet patterns or emerger patterns across and down, or even try stripping a nymph a bit. It works!

Late-summer days are made for stoneflies, especially here. Again, you'll enjoy a reprieve from microscopic fishing. Try size 12 and larger Golden Stoneflies. Fish yellow Stimulators to your heart's content till dark or after. With that said, if you're up for it, be prepared for an epic spinner fall of Blue-winged Olives and Sulphurs at dark thirty.

Being a tailwater, fall brings warmer than desired water temps, and the fish and the fishing will slow by late October and November. They're still catchable, but you'll possibly be relegated to fishing buggers slowly. My favorite pattern in the fall is the Muddler Minnow. Use size 8 all the way to size 14.

Remember that this is a tailwater—it can be technical, at least for the larger holdover fish. Think emergers and cripples all year, especially when going to bat during any of the mayfly hatches. You'll be rewarded.

➤ **Regulations:** The Hiwassee is a Delayed Harvest area. From March 1 through September 30, there is a seven-trout creel limit with only two being brown trout. There are no bait restrictions. From October 1 through the end of February, the rule is catch-and-release for all trout. Use artificial lures only.

➤ **Tackle:**
- 9-foot, 5- or 6-weight rods with floating or sink-tip lines
- Leaders 9–12 feet tapered to 6X
- Waders, wading boots, and wading staff are recommended

WANDA TAYLOR was the first woman to be certified as a Master Casting Instructor by the International Federation of Fly Fishers. She was awarded the 2005 SE IFFF Woman of the Year and the 2008 SE IFFF Council Award of Excellence, and she is an advisory staff member of www.tforods.com. In addition, Wanda is an ambassador of Georgia Women Fly Fishers, Casting for Recovery and Casting Carolinas. She is the owner of Wanda Taylor Fly Fishing.

Wanda Taylor in search of an early morning striper bite on Lake Lanier. Henry Cowan

CLOSEST FLY SHOPS

Reliance Fly & Tackle
588 Childers Creek Rd.
Reliance, TN 37369
423-338-7771
www.relianceflyshop.blogspot.com

Little River Outfitters
106 Town Square Dr.
Townsend, TN 37882
865-448-9459
info@littleriveroutfitters.com
www.littleriveroutfitters.com

CLOSEST GUIDES AND OUTFITTERS

Southeastern Anglers
149 McCormick Rd. SW
Cartersville, GA 30120
423-338-7368
danelaw@southeasternanglers.com
www.southeasternanglers.com
/contact-information.html

Dry Flyer Outfitters
500 E. Main St.
Blue Ridge, GA 30513
706-537-3254
https://www.facebook.com
/Dryflyeroutfitters/?rc=p

CLOSEST LODGING

Mountain Stream Cabins
1370 Childers Creek Rd.
Reliance, TN 37369
423-338-1070
www.mountainstreamlodging.com/

Hiwassee Outfitters Cabins
155 Ellis Creek Rd.
Reliance, TN 37369
423-338-8115
www.hiwasseeoutfitters.com

Lost Creek Cabins
328 Lost Creek Rd.
Reliance, TN 37369
423-338-0757
http://www.lostcreekcabins.com/

Welcome Valley Village
Whitewater Inn
120 Whitewater Dr.
Ocoee, TN 37361
423-338-1201
www.ocoeewhitewaterinn.com

Red Roof Inn
600 N. Tennessee Ave.
Etowah, TN 37331
423-781-7459

Hiwassee Outfitters
155 Ellis Creek Rd.
Reliance, TN 37369
423-338-8115

Gee Creek
404 Spring Creek Rd.
P.O. Box 5
Delano, TN 37325

Two Rivers
397 Dentville Rd.
Benton, TN 37307
423-338-7208
info@2riverscamping.com
http://2riverscamping.com/

CLOSEST RESTAURANTS

Lottie's Diner
5790 Old Hwy. 411
Benton, TN 37307
423-338-1322

Ocoee Dam Deli & Diner
1223 U.S. Route 64
Ocoee, TN 37361
423-338-8184
www.ocoeedamdeli.com

Michael's Casual Dining
862 Tennessee Ave.
Etowah, TN 37331
423-263-2603
www.michaelsgreatfood.com

Ocoee Gondolier
1603 Tennessee 64
Ocoee, TN 37361
423-338-7299

Castillo's Mexican Restaurant
331 Tennessee 33
Etowah, TN 37331
423-263-6562

CLOSEST HOSPITALS OR URGENT CARE

Woods Memorial
886 Tennessee 411 N.
Etowah, TN 37331
423-263-3600
www.starrregional.com

Bradley County Memorial
2305 Chambliss Ave. NW
Cleveland, TN 37311
423-559-6127

Erlanger Health Center
975 E. Third St.
Chattanooga, TN 37403
423-778-7000
www.erlanger.org

CLOSEST FLY-FISHING SCHOOLS

Wanda Taylor Fly Fishing
706-537-7444
http://wandataylorflyfishing.com

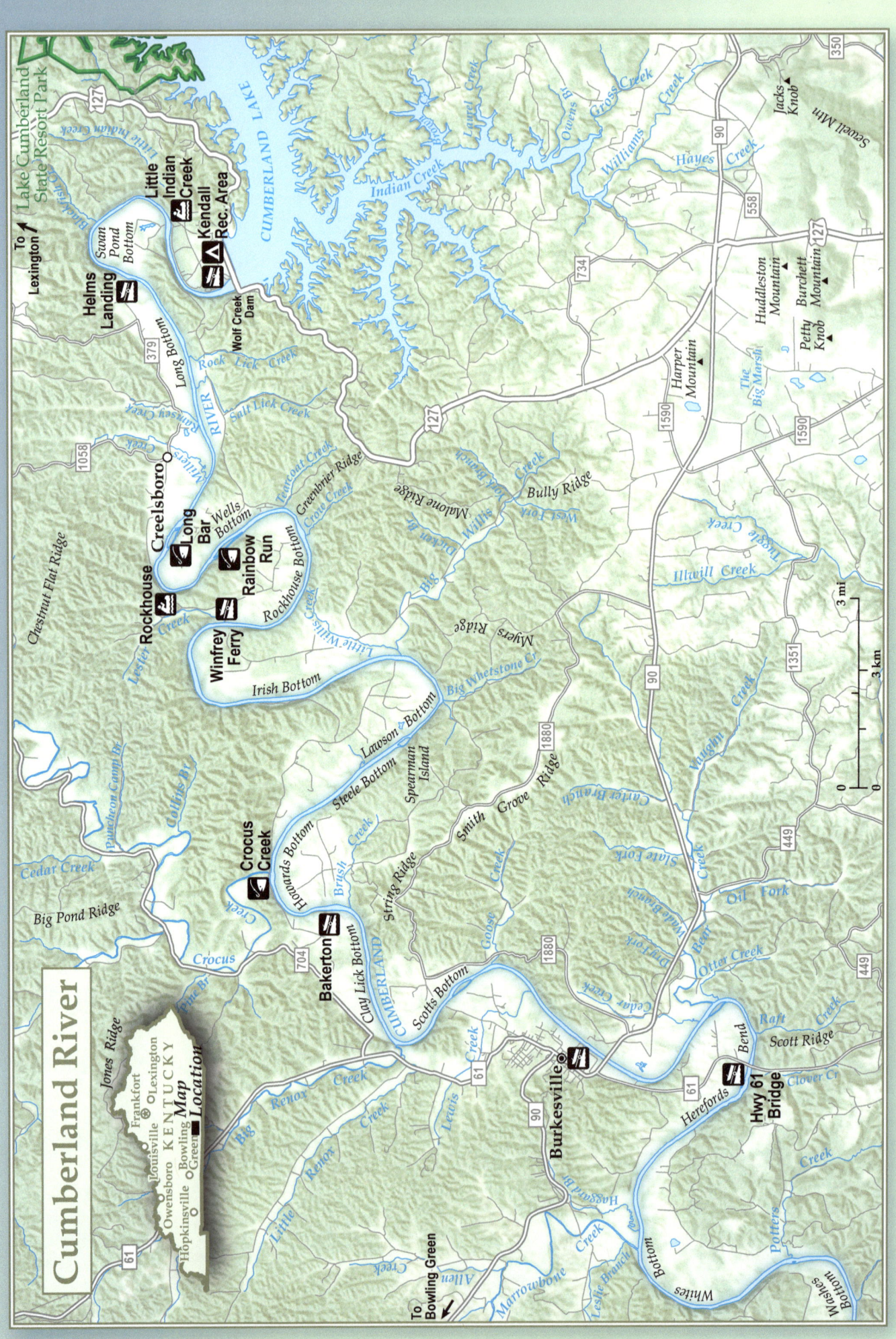

45 · Cumberland

➤ **Location:** The Cumberland River lies about 130 miles south of Louisville, Kentucky; 105 miles southwest of Lexington, Kentucky; 95 miles east of Bowling Green, Kentucky; and about 155 miles northeast of Nashville, Tennessee.

Some would argue the Cumberland River tailwater below Wolf Creek Dam is the best trout stream in the Southeast. If you haven't fished the "Cumby," then I can guarantee it's the best Southern trout stream that you haven't fished yet.

The Army Corps of Engineers originally constructed Wolf Creek Dam in the early 1940s to provide hydroelectric power and flood control to the region. This 258-foot tall, 5,736-foot long concrete and earthen dam created the largest man-made lake east of the Mississippi: Lake Cumberland. It is one of the larger hydroelectric dams in the area, with six 45-kilowatt units. The daily water releases that power the generators provide enough coldwater discharge to hold trout for over 70 miles downstream.

In the mid-Southern part of Kentucky, the Cumberland winds its way from Wolf Creek Dam through beautiful rolling foothills, farms, and pastures that dot the rural Kentucky landscape. It passes natural rock bridges and tumbles over long riffles and runs, full of fossils and geodes, down to the town of Burkesville, Kentucky. The river then continues to snake its way to the Tennessee border just northwest of Celina, Tennessee. The best way to describe the Cumberland River is that it is as if you took the best parts of several Southern tailwater trout streams and mashed them all together. It has the river miles of the White River, hatches like the South Holston River, cover that reminds you of the Clinch or Watauga Rivers, technical fishing and weed beds of the Caney Fork and Elk Rivers, and fish quality and quantity to rival all of them.

While the river offers plenty of walk-in wadable fishing opportunities, predominately in the upper 25 miles of the river, most Cumberland anglers fish the river out of some type of motorized boat. The most common style of fishing on the river is to motor to the top of a run, shut off, then drift down through the run, fire back up, and repeat. Wading anglers can get frustrated with boat anglers running through them and then drifting over them several times in a row. I have found if you ask boaters nicely to please not drift through your fishing area, most will happily adjust their drift. Drift boats, kayaks, pontoon boats, and other small watercraft can all be effective on the river, depending on flows.

Like all of the southern tailwaters that hold trout, the four essential fly patterns that catch fish all year are midges, blackflies, scud, and sow bugs. Midge fishing on the Cumberland can dominate July, August, and September. Terrestrials can

A lone wade angler at Rainbow Run on the Cumberland. Gene Slusher

also play an important role during the dog days of summer. Ants, beetles, grasshoppers, and cicadas can also produce well. (The river gets cicadas every 17 years; this is an epic experience that's hard to explain unless you have fished it!) The wonderful thing about the Cumberland is that it has multiple caddisflies, mayflies, and even stoneflies in the river. Baitfish patterns typically rule high-water fishing, pounding deeper water structure looking for trophy fish or trying to chase the world-class stripers that are also in the river.

Above. Looking out of Rock House Natural Arch during a passing storm. *Gene Slusher*

Inset. David Buxbaum with a Cumberland River brown. *Jim Mauries*

Cumby flies. Jim Mauries

The fishing that is often overlooked in the Cumberland, and most say doesn't exist, is the outstanding dry-fly fishing. I have had days dry-fly fishing on the Cumberland that rival any stream in the country. Most anglers overlook the hatches on this river, but the bugs are what draw me to the Cumby. I have experienced midge hatches that roll into caddis hatches that roll into mayfly hatches that roll back to caddis before the spinners fall just before dark, all on the same run. Heads-up sipping off the surface, sunup to sundown—heaven!

The Cumberland River is a year-round fishery. Wadable water levels are found during times of no water release. The Cumberland is always very cold, even during the hot summer months. In July and August, the water will still be in the low 50s, and wearing waders is a must. Fog is common and can be problematic on the Cumberland. Many people have missed the boat ramp or run into other boats (or even over wading anglers). Be careful! Water releases can reach volumes upward of 30,000 cubic feet per second, so it is very important to check water release schedules before planning to fish for the day. Water release schedules can be obtained online at www.tva.gov/river/lakeinfo/index.htm. Release schedules are always subject to change, so be sure to check it again in the morning before departure. Always be aware and alert to water rising during the course of the day's fishing. (Anglers should also be aware that cell phone coverage can be spotty along the Cumberland—plan accordingly.)

An unfortunate thing to note is the presence of the invasive *didymo algae (Didymosphenia geminata)* in the Cumberland. Inspect your gear, boats, trailers, and other equipment when you pull out of the river. Treat your wading boots, and anything that might hold this nasty algae, with a 2 percent bleach solution. Don't be the one who spreads didymo to the next stream or river system!

Summertime cicadas. Jim Mauries

Cumberland River rainbow. Gene Slusher

A foggy start to a day on the Cumberland. Gene Slusher

▶ **Regulations:** The Cumberland River is a year-round fishery with opportunities to both wade and float. All anglers must have a valid Kentucky fishing license and a trout permit (see www.fw.ky.gov for more information). The trout regulations for the Cumberland River, Hatchery Creek, and all its tributaries from Wolf Creek Dam to the Tennessee state line are as follows:

- Creel limit is five fish.
- Brown trout requirements include one fish daily creel limit, with fish longer than 20 inches only.
- Regarding rainbows, any fish 15 to 20 inches must be released (only one rainbow over 20 inches may be in creel).
- Brook trout regulations include one fish daily creel, with fish longer than 15 inches only.

▶ **Tackle:** Rods and reels should be 9-foot, 4- and 5-weights, loaded with floating lines, leaders 9–15 feet, and fluorocarbon tippet sizes 4–8X. In high water, rods should be 9-foot, 6- to 9-weights, loaded with floating lines and 15- to 30-foot type 6 sinking tips up to 350 grains.

George Mauries with a Cumberland River buffalo. Jim Mauries

Jim Mauries.

JIM MAURIES owns and operates Fly South, a full-service fly shop located in Nashville, Tennessee. He has been a professional fly tier and has guided and instructed fly fishers in the mid-South for more than 25 years.

CLOSEST FLY SHOPS

The Lexington Angler
119 Clay Ave.
Lexington, KY 40502
859-389-6552
www.lexingtonangler.com

Fly South
115 19th Ave. S.
Nashville, TN 37203
615-341-0420
flysouth@bellsouth.net
www.flysouth.net

CLOSEST GUIDES AND OUTFITTER

Cumberland Drifters
Brandon Wade
859-983-2907
brandonwade@gmail.com
Michael Wlosinski
859-492-7906
michaeldubya@gmail.com
www.cumberlanddrifters.com

CLOSEST LODGING

Lure Lodge
(at Lake Cumberland State Park Resort)
5465 State Park Rd.
Jamestown, KY 42629
270- 343-3111
http://parks.ky.gov/parks/resortparks/lake-cumberland/

Alpine Motel
700 Hill St.
Burkesville, KY 42717
270-864-7100
www.alpinemotel.com

Kendall Campground
80 Kendall Rd.
Jamestown, KY 42629
270-343-4660

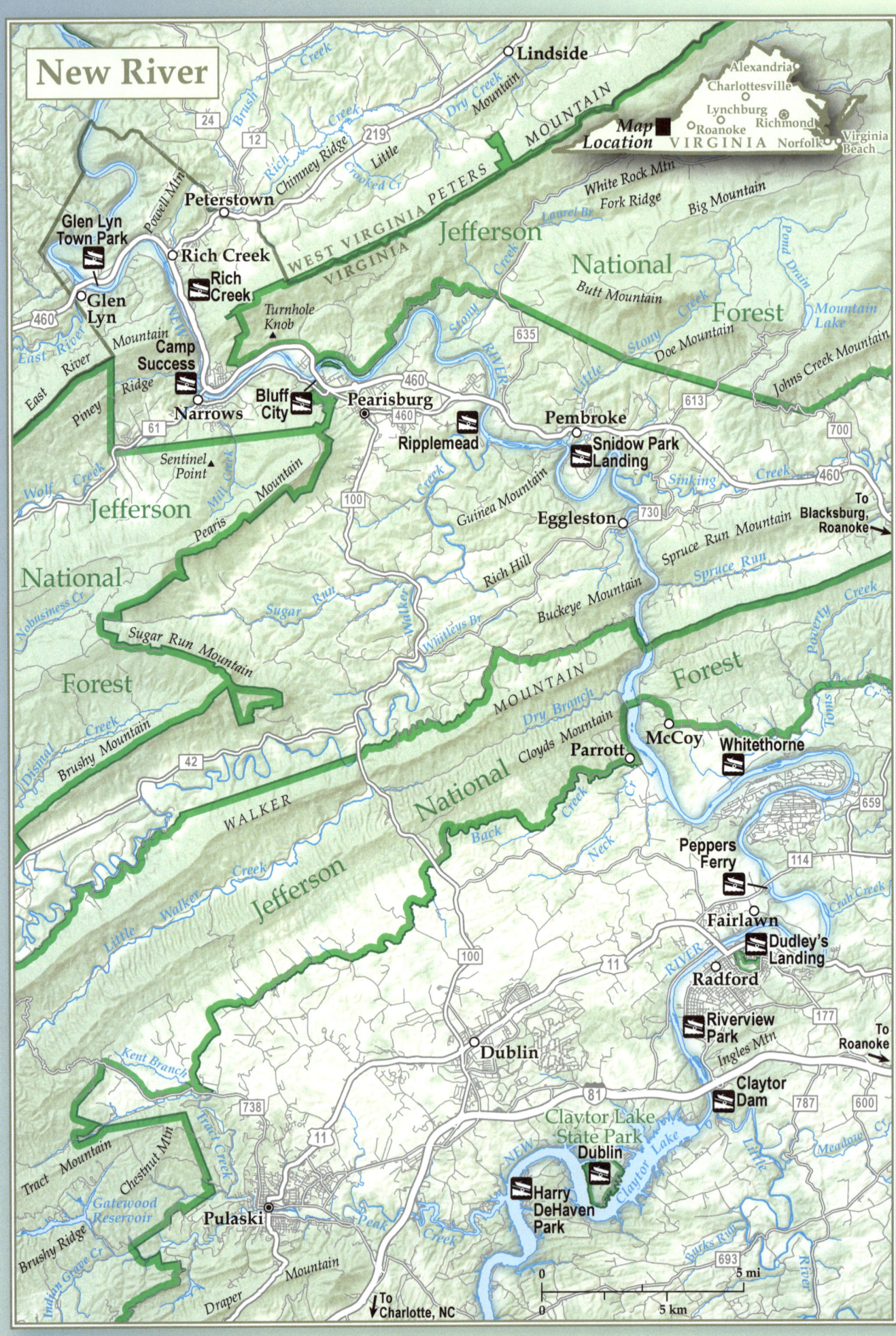

46 · New River

➤ **Location:** The New River is located one hour from Roanoke, Virginia, and three hours from Charlotte, North Carolina, Roanoke Blacksburg Regional Airport provides numerous flights in and out of the Southeast.

The New River, part of the Ohio River watershed, is a tributary of the Kanawha River, flowing about 320 miles long. The New River flows through the states of North Carolina, Virginia, and West Virginia. Much of the river's path through West Virginia is designated as the New River Gorge National River.

The New River below Claytor Lake in Virginia starts its long journey through mountainous regions full of long views and cliff-side dwellings that allow anglers to experience one of the last great remote sections of rivers in the Southeast. With great smallmouth and musky fishing, anglers can pick their quarry throughout this full-year fishery. The New River is large in proportion to a lot of rivers and streams listed in this guidebook, leaving limited wading access. Driftboat access is highly recommended. Anglers are welcome to consult with the Virginia DNR for boat ramps and other access points to plan out their fishing day.

This upper section of the New River can provide anglers with unreal fishing days and great scenery. Starting in Radford, Virginia, anglers can float through Radford University to Byers Park. This float is pretty much in the middle of the college towns of Radford University and Virginia Tech. Warm spring and summer weekend days can provide anglers with some traffic from tubing, recreational boaters, and fellow fishermen. Fishing on weekdays, anglers will find that the New River traffic and angling pressure can be light, and fishing can shine. Expect to float through long pools and shallow river-wide riffles. Fishing these riffles and huge tailouts, anglers can cast minnow pattern streamers and topwater flies. Remember to wait for the eat with topwater flies.

Smallmouth bass are the target species, but musky roam these waters as well. Targeting musky on a fly will be tough. Anglers will need to pay attention to larger pools and runs. Musky don't feed all day long, so numerous casts and the right tackle can help. The only way to catch these dinosaurs is to stay focused and keep casting. Patience and good drifts will hopefully produce musky.

From the one-stoplight town of Pembroke, Virginia, to the industrial town of Bluff City, anglers will see more gradient, large cliff walls, rock palisades, and larger rapids in the lower section of the New River. These lower floats have the remote characteristics that are worth the drive or flight. Floating this part of the New River needs to be taken seriously for the inexperienced oarsman or boater. Flowing through more remote sections than the upper section near Radford, these river sections will also provide great smallmouth and musky fishing. Smallmouth bass will seek shelter in the numerous broken ledges and Class II and Class III rapids.

The locations of the many boat ramps and access points can be obtained through the Virginia Department of Game and Inland Fisheries. Fishing some sections of the New River can be make an extremely long day, while some sections re-

David Howell releasing a new river smallie. Kevin Howell

David Howell with a New River smallmouth that fell victim to a black meat whistle near Pembroke. Kevin Howell

quire just a few hours. Refer to local river maps, and rely on experienced guides and fly shops to aim you in the correct direction. If you do not have your own whitewater fishing assault rig, try a guide to show you the way. Guides run large rafts, motorboats, and jet boats. Late spring and early summer can give anglers the greatest chance to catch smallmouths on streamers and topwater flies. As the water warms through the spring months, smallmouths will start to spread out, away from spawning grounds, and start to feed in summer patterns. During summer months, smallmouths will stage along structure and deeper pools, feeding on aquatic insects, terrestrials, and minnows. Smallmouths can make for a fantastic day of angling.

As fall sets in Virginia and the Southeast, water and air temperatures drop. Smallmouths and musky start to feed for the long winters of Virginia and the New River. Fall and winter fishing can be cold as Michigan, but fishing does not stop.

Musky fishing this time of year can be good, with slow, long retrieves. Musky feed on whatever they see that is easy to eat. Suckers and fallfish can be an easy lunch. Tying or buying flies that resemble a 5- to 12-inch baitfish pattern will work well to catch the attention of such a great fish. Staying focused fishing for musky, anglers can be rewarded at times with the freshwater fish of a lifetime.

Water levels will fluctuate from Claytor Dam, at times, making fish move from day to day. Checking the release schedules and water levels through the Virginia USGS stream flow data page will help anglers plan where to float from day to day. Reading, research, and getting the water levels correct can be tricky, but more experience with water flows will make fishing easier in the future.

▶ **Tackle:** Smallmouth anglers will need fly rods ranging from 9-foot, 5-weights to 9-foot, 7-weights. Floating lines will work great for topwater flies, small streamers, and crayfish flies. Intermediate lines are great for days when smallmouth are not looking for topwater bugs.

Musky anglers will want to have a few fly lines readily available. Floating lines will work for warmer days. As water temperatures drop, anglers may need to trade floating lines for heavy-grain intermediate lines or full-sink lines. RIO Products has revolutionized musky lines with the Outbound Short. Casting heavier grain lines, along with heavy shooting tapers, will help anglers chuck large flies made of chicken feathers and deer hair. Leaders and tippet sizes will vary with water levels and water clarity. Smallmouth leaders should range from 9 feet to 10 feet. Tippets should be 2–4X.

Take a break from the smallmouths. Try the colorful bluegill and redeye bass in the shade during summer months. Dropping a tungsten damselfly nymph under a popper can provide anyone with a few hours of bluegill bustin'.

Musky leaders should be ready for a toothy attack and an erratic battle. Musky leaders can be really simple. I suggest a 4-foot piece of 40-pound fluorocarbon with a 2-foot piece of 60- to 80-pound bite tippet. Knottable wire works well as a bite tippet also, but some tend to kink after a few hours. RIO Products seems to have the best 20- to 40-pound Powerflex wire bite tippet.

- Smallmouth Bass Topwater Flies (fly colors and sizes will vary from day to day with cloudy or clear skies; fly sizes from 1/0 to 6)
    Boogle Bug, sizes 4-6
    Dahlberg Diver, sizes 1-6
    Chocklett's Disc Slider, size 4
    Floating Gummy, sizes 4-8
    Hair bugs, sizes 1-8
    Cicada patterns, sizes 4-6
    Umpqua Swimming Minnow, sizes 1-4
    Chocklett's Cicada, sizes 4-6
    Sneaky Pete, sizes 6-8
- Smallmouth Bass Streamer Flies
    Gummy Minnow, sizes 1-8
    Zoo Cougar, sizes 4-6
    Clousers, sizes 1-4
    Half & Half, sizes 1/0-4

David Howell with a light-colored summertime smallmouth. Kevin Howell

Guide Blaine Chocklett with a nice New River musky. Blane Chocklett

    Walker's Wiggler, sizes 4-6
    Zonkers, sizes 4-8
- Smallmouth Nymphs
    Howell's Big Nasty, sizes 4-6
    Bitch Creek, sizes 4-6
    Near 'Nuff Crawfish, sizes 4-6
    Scorpion, sizes 4-6
    Large stonefly patterns, sizes 4-8
    Feather jigs, sizes 4-10
    Whitlock's Damselfly Nymph, sizes 2-6

- Musky Flies
    T-Bone, sizes 3/0-5/0
    Game Changer, sizes 2/0
    Beaufort Fly, sizes 3/0-5/0
    Hang Time Optic Minnow, sizes 3/0
    Half & Half, sizes 1/0-5/0
    Clouser Minnow, sizes 2/0-5/0

Walker Parrott with a Madison River brown trout. Kevin Howell

Growing up on the South Carolina coast, **Walker Parrott** was introduced to fishing as a child, catching redfish, trout, jacks, and other inshore species. While completing high school in Sandpoint, Idaho, Walker was introduced to mountain trout fishing. He wanted to stay in the mountains, but live in the Southeast. After completing Brevard College with a bachelor's degree in experimental education, Walker settled in Brevard, North Carolina where he could fish the streams and rivers for trout and bass. After college, Walker took a job with an environmental engineering firm, which he soon left to pursue his passion of fishing, landing at Davidson River Outfitters. Now, too many years later, Walker is managing Davidson River Outfitters guide service and guiding and hosting anglers to Andros Bahamas, Argentina, and Montana. Between working with a great staff in the shop and guiding trout, smallmouth, and musky trips, he has the perfect balance. While trout are the staple, Walker likes to float for smallmouth bass and musky in Tennessee, North Carolina, and Virginia. When Walker is not guiding or pacing the fly shop, Walker can be found mountain biking, kayaking, taking long walks on the beach, fishing, and hanging out with his wife Nicole, and dogs, Mojo, Mia, Cassidy, and Catch 'em.

CLOSEST GUIDES AND OUTFITTERS

New Angle Fishing Company
Blane Chocklett
Troutville, VA
540-354-1774
bchocklett@comcast.net

Tangent Outfitters
201 Cascade Dr.
Pembroke, VA 24136
540-626-4567
www.tangentoutfitters.com

CLOSEST RESTAURANTS

The River Company Restaurant and Brewery
6633 Viscoe Rd.
Fairlawn, VA 24141
540-633-3940
www.therivercompanyrestaurant.com

BT's
218 Tyler Ave.
Radford, VA 24141
540-639-1282
btsradford@msn.com
www.btsradford.com

CLOSEST LODGING

Best Western Radford Inn
1501 Tyler Ave.
Radford, VA 24141
540-639-3000

Hilton Garden Inn Blacksburg
900 Plantation Rd.
Blacksburg, VA 24060
540-552-5005

Clay Corner Inn
401 Clay St. SW
Blacksburg, VA 24060
540-552-4030

River City Grill
103 Third Ave.
Radford, VA 24141
540-629-2130
Rivercitygrillva.com

Nagoya Sushi
1144 E. Main St
Radford, VA 24141
540-633-6008

47 · James River

▶ **Location:** The James River, near the town of Roanoke, Virginia, formerly known as Big Lick, has plenty of ways to travel in and out of the area. Roanoke Airport can make this angling destination really easy with multiple domestic and international flights available. For people who prefer to drive, Interstate 81 runs through Roanoke.

Sitting in the shadow of the Blue Ridge Parkway, Roanoke can be a great town in which to fish, canoe, mountain bike, and just relax.

The James River is rich in American history, and it is regarded as one of the key elements our country was founded on. With a rich history and ongoing legacies of farming and local industry, the James River is one of the best fisheries in Virginia. The early settlers in Jamestown used the fertile water of the James River to help sustain living conditions, from hunting and fishing to agriculture. The James River starts flowing on an eastern path through the Blue Ridge and Allegheny Mountains of Southern West Virginia, finally spilling into the Chesapeake Bay. There are many of places to stay near or around the river as it runs close to bigger cities like Roanoke, Lynchburg, and Charlottesville. The dining and nightlife in and around the area is very good, with many options available. There are also many sightseeing opportunities, as the James River flows through beautiful country and many historic sites.

The James River is broken in to three parts: the upper, middle, and lower sections. Due to limited space, I'll focus on the upper section. There are many diverse species of fish to catch in its entire length of more than 340 miles. There are large and smallmouth bass, sunfish, catfish, gar, striped bass, sturgeon, musky, carp, and American and hickory shad, to name a few. At times, the river can hold trout that fall out of the many tributary streams that flow into the James River.

I have had the fortune of growing up on the James River near my home in Troutville, Virginia. Not only did I grow up fishing, floating, and wading these waters, but I have also used the river to make a career, guiding fisherman for over 22 years. The part of the James River I am most familiar with is its very beginning, which flows close to Lynchburg, Virginia. The James River flows through beautiful mountains and valleys and the views can rival any western waters.

The character of the James doesn't change too much as it falls and winds through this mountainous region. The James includes numerous rapids, runs, and long pools that carve out what is, in my opinion, the perfect river. What I mean by *perfect* is that the section of the James on which I fish and guide is the perfect size. The fish structure, food base, and awesome flows combine to create an optimal fishing experience.

The James River has excellent habitat for the many gamefish that call the river home. Many boulder-strewn rapids and runs with back eddies followed by mid-river rock ledges give ample opportunity to catch fish. (Not to mention the mountains come right down to the river's edge, exposing rock cliffs and beautiful vistas.) The one problem anglers can have is deciding where to cast next, because every piece of water looks so great. The most prized fish in the upper James would be the smallmouth bass. The smallmouth bass is a great fighting fish and does extremely well in the upper reaches of this section.

There are also musky, flathead catfish, all types of sunfish, carp, and a few channel catfish to be had on any given day. The best time for fishing the James River for smallmouth bass is early spring (with its higher water flows), summer, and fall. The spring season offers a great opportunity for big prespawn smallmouth bass. Smallmouths tend to be very aggressive and

James River smallie caught on the ever popular Game Changer. Blane Chocklett

Blane Chocklett displaying a large James River muskie. Blane Chocklett

hit a variety of subsurface streamer-style flies. The water levels this time of year tend to be higher, so be careful while boating. Smallmouths tend to hold near or adjacent to their spawning areas. Look for breaks in current and ledges where smallmouths can hold out of the current and ambush their prey.

Water temps and water levels will vary from season to season. Summer water levels and water temps will move smallmouths into different locations on the river, so keep an eager eye out for smallmouths that will travel with these changing patterns. If you are a do-it-yourself angler, access can be challenging. I would recommend finding a guide for the upper and lower sections of the James. The James is a great river with little development and light angling pressure. Both of these factors help create a world-class fishery.

▶ **Tackle:** My favorite summer flies are minnow imitations and crayfish-style flies. Having two rods rigged helps. When the smallmouths are picky, I can fish a crayfish pattern deep. When smallmouths are happier and on the move, I switch out to various minnow patterns.

The best rod weights I recommend are 6- to 8-weight, 8- to 9-feet in length. Fly lines will generally be intermediate and sinking in the 150- to 350-grain range.

Leaders are short, from 3 to 6 feet, and will work best in the 2–0X range. A good large arbor reel with a smooth drag will work fine.

Late spring also will add more opportunities, as musky come off the spawn. After spawning from mid-March through April, the musky are ready to start putting on the feedbag. The best flies are large streamers from 8 to 14 inches, representing suckers and fallfish. The best rod sizes will be 10- to 12-weights and sinking lines ranging from 350- to 500-grain weight.

Summer marks the best time of year for the fly angler wanting to fish the James River for smallmouths. This marks what we call "bug season." At this time of year, the river is usually low and clear, making it easy to fish. There are all types of insects and baitfish available for the fish to feed on, including stoneflies, hellgrammites, mayflies, cicadas, terrestrials, fallfish, suckers, and many other nongame species.

During summertime, the smallmouths will be spread all over the river, from riffles to runs and everything between. The best lines to use are floating bass-style lines and intermediate for streamer fishing. Rod sizes from 6- to 8-weight and 8 to 9 feet in length work best. I recommend leaders from 9 feet in the 2X to 0X range for floating lines. For intermediate lines for subsurface fishing, use short leaders from 3 to 6 feet in length.

The fall brings cooler water temperature with low, clear water. These conditions signal the smallmouth and musky that winter is on its way. The bass fishing can be very good at times, with topwater and subsurface fishing available. The best fishing is usually during the middle of the day for smallmouths. The water temperatures are at their highest at this time of day, revving up the fishes' metabolism.

The musky really start moving around during the fall, looking for good feeding opportunities. Musky can be very challenging at this time of year, due to the low, clear water. However, musky are looking to feed more because of the cooler water and weather.

Fly retrieval and smaller flies can work best on a fast retrieve. I recommend fishing flies in the 7- to 9-inch range in natural colors.

Wintertime brings the prime time for musky fly anglers. This time of year is best to pursue musky if you really want to target them. Musky are in a prespawn mode through the winter months and can get very aggressive. The best flies for musky during the winter are 10- to 17-inch flies in a variety of colors ranging from natural to bright fire tiger. (The water levels during the winter are generally high to medium in flows and need to be respected.) Leaders should be 2 feet long and 20–30 pounds, with a wire bite guard of 18 inches and 30 to 60 pounds. Full-sinking lines of 350–550 grain, 9 feet long, and 10- to 12-weight will do fine.

Blane Chocklett.

Since 1996, **Blane Chocklett** has been a full-time fly-fishing guide based in Troutville, Virginia. Operating New Angle Fishing Company, Blane has also set the fly-tying world on fire with innovative fly patterns. Working with Umpqua Feather Merchants, Blane has many commercial fly patterns, such as the Gummy. Because he develops select custom patterns for musky, smallmouth, and trout, not much in the fishing and catching world gets past Blane.

CLOSEST FLY SHOPS

Mossy Creek Flyfishing
1790-92 E. Market St.
Harrisonburg, VA 22801
540-434-2444
store@mossycreekflyfishing.com
www.mossycreekflyfishing.com

Orvis
19 Campbell Ave. SE
Market Square
Roanoke, VA 24011
540-345-3635

CLOSEST GUIDES AND OUTFITTERS

New Angle Fishing Company
Blane Chocklett
Troutville, VA
540-354-1774
bchocklett@comcast.net
www.newanglefishingcompany.com

Mossy Creek Flyfishing
1790-92 E. Market St.
Harrisonburg, VA 22801
540-434-2444
store@mossycreekflyfishing.com
www.mossycreekflyfishing.com

CLOSEST LODGING

Hampton Inn & Suites
5033 Valley View Blvd. N.
Roanoke, VA 24012
540-366-6300

Country Inn & Suites
7860 Plantation Rd.
Roanoke, VA 24019
540-366-5678

Hyatt Place
2100 Bond St.
Charlottesville, VA 22901
434-995-5200

CLOSEST RESTAURANTS

Pink Cadillac Diner
4743 S. Lee Hwy.
Natural Bridge, VA 24578
540-291-2378
www.pinkcadillacdineronline.com

Mel's Cafe
719 W. Main St.
Charlottesville, VA 22903
434-971-8819

Shakers Good Food & Drink
1909 Valley View Blvd. NW
Roanoke, VA 24012
540-366-4783

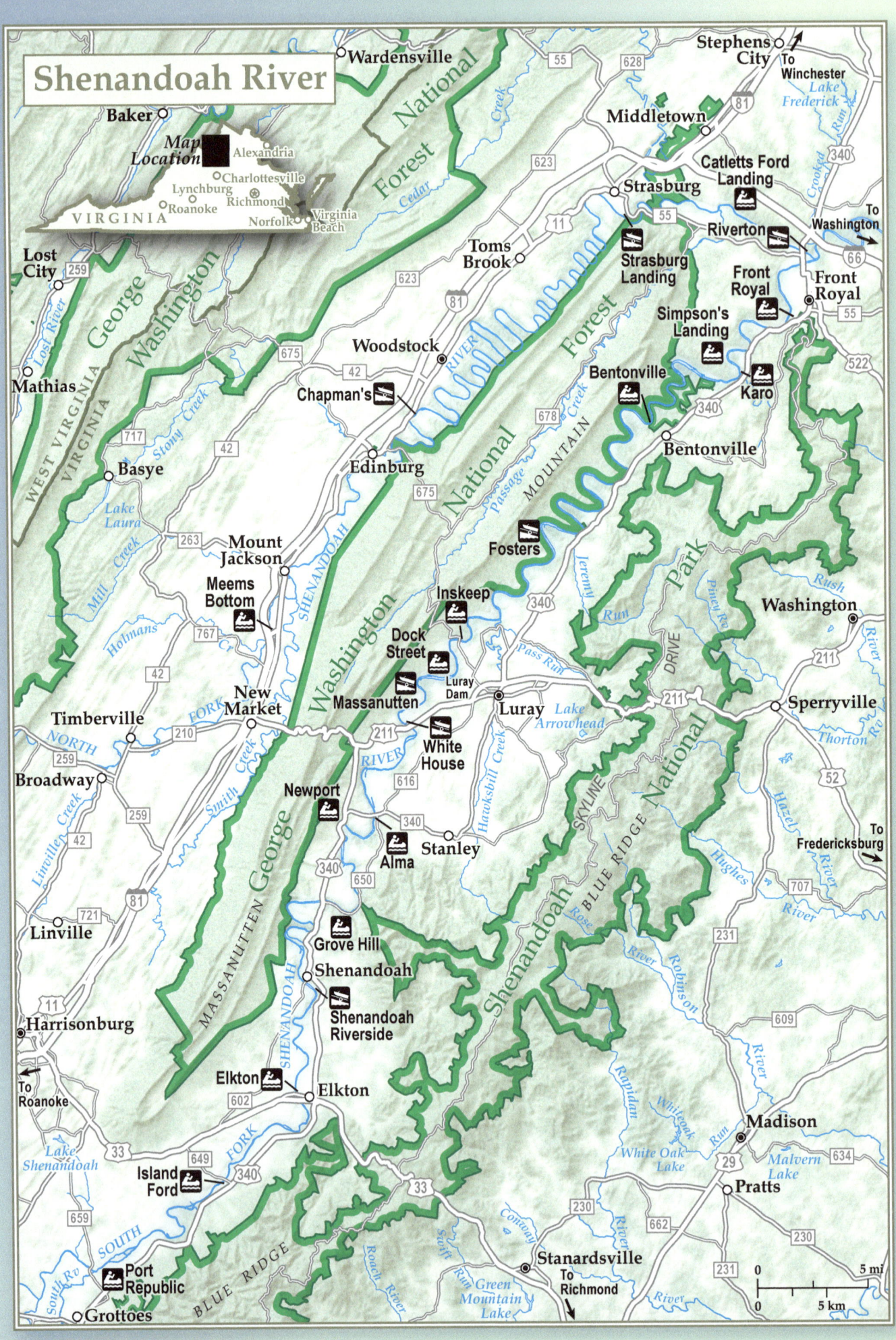

48 · Shenandoah River

➤ **Location:** The Shenandoah River consists of three sections, the North Fork, South Fork, and the main stem. The South Fork of the Shenandoah originates at Port Republic, Virginia, where the North River and South River meet. The South Fork flows north on the east side of Massanutten Mountain and west of the Blue Ridge Mountains 97 miles and meets the North Fork of the Shenandoah in Front Royal, Virginia.

The North Fork originates in Rockingham County and flows 116 miles north on the west side of Massanutten Mountain to Front Royal.

The main stem of the Shenandoah flows north from Front Royal 57 miles to the confluence with the Potomac River in Harpers Ferry, West Virginia. Thirty-five miles of the main stem is located in Virginia. The South Fork and main stem are paralleled closely by U.S. Route 340 through its entire length. The North Fork of the Shenandoah runs north along the Interstate 81 corridor. There are small towns about every 20 river miles with lodging and restaurant options for traveling anglers.

Anglers can easily make day trips to sections of the Shenandoah River system from the major metropolitan areas. The Shenandoah is one to two hours from Richmond; Washington, D.C., Fredericksburg; and Roanoke. Major airports include Washington Dulles International, Reagan National Airport, and Richmond International Airport. Regional airports include Charlottesville-Albemarle Airport and Shenandoah Valley Regional.

The Shenandoah River is considered one of the most historic and scenic rivers in the country. All forks of the Shenandoah River are relatively low gradient and slow moving. These waters flow adjacent to the George Washington National Forest, as well as woods and pastureland. It is a popular river to float, with easy navigation in canoes, kayaks, rafts, and drift boats. Class I and Class II rapids are common between the long flat pools, and only a few Class III rapids exist during spring runoff events.

There are a number of dams along all sections of the Shenandoah River system, but portages are available for smaller watercraft. There are public boat ramps every 6 to 15 miles on the entire South Fork and main stem, allowing for easy access to most stretches. (Access to the North Fork is a bit tricky, with many low-water bridges and dams impeding the six access points.) The South Fork and main stem are the more popular sections to float and fish. Anglers regularly use the towns of Harrisonburg, Elkton, Shenandoah, Luray, Bentonville, Front Royal, Woodstock, Edinburg, Winchester, and Harpers Ferry for convenient lodging and access to the river.

The smallmouth bass fishery is what has made the Shenandoah River so popular. It is considered one of the best smallmouth bass destinations in the world. Famous for its numbers of fish, it is not uncommon for knowledgeable anglers to have 100–150 fish days on the water. Fly fishermen can enjoy quality fishing from mid-April through September. The smallmouth bass begin to spawn around mid-April and can be found behind the river's many big rocky ledges and backwater areas. The largest fish of the year can be landed on flies during this time if anglers learn where the best spawning areas are.

A nice Shanendoah smallmouth.

Fall can be great time on the Shenandoah for muskie and smallies. Colby Trow

Once springtime waters recede, the smallmouths distribute well throughout their summer haunts. Anglers will primarily fish floating fly lines with crayfish, baitfish, or topwater patterns on 6- to 8-weight rods. In the peak of the summer season, anglers can conservatively expect to land 30–40 fish in an eight-hour day.

The best part of the Shenandoah's fishery is that smallmouth bass aren't the only fish you are going to catch! Diversity is an incredible asset to the Shenandoah. Huge largemouth bass, common river carp, channel catfish, sunfish, rock bass, and musky are available to anglers. Most anglers don't associate rivers with really good largemouth bass. However, Florida-strain largemouth dominate the river and fish up to 10 pounds have been caught by fly fishermen! It is common for bass anglers to regularly land largemouth in the 4- to 6-pound range during the proper seasons.

Crayfish patterns fished deep will catch just about anything that swims. Big channel catfish up to 15 pounds love big crayfish flies and provide anglers with an incredibly strong fight on a light rod. Rock bass and a variety of sunfish species readily attack flies through the spring and summer months.

Fly fishing for musky is continually becoming more popular in the mid-Atlantic states. The Shenandoah doesn't boast the largest population density compared to the James or New

While the ambient temprature may be cold winter time Musky fishing on the Shanendoah can be really good. Albemarle Angler.

rivers, but it does contain a quality destination fishery. The musky in the Shenandoah River system grow very big, and fish up to 48 inches have been landed on flies. The average fish in the Shenandoah watershed runs 38 to 41 inches. Anglers will need to come prepared with 9- to 11-weight fly rods, intermediate or sinking lines, stout leaders with bite tippet, and large flies. Most of the musky can be found in the long, deep, slow-moving pools. It is recommended to use a guide or outfitter on your first musky trips to the Shenandoah, as it doesn't fish like other popular musky rivers—fish aren't evenly distributed throughout the watershed.

For the technical anglers, carp fishing can be excellent, especially in the summer and early fall during low, clear water conditions. These fish frequent the shallow, silty flats and edges of the miles of water willow that parallel the river edges. These fish feed primarily on small crustaceans, nymphs, and worms, allowing anglers to target them with long leaders and small flies. While the common carp averages 8–12 pounds, fish up to 27 pounds are known to have been landed on flies. You will need to bring your A-game as the big carp in the Shenandoah are extremely spooky and difficult to approach.

Early spring on the Shanendoah. Albemarle Angler

Summertime smallmouth on the Shanendoah. Albemarle Angler.

Colby is co-owner of Mossy Creek Fly Fishing. He serves as a board member for the American Fly Fishing Trade Association and the Massanutten Trout Unlimited. He is a technical advisor for the Fly Fishers of Virginia. Colby and his brother, Brian, opened Mossy Creek Fly Fishing together in 2003. He started guiding and instructing in Virginia in 1999, and has fished almost every day since 2003. When he isn't fishing, he's at the vise tying flies. He started tying flies for local Virginia fly shops at age 13 and was featured at many fly-fishing trade shows through his teen years.

▶ **Regulations:** From the confluence of North River and South River at Port Republic, Virginia, downstream to the Shenandoah Dam near the town of Shenandoah, the regulations are as follows:
- Bass
  All bass 11 to 14 inches must be released.
  Daily creel limit is five bass per day.

From the base of the Shenandoah Dam near the town of Shenandoah downstream to Luray Dam near Luray, Virginia, the regulations are as follows:
- Bass
  All bass 14 to 20 inches must be released.
  Only one bass longer than 20 inches may be harvested per day.
  Daily creel limit is five bass per day.

From the base of Luray Dam near Luray, Virginia, downstream to the confluence with North Fork of the Shenandoah River at Front Royal, Virginia, the regulations are as follows:
- Bass
  All bass 11 to 14 inches must be released.
  Daily creel limit is 5 bass per day.
- Sunfish
  No minimum size limit.
  Daily creel limit is 50 sunfish per day in aggregate (combined).
- Rock Bass
  No minimum size limit.
  Daily creel limit is 25 rock bass per day.
- Crappie
  No minimum size limit.
  Daily creel limit is 25 crappie per day.
- Muskellunge
  Minimum size limit is 30 inches minimum size limit; all musky less than 30 inches must be released.
  Daily creel limit is two muskellunge per day.
- Channel Catfish
  No minimum size limit.
  Daily creel limit is 20 channel catfish per day.

▶**Tackle:** I suggest using 9-foot, 6-weight through 9-foot, 8-weight rods with weight-forward floating or sink-tip lines for smallmouth, largemouth, and carp. For musky, use 9-foot, 9-weight through 9-foot, 11-weight rods with intermediate or full-sinking lines.

CLOSEST FLY SHOPS

Mossy Creek Flyfishing
1790-92 E. Market St.
Harrisonburg, VA 22801
540-434-2444
store@mossycreekflyfishing.com
www.mossycreekflyfishing.com

Murray's Fly Shop
121 S. Main St.
Edinburg, VA 22824
540-984-4212
info@murraysflyshop.com
www.murraysflyshop.com

Orvis
2020 Bond St.
Charlottesville, VA 22901
434-975-0210

Orvis
1614 Village Market Blvd. SE, Ste. 110
Leesburg, VA 20175
703-777-5305

CLOSEST GUIDES AND OUTFITTERS

Mossy Creek Flyfishing
1790-92 E. Market St.
Harrisonburg, VA 22801
540-434-2444
store@mossycreekflyfishing.com
www.mossycreekflyfishing.com

Murray's Fly Shop
121 S. Main St.
Edinburg, VA 22824
540-984-4212
info@murraysflyshop.com
www.murraysflyshop.com

Shenandoah River Adventures
415 Long Ave.
Shenandoah, VA 22849
888-309-7222
shenandoahcanoes@aol.com
www.shenandoahriveradventures.com

Downriver Canoe Company
884 Indian Hollow Rd.
Bentonville, VA 22610
800-338-1963
somebody@downriver.com
www.downriver.com

Front Royal Canoe Company
8567 Stonewall Jackson Hwy.
Front Royal, VA 22630
540-635-5440
www.frontroyalcanoe.com

CLOSEST LODGING

By the Side of the Road Inn & Cottages
491 Garbers Church Rd.
Harrisonburg, VA 22801 (540-801-0430)
stay@bythesideoftheroad.com
www.bythesideoftheroad.com

Stonewall Jackson Inn
547 E. Market St.
Harrisonburg, VA 22801 (540-433-8233)
info@stonewalljacksoninn.com
www.stonewalljacksoninn.com

Wintergreen Resort
39 Mountain Inn Loop
Nellysford, VA 22958 (855-699-1858)
www.wintergreenresort.com

Massanutten Resort
1822 Resort Dr.
McGaheysville, VA 22840 (540-289-9441)
www.massresort.com

Hampton Inn
85 University Blvd.
Harrisonburg, VA 22801 (540-432-1111)

Courtyard
1890 Evelyn Byrd Ave.
Harrisonburg, VA 22801 (540-432-3031)

Shenandoah River Adventures
415 Long Ave.
Shenandoah, VA 22849 (888-309-7222)
shenandoahcanoes@aol.com
www.shenandoahriveradventures.com

Kite's Store Campground
4258 U.S. Route 340
Shenandoah, VA 22849 (540-652-8174)
www.virginia.org/listings/OutdoorsAnd-Sports/RiversideCamping/

Outlanders River Camp
4253 U.S. Hwy. 211 W.
Luray, VA 22835 (540-743-5540)
reservations@outlandersrivercamp.com
www.outlandersrivercamp.com

Low Water Bridge Campground
192 Panhandle Rd.
Bentonville, VA 22610 (540-635-7277)

Shenandoah River State Park
350 Daughter of Stars Dr.
Bentonville, VA 22610 (540-622-6840)
shenandoahriver@dcr.virginia.gov
www.dcr.virginia.gov/state-parks/shenandoah-river

CLOSEST RESTAURANTS

Cuban Burger
70 W. Water St.
Harrisonburg, VA 22801
540-434-1769

Clementine
153 S. Main St.
Harrisonburg, VA 22801
540-801-8881
www.clementinecafe.com

Harrisonburg Union Station Restaurant & Bar
128 W. Market St.
Harrisonburg, VA 22801
540-437-0042
www.unionstationdowntown.com

Local Chop & Grill House
56 W. Gay St.
Harrisonburg, VA 22802
540-801-0505
www.localchops.com

Billy Jack's Wing & Draft Shack
92 S. Main St.
Harrisonburg, VA 22801
540-433-1793
aaron@jackbrownsjoint.com
www.billyjacksshack.com

Capital Ale House
41-A Court Square
Harrisonburg, VA 22801
540-564-ALES
www.capitalalehouse.com

Jack Brown's Beer and Burger Joint
80 S. Main St.
Harrisonburg, VA 22801
540-433-5225
www.jackbrownsjoint.com

CLOSEST HOSPITALS OR URGENT CARE

Sentara RMH Medical Center
2010 Health Campus Drive
Harrisonburg, VA 22801
540-689-1000
www.sentara.com/harrisonburg-virginia/hospitalslocations/locations/sentara-rmh-medical-center.aspx

Augusta Medical
78 Medical Center Dr.
Fishersville, VA 22939
540-932-4000
www.augustahealth.com/

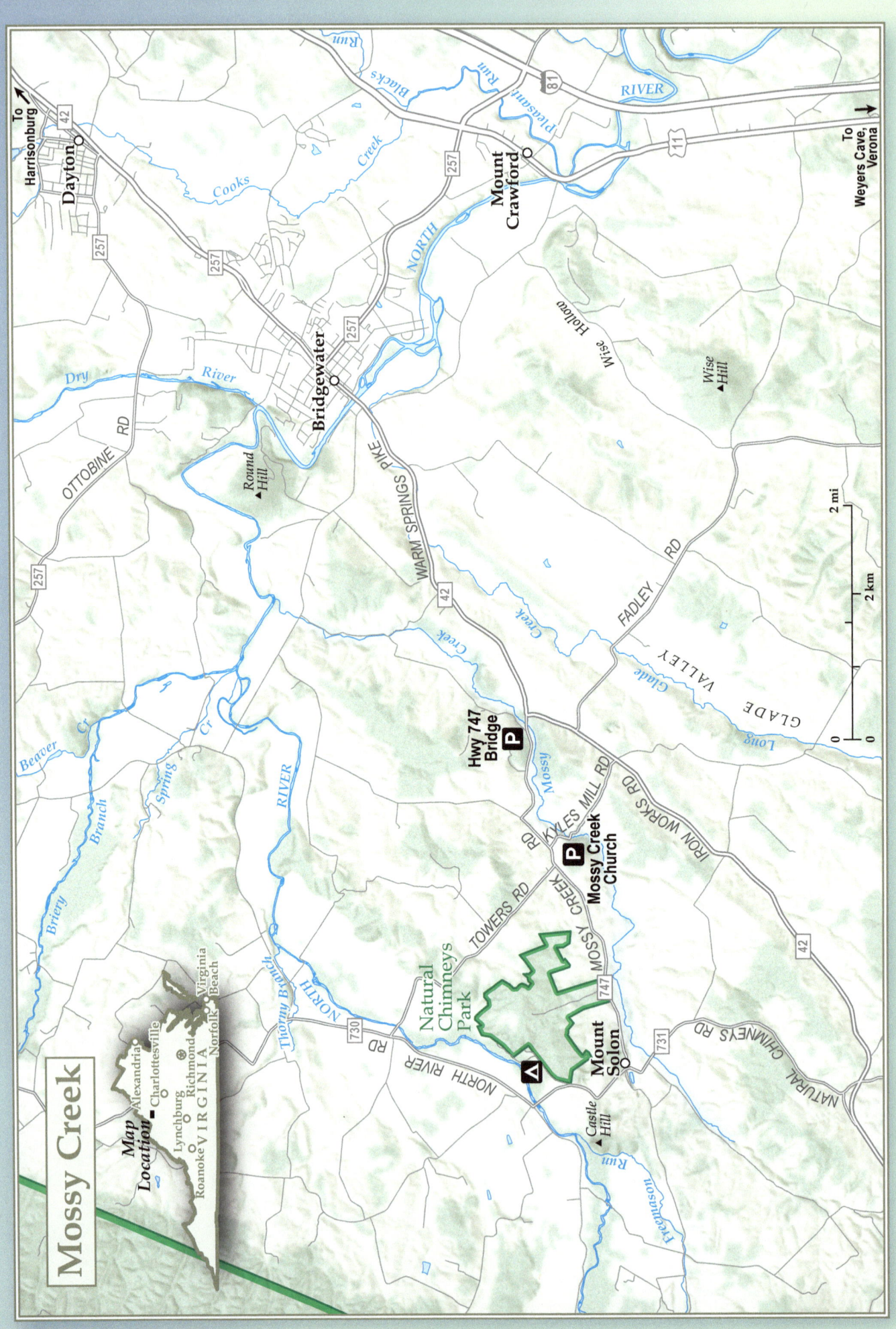

49 · Mossy Creek

▶ **Location:** Mossy Creek is a small limestone spring creek that flows eight miles from its spring sources around Mount Solon, Virginia, to the North River just outside of Bridgewater, Virginia. Roughly four miles of water are open to the public, from Joseph's Spring to the Rockingham-Augusta County line. There are two main parking areas for Mossy Creek: one is adjacent to the Mossy Creek Presbyterian Church and one is downstream by the concrete bridge at the intersection of Mossy Creek Road and Iron Works Road immediately off U.S. Route 42. This section of blue-ribbon trout water carries fly-fishing-only, catch-and-release regulations (one trout longer than 20 inches may be kept, however). It is located two hours from Richmond; two hours from Washington, D.C.; and just minutes off of Interstate 81. Shenandoah Valley Regional Airport is just ten minutes down the road in Weyers Cave.

Mossy Creek is unique in that it is one of a small number of true limestone spring creeks open to public fishing access in Virginia, thanks to an arrangement between landowners, Trout Unlimited, and the Virginia Department of Game and Inland Fisheries (VDGIF). To legally fish Mossy Creek, anglers must obtain a free landowners permit from the VDGIF (in addition to their Virginia freshwater license). This can be done either online at the VDGIF website or in person at the VDGIF office in Verona. The permit allows access to the creek 365 days a year, from sunup to sundown. Trees and fence lines are marked well with special-regulations signs to ensure anglers do not trespass onto private property. Anglers must stay within 30 feet of the creek and use fence crossings and stiles. Anglers should not open or cross fences, except in designated areas. Walking the creek is low-impact and easy. Wading is not permitted, but waders are commonly worn as the surrounding springs and creek edges can be swampy and muddy.

Contrary to the information given in some regional publications, Mossy can be an extremely challenging stream and is not recommended for novice anglers. Dry-fly fishermen, familiar with Mossy's moods, fish it carefully and slowly, often crouching or kneeling along the bank.

It is the summer dry-fly fishing for which Mossy is most famous. Most of the public section runs through open grassy meadows with overhanging multiflora rose bushes. By late July, trout are used to seeing grasshoppers, crickets, beetles, and ants falling into the water, and the fish become very aggressive. The average fisherman has his or her best chance of seeing and hooking really big fish in Mossy at this time. It is not uncommon to start your day fishing small emergers and drys during the Trico hatch, big terrestrial patterns during the heat of the day, and large drakes, Hex, or mouse patterns during the last bit of daylight.

Streamer fishing on Mossy can also bring about some action from the largest fish. The best opportunity to landing the largest browns of the year is during a high-water event.

Posing with a fall brown trout for a quick picture before being released. Colby Trow

Heavy spring rains or tropical systems that move over the area, dumping multiple inches a day, will stain the water and increase the flow. The biggest browns will emerge from the undercuts and holes and move to the shallow moss beds and ambush disoriented bait washing downstream. Don't be afraid to throw flies in the 5- to 7-inch range to entice a strike by some of these monsters. Fish over 6 pounds and up to 28 inches long are caught annually. These large trout present a challenge, but the possibility of drawing one out from the depths on any cast is what brings anglers back to the creek on a regular basis.

Be prepared to bring multiple rods if you plan on fishing Mossy Creek. Streamer fishing is almost always good on overcast, rainy days, and insects could hatch almost any time out there. You may start off fishing a 3-weight rod with 7X tippet

Releasing a Mossy Creek brown trout. Colby Trow

Looking for risers on Mossy Creek. Colby Trow

and small ant and end up throwing 0X fluorocarbon on a saltwater 6-weight with an articulated streamer 6 inches long. Conditions may change rapidly and spring creek brown trout can be notoriously picky, so come prepared! Mossy Creek has earned a reputation as a challenging but fun spring creek and is still listed as one of the top 100 trout streams in the United States by Trout Unlimited.

▶ **Hatches:** Like many limestone streams, there are many reliable hatches of mayflies, caddis, and midges on Mossy Creek. Surface action can take place all year, with tiny olives and midges hatching sporadically throughout the winter. By mid-April, hatches of larger Blue-winged Olives and Sulphurs become regular. Trico action usually begins around Memorial Day and can last until Halloween. Large Green Drakes swarm during the evening hours around the end of May and add to the surface action with the Trico hatch. Large Yellow Drakes are present into July, and the Hex mayflies end the evening hatch during the end of August.

▶ **Regulations:** We believe in 100 percent catch and release. However, the following state regulations do apply.
- Brook, brown, and rainbow trout
    Creel limit is 1 trout per day
    Fish must measure 20 inches or longer
- Mossy Creek is fly fishing only
- Use only single-hook artificial flies
- Dropper flies are allowed
- Leaders may not exceed 15 feet in length
- Creel limit is 1 fish per day
- All fish less than 20 inches must be immediately returned to the water unharmed; no fish less than 20 inches may be in possession while fishing these waters
- No bait may be in possession while fishing these waters
- Fishing is permitted year-round on these waters
- Access must be at designated parking and fence crossings

Aquatic vegetation can make landing trout on light tippet difficult. Colby Trow

Winter time on Mossy Creek. Colby Trow

- Wading, camping, and fires are not permitted
- Written permission is needed (landowners permit)
- Fishing is allowed from a half hour before sunrise to a half hour after sunset
- No dogs are allowed
- Do not disturb livestock or open any fences (crossings are available for anglers to navigate fences)
- Trout stamp is not required
- Please respect landowners' property; violators will lose their right to fish (presently, there is no fishing on Mossy Creek above or below the special regulation areas without permission from individual landowners)
- Anglers must have the free, signed landowner permission card in addition to their fishing license. These permits can be obtained by visiting the Verona Regional Office between 8:15 a.m. and 5:00 p.m., Monday through Friday:
  517 Lee Hwy.
  Verona, VA 24482
- Anglers may also obtain their landowner permission cards by sending a self-addressed stamped envelope to:
  Fisheries Division, DGIF
  P.O. Box 996
  Verona, VA 24482
- Anglers who prefer to conduct business online can visit the special-regulations landowners permit page on the VDGIF website: http://www.dgif.virginia.gov/

➤ **Tackle:** I recommend employing 8-foot, 3-weight fly rods to 9foot, 6-weight fly rods with weight-forward floating or sink-tip lines. Use leaders 0–7X in varying lengths. As noted previously, wading is not allowed in Mossy Creek, but I still suggest waders as it can be very muddy and swampy in spots. Fly choices range from small dry flies to large streamers, so we typically bring a few rods, depending on fishing conditions.

Headed home. Colby Trow

CLOSEST FLY SHOPS

Mossy Creek Fly Fishing
1790-92 E. Market St.
Harrisonburg, VA 22801
540-434-2444
store@mossycreekflyfishing.com
www.mossycreekflyfishing.com

Angler's Lane
Graves Mill Center
18013 Forest Rd. E04
Forest, VA 24551
434-385-0200
www.anglerslane.com

Murray's Fly Shop
121 S. Main St.
Edinburg, VA 22824
540-984-4212
info@murraysflyshop.com
www.murraysflyshop.com

Orvis
2020 Bond St.
Charlottesville, VA 22901
434-975-0210

Orvis
1614 Village Market Blvd. SE, Suite 110
Leesburg, VA 20175
703-777-5305

Orvis
11800 W. Broad St., Suite 1650
Richmond, VA 23233
804-253-9000

CLOSEST GUIDES AND OUTFITTERS

Mossy Creek Fly Fishing
1790-92 E. Market St.
Harrisonburg, VA 22801
540-434-2444
store@mossycreekflyfishing.com
www.mossycreekflyfishing.com

Angler's Lane
Graves Mill Center at U.S. Route 221
Forest, VA 24551
434-385-0200
www.anglerslane.com

Murray's Fly Shop
121 S. Main St.
Edinburg, VA 22824
540-984-4212
info@murraysflyshop.com
www.murraysflyshop.com

CLOSEST LODGING

By the Side of the Road Inn & Cottages
491 Garbers Church Rd.
Harrisonburg, VA 22801
540-801-0430
stay@bythesideoftheroad.com
www.bythesideoftheroad.com

Stonewall Jackson Inn
547 E. Market St.
Harrisonburg, VA 22801
540-433-8233
info@stonewalljacksoninn.com
www.stonewalljacksoninn.com

Wintergreen Resort
39 Mountain Inn Loop
Nellysford, VA 22958
855-699-1858
www.wintergreenresort.com

Massanutten Resort
1822 Resort Dr.
McGaheysville, VA 22840
540-289-9441
www.massresort.com

Crimson Inn
116 N. Main St.
Bridgewater, VA 22812
540-828-4661
crimson@goodmanagement.com
www.crimsoninn.com

The Village Inn
4979 S. Valley Pike
Harrisonburg, VA 22801
540-434-7355
www.thevillageinn.travel

Hampton Inn
85 University Blvd.
Harrisonburg, VA 22801
540-432-1111

Courtyard
1890 Evelyn Byrd Ave.
Harrisonburg, VA 22801
540-432-3031

COLBY TROW is co-owner of Mossy Creek Fly Fishing. He serves as a board member for the American Fly Fishing Trade Association and the Massanutten Trout Unlimited. He is a technical advisor for the Fly Fishers of Virginia. Colby and his brother, Brian, opened Mossy Creek Fly Fishing together in 2003. He started guiding and instructing in Virginia in 1999, and has fished almost every day since 2003. When he isn't fishing, he's at the vise tying flies. He started tying flies for local Virginia fly shops at age 13 and was featured at many fly-fishing trade shows through his teen years.

Natural Chimneys
540-245-5727
camping@co.augusta.va.us
www.co.augusta.va.us

Hone Quarry Campground
888-265-0019
www.fs.usda.gov

North River Campground
888-265-0019
www.fs.usda.gov

CLOSEST RESTAURANTS

Cuban Burger
70 W. Water St.
Harrisonburg, VA 22801
540-434-1769

Clementine
153 S. Main St.
Harrisonburg, VA 22801
540-801-8881
www.clementinecafe.com

Harrisonburg Union Station Restaurant & Bar
128 W. Market St.
Harrisonburg, VA 22801
540-437-0042
www.unionstationdowntown.com

Local Chop & Grill House
56 W. Gay St.
Harrisonburg, VA 22802
540-801-0505
www.localchops.com

Billy Jack's Wing & Draft Shack
92 S. Main St.
Harrisonburg, VA 22801
540-433-1793
aaron@jackbrownsjoint.com
www.billyjacksshack.com

Capital Ale House
41-A Court Square
Harrisonburg, VA 22801
540-564-ALES
www.capitalalehouse.com

Jack Brown's Beer and Burger Joint
80 S. Main St.
Harrisonburg, VA 22801
540-433-5225
www.jackbrownsjoint.com

CLOSEST HOSPITALS OR URGENT CARE

Sentara RMH Medical Center
2010 Health Campus Drive
Harrisonburg, VA 22801
540-689-1000
www.sentara.com/harrisonburg-virginia/hospitalslocations/locations/sentara-rmh-medical-center.aspx

Augusta Medical
78 Medical Center Dr.
Fishersville, VA 22939
540-932-4000
www.augustahealth.com

WEST VIRGINIA

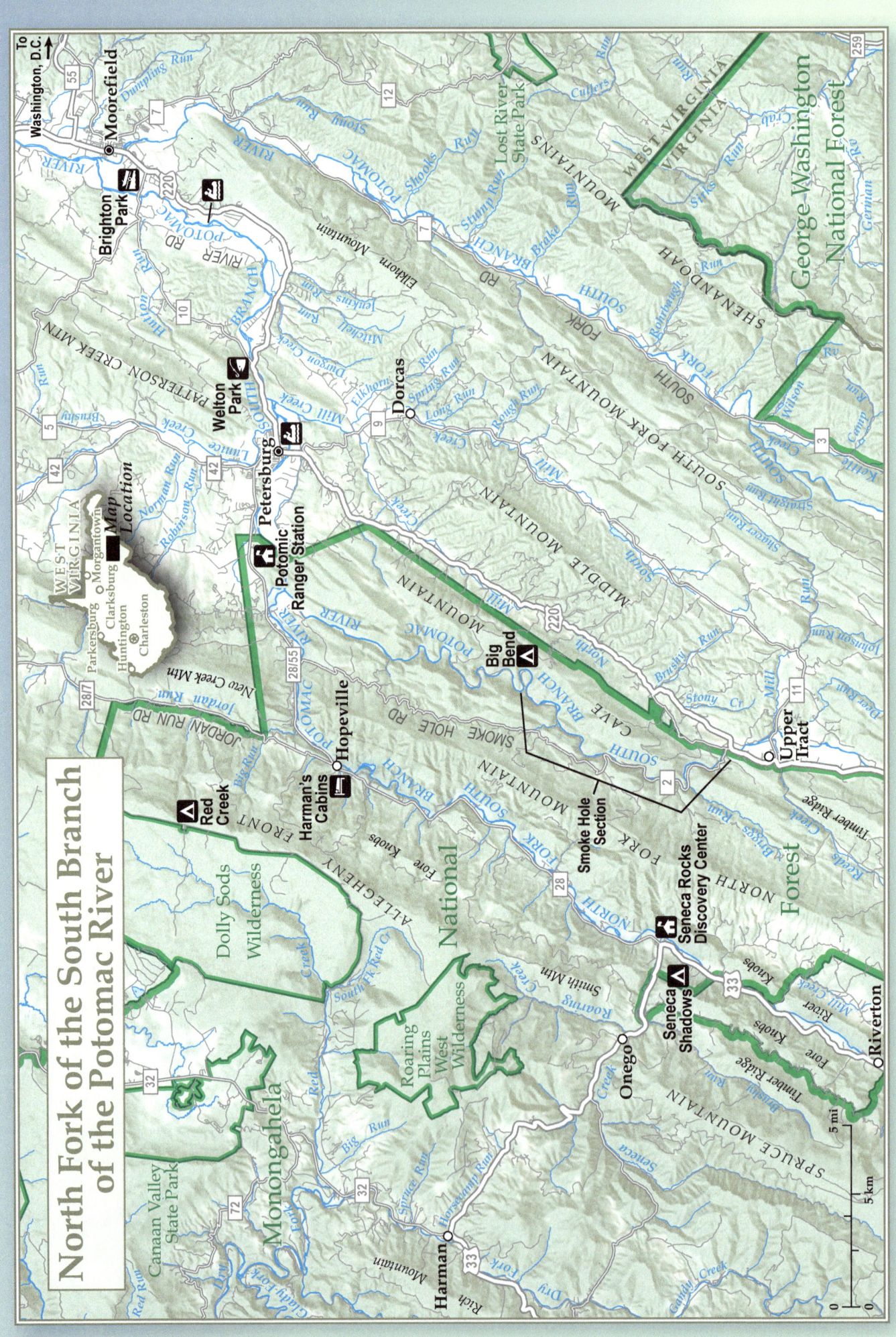

50 · North Fork of the South Branch of the Potomac River

▶ **Location:** The North Fork of the South Branch of the Potomic River is located near Petersburg,, West Virginia, approximately 122 miles west of Washington, D.C.

Though many anglers float the Potomac in Maryland and Virginia, excellent access for wading anglers exists primarily off U.S. Route 28/55 in West Virginia. Those who wish to fish the North Fork of the South Branch of the Potomac River will find a healthy mix of trout here—mostly browns and rainbows with the occasional broodstock brookie, because it's so easy to stock this river. That sudden jolt on your line, however, may come from a smallmouth bass. The state's record fish, which weighed in at a whopping 9 3/4 pounds, was caught in the Potomac.

Heading south on U.S. Route 28/55, you'll lose all cell phone service once you leave the town of Petersburg. In exchange, however, you'll gain excellent wading water. You'll find numerous cutouts all along the road; they are easy to spot, and parking is abundant. If you prefer to float the river in a canoe or kayak, one of the first places you can put in is Welton Parkin Grant County. The National Park Service also designates several points at which boats may be launched.

The North Fork is loaded with big rocks, many of which can't be seen when the river is running with high flows. I highly recommend going with a guide or contacting an outfitter. The closest that offers shuttle service on the North Fork is Eagle's Nest Outfitters just outside Petersburg.

About a mile and half from U.S. Route 28/55 is a defunct dam. For safety's sake, avoid the area directly adjacent to the dam and instead search the nearby shoreline, which offers long flats both above and below the old dam. You'll find deeper water opposite where you parked. In this part of the river, a 10- to 14-inch rainbow is a good fish.

The "Smoke Hole" section of the Potomac River is well-known and easily accessed off of Smoke Hole Road (West Virginia 2). This is a left-hand turn off of U.S. Route 28/55 when heading south from the town of Petersburg. Although the origin of the area's peculiar name remains obscure, I can say with certainty that the fishing here can be excellent. You'll

Anna from WVU with a North Fork rainbow, caught during the Harman's Invitational. Todd Harman

Wading anglers can also gain access from River Road just a few hundred yards south of Cheat-Potomac ranger station. This is a hard-surface road that eventually becomes a gravel road as you head toward the river. The area is popular with campers, but anglers seem to overlook it, probably because one can't see the river from the road at this point. Most anglers unknowingly drive right past this good river access despite the road's telling name.

drive about 13 miles before you hit the river here, but stay on the paved road and you'll find great water and camping sites. This area has a mile of catch-and-release water. The trout bite slacks off near the end of May, but the smallmouth bass more than make up for the trout's lockjaw. Smoke Hole's stunning rock walls and canyon are worth a visit, even by the non-angler.

Curtis Fleming with a golden trout from the North Fork near Harman's Cabins. Todd Harman

Continuing south on U.S. Route 28/55, you'll eventually arrive at Harman's Luxury Log Cabins on your left. Harman's makes the perfect base of operations from which to explore the area's myriad fishing options. Harman's private mile of catch-and-release fishing is excellent; in fact, I began writing my book Fly Fishing the Mid-Atlantic: A No Nonsense Guide to Top Waters in one of their cabins. Harman's is so accessible and boasts such plentiful trout that Project Healing Waters, a nonprofit group that helps rehabilitate injured veterans through fly fishing, books this location at least twice a year for their group outings. I was lucky enough to land a 20-inch rainbow during one of my visits, but I can honestly say that my wife and kids love Harman's as much as I do because of the scenery and the solitude. The Harman family recently constructed a beautiful log cabin store that carries snacks as well as a selection of local patterns and other necessary fly-fishing gear, like waders and a limited selection of rods.

Upstream from Harmon's is Spruce Knob-Seneca Rocks National Recreation Area. Seneca Rocks is West Virginia's rock-climbing capital, so don't be surprised if you see fully outfitted climbers walking near the river or hanging off the face of this 900-foot towering stone wonder. Take your time here and work the pocketwater well. You'll find a mile of public catch-and-release water on national forest land, which sees some pressure from both fly anglers and tourists hiking along its easily accessible riverbanks. Do yourself a favor and bring along extra flies for the hungry canopy of trees.

Finally, Seneca Creek joins the North Fork near the Seneca Rocks Discovery Center. This visitor center is operated by the Monongahela National Forest and has an exhibit of Native American artifacts, maps of hikes in the nearby Dolly Sods Wilderness, restrooms, and friendly rangers who can point you in the direction of local campsites, as well as fishing opportunities in the small streams of the national forest. You're much more likely to find "wild" rainbows and native brook trout here in Seneca Creek, because its small size means that it gets much less pressure. Seneca Creek is ideal for 2- to 3-weight fly rods or the tenkara style of fly fishing.

Unlike other sections of the North Fork, the U.S. Route 28 stretch is narrower and therefore generally doesn't allow for long casts. Instead, think short, technical casts in the 20- to 30-foot range. Streamer fishing is effective at Harman's and other locations along Route 28, where you can find deep water. Some pools can be as much as 40 feet wide and hundreds of feet long. Dry-fly fishing can be tough here since the water clarity is generally very good. Keep in mind that sloppy casting and poorly presented dry flies will put these fish down in a heartbeat.

Curtis Fleming with a North Fork rainbow trout. Todd Harman

Beau Beasley.

▶ **Tackle:** The trout in the North Fork of the South Branch of the potomic are opportunistic feeders and anglers will very seldom need to match a hatch. Most anglers will find that attractor-style dries, such as stimulators, will work as well (if not better) than any other pattern. However, anglers should always come prepared with a few terrestials, such as Fat Alberts in sizes 10-16, beetles in sizes 12- 18, and green inchworms for the late spring- early fall season. During the cooler months, basic nymphs such as girdle bugs in sizes 8-12, Sheepflies in sizes 8-12, or Howell's Trip Savers in size 12-16 will produce a lot of fish. Leaders should range in size from 9-foot 4X to 12-foot 6X depending on water clarity and levels. An 8-foot-6-inch or 9-foot 4- to 5-weight rod will work for most of the trout fishing in the Cabins, West Virginia area.

BEAU BEASLEY is an award-winning conservation writer, the director of programs for the Virginia Fly Fishing & Wine Festival, and the author of Fly Fishing Virginia and Fly Fishing the Mid-Atlantic. He lives with his wife and children in Warrenton, Virginia.

Note: Anglers traveling to this area will need to be somewhat self sufficient. Harman's has a small selection of tackle for emergency purposes, but there are no major fly shops, outfitters or guides within an hour of this area.

CLOSEST LODGING
Harman's North Fork Cabins
10042 N. Fork Hwy.
Cabins, WV 26855
304-257-2220
www.wvlogcabins.com

Harman's North Fork Cabins
10042 N. Fork Hwy.
Cabins, WV 26855
304-257-2220
www.wvlogcabins.com

Smoke Hole Cabins
8290 N. Fork Hwy.
Cabins, WV 26855
800-828-8478
www.smokehole.com

CLOSEST RESTAURANTS
Belle Vita
203 Virginia Ave.
Petersburg, WV 26847
304-257-1713

Anthony's Italian Restraunt
330 Keyser Ave.
Petersburg, WV 26847
304-257-2222

Brook Trout fishing high in the Balsam Mountains of North Carolina. Patrick Williams

Philanthropy

We at Stonefly Press feel that it's important to view ourselves as a small part of a greater system of balance. We give back to that which nourishes us because it feels natural and right.

Stonefly Press will be donating a portion of our annual profits to conservation groups active in environmental stewardship. We encourage all our readers to learn more about them here, and encourage you to go a step further and get involved.

American Rivers
(americanrivers.org)

Bonefish & Tarpon Trust
(bonefishtarpontrust.org)

California Trout
(caltrout.org)

Coastal Conservation Association
(joincca.org)

Friends of the White River
(friendsofwhiteriver.org)

Riverkeeper
(riverkeeper.org)

Trout Unlimited
(tu.org)

Western Rivers Conservancy
(westernrivers.org)